TAKING CONTROL OF GOODS

Bailiff's Powers after the

Tribunals, Courts and Enforcement Act 2007

John Kruse

PP

Disclaimer

This work is not intended to be comprehensive and is intended to be a general guide to the law and cannot be a substitute for appropriate legal advice. Neither the author not the publisher accept any responsibility for loss occasioned to any person acting or refraining from acting as a result of material contained in this publication. The comments or views expressed by the author are not necessarily the comments or views of any organisation in which the author is employed.

Book ISBN 9781858116044
EBook 9781858116051   Printed & typeset in the UK

PP Publishing

Suite 74, 17 Holywell Hill

St Albans AL1 1DT, UK   www.peerpractice.co.uk

Contents

Table of Cases

Berliner Industriebank Aktiengesellschaft v Jost [1971] 1 QB 278, 124fn31
Berry v Farrow [1914] 1 KB 632, 140fn116
Bessey v Windham (1844) 6 QB 166, 293fn118
Bevils Case 4 Co Rep 11b, 107fn35
Bevir v. British Wagon Co Ltd (1935) 80 L Jo 162, 108fn43
Bhatnagar & Elanrent v Whitehall Investments (1996)5 CL 166, 357
Bibby v Chief Constable of Essex [2000] Casetrack, April 6th, 173
Biggins v Goode (1832) 2 C&J 364, 283
Bignell v Clarke (1860) 5 H&N 485, 184fn8
Billing v Pill [1954] 1 QB 70, 238fn122
Re: Binns [1875] 1 ChD 285, 77fn82
Birch v Dawson (1834) 2 A&E 37, 241fn148
Bird v Hildage [1948] 1 KB 91, 131fn73
Ex p Birmingham Gaslight & Coke Co, In Re:Adams [1870] 11 Eq 204, 65fn8
Birstall Candle Co v Daniels [1908] 2 KB 254, 127fn48
Re: Bishop deceased [1965] Ch 450, 253
Bishop v Bryant [1834] 6 C&P 484, 280fn43
Bishop v Elliot [1885] 11 Exch 113, 241fn148
Bishop of Rochester v Le Fanu [1906] 2 Ch 513, 75fn74
Bissett v Caldwell (1791) Peake 50, 188fn19,223fn32
Bissett v Caldwell 1 Esp 206, 243fn161
Black v Coleman (1878) 29 CP 507, 206fn83
Blackburn v Bowering [1994] 3 All ER 380 CA, 111fn61
Blackpool Aero Club v Fylde BC [1990] 1 WLR 1195, 341fn49
Blades v Arundale [1813] 1 M&S 711, 245fn179
Blades v Higgs (1861) 10 CBNS 713, 107fn37
Blake v Newburn (1848) 17 LJQB 216, 325fn57
Blankenstein v Robertson [1890] 24 QBD 543, 255fn225
Re: Blue Bird Mines [1942] 44 WALR 85, 83fn101
Bluston & Bramley Ltd v Leigh [1950] 2 KB 554, 72fn48,87fn130
Bolt & Nut Co (Tipton) Ltd v Rowlands, Nicholls & Co [1964] 2 QB 10, 273
Bolton v Canham (1670) Pollexfen 20, 130fn71
Re: Bond Worth [1979] 3 All ER 919 CA, 258fn242
Booth v Walkden Spinning & Manufacturing Co Ltd [1909] 2 KB 368, 89fb138
Borden (UK) v Scottish Timber Products Ltd [1979] 3 All ER 961 CA, 258fn242
Boswell v Crucible Steel Co [1925] 1 KB 119, 236fn108
Boucher v Wiseman (1595) Cro Eliz 440, 128fn57
Boulton v Reynolds (1859) 2 E&E 369, 273fn11
Bott v Ackroyd (1859) 23 JP 661, 331fn1
Bourgoin SA v Ministry of Agriculture [1986] 1 QB 716, 370fn126
Bowden v Waithman (1821) 5 Moore CP 183, 337fn37
Bower v Hett [1895] 2 QB 337, 206fn87
Bowkett v Fullers United Electrical Works [1923] 1 KB 160, 85fn118
Bower & Co v Hett [1895] 2 QB 51, 73fn64
Re: Bowman (1931) 4 ABC 155, 71fn40
Boyd v. Bilham [1909] 1 KB 14, 224fn38
Boyd v Profaze (1867) 16 LT 431, 160fn65
Boyd v Shorrock [1867] 5 Eq 72, 236,238fn123
Bradby at p.275 cites Coke 2 Inst 107, 356fn81
Bradford MBC v. Arora [1991] 2 WLR 1377 CA, 356fn86
Braithwaite v Cooksey & Another 1 H Bl 465, 130fn71
Braithwaite v Marriott [1862] 1 H&C 591, 320fn39
Branscomb v Bridges (1823) 1 B&C 145, 273fn12
Bray v Fitzwilliam (1863) *The Times*, July 16th, 13c (Nisi Prius) *The Times* November 14th
  1872 9e & July 30th 1873 11d, 223fn29

Grunnell v Welch [1906] 2 KB 555, 297fn135
Grymes v Boweren (1830) 6 Bing 437, 241fn148
Guardians of Naas Union v. Cooper 18 LR Ir 242, 289fn96
Guest v Cowbridge Railway Co (1868) 6 Eq 619, 127fn47
Gunn v Bolckow, Vaughan & Co [1875] 10 Ch App 491, 273fn8
Re: Gurden (1894) 2 PMR 872, 28fn14,30fn23
Re: Gwynn ex p Veness [1870] 10 Eq 419, 72fn49

Haddow v Morton [1894] 1 QB 565, 350fn58
Hale v Saloon Omnibus Co (1859) 4 Drew 492, 112fn66
Hall v Roche (1799) 8 TR 187, 122fn14
Hall v Rover Financial [2002] EWCA Civ 1514, 323fn49
Halliday v Nevill [1984] 155 CLR 1, 154fn36,157fn45
Hammond v Mather (1862) 3 F&F 151, 203fn75
Harding v Hall (1866) 14 LT 410, 319fn29
Harpelle v. Carroll (1896) 27 OR 240, 108fn41
Harper v. Carr (1797) 7 TR 270, 140fn113.332fn6
In Re: Harpur's Cycle Fittings [1900] 2 Ch 731, 89fb144
In Re: Harris [1931] 1 Ch 138, 71fn34
Harris v Shipway (1744) Bull NP 182a, 131fn78
Harrison v Mearing (1843) The Times, May 10th, 8b (Exch), 30fn28
Harrison v Paynter (1840) 6 M&W 387, 292fn114
Harvey v. Mayne [1872] Ir 6 CL 417, 110fn53
Harwell v Burwell Sir W Jones 456, 245fn179
Haselar v Lemoyne (1858) 5 CBNS 530, 337fn40
In Re: Hassall ex p Brooke [1874] 9 Ch 301, 74fn65
Hatch v Hale (1850) 15 QB 10, 273fn11
Hawes v. Watson (1892) 94 LT 181, 30fn27
Hawkins v Walrond [1876] 1 CPD 280, 288fn86
Hawtry v Butlin [1873] 8 QB 290, 256fn229
Hayne's Case (1614) 12 Co Rep 113, 251fn206
Hayoz v. Patrick (1961) 30 DLR 742, 224
Haythorn v Bush (1834) 2 Cr& M 689, 245fn176
Haywards Builders Supplies Ltd v MacKenzie [1956] 20 WWR 591, 226fn50
Headland v Coster [1905] 1 KB 219 (confirmed on appeal [1906] AC 286 HL), 320fn39
Heathcote v. Livesey [1887] 19 QBD 285, 71fn37, 72fn46
Heaton v Dugard Ltd & Cutting Bros Ltd [1925] 1KB 655, 91fn153,259ff252,253
Heeles v Creditors' Trustee of Samson (1880) UB&F(SC) 196, 84fn104
Hellawell v Eastwood (1851) 6 Exch 295, 236,237fn113
Henderson v. McGuigan & Thompson [1933] 3 WWR 230, 163fn77
Re: Henley ex p Fletcher [1877] 5 Ch D 809, 199fn46
Hentrich v. France (1995)
Re: Herbert Berry [1977] 1 WLR 617, 84fn106
Herries v Jamieson (1794) 5 TR 553, 145fn2,247fn191
Heseltine v Heseltine [1971] 1 All ER 952 @ 956, 253fn216
Heseltine v Simmons [1892] 2 QB 547, 256fn230
Hessey v. Quinn [1910] 21 OLR 519, 356fn82
Hetherington v Groome [1884] 13 QBD 789, 255fn225
Heward v. Mitchell [1853] 10 UCQB 535 (CA), 256fn234
Hickman v Maisey [1900] 1 QB 752, 321fn47
Higgins v M'Adam (1829) 3 Y&J 1, 72fn50
In re: High Bailiff of Brompton county court (1893) The Times, May 12th, 14a (QBD), 30fn25
Ex p Hill, In Re: Roberts [1877] 6 Ch D 63, 69fn26
Re: Hill Pottery [1866] LR 1 Eq 649, 84fn111

Taking Control of Goods

Kirkpatrick v Kelly (1781) 3 Doug KB 30, 152fn30
In Re: Knight ex p Voisey [1882] 21 Ch D 442, 131fn80
Knotts v Curtis (1832) 5 C&P 322, 283fn56
Knox v Anderton [1983] Crim LR 115, 154fn36
Koppel v Koppel [1966] 2 All ER 187, 253
Koppers Co v. Dominion Foundries & Steel Ltd (1965) 8 CBR(NS) 49, 71fn42
Kotchie v The Golden Sovereigns Ltd [1898] 2 QB 164, 350fn60
Re: Kreutzweiser [1967] 2 OR 108, 227fn56

Lady Branscomb v Fleming & Bridges (1822) *The Times*, December 7th, 3a (KBD), 31fn32
W T Lamb & Sons v Rider [1948] 2 KB 331, 124fn31
Lamb v Cloves (1847) 10 LT 231, 283fn58
Loring v Warburton (1858) EB&E 507, 274fn14
Lyon v Tomkies (1836) 1 M&W 603, 292fn114
Laidler v Elliott (1825) 3 B&C 738, 335fn28
Lambert v Roberts [1981] 2 All ER 15, 154fn34,fn36,157,158fn56
Lampleigh v Brathwaite 1 Sm LC 151, 353fn73
In Re: Lancashire Cotton Spinning Co [1887] 35 Ch D 656, 85fn118
Langdon v. Traders Finance Corporation [1966] 1 OR 655, 220fn19,226
Langford v Selmes (1857) 3 K&J 220, 10fn36
Langtry v. Clark (1896) 27 OR 280, 288fn91
Lanphier v Phipos (1838) 8 C&P 475, 335fn27
Late v McLean [1870] 8 NSR 69, 249fn198
Lavell & Co v O'Leary [1933]2 KB 200, 108
Lavell v Ritchings [1906] 1 KB 480and *The Times* Feb. 24th, 3c, 221,227fn61,231fn76
In Re: Lavies ex p Stephens [1877] 7 ChD 127, 241fn151
Lawton v Lawton (1743) Atk 13, 240fn140
LB Hackney v White [1995] 28 HLR 219, 124fn31
LCP Retail v Segal [2006] EWHC 2087, 65fn8,109,205
Ledger v DPP [1997] Crim LR 439, 106fn30
Lee v Cooke [1858] 3 H & N 203, 297fn132
Lee v Dangar & Co [1892]1 QB 231, 170fn113
Lee v Dangar, Grant & Co [1892] 2 QB 337, 298fn139
Lee v Gansel (1774).1 Cowp 1, 152
Lee v Gaskell [1876] 1 QBD 700, 239fn126
Lee v Smith (1854) 9 Exch 662, 131fn78
Lee v Walker [1872] 7 CP 121, 335fn27
Leery v Goodson (1792) 4 TR 687, 325fn60
Legg v. Evans (1840) 6 M&W 36, 254fn219
Lehain v Philpott (1876) 35 LT 855, 16fn59
Leicester v Plumtree Farms [2003] EWHC 206 (Ch); [2004] BPIR 296, 68fn23
Leigh v Taylor [1902] AC 157, 237fn119
Levitt v. Dymoke (1868) 3 Ir CL 1, 163fn76
Lewandowski v Poland (1999)appl 43457/98, 52
Lewis v Baker [1905], 10
Lewis v Read (1845) 13 M&W 834, 337fn40
Lewis v Owen [1894] 1 QB 102, 110fn56
Liepins v Spearman [1986] RTR 24, 106fn32
Liford's Case (1614) 11 Co Rep 46b, 237fn113
Linotype-Hell Finance Ltd v Baker [1993] 1 WLR 321, 99fn8
Ex p Lithgow In Re: Fenton [1878] 10 Ch D 169, 73fn61
Ex p Liverpool Loan Co In Re: Bullen [1872] 7 Ch App 732, 73fn61
Liverpool Marine Credit v Hunter [1868] LR 3 Ch App 479, 325fn55
Lloyd v Sandilands (1818) 8 Taunt 250, 200fn58

Master v Fraser (1901) *The Times*, November 8th, 14e, 228fn69
Mathews v Dwan [1949] NZLR 1037, 158fn53
Matthews v Buchanan [1889] 5 TLR 373, 255fn227
May v Hadley & East (1878) Aug.3rd, 4c (CP), 334fn19
May v May (1863) 33 Beav 81 @ 87, 251fn208
Mayner & Mayner v Cariboo Fir Co Ltd [1956]19 WWR 233, 226fn48
Mavor v Croome (1823) 7 Bing 261, 76fn78
Re: Maywald (1933) 7 ABC 9, 71fn40
McArdle v Wallace [1964] Crim LR 467, 154fn38,158
McGowan v. Betts [1871] 13 NBR 296, 371
McGregor v. Klotz [1929] 4 DLR 792, 320fn42
McKinnon v McKinley [1856] 1 PEI 113, 163fn80
McLeod v Girvin Central Telephone Association (1926) 1 DLR 216, 224fn34
McLeod v UK (1998) application no. 72/1997/856/1065; [1999] 1 EHRLR 125, 54,174fn128.
McLorie v Oxford [1982]1 QB 1290, 158fn57
McMillan v. Jones [1923] 3 DLR 821, 115fn82
McPherson v Temiskaming Lumber Co Ltd [1913] AC 145, 128fn61
McQuarrie v Jaques (1954) 92 CLR 262, 72fn55
Re: Mead ex p Cochrane [1875] 20 Eq 282, 76fn80
Mears v Callender [1901] 2 Ch 388, 240ff144,146
Mechelen v Wallace (1836) 7 Ad & El 54n, 11fn41
Re: Meehan [1879] 6 Nfld LR 172, 199fn45
Meggy v Imperial Discount Co Ltd [1878] 3 QBD 711, 196fn40
Megson v Mapleton [1884] 49 LT 744, 320fn39,334fn19,336fn35
Melluish v BMI (No 3) [1994] 2 WLR 795, 238fn124
Re: Memco [1986] Ch 86, 82
Metro-Cab v Munro (1965) 1 OR 555, 226fn49
Meux v. Howell (1803) 4 East 1, 112fn68
Meux v Jacobs [1875] 7 App Cas 481, 239fn131
M'Fadden v Jenkyns (1842) 1 Ph 153, 114fn76
M'Guckin v Dobbin (1863) 15 Ir Jur 311, 358fn92
Miailhe v France (1997) 23 EHRR 491, 51fn9
Miles v Furber [1873] 8 QB 77, 16fn53
Milgate v Kelley & Gooding (1828) The Times, August 16th, 3f (KBD), 30fn25
Miller v Curry [1893] 25 NSR 537, 162fn73
Miller v Parnell [1815] 5 Taunt 370, 298fn139
Miller v Solomon [1906] 2 KB 91 @ 96, 115,233fn84,350fn59
Ex p Millwood Colliery Co (1876) 24 WR 898, 84fn107
Milner v Rawlings [1867] 2 Exch 249, 202ff69-70
Milton v Green 2 B&P 158, 332fn10
Minor- Smith v Smith [1971] 115 Sol Jo 444, 102fn20
Mitchell v Buckingham International plc [1998]EWCA Civ 247/ 2 BCLC 369, 85fn116
Re: Modern Jet Support [2005] 1 WLR 3880, 70fn31
Moffatt v Lemkin (1993), High Court, unreported, 229,369fn119
Molsons Bank v McMeekin ex. p. Sloan (1888) 15 AR 535, 203fn73
Money v Leach (1765) 3 Burr 1742, 333fn14
Montague v Davies Benachi & Co [1911] 2 KB 595, 89fb141
Montgomery v. Hellyar (1894) 9 Man LR 551, 337fn41
Mooney v Prince Albert Credit Union (1994) 121 Sask LR 318, 227fn52
Moore v Drinkwater (1858) 1 F&F 134, 239fn129
Moore v. Lambeth County Court Registrar [1970] 1 All ER 980, 356fn86
In Re: Morgan [1881] 18 ChD 93, 243fn166
Morris v Beardmore [1980] 2 All ER 753, 154,156,157fn45,fn47
Morris v Matthews (1841) 2 QB 293, 361fn99
Mortimer v Cragg (1879) 3 CPD 216, 319fn32

Morton v Woods [1869] 4 QB 293, 11fn39
Moseley v Rendell [1871] 6 QB 338, 244fn168
In Re: Moser [1884] 13 QBD 738, 241fn152
Moss v Gallimore (1779) 1 Doug KB 279, 209fn98
Mostyn v Stock [1882] 9 QBD 432, 73fn62
Mullet v Challis (1851) 16 QB 239, 199fn51
Munk v Cass (1841) 9 Dowl 332, 202fn71
Munroe & Munroe v Woodspring District Council (1979) (1979) CLY 2226, 162
Murgatroyd v Dodworth & Silkstone Coal & Iron Co.[1895] 65 LJ Ch 111, 132fn86
Murgatroyd v Wright [1907] 2 KB 333, 127fn49
Mutter v Speering (1903) 119 LT 134, 29
Mutton v Sheppard (1905) 66 EG 806, 29fn16
Myers v Washbrook [1901] 1 KB 360, 115fn7

Nantes v Corrock 9 Ves 177, 235fn95
Nash v Dickinson [1867] 2 CP 252, 201
Nash v Lucas (1867) 2 QB 590, 163
National Westminster Bank v Powney [1990] 2 WLR 1084, 124fn31
Needham v Rivers Protection & Manure Co [1875] 1 Ch D 253, 89fb139
Neilson v James [1882] 9 QBD 546, 335fn25
Neumann v Bakeaway [1983] 1 WLR 1016, 289fn98
Never Stop (Railway) Ltd v British Empire Exhibition (1924) Inc [1926] Ch 877, 240fn142
Nevill v Halliday [1983]2 VR 553, 156,157
Re: New City Constitutional Club Co ex p Russell [1887] 34 ChD 646, 258fn243
Re: New York Life Assurance Association Co. & Fullerton [1919] 45 OLR 244, 234fn90
Newman t/a Mantella Publishing v Modern Bookbinders Ltd The Independent, February
     3rd, 2000, 53fn12
Re: Nink (1955) 17 ABC 13, 72fn47
Noble Investments Ltd v. General Collections Ltd (1965) 48 DLR (2d) 638, 320fn41
Re: North Wales Produce & Supply Co Ltd [1922] 2 Ch 340, 256fn229
Re: North Yorkshire Iron Co [1878] 7 Ch D 661, 85fn123,86f125,n126
Re: Norton ex p Todhunter [1870] 10 Eq 425, 71fn37
Noseworthy v Campbell [1929] 1 DLR 964, 198fn44
Notley v Buck (1828) 8 B&C 160, 74fn67
Nott v Bound (1866) 1 QB 405, 325fn58
Novello v Toogood (1823) 1 B&C 554, 146
Nutting v Jackson (1773) Bull NP 24, 332fn6
Nyman v Ward (1862) *The Times* August 18th, 11a (Assizes), 227fn59

Re: Oak Pits Colliery [1882] 21 ChD 322, 86fn124
Observer Ltd v Gordon [1983] 1 WLR 1008, 293
Official Assignee of Casey v. Bartosh [1955] NZLR 287, 256fn234
Official Assignee of Slattery v. Slattery (1897) 16 NZLR 332, 115fn81
Re: Opera [1891] 3 Ch 260, 259fn251
Re: Oshawa Heat, Light & Power Co (1906) 8 OWR 415, 73fn58
Ostler v Elliott [1980] Crim LR 584, 106fn32
Oxenham v Collins (1860) 2 F&F 172, 16fn53
In Re: Oxley [1914] 1 Ch 602, 244fn172
Owens v Wynne [1855] 4 E&B 579, 296fn126

Paget v Perchard (1794) 1 Esp 205, 196fn37
Palmer v Bramley [1895] 2 QB 405, 273fn7
Palmer v Crone [1927] 1 KB 804, 331fn2,332fn3
Palmer v Meux (1857) *The Times* December 17th 1857, 8d, 220
Palmer v Stanage (1661) 1 Lev 43, 132fn85,297fn129

Pamplin v Fraser [1981] RTR 494, 157
Pape v Westacott [1894] 1 QB 272, 16fn56
Park v Hammond (1816) 6 Taunt 495, 335fn26
Parker v Harris 1 Salk 262, 131fn79
Parke & Moss v. Howe, Dalton, p.529, 243fn162
Parking Brixen GmbH v Gemeinde Brixen und Stadtwerke Brixen AG [2005] ECR 1-08585,
    340fn48
Parsons v Hind (1866) 13 WR 860, 238fn125
Re: D S Paterson & Co Ltd [1931] OR 777, 83fn101
Payne v Drew [1804] 4 East 523, 128fn52,128fn58,fm59,fn60
Pead's Ltd v Yeo (1980) 31 NBR 581, 226fn48
Peake v Carter [1916] 1 KB 652, 248fn194
Re: Pearson ex p West Cannock Colliery Co (1886) 3 Morr 157, 71fn42
Pearson v Graham (1837) 6 A&E 899, 71fn34
Peel Land & Property (Ports No.3) Ltd v TS Sheerness Steel Ltd [2013] EWHC 1658 (Ch), 237
Pegge v. Neath District Tramways [1895] 2 Ch 508, 259fn255
Re: Penny Lumber Co (1921) 2 CBR 113, 73fn58
Penoyer v Bruce (1697) 1 Ld Raym 244, 145,247fn190
Penton v Browne (1664) 1 Keb 698), 165fn93
Penton v Robert (1801) 2 East 88, 240fn144
Re: Perkins Beach Lead Mining Co [1878] 7 Ch D 371, 85fn114
Perkins v Butterfield [1627] Het 75, 282fn49
Perring & Co v. Emerson [1903] 1 KB 1, 30fn24
Phillips & Another v Rees [1889] 24 QBD 17, 306fn2,320fn40
Phillips v General Omnibus Co (1880) 50 LJQB 112, 68fn22
Philips v Thompson (1684) 3 Lev 191, 72fn44,128fn59
Phillips v Viscount Canterbury [1843] 11 M&W 619, 320fn39
Phipps v Boardman [1965] Ch 992, 336fn31
Pickard v Marriage [1876] 1 Ex D 364, 256fn231
Pickard v Sears (1837) 6 A&E 469, 249fn200
Piggot v Wilkes (1820) 3 B & Ald 502, 152fn30
Piggott v Birtles (1836) 1 M&W 441, 356fn82,358fn91
Pilling v Stewart [1895] 4 BCR 94, 369fn121
Pilling v Teleconstruction Co Ltd [1961] 111 L J 424, 293
Pinero v Judson (1829) 6 Bing 206, 11fn40
Pit v Hunt [1681] 2 Cas in Ch 73, 233fn86
Pitcher v King (1844) 5 QB 758, 233fn83
Pitt v Yalden (1767) 4 Burr 2060, 335fn28
Place v Flagg (1821) 4 M&R 277, 241fn149
Planet Earth Productions Inc. v. Rowlands [1990] 69 DLR 715, 216fn6,232fn81
Planned Properties v Ramsdens Commercials (1984) *Times* March 2nd, 188fn20
Re: Plas-yn-Mhowys Coal Co [1867] LR 4 Eq 689, 84fn111
Plomer v Ball (1837) 5 A&E 823, 122fn16
Ex p Plummer (1739) 1 Atk 103, 76fn79
Polkinhorn v Wright (1845) 8 QB 195, 158fn55
Re: Pollock (1902) 87 LT 238, 71fn42
Pool v Crawcour (1884) 1 TLR 165, 112fn64
In Re: Poole Firebrick & Blue Clay Co [1873] LR 17 Eq 268, 89fb145
Pooles Case (1703) 1 Salk 368, 240fn138
Potter v Bradley & Co (1894) 10 TLR 445, 16fn58
Potter v North (1669) 1 Wms Saund 347(c), 337fn42
In Re: Poverty Bay Farmers' Co-operative Association Ltd (1898) 16 NZLR 695, 85fn113
Poynter v Buckley (1833) 5 C&P 512, 288fn88
Preece v Corrie (1828) 5 Bing 24, 10fn36
Re: Prescott Elevator Co (1902) 1 OWR 161, 84fn109

Re: Zoedone (1884) 32 WR 312, 89fb140
Zouch v Willingdale 1 H Bl 311, 132fn86

Table of Statutes

Table of Statutory Instruments and Rules

Table of Statutory Instruments and Rules

Chapter 1

Foreword

A third edition of this book was required in response to a major change in the legislation. The Tribunals, Courts and Enforcement Act 2007 (TCEA) has substantially reformed the law on the enforcement of debt by the seizure of goods and all practitioners in the field will require a revised handbook. As s.65(1) of the Act says, all previous common law rules on the exercise of powers are replaced by the powers created by Sch.12 of the Act. Much of the existing case authority and principles on these issues are replaced by a statutory code for those debts covered by the new Act.

In response to all these matters this text aims to provide a pragmatic step by step manual to assist those confronted with enforcement by seizure of goods under the new Act. The first part of the book puts the process of taking control of goods in its legal context and considers the impact of such general measures as public law and the Human Rights Act. The second part examines how enforcement action may be avoided, whether by negotiation or by the more extreme solution of insolvency. The third part goes through the procedure blow by blow, from the issue of a warrant to sale. At each stage the parties' rights and responsibilities are described, both in respect of the general principles of the law and in light of the particular debt being levied; remedies are discussed and issues of legal controversy are explored.

The book is designed for practitioners assisting the following groups:

- *debtors*: whether they are individuals, members of partnerships or limited companies;
- *the debtor's relatives*: whether spouses, cohabitees, children or other family members who might find themselves involved in enforcement;
- *tenants & lodgers of debtors* (or their families);
- *creditors*;
- *enforcement agents*; or,
- *third parties* with an interest in property on the debtor's premises, whether they are landlords, holders of bills of sale or debentures, trustees or liquidators in an insolvency, finance companies who have let property on lease or hire purchase, manufacturers with claims under retention of title clauses, other creditors of the debtor or any other third party whose goods might be threatened.

Note: Because of the substantial changes made to the law by the TCEA this third edition of *Law of seizure of goods* wholly replaces the first edition for the purposes of the main debts which readers will encounter- local taxes, fines, parking penalties etc. There will nonetheless be a transitional period, though relatively short, during which seizures issued under the old rules may continue; the new Act provides for this in s.58. In addition there are a few less common debts to which the content of the first edition will continue to apply (see later).

The Act seeks to break with the past by replacing all common law rules with a statutory enforcement code. That said, many existing procedures are preserved in the new legislation, often as a result of applying one feature from a previous form of seizure (especially civil courts) to all debts now to be enforced under the new process of 'taking control.' Additionally, as the established learning is that the best analogy for statutory seizure of goods is the practice in executions, and as taking control is wholly a statutory remedy, case authorities relating to executions may still be useful for reference purposes. As a result, the associated case law is preserved in the text for the purposes of analogy until new authorities are established. Equally, most of the existing law on liability for rent and other debts, the right to seize certain goods and on insolvency is preserved largely un-amended. All the existing case authorities that have been deemed relevant remain in the text.

Note: Criminal Procedure Rules

At the time of writing (May 2014) amendments had yet to be made to bring the Criminal Procedure Rules into line with the new taking control of goods process. This work was underway but not completed.

Part 52 of the Rules are affected and require amendment, specifically:

- *Part 52.7 form of warrants* - there may be no need to alter this rule although Ministry of Justice may bring 52.7(3) more closely into line with Sch.12 para.68 of the Act;
- *Part 52.8 execution of warrants* - several parts of this rule require attention. The duties of the enforcement agent to explain the warrant and its affect supplement but do not contradict the 2007 Act. Rule 52.8(2)(d) on the manner of impounding and rules 52.8(3) and (4) on exempted goods and removals are redundant; and,
- *Part 52.9 sale* - the rules on the conduct and timing of sales and on the distribution of proceeds are redundant.

[1] My book *Sources of bailiff law*, PP Publishing, 2012, will therefore remain useful to readers for some time to come.

Chapter 2

Forms of enforcement and enforcement agent

Section one: Scope & terminology

2.1 Legislation
The new Act aims to provide a wholly new regime for the recovery of debt by the seizure of goods. Accordingly all existing powers are replaced by those contained in Sch.12 of the Act.[1] Almost all enforcement instruments are renamed by s.62(4) -

- *writs of fieri facias* become writs of control (writs of *fieri facias de bonis ecclesiasticis* are excepted from this - see section 3 later);
- *warrants of execution* become warrants of control; and
- *warrants of distress* (unless the power they confer is exercisable only against specific goods) become warrants of control.

These new writs and warrants may only be executed by following the new procedure laid down in Sch.12. This new power of 'taking control' will, if for no other reason than variety, also continue to be described in this book as seizures of goods and levies, using terms formerly applied to distress and execution. The process of taking control of goods in respect of civil court orders (High Court, county court and road traffic penalties) will continue to be termed collectively execution, not least because these procedures continue to be treated as a separate class in insolvency (see c.5). The detailed provisions implementing the 2007 Act are found primarily in the Taking Control of Goods Regulations 2013 and in the Civil Procedure Rules.[2]

2.2 Definitions
The new provisions contain definitions of various key concepts which are repeatedly applied in the legislation.[3] These include the following:

- A child is a person under 16 years of age rather than under 18 years as might be expected. This is because some debtors may be aged 17 or 18;
- A co-owner of goods is any person other than the debtor who has an interest in particular goods. However, to qualify under this description a person must be able to show that the enforcement agent is aware of their interest or would have been had reasonable enquiries been made;
- A disabled person is defined as being anyone whose sight, hearing or speech is substantially impaired, anyone with a mental disorder

or anyone who is substantially physically disabled by any illness, impairment since birth or otherwise. Clearly this particular definition incorporates a considerable degree of subjectivity and differences may well arise between debtors and agents and creditors over the degree of a person's disability;

· Goods includes all property of every description except land;
· An 'older person' is one aged over 65 years; and,
· Premises means any place including vehicles, vessels, aircraft, hovercraft, tents and other moveable structures.

2.3 Character of the reforms
Before we commence our examination of the new regime, it may be helpful to attempt a summary of its overall character and how it differs from the previous law. The purpose of the reforms was to modernise and to unify enforcement law and these aims very substantially have been met. This consolidated and updated nature is one clear characteristic of the new Act.

Secondly, even a brief reading of the Act and Regulations will disclose two central themes to the new rules- openness and clarity. Ensuring that debtors are informed as to what is being done, what stage has been reached and what the cost will be has moved from being good practice under the earlier law to a formal aspect of its replacement. This operates generally through the existence of the single code of bailiff powers and, in detail in individual levies, through the notices that now must be served at successive stages of the recovery process.

Section two: Debts enforceable under the new Act

The active forms of taking control may be divided into three categories as follows.

2.4 Court orders
This category was formerly described as execution, a term which referred generally to the process of enforcement of civil court judgments, whether by charging order, attachment of third party debts, attachment of earnings and more narrowly by the seizure of goods to recover judgment debts. Although the procedure for enforcing judgments by taking control is now identical to that for recovering those debts where a court has not been involved, it may still be useful to distinguish those cases where a prior order of a civil court is required and where it is not.

2.4.1 High Court

The High Court enforcement officer may enforce the following judgments by seizure and sale of the defendant's goods:

- High Court judgments of any amount;
- all county court judgments for over £5000 where the debt does not arise from an agreement regulated by the Consumer Credit Act 1974; and,
- county court judgments of between £600 and £5000 which do not arise from an agreement regulated by the Consumer Credit Act 1974 and where the creditor requests transfer from the county court to the High Court for this purpose.[4]

High Court enforcement officers are private bailiffs, but are also officers of the Supreme Court. They are regulated by the Courts Act 2003, the High Court Enforcement Officers Regulations 2004 and by the Civil Procedure Rules.

2.4.2 County court

HM Court Service employs bailiffs in each county court who are responsible for enforcing all warrants and serving process within that court's area. The bailiff is under control of an authorised officer in the court and may enforce the following judgments by seizure and sale of the defendant's goods:[5]

- all judgments based on debts arising from agreements regulated by Consumer Credit Act 1974;
- all county court judgments of less than £600; and,
- any other judgment of an amount up to £5000.[6]

County court bailiffs are the only bailiffs who are employed as such by a government department or agency. They are civil servants employed by Court Service and are generally regarded as being well trained and well controlled.

It is possible to transfer a High Court judgment to the county court for the purposes of enforcement by a warrant of control. It will thereafter be treated as a county court judgment- in other words, interest will cease to accrue - which is one of the reasons why this will very rarely happen.[7]

2.4.3 Road traffic debts

This is an area of considerable recent growth and now comprises several forms, all modelled upon the first for the recovery of decriminalised parking penalties:

- road traffic penalties: local authorities may use private bailiffs to levy for unpaid orders for road traffic penalties issued under the Traffic Management Act 2004. Any sum payable for a parking offence in England & Wales is recoverable by a warrant of execution as if payable under a county court order.[8]
- vehicle emissions - penalties due under Road Traffic (Vehicle Emissions) (Fixed Penalty)(England) Regulations 2002;[9]
- for violations of red routes and bus lanes by Transport for London under s.144 Transport Act 2000; and,
- the congestion charge in central London under reg.20 Road User Charging (Enforcement & Adjudicator)(London) Regulations 2001.[10]

All of the above penalties are enforced following a county court order. What are now called 'local authority warrants of control' are bulk issued by the Traffic Enforcement Centre at Northampton county court, but are executed by private enforcement agents contracted to the relevant enforcement authority rather than by a county court bailiff.

2.5 Seizures under statute

The power to recover some of the most significant debts arises under statute. The new Act has either amended the existing statute or, where the power to distrain was previously contained in secondary legislation, has set out the power to take control of goods in the statute itself. These liabilities are as follows.

- *Local taxes*: both council tax and national non-domestic rates (NNDR) are enforceable by seizure of goods. Arrears may be levied by either local authority officers or by private enforcement agents. The legislation is expanded upon by guidance such as local authority codes of practice (see c.4) and those issued by trade bodies and government.[11]
- *Drainage rates*: under Land Drainage Act 1991 s.54(1) a drainage board may recover arrears of drainage rates by taking control of goods in the same manner as a local authority may recover NNDR. Rates are raised by assessment on agricultural land and buildings and special levies on non-agricultural properties in order to finance flood defences and the like. The occupier of a chargeable agricultural property may appeal to the valuation tribunal about the determination of the annual value.[12] Any other matter can be appealed to the Crown Court.[13] These matters cannot be raised as a defence in recovery proceedings. A liability order made by the magistrates' court may be enforced by taking control only of the goods and chattels of the liable person though the drainage board need not enforce if it feels that the expenses of collection will not be met.[14] The procedure for recovery has now been brought within

the new Act.[15] Special drainage charges levied and collected by the Environment Agency under the Water Resources Act 1991 are likewise recovered by taking control of goods.

- *Assessed taxes*: note that the situation in respect of income taxes and indirect taxes was changed by the Finance Act 2008.[16] With the consolidation of tax assessment and collection in one body, HM Revenues and Customs, the decision was taken to consolidate their powers to seize goods to recover arrears under Schedule 12 of the 2007 Act. All separate regulations and unique powers were repealed. This applies to income tax, VAT, NICs and all the other taxes described in the following paragraphs. The Finance Act 2008 changes came into effect on April 6th 2014.[17]

  - *Income taxes*: the Collector of Taxes may take control of goods to collect any unpaid taxes under Taxes Management Act 1970 s.61 as amended by TCEA.[18] Seizure is regularly used by the Revenue but in the majority of cases it is against companies who have not paid PAYE.
  - *National insurance contributions* are enforceable by seizure of goods under s.121A Social Security Administration Act 1992. This procedure is amended to bring it within the new provisions for taking control of goods.[19]
  - *Tax credit overpayments*: tax credits are assessed and paid by HMRC and overpayments are collected in the same manner as tax arrears, including by taking control of goods;[20]
  - *VAT*: HMRC have the power to take control of goods for arrears of VAT under para.5(4) Sch.11 VAT Act 1994. The enforcement agent may be any collector or officer empowered by a warrant signed by a Customs Officer of rank not below Higher Executive Officer.[21] Alternatively a warrant may be issued by the HEO direct to an 'authorised person' to levy. The levy must be executed by or under the direction of the authorised person. Finance Act 1997 s.51 is amended to bring VAT enforcement within the new procedure.[22] Also amended at the same time and in the same manner is the enforcement procedure for the following:
  - *Insurance premium tax*: Customs may also levy distress to collect tax due from any insurer which they are refusing to pay.[23] The tax is charged at 2.5% on any taxable insurance contract. These contracts include most policies except those for motor vehicles for the disabled, credit facilities and various ships and aircraft. Like VAT insurance premium tax may be assessed in the absence of a return, there is a right of appeal to tribunal, and various penalties for non-payment and non compliance. Like VAT these include a penalty for breach of

a controlled goods agreement. The tax is enforced by taking control of goods in the same manner as VAT.[24]

· *Landfill tax*: is also collected by HMRC under Part III, Finance Act 1996. It is a tax on the disposal of waste in landfill sites throughout the UK. Site operators are liable for the tax per tonne of landfill disposed. Tax can be assessed where HMRC feel that too little is being paid. There is again a right of appeal to tribunal, interest and penalties for non payment and a penalty of 50% of the tax due for breach of a controlled goods agreement. The tax is enforced by a taking control of goods in the same manner as VAT.[25]

· *Aggregates levy:* this is a tax upon the mining and processing of aggregates and is recoverable under Finance Act 2001 Sch.5. The tax is enforced by taking control of goods in the same manner as VAT.[26]

· *Climate change levy*: this is a tax upon fuel supplies and is recoverable under Finance Act 2000 Sch.6. The tax is enforced by taking control of goods in the same manner as VAT.[27]

· *Stamp duty land tax* this is a tax upon land transactions levied and collected by HM Revenues. It is enforceable using the new procedure of taking control of goods under Finance Act 2003.[28]

· *Any other excise duties*: HMRC can distrain on defaulting excise traders' stock and assets under s.117 Customs & Excise Management Act 1979. All other such powers to seize goods are brought within the new procedure by TCEA which amends Finance Act 1997 s.51.[29]

· *Magistrates' court orders*: private bailiffs or court employed civilian enforcement officers (CEOs) may be used by magistrates' courts to enforce a range of magistrates court orders.[30] The sums recoverable by this means are civil debts (tax and national insurance contributions and criminal legal aid contributions),[31] damages, compensation orders and fines, including those from the Crown Court, Court of Appeal and House of Lords. Fines may be enforced by various means other than seizure of goods. Section 14.1 specifically describes the power to immobilise vehicles in enforcement of a fine. Details of warrant enforcement are also to be found in the Magistrates' Courts Rules 1981 (civil debts) and the Criminal Procedure Rules Part 52 (fines).[32]

· *Child support maintenance*: the Secretary of State for Social Security is empowered to take control of goods to collect arrears of maintenance due to the Child Support Agency (CSA).[33] Recent criticism of the CSA's success in recovering maintenance owes has led to an increased emphasis upon arrears recovery and will result in a likely rise in the use of seizure of goods.

2.6 Commercial rent arrears recovery

The power of distress for rent has been abolished by s.71 of the Act. There will no longer be any power to take control of goods for rent arrears arising from domestic premises. However section 72 of the new Act provides that a landlord of commercial premises may instead use the Sch.12 procedure of taking control to enforce rent arrears due under a lease. This power is referred to as commercial rent arrears recovery, abbreviated to the inelegant acronym of CRAR. It is a form of taking control of goods identical to all other debts so far described, but some special extra rules are made in respect of the landlord and tenant relationship.

2.6.1 Landlord

Section 73(1) defines landlord, but with certain provisos. The definition of landlord is important as it determines who may lawfully levy CRAR. A landlord is the person for the time being entitled to the immediate reversion in the property comprised in the lease. In most cases it will be clear who is entitled to the immediate reversion of the property but provision is made for a number of situations where this may be less clear. These are:

- *Tenancies by estoppel:* these are tenancies granted by a person when s/he has no right to make such a grant. A landlord and tenant relationship will exist between the two parties and as a result, even though the landlord may not have a legal estate in the land comprised in the lease and therefore will not be entitled to immediate reversion of the property, s.73(3) states a person is treated as being "entitled to the immediate reversion" if he is entitled to it as between himself and the tenant.
- *Joint tenants*: if there are joint tenants of the immediate reversion, or if a number of persons are entitled to the immediate reversion as between themselves and the tenant the "landlord" means any one of them and CRAR may be exercised to recover rent due to all of them.
- *Mortgaged properties*: if the immediate reversion is mortgaged, "landlord" means the mortgagee, if he has given notice of his intention to take possession or enter into receipt of rents and profits on the existing lease; otherwise, the person entitled to exercise CRAR will be the mortgagor. This applies whether the lease is made before or after the mortgage is created, but CRAR is not exercisable by a mortgagee in relation to a lease that does not bind him because there will be no relationship of landlord and tenant between lender and tenant. A non-binding lease may be one which has not been made in line with the terms of the mortgage or s.99 Law of Property Act 1925.

- *Receivers*: where a receiver is appointed by a court in relation to the immediate reversion, CRAR is exercisable by the receiver in the name of the landlord.[34]
- *Other cases*: These provisions apply to any other person entitled under statute to exercise CRAR as they apply to the landlord- for example a trustee or administrator in insolvency.

The older case law held that the landlord had to hold the reversion, no matter how short it might have been, even if (for example) s/he was a tenant who had sublet for their term less just one day. The reversion had to be vested in the landlord at the time the rent fell due, even though it was not necessary to hold the reversion for the whole period over which it accrued. A joint landlord could distrain for the full sum due, with or without the consent of the other joint landlords.[35] If there had been an assignment of the lease, the distrainor must have reserved the express power to distrain if assigning his/ her whole interest. A demise of the whole term or longer equals an assignment.[36] Thus in *Lewis v Baker* [1905], the defendant sublet the property for a term exceeding the original lease. When he levied distress for the rent, the court held it to be illegal. See too *Tadman v Henman* [1893] in which a reversion by estoppel was held to justify distress, but not against third party goods.[37]

2.6.2 Lease

A lease is defined in s.74 as a tenancy in law or in equity, including a tenancy at will, but not including a tenancy at sufferance in which a tenant holds over after the end of a lease but who is contracted out of the protection of the Landlord & Tenant Act 1954 (*see 7.4.1*). All forms of lease are included - long leases, short tenancies, tenancies by estoppel (*see 2.6.1*) and other equitable leases. The lease must, however, be evidenced in writing in order to ensure that all the terms upon which a power of CRAR may be exercised are clear and certain. References to a lease are to a lease as varied from time to time (whether or not the variation is in writing).

CRAR only applies to commercial premises and s.75 elaborates upon this restriction. A lease is treated as a lease of commercial premises if no part of the demised premises is let as a dwelling, if none is let under an inferior lease as a dwelling, or if none is in fact occupied as a dwelling. As a result a lease of a shop with a flat above will not be a lease of commercial premises provided that the flat is used as a dwelling or is required to be used in this manner by the terms of the lease. If the lease does not impose such conditions, and the flat is used for other purposes, then the lease will be one in respect of which CRAR may be used. The "demised premises" include anything on them.

"Let as a dwelling" is defined as meaning that premises are let on terms permitting only occupation as a dwelling or other use combined with occupation as a dwelling. As the basis of the remedy is the written lease, it appears that the fact that the tenant does not actually use the residential accommodation (or does not do so at the time of the bailiff visit) will not permit CRAR to be used. Conversely, if the lease makes no reference to the intended usage of the upper part of premises, even though they may be arranged or furnished as living accommodation, it may mean that CRAR will not be excluded. Premises are not within the exception if letting them as a dwelling is a breach of a superior lease.[38] This provision is designed partly to avoid evasion by tenants subletting part of their premises for residential purposes and then using this as a defence against a levy of CRAR. The other purpose is to prevent landlords who are themselves commercial tenants relying on their own breach of their lease to use CRAR against any subtenants to whom they have let the premises for residential purposes. As the sub-tenancy was for commercial premises, CRAR cannot be employed.

The case law for distress for rent confirmed that the nature of the tenancy was immaterial to the right of seizure of goods: it may have been a tenancy at will or a normal weekly tenancy. If several tenants occupied the land subject to one rent, the landlord could levy on any one for the rent due from all.[39] A contract for a lease was not sufficient to entitle a person to levy distress, nor was entry by a tenant in anticipation of a grant of a lease or an agreement for a lease, unless the conditions for a tenancy at a fixed rent could be implied or unless there was subsequent execution of the lease or a clause in an agreement permitting distress.[40] A landlord also could not distrain if conditions precedent to a tenancy were yet to be satisfied - for example if a house was to be furnished by the landlord prior to the letting, he was unable not distrain until this had been done.[41] Another principle previously applicable to distresses was that if there were several tenancies in one tenant's name, arrears of rent on each had to be distrained for separately; this is likely still to apply.[42]

2.6.3 Rent

Section 76 of the Act defines rent for the purposes of CRAR. Rent means the amount payable under a lease (in advance or in arrear) for possession and use of the demised premises, together with any interest payable on that amount under the lease, and any VAT chargeable on that amount or on the interest. The amount payable for possession and use of the demised premises, where it is not otherwise identifiable, is to be taken to be so much of the total amount payable under the lease as is reasonably attributable to possession and use. Where an interim rent is payable for business premises under or by virtue of Part 2 of the Landlord and Tenant Act 1954, the amount payable under the lease for possession and use of those premises is to be taken to be that rent.

The Act makes it very clear that CRAR applies solely to 'pure' rent and is not available for other liabilities due from a tenant. "Rent" does not include any sum in respect of rates, council tax, services, repairs, maintenance, insurance or other ancillary matters (whether or not called "rent" in the lease). These provisions of s.76(2) deliberately reverse the recent case law on this matter,[43] reverting to earlier principles. Formerly the courts held that if separate agreements exist between landlord and tenant, related to, but distinct from, the letting of the land, these could not be the subject of a distress. See, for example, *Stevens v Marston* (1890) in which brewers who were landlords of pub premises sought to distrain in respect of sums due under agreements to supply drink to the licenced premises.[44]

2.6.4 Contracting out

The Act states that a provision of a contract is void to the extent that it would do any of these - confer a right to seize or otherwise take control of goods to recover amounts within subsection (2); modify the effect of section 72(1) which creates the remedy of CRAR, except in accordance with subsection 85(3), or confer a right to sell goods to recover amounts within subsection (2).[45] Subsection 2 states that the amounts in question are any amounts payable by a tenant whether they are paid:

- as rent;
- under a lease (other than as rent);
- under an agreement collateral to a lease;
- under an instrument creating a rentcharge. Land, rent and rentcharge all have the meaning given by section 205(1) of the Law of Property Act 1925- this section along with the repeal by Sch.13 of s.121 of the Law of Property Act 1925 significantly abolishes the power to levy for rentcharges;
- in respect of breach of a covenant or condition in a lease, in an agreement collateral to a lease or in an instrument creating a rent charge; or,
- under an indemnity in respect of any of the above payments.

These provisions aim to prevent landlords evading the Act by trying to enlarge their powers to seize goods. Contractual terms seeking to resurrect a right of distress for residential premises, creating a right of seizure for payments which are not rent, or modifying the procedure laid down in the Act, will all be prevented. That said, a provision in a contract is not void to the extent that it prevents or restricts the exercise of CRAR.[46] Landlords will be free to place extra limits upon the remedy, for example upon the amounts or periods recoverable or upon the goods seizable.

Finally it is made clear that in this section "lease" also includes a licence to occupy. This confirms the previous case law that distress could not be used if a person with a license to occupy was involved.[47]

2.6.5 Subtenants' rights

The bill has perpetuated the procedure created by the Law of Distress Amendment Act 1908 whereby landlords could claim rent from the subtenants of lessees in arrears.

Where a landlord exercises a right of CRAR against a tenant he may under s.81 serve a notice on any sub-tenant stating the amount of rent which the landlord has the right to recover from the immediate tenant.[48] The notice has effect 14 clear days after it has been served on the sub-tenant. When the notice takes effect it transfers to the landlord the right to recover, receive and give a discharge for any rent payable by the sub-tenant under the sub-lease, until either the notified amount of the arrears has been paid, or the notice is replaced or withdrawn. Under the notice the landlord will be entitled to use CRAR against the subtenant. However, no notice can be served upon any inferior subtenant (*see later*).

The notice to the sub-tenant should be in writing, should be signed and dated by the landlord and should set out the following details:

· the landlord's name, contact details and reference;
· the amount of rent arrears that the landlord is entitled to recover from the immediate tenant (called the 'notified amount');
· instructions that, whilst the notified amount remains unpaid, the sub-tenant should pay rent directly to the landlord rather than the intermediate tenant. These payments will have the effect of discharging any rent owed by the sub-tenant under his/her lease. These payments will continue until the notified amount of rent arrears is cleared or until the notice is withdrawn or a new notice is issued; and,
· finally, the notice will confirm that the landlord may withdraw the notice to the subtenant under reg.55. This confirms that the landlord may cancel any notice to a sub-tenant under s.81(2) of the Act by service of written notice to that effect.[49]

The notice to the sub-tenant may be served by one of several methods:[50]
- · by post addressed to the sub-tenant at one of the addresses at which s/he usually resides or trades;
- · by fax or other electronic means;
- · by hand delivery through a letter box at one of the addresses at which s/he usually resides or trades;
- · personally to the sub-tenant if s/he is an individual rather than a company or partnership; or,
- · where companies, corporations or firms are involved, by delivery to the registered office or one of the addresses at which the debtor usually carries on business.

In determining, for the purposes of exercise of this right, whether CRAR is exercisable by the landlord, s.77 (see 2.6.3 earlier) applies with modifications: if notice of enforcement has not been given, references to that notice are to be read as references to the notice to the sub-tenant under s.81; if control has not been taken of goods, section 77(3)(b) does not apply.

Section 82(1) provides that from any amount that a sub-tenant pays under a notice under section 81, he may deduct an equal amount from the rent that would be due to his immediate landlord under the sub-lease. If an amount is deducted from rent due to a superior sub-tenant, that sub-tenant may deduct an equal amount from any rent due from him under his sub-lease. This right applies even if the sub-tenant's payment, or part of it, is not due under the notice, if it is not due because the notified amount has already been paid (wholly or partly otherwise than under the notice), or if the notice has been replaced by a notice served on another sub-tenant. Any sums paid under a notice by a subtenant to a superior landlord will be deductible from the rent owed to the immediate landlord. These deductions can be passed up a chain of subtenants until they reach the defaulting tenant whose arrears have precipitated the process.

The subtenant's right to make deductions from his rent payments to his immediate landlord does not apply if the superior landlord withdraws the notice before the payment is made. Where the notified amount has already been paid (or will be exceeded by the payment), the right to make deductions does not apply (or does not apply to the excess) if the sub-tenant has notice of that when making the payment. The right also does not apply if, before the payment is made, payments under the notice at least equal the notified amount. Lastly, the sub-tenant's right does not apply to a part of the payment if, with the rest of the payment, payments under the notice at least equal the notified amount. Where the notice has been replaced by one served on another sub-tenant, there is no right to make deductions if the sub-tenant has notice of that when making the payment. Payments under a notice will continue to be deductible from rent even after the rent arrears have been paid or a new notice has been served upon another subtenant, as long as the paying subtenant is unaware of those facts. Payments are not deductible where a notice has been withdrawn, where the subtenant knows s/he has cleared the arrears stated in the notice or s/he knows that those arrears have been cleared by other means.

A notice under section 81 is automatically replaced if the landlord serves another notice on the same sub-tenant for a notified amount covering the same rent or part of that rent.[51] A notice served on one sub-tenant is also replaced if the landlord serves a notice on another sub-tenant for a notified amount covering the same rent or part of that rent, and, in relation to any of the premises comprised in the first sub-tenant's sub-lease, the second sub-tenant is an inferior or superior sub-tenant. There should not normally be two notices in force at once. The only exception to this would be where a tenant physically divides the rented premises and lets to several subtenants. None of these would be inferior to any other and they would each be liable to pay under a notice served on each by the landlord.

The landlord must withdraw a notice under section 81 if any of these following events happens- if either the notice is replaced or if the notified amount is paid, unless it is paid wholly by the sub-tenant. A subtenant paying under a notice should always know when the stated arrears have been cleared and that the notice will therefore be liable to lapse. However payment by the defaulting tenant or service of a notice on another subtenant need not necessarily come to the subtenant's attention - hence the duty on the landlord to keep the subtenant informed.

For the purposes of the recovery of sums payable by a sub-tenant under a section 81 notice, the sub-tenant is to be treated as the immediate tenant of the landlord, and the sums are to be treated as rent accordingly. This means that the landlord may use CRAR against the subtenant. But those sums (as opposed to rent due from the immediate tenant) are not recoverable by notice under section 81 served on an inferior sub-tenant. Any payment received by the landlord that the sub-tenant purports to make under a notice under section 81, and that is not due under the notice for any reason, is to be treated as a payment of rent by the immediate tenant, for the purposes of the retention of the payment by the landlord and (if no rent is due) for the purposes of any claim by the immediate tenant to recover the payment. However this does not affect any claim by the sub-tenant against the immediate tenant.

2.6.6 Old rules on liability for rent

There are certain situations where the courts have held that the landlord might not distrain, and it is presumed that these principles will also still apply.

- *if new premises were involved.* If a new lease had been granted or if an action had been commenced against the ex-tenant as a trespasser.[52]
- *if the tenant had been led to believe that the remedy would not be used* by the landlord or if agreement was made to postpone distress.[53]
- *if the tenant had been given notice to pay the rent due* and was still within the period of 'grace' granted by the notice. To then distrain was premature and was trespass ab initio.[54]
- *if the tenancy had been terminated by death.* In *Scobie v Collins* [1895] a tenancy at will ceased on the death of the tenant therefore a distress was trespass. However if a tenant died and their personal representative entered and held over, distress might be levied. This could not be done if a spouse alone remained in occupation.[55]
- *against the assignee of a lease* if the landlord had consented to the assignment, knowing the assignor owed rent.[56] However the assignee was bound by the power of distress in the pre-existing lease and could not object to its use against them.[57]
- *if court action had been commenced for the rent due.*[58] Conversely the landlord could not sue so long as distress was held, even if it was insufficient, because as long as the distress was held the debt was regarded as being suspended.[59]

If a tenant wishes to dispute the right of the landlord to levy distress, this should be done by a claim for trespass.

Section 3 - Debts not enforceable under the new Act

In addition to the forms of seizure already described, numerous other forms of distress exist which have largely fallen into disuse. They have not however been abolished by the new Act, nor have they been brought within the new procedure of taking control of goods. As a consequence, though rarely seen, the following debts will continue to be enforced under the old laws on the seizure of goods:

- *market tolls and stallages*: may be collected by distress by a market owner (a person or council) under s.38 of the Markets & Fairs Clauses Act 1847. This is amended by TCEA to make market rents enforceable by CRAR, but the recovery of tolls and stallages remains unreformed;[60]
- *various maritime liabilities* including tonnage rates, wreck removal costs and damage to harbour works under the Harbours, Docks & Piers Clauses Act 1847, dockyard charges, lighthouse dues and various fines upon shipping for such offences as oil pollution and sea fishery violations;
- *distress damage feasant* - this is a self help right of distress to deal with trespassing chattels; and,
- *ecclesiastical executions* levies against the goods of a clergyman remain enforceable by writs of *fieri facias de bonis ecclesiasticis* under CPR 83.3. Because of the unique role of the diocesan bishop in this procedure, these writs have been excluded from the TCEA.

The law applicable to these debts is discussed in detail in my book, *Powers of distress*.[61] The new Taking Control of Goods Regulations 2013 are also explicit in stating that they only apply to the process of taking control of goods for the specific debts covered by the 2007 Act.[62]

Section 4 - Transitional Provisions

Inevitably, there will cases of enforcement part completed at the time of the change over from the old to the new law. The legislation lays down procedures for the handling of these.

2.7 Levied debts

The main provision is section 66 of the Act, which states that where:

"before the commencement of [the Act], goods have been distrained or executed against, or made subject to a walking possession agreement, under the power, this Part does not affect the continuing exercise of the power in relation to those goods."

The effect of this concession is, that if enforcement agents are already in possession of goods taken in distress, they will be able to carry the process of distraint through to its natural conclusion. What is envisaged is the following:

- Goods impounded in walking possession and subject to a signed agreement with the tenant;
- Goods impounded on the premises (perhaps by securing them in a room or outbuilding) in line with section 10 of the Distress for Rent Act 1737;
- Goods that have been impounded by immediate removal from the premises to a place of secure storage; or,
- Goods that have been removed from the premises with a view to their imminent sale.

These levies will remain valid and will have to be resolved by payment or sale. Specific provisions are also made for particular debts, as described in the following paragraphs.

2.8 Civil court judgments

The Civil Procedure Rules also lay out rules for the courts to follow. Where in respect of a writ or warrant of control permission for the issue of the writ or warrant was sought before 6th April 2014 or permission was not required for the issue of the writ or a warrant, but a request for issue was filed before 6th April 2014, the new rules do not apply. Secondly, the new rules do not apply to any enforcement action, or any action taken in relation to that enforcement action, where the right to take the enforcement action becomes exercisable otherwise than by virtue of a writ or warrant issued by a court, and the enforcement action is begun before 6th April 2014.[63]

Where, before 6th April 2014 a writ of *fieri facias* has been issued, a High Court Enforcement Officer has made at least one journey to seize goods pursuant to the writ and no goods have been seized and no walking possession agreement has been entered into, but the debtor entered into an agreement to pay the judgment debt and costs and has those payments, the action taken by the HCEO is to be regarded as constituting the compliance and first enforcement stage under the Taking Control of Goods (Fees) Regulations 2014. However, the fees for those stages will not be payable and instead, there may be recovered, as appropriate, the following fees allowed by Sch.3 of the High Court Enforcement Officers Regulations 2004 - the mileage fee, the percentage fee and, if the agreement provided for the payment of such a fee, a miscellaneous fee under para.12 of the scale.[64]

2.9 Liability orders & road traffic debts

Where, before 6th April 2014 a liability order has been made or an authority has issued a warrant, for the enforcement of business rates, council tax, child support maintenance or road traffic penalties and visits have been made, or premises have been attended, to levy distress or with a view to levying distress but no goods have been seized or taken into possession the following rules apply. The action taken is to be regarded as constituting the compliance stage under the Taking Control of Goods (Fees) Regulations 2014, but the fee for the compliance stage will not be payable. Instead, the bailiff may recover the fees set out below, as appropriate:

- for visits under heads A(i) and A(ii) in paragraph 1 of Schedule 3 to the Non-Domestic Rating (Collection and Enforcement) (Local Lists) Regulations 1989;
- for visits under heads A(i) and A(ii) in paragraph 1 of Schedule 3 to the Council Tax (Administration and Enforcement) Regulations 1992;
- the fees for visits under heads A and BB in paragraph 1 of Schedule 2 to the Child Support (Collection and Enforcement) Regulations 1992; or,
- the fees for visits under heads 1 and 3 in Schedule 1 to the Enforcement of Road Traffic Debts (Certificated Bailiffs) Regulations 1993.[65]

2.10 Distress for rent

Where, before 6th April 2014, a bailiff has attended premises to levy distress for rent but a levy has not been made, and possession has not been taken of any goods, the action taken is to be regarded as constituting the compliance stage within the meaning of the Taking Control of Goods (Fees) Regulations 2014. The fee for the compliance stage will not be payable and instead the fee in paragraph 2 of Appendix 1 to the Distress for Rent Rules 1988(g) may be recovered.[66]

2.11 Distraint for fines

Where, before 6th April 2014 a warrant of distress has been issued under section 76(1) of the Magistrates' Courts Act 1980 and a bailiff has sent to the debtor a letter or notice requiring payment of the sum within a specified period and/ or has attended premises to levy the sum, but the levy has not been made, and possession has not been taken of any goods, the action taken is to be regarded as constituting the compliance stage under the 2014 Fees Regulations. The compliance fee will not be payable and instead there may be recovered the appropriate fee for the action taken allowed by any contractual or other binding arrangement in force between the creditor and the bailiff at that time.[67]

Section 5 - Commentary

The origin of the 2007 Enforcement Act was a study undertaken on behalf of the Department of Constitutional Affairs in 2000 entitled A single piece of bailiff law. It will already have been observed that the subsequent statute failed to achieve this aspiration - some forms of seizure of goods remain outside the new Act for reasons which remain unclear. It may be argued that they are seldom used, but this is just as much a reason for incorporating them as not. Failure to bring them within the new procedure leaves us with the old common law rules and statutes still existing alongside the new regime, adding to the complexity and confusion rather than alleviating it.

Additionally, as will appear in future chapters, the new Act preserves several of the distinctions between debts that operated under the old law. The only justification for these is that the government has preserved its preferential status as a creditor.[68] This may well make economic sense, but in pure jurisprudential terms it is nonsensical as it leaves in place distinctions between the recovery of different debts based solely on the identity of the creditor rather than any more substantive differences.

1 s.62(1)-(3).
2 SI 2013/ 1739 & 1894.
3 Sch.12 para.3(1) & reg.2.
4 Article 8 High Court & County Courts Jurisdiction Order 1991; CPR 83.19.
5 s.59 TCEA.
6 As fn.5.
7 CPR 83.17.
8 Traffic Management Act 2004; see also Enforcement of Road Traffic Debts Order 1993 as amended by Tribunals, Courts & Enforcement Act 2007 (Consequential, Transitional & Saving Provision) Order 2014 Sch. Para.5.
9 SI 1808.
10 SI 2313 as amended by SI 2003/108.
11 Local Government Finance Act 1992, Council Tax (Administration & Enforcement) Regs 1992 & Non-domestic rating (Collection & Enforcement) Regulations 1989 as amended by TCEA Sch.13 paras 87-89 & 105-107 and by Tribunals, Courts & Enforcement Act 2007 (Consequential, Transitional & Saving Provision) Order 2014 Sch.para.2 & 3.
12 s.45.
13 s.51.
14 s.54(5)(a) & s.54(6)).
15 Sch.13 para.100.
16 Finance Act 2008 ss.127 & 129 and Sch.43 Part 1.
17 Finance Act 2008, Section 127 and Part 1 of Schedule 43 (Appointed Day) Order 2014, S.I.906/2014.
18 Sch.13 paras 32-34.
19 Sch.13 para 101-102.

20 Tax Credits Act 2002 s.29(3) - overpayments are recoverable like unpaid tax under Part 6 of the Taxes Management Act 1970.

21 reg 65(1).

22 Sch.13 para.119-126.

23 Sch 7 Part III para 7(7) Finance Act 1994.

24 para 19, Sch 7; TCEA Sch.13 para.114.

25 Part V, para 24, Sch 5; TCEA Sch.13 para.123.

26 TCEA Sch.13 para.140.

27 TCEA Sch.13 para.136.

28 Sch.13 para 147.

29 Sch.13 para.126.

30 ss75-78 Magistrates Court Act 1980 as amended by TCEA Sch.13 paras 45-65.

31 Criminal Legal Aid (Contribution Orders) Regulations 2013 reg.46.

32 The 1981 Rules are amended by Tribunals, Courts & Enforcement Act 2007 (Consequential, Transitional & Saving Provision) Order 2014 Sch.para.1.

33 Section 35(1) Child Support Act 1991 as amended by TCEA Sch.13 paras 93-94

34 s.73(7).

35 Respectively - length of reversion - *Wade v Marsh* (1625) Lat 211 & The'r v. Barton (1570); vesting in landlord - *Thompson v Shaw* (1836) 5 LJCP 234; joint landlords - *Pullen v Palmer* (1696) 3 Salk 207 & *Robinson v Hoffman* (1828) 4 Bing 562.

36 *Preece v Corrie* (1828) 5 Bing 24; *Langford v Selmes* (1857) 3 K&J 220.

37 1 Ch 46; 2 QB 168.

38 Section 75(3)-(5).

39 Respectively a tenancy at will - *Morton v Woods* [1869] 4 QB 293, a weekly tenancy - *Yeoman v Ellison* [1867] 2 CP 681& multiple tenants - *Woodcock v Titterton* (1864) 12 WR 865.

40 Respectively: contract - *Dunk v Hunter* (1822) 5 B & Ald 322; entry - *Pinero v Judson* (1829) 6 Bing 206; subsequent execution - *Carrington v Saldin* (1925) 133 LT 432 and *Manchester Brewery v Coomb* [1901] 2 Ch 608.

41 *Mechelen v Wallace* (1836) 7 Ad & El 54n.

42 *Rogers v Birkmire* (1736) 2 Stra 1040.

43 *Concorde Graphics v Andromeda Investments* [1983] 265 EG 386; *Escalus Properties v Robinson* [1995] 31 EG 71.

44 60 LJQB 192 or see *Pulbrook v Ashby* (1887) 56 LJQB 376.

45 s.85.

46 s.85(3).

47 *Rendell v Roman* (1893) 9 TLR 192; *Provincial Bill Posting Co v Low Moor Iron Co* [1909] 2 KB 344; *Interoven Stoves Co Ltd v F W Hubbard* [1936] 1 All ER 263.

48 Reg.53(1) TCG Regs.

49 Reg.54 TCG Regs.

50 Reg.53(2) applying reg.8(1) TCG Regs.

51 s.83.

52 *Bridges v Smyth* (1829) 5 Bing 410.

53 *Miles v Furber* [1873] 8 QB 77; agreement - *Giles v Spencer* (1857) 3 CBNS 244 & *Oxenham v Collins* [1860] 2 F&F 172

54 *Purple Daisy Ltd v. Frobisher Developments Ltd* [1990] NWTR 375.

55 1 QB 375; spouse alone - *Turner v Barnes* (1862) 2 B&S 435.

56 *Pape v Westacott* [1894] 1 QB 272; *Wharfland v South London Co-operative Building Co* [1995] Times 25/4.

57 *Daniel v Stepney* [1874] 9 Exch 185.

58 *Chancellor v Webster* [1893] TLR 568; *Potter v Bradley & Co* (1894) 10 TLR 445.

59 *Edwards v Kelly* 6 M&S 204; *Lehain v Philpott* (1876) 35 LT 855.

60 Sch.14 para.11. All these remedies were described by the author in *Lloyds Maritime & Commercial Law Quarterly* [2000] pp.113-121.

61 *Powers of distress*, Wildy, Simmonds & Hill, 2009.

62 Reg.3(1).

63 CPR 69th update, PD amendment paras.(2) & (3).

64 Article 4(1) & (2) Tribunals, Courts & Enforcement Act 2007 (Consequential, Transitional & Saving Provision) Order 2014.

65 Art.4(3) & (4) Tribunals, Courts & Enforcement Act 2007 (Consequential, Transitional & Saving Provision) Order 2014.

66 Art.4(5) & (6) Tribunals, Courts & Enforcement Act 2007 (Consequential, Transitional & Saving Provision) Order 2014.

67 Art.4(7) & (8) Tribunals, Courts & Enforcement Act 2007 (Consequential, Transitional & Saving Provision) Order 2014.

68 See my discussion of these issues in *Weapon of authority*, KDP, 2013.

Chapter 3

Licencing of bailiffs

3.1 Certification

The major failure of the new legislation is to provide a new, comprehensive and robust system of regulation for the entire enforcement sector. Rather we have a continuation of the previous system that distinguishes (no longer for any profound reason) between bailiffs and HCEOs, albeit it with a modestly reformed system of certification for bailiffs.

3.1.1 Introduction

Sections 63 and 64 of the Act provide for new rules to be made for the regulation of bailiffs. A revised system of certification of bailiffs is introduced. An individual may only act as an enforcement agent exercising the enforcement powers created by the Act if one of the following conditions applies:

- s/he acts under a certificate under section 64;
- s/he is exempt from the need to hold a certificate; or,
- s/he acts in the presence and under the direction of a person to whom either of the preceding paragraphs applies.[1]

An individual is exempted from the need to be certificated only if s/he acts in the course of his/her duty as one of the following capacities:

- a constable. Police officers are mentioned because of their role in assisting with forced entries under court warrants (*see 8.7 below*);
- an officer of HM Revenue and Customs;
- a person appointed by the Lord Chancellor as court officers and staff under section 2(1) of the Courts Act 2003 (which will include HCEOs appointed under s.99 and Sch.7 of the 2003 Act). Although authorised HCEOs do not require certificates, their staff will do so;
- in the course of his duty as an officer of a government department; and,
- if the individual is a civilian enforcement officer, as defined in section 125A of the Magistrates' Courts Act 1980.[2]

A person is guilty of an offence if s/he purports to act as an enforcement agent without being authorised to do so (*see 3.5 below*).

3.1.2 *Application process*

An application for the issue of a certificate must be made to the County Court Business Centre in Northampton, using the prescribed form EAC1.[3] The application must specify one of the county court hearing centres listed in Practice Direction 84 as the centre at which the application is to be heard. There are 24 of these in total; the country is divided into seven regions with three or four courts generally allocated to each.

The application must provide evidence that the applicant fulfils the requirements of regulation 3(b) of the Certification Regulations: that the applicant is a fit and proper person to hold a certificate and that s/he possesses sufficient knowledge of the law and procedure of taking control of goods. In particular the applicant will have to provide copies of various documents specified in the Practice Direction 84. These are as follows:

- two references, of which one may be from the applicant's employer or an approved officer of the Civil Enforcement Association or of the High Court Enforcement Officers' Association and one must deal with the applicant's knowledge of the law and procedure relating to powers of enforcement by taking control of goods and commercial rent arrears recovery, and the applicant's experience of, and conduct in, exercising such powers;
- a certified copy of the result of a search (which must be no more than one month old) of the Register of judgments, orders, fines and tribunal decisions against the applicant's full name; and the applicant's home and business addresses for the last six years;
- two passport sized photographs of the applicant (one of which is retained on the court file, the other fixed to the certificate if issued);
- a copy (which must conform to the design and layout prescribed in the Schedule to the Certification Regulations and be on paper of durable quality and in a clear and legible printed or typewritten form with a font size no less than 10 point) of each of the following forms required by the TCG Regulations and intended to be used by the applicant when exercising powers of taking control of goods or commercial rent arrears recovery -
  - enforcement notice;
  - controlled goods agreement;
  - immobilisation warning;
  - notice of re-entry;
  - notice after entry or taking control of goods on a highway and inventory of goods taken into control;
  - notice of removal for storage or sale;

- inventory;
- notice of sale;
- notice of abandonment;
- proof that the applicant has achieved at least a qualification on Taking Control of Goods at (or above) Level 2 of the Qualifications and Credit Framework or equivalent as determined by a nationally accredited awarding body or that s/he has been authorised to act as an enforcement officer in accordance with the High Court Enforcement Officers Regulations 2004; and, lastly,
- If any objections have been submitted to the court in response to publication of the notice of the application (see later), a copy of those reasons must be sent to the applicant at least seven days before the hearing, and the applicant may respond to them both in writing and at the hearing.

The applicant must also file such further evidence as the court may direct before the date scheduled for the hearing.

The penultimate bullet point in the last list refers to the need for a bailiff to have obtained a qualification. Four are available for potential applicants to study which have been endorsed by Ofqual, the Office for Qualifications and Examinations Regulation. These are:

- Institute of Credit Management (ICM) level 4 certificate for HCEOs;
- ICM level 4 diploma for HCEOs;
- ICM level 5 diploma for HCEOs; and,
- Institute of Rating, Revenues and Valuation level 2 certificate in debt enforcement. This is the qualification that will apply to the bulk of those wishing to take control of goods in future.

None of the qualifications are at a particularly high academic level, but the fact that they are required at all under the new regime is a significant step forward.

Before a certificate can be issued, any applicant must lodge in court security totalling £10,000 by way of bond or, alternatively, satisfy the judge that security totalling that amount is already subsisting by way of bond. This security must be retained once the certificate has been issued for the purpose of securing the certificated person's duties as an enforcement agent and the payment of any reasonable costs, fees and expenses incurred in the investigation of any complaint made to the court against the certificated person in the capacity of an enforcement agent (see 3.1.5 & 13.11). It must be maintained throughout the duration of the certificate (see 3.1.4) and, if at any time during this period the security no longer exists, or is reduced in value to less than £10,000, the certificated person must, by such time as the court may direct, provide fresh security to the satisfaction of the court.

Finally, the court must publish, on the HMCTS website, notice of every application made to the court for the issue of a certificate. This notice must contain the following information:

- the applicant's name;
- the name of the applicant's employer, if any;
- the date on which the application will be heard, which must be at least eight days after the deadline for filing objections to the application;
- that any person who knows of any reason why the applicant may not be a fit and proper person to hold a certificate may give the written details to the court; and,
- the date by which a person must file their objections, which must be at least 30 days from the date on which the notice is published on the website.[4]

3.1.3 Hearing of applications

Certificates to act as an enforcement agent may be issued by either:

- by a judge assigned to a county court district; or,
- in prescribed circumstances, by a district judge. In fact, this will be the normal practice of the courts in future.[5]

The hearing of an application at one of the county court hearing centres cannot be scheduled to take place until at least eight days after the deadline for members of the public to file objections (see the previous section).[6]

The applicant must attend for examination on the day of the hearing. S/he will have to provide copies of all the documents referred to in the previous section plus the following:

- a certified copy of a one of the following - a criminal conviction certificate, a criminal record certificate or an enhanced criminal record certificate- which has been issued pursuant to Part V of the Police Act 1997 and which is not more than one month old; and,
- written evidence of the lodging by way of bond of the security required by regulation 6 of the Certification Regulations.

A judge cannot grant a certificate to an applicant unless s/he has been satisfied that:

- the applicant is a fit and proper person to hold a certificate;
- the person possesses sufficient knowledge of the law and procedure relating to powers of enforcement by taking control of goods and of commercial rent arrears recovery to be competent to exercise those powers;
- the forms which the applicant intends to use when exercising powers of taking control of goods or commercial rent arrears recovery conform to the design and layout prescribed in the Schedule to the Certification Regulations 2014;
- the applicant has lodged the security required or such security is already subsisting; and,
- the applicant does not carry on, and is not and will not be employed in, a business which includes buying debts.

The hearing should involve a thorough and searching examination of the applicant, testing their knowledge and challenging their fitness to undertake the intended role.

Courts must compile and maintain a list of all certificated persons who hold a certificate which has not expired or been cancelled. This list must contain, for each certificated individual, the person's name, the name of the person's employer (if any), the date of issue of the certificate and the date on which the certificate ceases to have effect. The list complied from this information must be published on a website maintained by or on behalf of Her Majesty's Courts and Tribunals Service.[7]

3.1.4 Duration & amendment

A certificate granted upon a successful application remains valid, unless it is cancelled, for two years from the date on which it was issued, subject in the case of a replacement certificate (see below). Every certificate must state the date on which it ceases to have effect.[8]

When a certificate expires, it must be surrendered to the court, unless the judge directs otherwise. If a certificated person ceases to carry on business as an enforcement agent, s/he must (unless a judge has ordered otherwise) surrender the certificate to the court. It will be treated as if it had expired on the date on which it was surrendered. At the same time the security must be cancelled and the balance of any deposit returned to the individual.[9] If a certificate has expired and, before the date of expiry, the certificated person took control of goods then, unless the court orders otherwise, the goods continue to be controlled goods and the certificate continues to have effect, for the purposes of completing the levy.[10]

If there is any change in the name, business address and employer of a certificated person, the certificated person must as soon as possible send written notice to the county court hearing centre that issued the certificate and produce the certificate to the court. When this happens, the old certificate must be cancelled and a replacement certificate must be issued to the certificated person, as soon possible. The replacement certificate must reflect the change notified, but in all other respects, including the date on which it ceases to have effect, must be the same as the cancelled certificate. No fee is payable for cancellation of a certificate or for the issue of a replacement certificate under this regulation.[11]

3.1.5 Complaints

The Act provides in section 64(3)(d) for there to be a complaints procedure against certificated individuals. This is described in detail later at 13.11.

3.1.6 Duties of certificated bailiffs

From the early case law developed in the decades after the creation of certification, it is possible to assert that certain standards must be expected of certificated bailiffs if they are to continue to satisfy the tests of fitness and propriety imposed by the court. Certificated bailiffs should, in general, maintain the highest standards of personal behaviour when levying, avoiding drunkenness, rudeness and violence. In the exercise of their powers, bailiffs should show discretion and discrimination. HHJ Parry at Manchester county court in 1910 warned that certificate holders had duties to all the parties involved - to the creditor, to the debtor, to the wider community and the court that awarded the certificate by ensuring that the poor were protected and that exempt goods were not seized in distress.[12] These duties coincide with requirements of the new Act and have lost none of their relevance.

Over the years the courts have laid down a set of standards of behaviour which those applying for certificates should attain and which those holding certificates should maintain:

· *Being a fit and proper person* - as "officers of the law" bailiffs have a legal and professional duty to maintain the highest standards of conduct.[13] The kinds of unfit behaviour which the court will take into account when considering revocation or renewal include illegal levying, the charging of illegal or excessive fees, abuse of position or improper conduct.[14] Improper conduct will, for example, include bailiffs deliberately misleading a person about their powers or authority (for which see the revised NSEA) or about their intentions. It is unprofessional and improper conduct for an enforcement agent to state that s/he will not levy - and then forthwith to go against that promise[15] - or to make statements which persuade an individual to act in such a way that they become subject to further enforcement action.[16] As well as any threat to the agent's authorisation, such actions on the part of the bailiff may render a levy illegal and may entitle the aggrieved party to a refund of fees or to exercise the right to rescue the goods wrongfully taken into control. Improper conduct which may prejudice a certificate will even include wrongful acts when undertaking un-certificated work;[17] and,

· *Knowing the laws of distress adequately* - it was stressed by one county court judge that "it is of great importance, considering the enormous amount of injustice suffered by poor people in this matter, that certificated bailiffs should thoroughly master the law which regulates their powers."[18] Balancing these remarks, it was accepted that the law can be "obscure and difficult" and that in many instances bailiffs cannot be expected "to express a very definite opinion on it". Of course, under the new statutory code certainty as to powers and duties is much greater than formerly, so that it is likely that higher standards of knowledge and compliance may be expected from individuals. All the same, they have duties both to the community they serve and to the state which has granted them a licence to practice to protect the poor from abuse. As a consequence, they should normally err on the side of caution and give generous treatment to debtors.[19] This reinforces the provisions of the Act relating to vulnerability.

However, over and above this, judges granting certificates and other members of the judiciary hearing cases relating to bailiffs' conduct have set out a range of additional principles which should guide their daily practice in particular areas. Many certification complaints have been founded upon grievances about improper fees. Certificated bailiffs should particularly not:

· *Take excessive fees.* In *Re: Longstaffe ex. P. Robinson* (1896) a certificate was revoked because the bailiff had charged extortionate fees and had also left no inventory of the goods seized (in breach of his statutory duty) and had sold the goods at an undervalue to an associate;[20]
· *Charge for actions not taken.* In *Duncombe v. Hicks* (1898) the bailiff lost his certificate for charging fees for work not actually done by him;[21] or,
· *Charge extra-statutory fees.* In *Mutter v. Speering* (1903) revocation

was ordered because fees not authorised by the fee scale had been charged.[22]

Certificates can be lost for other unfit or improper behaviour. This has included criminal acts such as assault, civil wrongs such as negligence and the detention of goods despite payment by the debtor and the misappropriation or mishandling of monies received.[23]

Part of the point of certification is to ensure that the aggrieved person has a named individual against whom to make a complaint and, through the bond requirement, to ensure that individuals can provide compensation if appropriate. The right to initiate a complaint lies not only with the debtor, but with the creditor, and, indeed, affected third parties, such as hire purchase lenders whose goods are wrongfully levied.[24]

As well as the broad stipulations as to fitness and propriety which must be satisfied in order to obtain and retain a certificate, specific duties have been identified by judges throughout the levy process:

- *Appointing reputable staff* - whether taking on employees or bringing in other contractors, it is important to ensure that their training and conduct matches the standards expected by the courts.[25] In particular, it is the duty of a certificated bailiff to ensure that only certificated staff should undertake those functions for which a certificate is required by statute.[26] It is certain that un-certificated bailiffs cannot undertake certificated work; also a certificated bailiff is liable for any trespass by his non-certificated assistant. It is further arguable that no un-certificated bailiff should be involved in any way with work for which a certificate is required.[27]
- *Behaving impartially* - bailiffs are agents of the creditor, but also have duties to protect the debtor and other parties involved, so they must constantly have regard to the competing interests in a case and certainly should not allow their own interests (such as fees) to influence their conduct.[28]
- *Protecting exempt goods* - the bailiff's duty is to consider the interests of debtors as well as those of creditors. This means that, although no claim for exemption might be made during a levy, the bailiff ought to make "reasonable and proper enquiry" as to the possible existence of any tools of the trade on the premises and should enquire "properly and carefully" about basic household items. If any doubts exist, erring on the side of the debtor is the bailiff's best course of action. Failure to make enquiries about exempt items could endanger a certificate. The courts have suggested strategies for bailiffs to employ to deal with this issue.[29]

Taking Control of Goods

- *Completing full inventories* - in *Streek v Gill* in 1829 the Lord Chief Justice advised the jury that "it was certainly the duty of brokers [bailiffs] to specify in the inventory the whole of the articles distrained..." He repeated this one year later in his judgment in *Green v Chapman*, expanding the advice by saying that "in the inventory of goods distrained every article ought to be particularised and not included under any such general head as sundries."[30] Levies in which no adequate inventory is prepared or during which goods not on the inventory are removed are likely to be unlawful but an additional sanction may exist against the certificate.[31]
- *Avoiding excessive levies* - in 1822 the Lord Chief Justice stated in a case that "it is a very improper practice for brokers [bailiffs] to seize in the first instance much more than could be necessary to satisfy the arrears distrained for." In 1860 the Court of Exchequer revisited this issue, warning that it was necessary for a close eye to be kept on conduct at this stage in the process to avoid harsh or wrongful treatment of debtors.[32]
- *Ensuring public health and safety* - a number of cases illustrate the additional duties and expectations which may fall upon enforcement agents as public officers. The first might be viewed as a manifestation of the duty under the National Standard to protect the vulnerable, but a more general responsibility to report neglect and severe hardship when it is discovered may be identified.[33] Secondly, agents will have a duty to prevent the spread of infectious diseases. Under The Public Health (Control of Diseases) Act 1984, section 17, it is an offence punishable by fine for a person to 'give, lend, sell, transmit or expose, without previous disinfection, any clothing, bedding or rags which he knows to have been exposed to infection from any disease, or any other article which he knows may have been so exposed and which is liable to carry such infection.' The diseases in question include scarlet fever and diphtheria (bailiffs have been fined for potentially spreading both of these),[34] but a long list is published by the Health Protection Agency which also mentions typhoid, cholera, small pox and the plague. Lastly, bailiffs must always bear in mind the need to protect the health and safety of households: for example, in 1926 a toddler in Ashton under Lyne died from burns following seizure from the home of a fireguard.[35]

All of the above duties might be enforced through a certification complaint, as breach would indicate a lack of familiarity with the basics of enforcement law. Complaints also might arise under the agency relationship between bailiff and creditor (*see 13.2*).

3.1.7 Transitional provisions

As readers will appreciate, in the transition from the old legislative regime to the new one, most bailiffs in the profession will have obtained their authorisation under the old Rules. The new Regulations make allowance for this and for a gradual change-over from distress to taking control of goods.[36]

The Distress for Rent Rules 1988 continue to apply in relation to any application for the grant of a new certificate made before 6th April 2014 by a person who does not hold a certificate and which was not determined by the court before that date. The old Rules also still apply to any application for the grant of a certificate to replace an existing one which ceases to have effect on or before 6th August 2014. Certificates granted under these provisions on or after 6th April 2014 will be valid under section 64 of the 2007. A certificate issued under section 7 of the Law of Distress Amendment Act 1888 Act which is in force on 6th April 2014 shall have effect for the period provided for when it was granted- in other words, it will run its full two year duration before the holder has to renew under the new rules already described.[37]

3.2 Magistrates' court approval

Private bailiffs need to be approved to execute warrants of control issued by magistrates' courts. These provisions supplement and reinforce the certification rules. Section 125B(1) of the Magistrates Court Act 1980 (MCA) provides that warrants may be executed anywhere in England & Wales by any one of the following:

- an individual who is an approved enforcement agency;
- a director of an approved company;
- a partner of a partnership which is approved; or,
- an employee of an approved agency.

Section 31A Justices of the Peace Act 1997 deals with the approval of such agencies and requires magistrates' court committees (MCCs) to maintain a register showing all persons or bodies approved by them or stating that none have been approved. This register will be open for public consultation. Approval is by the process set out in the Approval of Enforcement Agencies Regulations 2000. Enforcement agencies may only be approved if they satisfy the conditions laid down in the Regulations and if the procedure prescribed there is followed.[38]

Note that defects in the approval process do not invalidate warrants. As a result a bailiff will not be acting illegally in enforcing a warrant even though the MCC may have made errors in the process of approving them.[39]

3.2.1 Tendering process

Written tenders from agencies will be requested by MCCs. These must follow the MCC's financial guidelines and agencies must supply with them a copy of their proposed standards of service. Tenders from agencies should contain such details as:[40]

- their history and experience;
- the number of staff to be engaged on work for the court in question;
- copies of audited or certified accounts for the business for the last three years or a shorter period if the firm has not been trading as long as this. The applicant should also supply accounts for other businesses with which the s/he has been associated during this period;
- any past judgments, orders or adverse determinations by any court, tribunal, complaints panel or professional or trade body against the applicant or any individual employee relating to unprofessional conduct. This will undoubtedly include successful complaints against county court certificates and judgments for damages arising from successful claims for wrongful levies and also encompasses adverse determinations under the ESA and ACEA complaints procedures;
- any insolvency proceedings which have been taken against the applicant, such as individual or partnership bankruptcy, a deed of arrangement or voluntary arrangement, proceedings under the Company Directors Disqualification Act 1986 or a county court administration order;
- whether the applicant holds a county court certificate and whether any complaints about the individuals fitness to hold such a certificate have been made (and their outcome);
- any court judgments or orders or tribunal decisions arising from non-payment of tax or contributions. This will include not only enforcement proceedings in the county or magistrates courts but also unsuccessful appeals against assessed liabilities before the General Commissioners of the Inland Revenue;
- any court or tribunal decisions arising from failure to comply with responsibilities as an employer (presumably primarily non-compliance with PAYE and National Insurance obligations on behalf of employees); and,
- names and addresses of referees who may be approached. These will be at least three of the agency's existing customers, the agency's bankers and accountants and individual referees attesting the character and work experience of each individual member of staff who will be undertaking the warrant work.

Applicant agencies will be required to advertise the fact that they have sought approval from the MCC. Adverts will be placed in up to three local or regional newspapers specified by the MCC whilst each court will display notice of the application in a public area.[41]

3.2.2 Criteria and consideration

In order to enter into a contract with an agency, the MCC must be satisfied that it meets each of the following conditions. An approved agency should:

- have an adequate accounting procedure so as to enable the agency to produce annual accounts that will satisfy professional accounting standards and also comply with requirements of the Companies Acts (if appropriate) and the Taxes Acts. As will be noted, protecting the financial interests of MCCs is a central feature in the new regime of approval and contracting;
- provide 'adequate' training for staff on warrant enforcement, human rights law (aspects of which relevant to arrest will be discussed throughout the text) and on health and safety procedures;
- have adequate systems in place to assess the health and safety risks to staff when enforcing warrants;
- operate adequate complaints handling procedures in house. No doubt individual or corporate membership of the CIVEA and compliance with their complaints procedures will be sufficient. The agency must also show that it can cooperate with the MCC's own complaints procedures;
- provide security (normally in the form of a bank bond or indemnity policy) to the MCC for an amount to be determined by the MCC but of not less than £10,000. This is to cover any loss that use of the agency's services may cause to the MCC. The losses envisaged presumably include monies lost as a result of insolvency or fraud on the part of an agency and damages awarded against the court as a consequence of a successful claim in tort relating to the enforcement agency's activities;
- have indemnity insurance for an amount and on terms to be approved by the MCC; and,
- have adequate accounting and financial management systems.[42]

Approved individuals (whether company directors, partners or employees etc) should also satisfy certain personal conditions. They should:

- not have convictions for any offences leading to imprisonment or involving dishonesty or violence. Spent convictions do not have to be disclosed;

· not be liable for any overdue fines or court judgments. The LCD made it clear that an applicant may be subject to a fine (say for a motoring offence) which is payable by instalments, but as long as these payments are being maintained in line with the order it will not be a matter of concern to the MCC;

· not be undischarged bankrupts; and,

· not be engaged in buying or trading debts.[43]

Once received the tenders will be considered by each MCC. Applicants may supply missing information or supporting evidence. A short list will be prepared and, besides taking up the references supplied, a representative of the MCC will visit and inspect the applicant agency's premises. The MCC will then take a decision based on the information gathered.[44]

3.2.3 Approval of agencies

Along with the contract, the successful applicant will receive a 'certificate of approval' from the MCC which should be displayed in a public area at the agency's principal offices.[45] The enforcement agency will be notified which individual members of staff (if not all of those put forward) are being authorised to execute warrants, and each shall receive a 'certificate of authorisation' from the court. Further individuals may be authorised subsequently, by supplying the personal details mentioned below to the court.[46]

Each authorised individual shall be issued by the approved enforcement agency with an identity card bearing their photograph and a photographic reproduction of the authorisation from the court, and this should be carried at all times and shown to the person against whom the warrant is being executed- otherwise it produced on demand from any other individual when executing warrants.[47] Having executed any warrant a CEO or enforcement agent has a duty to produce identification on demand from the defendant. This should be done as soon as is practicable. The identification should be a written statement giving the person's name, employment details and, if they are a CEO or employee of an approved enforcement agency, their certificate of authorisation.[48]

3.2.4 Contracts

There must be a written contract between MCC and enforcement agency - it should of course be possible to obtain copies of these under the Freedom of Information Act. This shall contain a service specification covering the type and volume of work to be done by the agency, setting the standards of service and conduct to be achieved and allowing for the MCC to monitor compliance with these standards by the agency. Contracts will last three years, though they may be extended to allow for the tendering process for a new contract to take place.[49] The contract should allow for such matters as:

- regular inspection of client accounts by the MCC or Ministry of Justice;
- prompt payment over of money collected on behalf of either an MCC or courts within the MCC's area;
- the circumstances in which the MCC could call on the security provided by the agency. Provision should also be made to allow the security to be retained for a period of up to six months after the end of a contract to allow for any outstanding complaints or claims to be made and settled;
- termination of the contract in circumstances where the agency's approval is revoked (see later). This would include provision for recovery of monies outstanding to the MCC and return of unexecuted warrants;
- a requirement that the agency supplies to the MCC a list of all other MCCs by whom it is approved, plus details of any revocation or new approval. Any change to any of the criteria upon which the agency's approval was based should also be notified to the MCC;
- remuneration of the bailiffs- especially in respect of the execution of warrants of control; and,
- a complaints procedure should be devised by the court and shall be publicised by the MCC along with details of the agencies' procedure.[50]

3.2.5 Withdrawal of authorisation

The MCC may 'at any time' withdraw an individual's certificate of authorisation.[51] The circumstances in which this may be done are not specified, but clearly any custodial sentence or conviction for an offence involving violence or dishonesty, any judgment or successful complaint related to unlawful conduct of levies or even allegations of unprofessional or unacceptable conduct as referred to in reg. 12(3) (see below) are likely to lead to withdrawal. If an individual's authorisation is withdrawn, the certificate of authorisation and any identity card issued must be returned to the MCC and the agency should satisfy the MCC that all copies of these have been destroyed or defaced.[52] The same must be done if the approval of the agency as a whole is revoked (see next paragraph).

3.2.6 Revocation

Approvals may be revoked at any time if it is 'in the public interest' to do so. This can be done for instance where untrue information was given in the application, the agency has permitted unauthorised individuals to enforce warrants, the agency or an individual employee has behaved in an unprofessional or unacceptable manner or there has been some serious breach of contract- for instance failure to maintain adequate security, mishandling of funds collected or charging excess fees. The approval can also be revoked where the contract has expired, has been terminated or has 'ceased to be binding' for any reason whatever.[53] Equally, approval may be temporarily suspended if the MCC is considering revocation.[54]

Where revocation is being considered as a result of misconduct or breach of contract by the MCC it should give notice of this fact to the agency (unless the situation is urgent). The agency is then entitled to make representations to the MCC against revocation and to take steps to remedy the problem.[55]

If approval is revoked, the MCC must notify the agency in writing giving reasons for the decision, must advertise the revocation in at least two local or regional newspapers and must notify other MCCs by whom the agency is approved of the circumstances of the matter. The agency has a duty to return the certificate of approval and should satisfy the MCC that all copies have been destroyed or defaced.[56]

3.3 High Court enforcement officers

High Court enforcement officers (HCEOs) are appointed under the High Court Enforcement Officers Regulations 2004, made under paragraph 12, Schedule 7 of the Courts Act 2003. They are appointed by the Lord Chancellor on a district basis throughout England and Wales; the country is divided into 105 districts for these purposes.

To be authorised as an HCEO a person must not have a criminal conviction for dishonesty or violence, or which led to a prison term; s/he must have neither unpaid fines nor judgments outstanding and should neither be an undischarged bankrupt or disqualified company director. Once appointed, HCEOs are under a duty not only to execute all writs directed to them but also to maintain adequate insurances and banking arrangements and to undergo appropriate training. The Lord Chancellor may cancel an authorisation whenever it appears to be in the public interest to do so, and particularly whenever it emerges that the person lied upon his/ her application or has behaved in an "unprofessional or unacceptable" manner. No direct method exists for aggrieved individuals to raise such issues. They are obliged to complain to the HCEO's association and to rely upon their decision in the matter.

3.4 Distrainors under CRAR

Section 73(8) of the Act states that any authorisation of a person to exercise CRAR on another's behalf must be in writing and in addition must comply with the regulations which prescribe the form of the written instruction (*see 7.1*). Those persons instructed to levy CRAR must be certificated. Previously landlords personally as well as certificated bailiffs could levy distress for rent. This will now only be possible of the landlord personally holds a certificate.

3.5 Impersonation of court staff

A number of statutory provisions prohibit individuals passing themselves off as court bailiffs when they are. For example, it is an offence to impersonate a county court officer; the County Courts Act 1984 section 135 reads:

"Any person who -

a)   delivers or causes to be delivered to any person any paper falsely purporting to be a copy of any summons or other process of a county court knowing it to be false; or,

b)   acts or professes to act under any false colour or pretence of the process or authority of a county court,

shall be guilty of an offence and shall for each offence be liable on conviction on indictment to imprisonment for a term not exceeding seven years."

Section 136 of the Act also creates an offence of delivering a document "which was not issued under the authority of a county court but which, by reason of its form or contents or both, has the appearance of having been issued under such authority." The responsible person faces on summary conviction a fine not exceeding level three of the standard scale (£1000).

By way of an example of behaviour which may have constituted an offence under s.135, the author has personal experience of a certificated bailiff employed to enforce road traffic penalties by execution who had a rubber stamp made to use on the warrants he delivered to debtors.

This identified him as a "county court warrant officer." It seemed clear that he sought to suggest that, rather than just be authorised by a county court, he was employed by one and had powers of arrest in connection with the parking penalties he was collecting. This misrepresentation was the subject matter of a complaint against the individual's certificate (for which he was reprimanded by his employers and required to dispose of his stamp); the possibility of the offence could have been raised at the same time.

It will be necessary for the court to determine whether any document served by an enforcement agent purported to be a copy of a court claim or "other process" in breach of s.135(a) - though s.136(1) is worded rather more broadly. A letter giving a person notice to produce evidence did not constitute an offence,[57] but a letter, headed with the royal arms and apparently signed by a county court clerk and in respect of which the defendant demanded court fees in addition to the debt due, led to a conviction.[58] It is, of course, more likely that enforcement agents would be considered to have breached subsection (b) and to have falsely acted court authority. In *R. v. Richmond* (1859) the defendant obtained a blank county court form which he used to pass himself off as a county court officer, threatening the issue of execution of the debt were not settled. His conviction was upheld on appeal.[59]

Turning to the certification process, a person is guilty of an offence if, knowingly or recklessly, he purports to act as an enforcement agent without being authorised to do so. A person found guilty of this offence is liable on summary conviction to a fine not exceeding level 5 on the standard scale.[60] It is also criminal contempt for any person to pretend that they are a HCEO.[61]

3.6 Professional conduct

The National Standards for Enforcement Agents (*see 4.1.2*) lay down a number of important principles on professional conduct, company management and training. These are worth citing at length.

Enforcement agents are required must act within the law at all times, complying with all defined legislation and observing all health and safety requirements in carrying out enforcement. In circumstances where the enforcement agency requires it, and always where there have been previous acts of, or threats of violence by a debtor, a risk assessment should be undertaken prior to the enforcement agent attending a debtor's premises. Enforcement agents should be trained to recognise and avoid potentially hazardous and aggressive situations and to withdraw when in doubt about their own or others' safety.

Agencies must maintain strict client confidentiality and comply with data protection legislation and, where appropriate the Freedom of Information Act. Agents must carry out their duties in a professional, calm and dignified manner. They must dress and speak appropriately and act with discretion and fairness. Agents must not discriminate unfairly on any grounds including those of age, disability, ethnicity, gender, race, religion or sexual orientation.

Enforcement agencies should ensure that audited accounts are available on request, where it is appropriate that these are kept. An annual audit of the agency's accounts by independent accountants should be undertaken at least once a year for businesses where this is appropriate. Agencies must comply with statutory obligations, for example, the Companies Act, HMRC provisions, data protection, health and safety and the like. A separate account for monies due to the creditor should be maintained and accurate books and accounts should be kept and made available to establish monies owed to the creditor. Enforcement agencies must keep a complete record of all financial transactions in whatever capacity undertaken.

Agencies must maintain suitable and comprehensive insurance cover for both professional indemnity and other risks including employer's liability and public liability.

Enforcement agencies must ensure that all agents, employees and contractors are provided with appropriate training to ensure that they understand and are able to act, at all times, within the bounds of the relevant legislation. This training should be provided at the commencement of employment and at intervals afterwards to ensure that the agent's knowledge is kept up to date. Professional training and assessment should be to an appropriate standard. Enforcement agencies must ensure that all employees, contractors and agents will at all times act within the scope of current legislation, and have an appropriate knowledge and understanding of it and be aware of any statutory obligations and provide relevant training.

Footnotes
1 Section 63(2).
2 Section 63(3) to (5).
3 CPR 84.18; Practice Direction 84.
4 Certification of Enforcement Agents Regulations 2014 reg.4.
5 Section 64(1). In the 69th update to the CPR, the PD amendments, para.9(3) state that certification cases will be allocated to district judges.
6 Certification Regs reg.5.
7 Certification Regs reg.4(1).
8 Certification Regs reg.7.

9 Certification Regs reg.12.

10 Certification Regs reg.13.

11 Reg.8 & CPR 84.9.

12 *Taylor v. Ashworth* (1910) 129 LT 578.

13 *The Times*, June 11th, 1894, 10g.

14 *Woodward v Day* (1894) 2 PMR 753 & *Re: Gurden* (1894) 2 PMR 872 - bailiff drunk or assaulted debtor; *In Re: Longstaffe ex. p. Robinson* (1897) 49 EG 60 - bailiff charged double the permitted percentage for an auctioneer & (1896) 47 EG 49 & 17; *Duncombe v Hicks* (1898) 42 Sol Jo 393 - certificate cancelled because illegal possession fee charged; *Villenueva v Clark* (1890) 33 EG 458 - bailiff drunk; *London Central Meat Co v Rae* (1905) 13 PMR 825 - illegal distress; (1912) 20 PMR 972 & *The Times* December 3rd 1894 4c; *Manchester Guardian* Jan.31st 1935 - certificate revoked after several complaints of gross misconduct.

15 *Banks v Lovell* (1863) June 11th, 12f (Exch); *Siggers v Deacon* (1842) Feb.2nd, 6d (CP).

16 *Mahoney v Richards* (1850) May 11th, 7e (Exch) - a lodger was told his goods had not been levied, but when he moved house he was pursued for fraudulent removal; *Mutton v Sheppard* (1905) 66 EG 806 - a child was persuaded by the bailiff to bring a horse from a stable to the rented premises so that it might be distrained.

17 *James v Proctor* (1905) 13 PMR 442.

18 *Jones Sewing Machine Co v Porter & Stone* (1897) *The Times*, June 5th, 8f.

19 (1898) 104 LT 345; *Taylor v Ashworth* (1910) 129 LT 578.

20 49 Estates Gazette 60.

21 42 Sol. Jo. 393.

22 119 LT 134.

23 see for example *Villeneuva v. Clark* (1890) 35 Estates Gazette 458; *Re: Gurden* (1894) 2 Property Market Review 410 & 872; Estates Gazette vol.47 p.171 & vol.48 p.183.

24 *Perring & Co v. Emerson* [1903] 1 KB 1.

25 *Milgate v Kelley & Gooding* (1828) The Times, August 16th, 3f (KBD); *Barton v Hankey* (1880) *The Times* May 4th, 4e (CP) - a sheriff's case; *In re: High Bailiff of Brompton county court* (1893) *The Times*, May 12th, 14a (QBD).

26 *Freeman v Crowley* (1889) The Times, Feb.2nd, 13c.

27 *Hogarth v. Jennings* [1892] 1 QB 907; *Hawes v. Watson* (1892) 94 LT 181; *Thomas v. Millington* (1892) 2 Property Market Review 472.

28 *Harrison v Mearing* (1843) *The Times*, May 10th, 8b (Exch).

29 *Taylor v Ashworth* (1910) 129 LT 578.

30 *The Times*, July 13th, 1827, 3c, KBD & February 20th, 1830 6a, KBD; see too *Tait v Harris* (1833) *The Times*, June 19th, 6c (Exch) - an engineer's drawing materials and equipment were removed when they had not been included on the inventory.

31 See my *Sources of bailiffs' law* c.4 and *Allen v Rutherford* (1874) *The Times*, December 8th, 11f.

32 *Lady Branscomb v Fleming & Bridges* (1822) *The Times*, December 7th, 3a (KBD); *Wilkinson v Ibbett* (1860) *The Times* November 10th, 11b.

33 *The Times* Feb.17th 1829 p.4; *Manchester Guardian* March 24th 1913 p.12.

34 *The Times* Sept.15th 1876 9d; *Manchester Guardian* Oct.22nd 1904 p.13.

35 *Manchester Guardian* Sept.23rd 1926 p.5.

36 s.64(3) of the 2007 Act.

37 Certification Regulations regs 14 & 15; see too articles 2 & 6 Tribunals, Courts & Enforcement Act 2007 (Consequential, Transitional & Saving Provision) Order 2014.

38 SI 3279/ 2000.

39 Section 125B(3) MCA 1980.

40 Service standards - reg.7; tenders - reg.8.

41 See respectively regs 8(10) & 9(3).
42 See respectively reg.4(3)-(10).
43 See respectively reg.5(2)-(5).
44 See reg.9.
45 Reg.10(1).
46 Reg.11(2)-(4).
47 Reg.11(6) & (7)(b).
48 ss125A(4) & 125B(4); Pt 18.11(2) & 52(5)(c) & (d) Crim PR.
49 See regs 4(2), 6(2) & 6(3).
50 See respectively reg.6(4)-(12).
51 Reg.11(5).
52 Reg.11(8).
53 Reg.12(1)-(3).
54 Reg.6(14).
55 Reg.12(4).
56 Regs.12(5) & 10(2).
57 *R. v. Castle* (1857) 21 JP 775.
58 *R. v Evans* (1857) 21 JP 391.
59 (1859) 23 JP 325.
60 TCE Act s.63(6) & (7).
61 Sheriffs' Act 1889 s29(6).

Chapter 4

Codes and regulators

4.1 Contracts and codes

In many cases there will be a written contract between creditor and bailiff, though readers may be surprised how sparsely documented some of these commercial relationships can be. *See also 13.2 and 13.3 on this issue.*

4.1.1 Contractual terms

The bailiff's power to levy derives from the warrant that is issued. The purpose of the contract is to regulate the general administration of enforcement by distress and to ensure that distress is conducted in an acceptable manner. Contracts will normally be for a fixed period of time. Typical terms in a contract will cover such issues as timescales for enforcement (the period of time which is to be allowed for a bailiff to execute a warrant and the number of visits that should be made to try to do that), the charges to be made, cash handling (the frequency with which monies should be remitted to the creditor), monitoring of the bailiffs' activities and the conduct of levies themselves (this latter issue is normally governed by a code of practice - *see 4.1.4*).

The Freedom of Information Act could be used by debtors to obtain details of the arrangements between creditors and their enforcement agents. Contracts, service level agreements, codes of practice, field operations manuals and separately agreed fee scales can all be obtained by exercise of this right, usually without charge. Using these materials, it may be possible to identify the reason for wrongful actions (for example, the bailiff is simply complying with his principal's instructions) and then to take the appropriate remedial action, such as a public law challenge to the content of the contract. That said, it will not infrequently be found that, in fact, a council has no written contract with its recovery agents. This seems particularly to be the case for local authority parking departments.

Regardless of the detailed terms of the contract, the effect of it will be to make the bailiff the agent of the creditor so that, besides all the explicit terms of any agreement, there will be certain terms implied by common law as a result of the relationship of principal and agent. *For more detail on this, see chapter 13.*

4.1.2 National Standards

Ministry of Justice has provided a national code of practice for enforcement agents, the National Standard (NSEA), since April 2003. A third, revised edition of the Standard was issued in April 2014 to reflect the changes made by the new Act and to reinforce some of its themes.

4.1.3 Creditors' or local codes

It is now normal practice for local authorities and central government agencies to impose codes of practice on bailiffs as part of the contract agreed between them. Magistrates courts will not do this, relying instead on the firm itself having its own internal code, though the agreement made with the firm may well specify certain items that typically would be part of a code - for instance, those classes of debtors who should not face distraint, the information that should be given to a debtor when levying or the form and content of any standard letters to be used. The NSEA recognises that local agreements may wish to extend the law - for example in respect of goods protected from seizure - and condones this: "creditors may agree other restrictions with agents acting on their behalf."

Many codes are well-drafted and offer considerable additional protection, both by exempting vulnerable groups and by expanding upon the present legislation or clarifying or defining the law where it is either unclear or even absent. However criticisms may be made of some. In many local authorities codes are regarded as internal only, part of the private contracts between local authority and bailiff that may not be published. They are thus of little use either to the debtor or, indeed, to the creditor as a means of verifiable monitoring of bailiffs' activities. The solution to this is the use of the Freedom of Information Act; the argument against it is founded on the Human Rights Act (see later). Furthermore, in several cases known to the author, codes have endorsed practice by bailiffs that were either illegal or of dubious legality. Whatever the contents of any contract or code between bailiff and creditor, it cannot authorise illegal acts and with the bailiff acting as agent for the creditor, both will be liable for any wrongful act.

4.2 Administrative law principles

Both public bodies as creditors and bailiffs when acting as their agents in enforcement action must comply with the principles of administrative law.

4.2.1 Challengeable decisions

It is possible to use public law principles to challenge actions and decisions (both the mere fact of an action or the way it is done), a failure to act, a policy or guideline and (indeed) the written law itself. The sorts of matter which might be suitable for a public law challenge include:

- *ultra vires* decisions - the authority lacked the power to do something. The body must exercise its recovery powers in line with the statutory framework provided for that purpose. For example, a public body's contract cannot permit its agents to seize goods exempted by law or to make charges not permitted by the fee scale (though of course a contract may quite lawfully further restrict a bailiff's powers to act by adding conditions further to those included in statute);
- The decision was made on the wrong basis, for example based on an error of law, an error of fact (lack of evidence or incorrect facts) or was based upon irrelevant matters;
- The authority had 'fettered' the exercise of its discretion and had, for instance, refused to consider alternative remedies. For example, justices have been challenged over failures to exercise discretion as to the remedy used for fine enforcement. Note that the administrative court has said though, that in a complaint over illegal seizure, the justices may refuse, in the interests of justice, to hear a case which involves too many complex issues of fact, law and title to goods and upon which it would be better for the civil courts to adjudicate;[1]
- The authority had created a 'legitimate expectation' that a certain course of action would be pursued a result of giving an individual misleading or incorrect information. See for example the case of *R (on the application of Dolatabadi) v Transport for London* [2005]. The applicant's car was seized by bailiffs for non-payment of congestion charge and was only recovered on payment of around £3300. He was entitled to exemption from the charge as the holder of a 'blue badge', granted to him on the basis that he provided care to an elderly and disabled person. Transport for London failed to handle his application for renewal of his exemption correctly and failed to respond properly to his representations against the penalties issued. The Court accepted that Mr Dolatabadi had been led to believe that the matter was concluded and that the penalties had been cancelled and, accordingly, it quashed the court orders made against him and ordered refund of his payments with interest;[2]
- it failed to act in line with the Human Rights Convention (*see 4.3 below*);
- it is procedurally unfair. The authority has to act in line with the principles of natural justice, for example by giving adequate reasons for a particular decision or act; or,
- maladministration which includes bias and unfairness, neglect and inattention, delay, incompetence and ineptitude, arbitrariness and being inconsiderate and misleading. Maladministration is something which is legal (or at least is not clearly illegal) but which gives rise to bad treatment.

In comparing judicial review to the use of the ombudsman, the following should be considered.

· A complaint can be made about a matter which could not be judicially reviewed;
· Review can interpret the law whereas the ombudsman cannot;
· Court rulings are binding and enforceable;
· Decisions can be quashed by judicial review whereas the ombudsman cannot alter them;
· The court's decision can be appealed whereas ombudsman decisions are final; and,
· Compensation is not awarded in judicial review, but the court can make an injunction.

In contrast the ombudsman offers various advantages to complainants:

· The LGO has the ability to get documents and other evidence which the court cannot obtain;
· The investigation process is inquisitorial;
· Deadlines are not so tight;
· Out of time complaints are often allowed;
· There are no costs to the process; and,
· Changes to local administration systems can be recommended.

The significance of public law remedies to those advising on bailiffs' actions is likely to be considerably enhanced by the fact that the Act has abolished debtors' ability to challenge lawful acts by means of claims for trespass. Challenges to illegalities by means of judicial review may in future be the only way of having some of these issues brought before a court.

4.2.2 Monitoring officer

Every local authority is required to appoint a 'monitoring officer' under s.5 Local Government & Housing Act 1989. The officer's duty is to report on every proposal, decision or omission which may give rise either to any contravention of law which could therefore lead to judicial review, or to maladministration which may require an ombudsman investigation. Whilst a report is being prepared, no further recovery action can be taken.

Given the apparent unwillingness of some council departments to supervise or control the bailiffs they employ, a complaint to the monitoring officer can be an effective strategy to get a legally trained person to review the decision or policy being challenged.

4.2.3 Ombudsmen

Another (indirect) sanction may arise where there has been maladministration by a local authority by a local or central government department which has used a bailiff's services. The aggrieved debtor could complain to the relevant ombudsman, that is the Commission for Local Administration for local authorities, The Parliamentary Ombudsman for the CSA, the Revenue Adjudicator for the Inland Revenue and Customs & Excise. A person must complain within twelve months of the alleged injustice caused by maladministration. A response should be received within 4-6 weeks and the investigation should be completed within 12 months. Investigations are free and can lead to an apology, remedial action, payment of compensation or reimbursement of costs and changes to procedure. There is no right of appeal. If a complaint is upheld following investigation by the ombudsman it is usual to recommend review of and improvements in local administration and an award of compensation to the individual.

Local government ombudsman

Bailiff-related problems fairly frequently form the basis of complaints to the Local Government Ombudsman. These typically arise from maladministration such poor communications between the council and bailiffs and failure to keep adequate records and accounts. However the ombudsman can also sometimes criticise the bailiffs' conduct of the levy and make awards of compensation in cases where substantive legal remedies might also be available. For example in an investigation of parking penalty enforcement by L.B Ealing in 2000 the bailiffs were criticised for failing to provide breakdowns of charges or information on how to dispute them and for making charges that were hard to justify under the statutory scale.[3] They were also criticised for failing to deal adequately with letters of complaint from the debtors. In another complaint compensation of £100 was awarded to a woman who was wrongly visited by bailiffs when a tracing agency incorrectly supplied her address as being that of the liable person with the same surname.[4]

The ombudsman has criticised cases where bailiffs have been instructed where benefits claims are still unresolved. This something that the courts have not done in judicial review proceedings. Delays in processing the council tax accounts leading to belated instruction of the bailiffs have also been criticised. In the case of a Mrs Fry, a further part of the complaint was that the bailiffs threatened to seize a motor vehicle which was the property of her son, despite the debtor having evidence of ownership.[5]

The conduct of bailiffs when levying have also attracted criticism. In the case of Mr & Mrs Hutchinson bailiffs approached neighbours about Mr & Mrs Hutchinson's whereabouts and, having managed to enter their home, rang numbers found in their address book trying to locate them. These breaches of confidentiality were treated as maladministration and the council was ordered to pay £200 and to review its procedures. In another complaint the bailiffs were criticised for failing to take further instructions when it was found that the debtors were disabled. The bailiffs were criticised for failing to calculate charges correctly whilst the ombudsman also criticised the council for delay in dealing with a benefit claim. Compensation of £150 was ordered and the council was required to review its procedures for identifying and handling cases of potential vulnerability.[6]

The Adjudicator's Office

It is worthwhile considering making a complaint about bailiff action to recover taxes. In the Adjudicator's 1999 annual report two cases complaints of bailiff action were reported. In one £250 consolatory payment was made when bailiffs were sent to business premises for a VAT debt which was not due. This compensated for the upset, intrusion and out of pocket expenses such as telephone calls and letters. In another instance a settlement was mediated in a case where the pre-distraint warning letter was sent to the wrong address in respect of an incorrect sum.

4.2.4 Judicial review

The scope for the use of judicial review against ultra vires or otherwise wrongful or unfair decisions by government bodies in respect of their use of the power of distress is generally little explored. There appear to be grounds upon which judicial review could be employed: for instance to review a decision to use distress in circumstances when it was unlawful; to review an unreasonable use of the remedy, particularly where there has been a mistake as to the facts, or to review an improper policy, such as a code of practice, in its application to the individual client. It will be up to practitioners to explore the possibilities of the remedy, but one major restriction will be the expectation that other avenues of appeal will have been tried first. The loss of the right to sue in trespass for illegal distress may very well widen the scope for judicial review. There is little authority on its use, but there is one nineteenth century authority to the effect that the court will not grant prohibition against a magistrates' court issuing a warrant unless it has done so in excess of its jurisdiction.[7]

4.3 Human Rights Act 1998

The significance of the Human Rights Act (HRA) is that it applies to any decision or act of a public authority. A public authority is defined as any body exercising powers of a public nature and will include central and local government departments (such as magistrates courts and local authorities), those acting as the enforcement agents of public bodies and 'quangos' such as regulatory bodies. The Act also applies to the courts, so that their judgments and administrative decisions will have to comply with the HRA. The HRA therefore makes it clear that those, such as bailiffs, exercising the powers of public bodies are themselves to be treated as public bodies and are to be subject to the principles of public law and to public law remedies.

Typically the rights enshrined in the HRA will be enforced by means of a judicial review of the public body in question. A human rights defence may also be raised in proceedings brought by a public body against an individual. In addition the courts, as public authorities, are required to apply European Court of Human Rights (ECHR) principles in their day to day making of judgments and orders so that, as a result, the HRA will have an impact on claims made by private persons as well as litigation between a private persons and a public authority.

The Act itself is mainly concerned with the interpretation and application of the ECHR. It requires that all legislation (whatever its date) must be read and given effect in a way compatible with Convention rights. The Act makes it unlawful for any public authority to act in a way incompatible with Convention rights.

4.3.1 ECHR

The ECHR is incorporated into English law by means of making it an appendix (Schedule 1) to the Act. Broadly the ECHR is concerned with the rule of law and its quality. The Convention comprises a number of articles and various protocols (later additions to the ECHR) setting out individuals' rights. For those concerned with enforcement, the most significant provisions are likely to be those listed below, which will be discussed in more detail later.

- *Article 6(1) - the right to a fair trial*: "In the determination of his civil rights and obligations or of any criminal charge against him, everyone is entitled to a fair and public hearing within a reasonable time by an independent and impartial tribunal established by law."
- *Article 8 - right to respect for private & family life*: "(1) Everyone has the right to respect for his private and family life, his home

and his correspondence. (2) There shall be no interference by a public authority with the exercise of this right except such as is in accordance with the law and is necessary in a democratic society in the interest of … the economic well being of the country… or for the protection of the rights and freedoms of others."

· *First protocol, article 1 - protection of property*: "Every natural and legal person is entitled to the peaceful enjoyment of his possessions. No one shall be deprived of his possessions except in the public interest and subject to the conditions provided for by law and by the general principles of international law. The preceding provisions shall not, however, in any way impair the right of a State to enforce such laws as it considers necessary to … secure the payment of taxes or other contributions or penalties."

4.3.2 ECHR jurisprudence

The Act requires that Convention rights are interpreted in light of the judgments, decisions and opinions of the European Court of Human Rights and the Commission. Over the years the Court has developed a number of principles to be used in the interpretation and application of Convention rights. The most significant for present purposes are as follows:

Restrictions on rights
As will have been observed, the rights in article 8 and 1st protocol, article 1 may be curtailed in certain circumstances. These restrictions must be 'in accordance with the law'. It is further required that the law in question must be clear and accessible- i.e. that it is published in an accessible form (though it is accepted that recourse may be necessary to a lawyer in order to have the law interpreted). One criticism of the former law of distress and one reason for the new Act was that as so much of it relied on very old case law, rather than on statutory rules, and was therefore unclear, imprecise and inaccessible. The Act provides a statutory code which replaces most of the former common law rules and cases (TCEA s.57(1)).

Although statute law may be regarded as being in 'accordance with law', certain codes of practice may not. Many local authorities operate codes of practice regulating their use of bailiffs, but quite frequently these are not made available publicly, either to advice agencies or individuals. These policies may fall foul of the HRA as unpublished guidelines have already been criticised in judgments by the Court. Statute law must often be vague and its interpretation and application will be a matter of practice. But, where individuals' rights are to be interfered with, the scope of any discretion on the part of the executive must be clearly laid out and there must be effective control of its exercise.

Where instructions and guides to officials establish an administrative practice to be followed, whilst not having the force of law, they must be accessible to individuals likely to be affected. This is so as to give them an indication of the circumstances and conditions upon which a public authority will exercise its powers to interfere with their rights. By way of example, local tax regulations enable councils to seize all of a person's household goods except for basic, necessary items. Many councils' codes of practice will define what is understood by this and debtors are entitled to know whether the bailiffs are adhering to these categories.

Next, the purpose of any restriction on rights must also be legitimate and 'necessary in a democratic society'. A legitimate aim includes the protection of the rights of others (including those of private and state creditors)[8] and the economic well being of the nation. To show the necessity of the human rights restriction the public authority must demonstrate that there is a 'pressing social need', and furthermore must show that any interference with rights is 'proportionate' (see below). When considering this the Court will also take account of national practice and tradition, a practice known as the 'margin of appreciation'.

Another important aspect of the 'lawfulness' of provisions is their 'quality': there is not only a need for the law to precisely formulated, but it must comply with 'the rule of law'. This will include, for example, the question of whether there are any rights for an aggrieved individual to seek a review or other remedy in order to have protection from unfair or arbitrary use of a legal power, especially where there is discretion in its use by the public body in question. It may be questioned therefore whether the termination of rights of challenge in the courts effected by the TCEA is fully ECHR compliant.

In a number of cases the Court has indicated that the issue of warrants without any prior judicial authority is in breach of article 8 as it is not a process that is "necessary in a democratic society". It is disproportionate to the legitimate aim of the economic well being of the nation being pursued. The cases concerned warrants to enter and search premises and remove documents in respect of criminal customs offences and were held in breach of article 8 because they were so wide. This was despite the fact that a senior officer of the public authority supervised them, a police officer had to be in attendance at the entry, there were rules on procedure and there was the right of judicial appeal.[9] Generally it has been held that the permitted interferences with article 8 rights have to be narrowly interpreted and must be convincingly established case by case. Legislation and practice must provide adequate safeguards against abuse: in these cases the exclusive competence of the customs department to assess the need for, number of, length of and scale of searches was too lax and full of loopholes to satisfy the Court. If this was the Court's view of criminal process, it may view civil proceedings even more strictly. This may suggest scope for ECHR challenges of many forms of taking control where no court proceedings preceded enforcement.

Proportionality
This is a concept running through the interpretation of many Convention rights. The question to be addressed is this: is there a reasonable foundation for any legal rule, taking into account the importance of its aim and the actual circumstances of the case in question? The courts must be satisfied that any measure strikes a fair balance between the human rights of the individual and the public interest. In other words, are the means proportionate to the aims? Means which seem to be excessive, in light of the circumstances of the case, will not justify a legitimate end purpose. This concept will introduce a new test into English law. Previously the actions of public bodies were judged as to whether they were illegal or irrational. The new test is more stringent as there is a presumption in favour of the protection of an individual's rights. The concept may also draw in consideration of Article 14 of the ECHR. This prohibits discrimination on various grounds, including on the basis of property. If it could be shown that enforcement against those with only personal property seizable by taking control was disproportionately more burdensome than, say, a charging order against a homeowner (with the much lower likelihood of that being enforced), there may have been a breach of the Act and scope for a challenge. Similarly preferring seizure over deductions from benefit may be open to challenge on the grounds of proportionality. In order to defeat a challenge a local authority officer would need to show why the more serious remedy was to be preferred and that the interests of the debtor were properly considered when making the decision on enforcement. The NSEA reinforces this point, stating that "Creditors should act proportionately when seeking to recover debt, taking into account debtors' circumstances."

It is generally accepted that "bailiff's duties by their very nature [are] bound to cause some difficulties" for the debtor but, provided the enforcement action is in accordance with law and proportionate, it is unlikely to be open to challenge.[10] This is also illustrated by *Lewandowski v Poland* (1999). The applicant claimed breach of article 2 (the right to life) as his wife died from a pre-existing illness a month after bailiffs had called to levy a warrant that had been issued in error, the debt having been paid. The Polish authorities and the European Court found that no breach had occurred as the bailiffs had left as soon as they were told that payment had been made, they were neither rude nor used any force or threats so that there had been no risk of a breach of the peace, and that there was no causal link to be found between their visit and the wife's subsequent death.[11]

4.3.3 Human rights in practice

A reasonable body of case law has been built up, both within the United Kingdom and outside, to enable us to form an accurate view of how the ECHR may be successfully applied to enforcement work.

Article 6
This article probably has had the most impact on the law in England & Wales so far, in respect of local tax committal proceedings. It was also applied to contempt of court proceedings for rescue of goods seized in execution by the county court bailiff. The Convention was breached by the fact that the defendant was given no details of the accusation against him and no opportunity to apply for legal aid when it became apparent that he faced committal.[12]

It has been decided that the fair trial guarantees of article 6(1) apply to civil proceedings not only up to the point of judgment, but through to the enforcement stage. The human rights issues that arise at this stage will differ from those adjudicated upon in the proceedings before any order or judgment. Liability was the issue in the earlier stages: questions of property ownership and the like will arise during enforcement, and opportunities to raise these at a hearing within a reasonable time must exist. The loss of many forms of judicial challenge to seizures may increase the likelihood of article 6 challenges to the TCEA.

Note also that under s9 HRA 'judicial acts' which breach Convention rights may be challenged by way of appeal, judicial review or other prescribed forum. Compensation may be awarded for any act done in bad faith, whether by a member of the judiciary, JP, clerk or other court officer.

However the European Commission has repeatedly held that article 6(1) does not apply to proceedings for the recovery of income taxes and duties. Local taxes have been held to benefit from the same restrictions on ECHR rights. As a result the fairly perfunctory nature of the hearing of a liability order for local taxes will not be in breach of article 6(1). The hearing has been held to be more an administrative process which does not assess liability for the tax itself, but rather merely confirms the fact of non-payment.[13]

Article 8
This was applied in *McLeod v UK* (1998) which considered the powers of entry of the police in cases of an alleged breach of the peace (*see 8.12 below*).

First protocol, article 1
On the face of it, the protection of a person's enjoyment of their possessions is not a right that will override legal enforcement of judgments, court orders and other valid claims. This is because both article 8 and protocol 1, article 1 contain provisos for lawful enforcement which is in defence of the rights of others, in the public interest or in order to secure the payment of taxes and the like. That the lawful activities of bailiffs may be unlikely to be affected is illustrated by the case *Gasus Dosier-und Fördertechnik GmbH v Netherlands* (1995). In this case, the seizure and disposal of third party goods subject to a retention of title clause was held to be justified by the need to secure payment of taxes, even though it was acknowledged that this was a prima facie breach of rights over property and possessions. The Court explicitly considered whether a fair balance between the public interest and the owner's rights had been achieved, having particular regard to the 'margin of appreciation'. A difference was found between commercial creditors who can refuse credit or take extra security, and a state's revenue department, which has neither of those advantages. Next, it was noted that retention of title clauses are more concerned with securing payment in full than with actual retention of ownership. Finally it was noted that rights to seize third party goods are common in tax legislation and had been a statutory provision in the Netherlands since the mid-nineteenth century. In other words, the creditor was paying the consequences for a calculated commercial risk.[14]

If this fairly extreme case does not attract protection under the ECHR, clearly most other cases of lawful enforcement will not either, particularly where they are by local and central government departments in respect of statutory liabilities. In confirmation note that in *K v Sweden* (1991) as the Swedish Enforcement Code permitted entry to be forced in order to levy goods (including in some cases any goods of third parties found on the premises, just as in the Netherlands case referred to above), although these measures were on the face of it violations of a person's human rights, they were justifiable as being in accordance with law and proportionate.[15] Similar established rights in England & Wales are also likely to be immune to challenge as breaches of the HRA.

Extra judicial and arbitrary seizures of property in the enforcement of tax have been held to breach P1,1 but as execution on a civil judgment is not an "arbitrary confiscation" it cannot breach this article. Moreover, seizure and impounding of goods alone are not a 'deprivation of property' within the meaning of P1,1. There must be a permanent deprivation by sale for a potential breach to arise.[16]

4.3.4 Conclusions

Rather than the articles themselves, it is likely that the concept of proportionality is likely to be more important in the impact of the ECHR on enforcement law. The principle might be applied at two levels:

· in the choice of remedy by the issuing authority; and,
· in the choice of goods made by the enforcement agent.[17]

In order to determine whether there has been a breach of the Convention, readers should ask themselves:

1. is an article engaged- does the activity complained of come within its scope and has there been an interference with the rights protected?
2. is the interference prescribed by law- is it lawful and is that law clear and accessible?
3. does it have a legitimate aim as described by the article?
4. is it necessary in a democratic society? Is there a 'pressing social need' being met and is it proportionate or were other means to achieve the same end available?

4.4 Equality Act 2010

Like the Human Rights Act, the Equality Act 2010 is another public law statute in that it has a general impact upon the activities of public authorities in all aspects of their decision making. As a consequence, it will apply to the activities of their enforcement agents and must be borne in mind by bailiffs at all stages in the recovery process.

4.4.1 Scope of the Act

We will mainly be concerned here with the impact of the Equality Act on public bodies and those organisations performing public functions. Official guidance makes it clear that public functions include such activities as law enforcement and tax collection. A private organisation which performs public functions on behalf of a public body has the same duties under the Act as the central or local government department for whom they work. It will be apparent that most bailiff work, collecting local and national taxes, fines, road traffic penalties and judgments, is included in this; only distress for rent work for private landlords will not be.

More broadly, any bailiff company in the role of employer will have to comply with the Act and avoid discrimination. Equally, where facilities are provided to enable members of the public to come to premises to make payments or to attend auction sales, the Act will apply.[18] Where information is provided to debtors, firms will have to consider its provision in accessible formats (Braille etc).

Further guidance on the application of the Act is available from the government Equalities Office or from the Equalities & Human Rights Commission.[19]

4.4.2 Unlawful discrimination

The Act makes it unlawful to discriminate against people on a number of grounds. These are listed in section 4 of the Act and are called "protected characteristics." They are:

- Age;
- Disability (either physical or mental impairment);
- Gender reassignment;
- Pregnancy & maternity;
- Race;
- Religion & belief;
- Sex;
- Sexual orientation; and,
- Marriage & civil partnership.

Note that, in the provision of public functions, discrimination on the grounds of age or marriage/civil partnership does not apply.[20] If a person is a victim of discrimination on one of these grounds, s/he may be able to apply to a county court for damages and/ or an injunction. Judicial review of public bodies' actions and policies may also be possible.

Discrimination can, of course, occur on the grounds of several protected characteristics in a single case. There is also a concept of 'discrimination by association' - a person such as a carer or relative can suffer because of a link to a person with a protected characteristic.

4.4.3 Types of discrimination

The Act identifies two types of discrimination that can take place:

Direct discrimination
This is defined in s.13 and arises where a person discriminates against another because of a protected characteristic and treats that person less

favourably as a result, putting that person at clear disadvantage. This may in turn lead to harassment or victimisation, both of which are also illegal under the Act. Obvious examples would be mistreating a debtor because of his/her sexuality or race. Probably, direct discrimination will arise rarely and will normally be the result of the conduct of an individual member of staff. It is obviously up to employers to ensure that their staff conduct their business without unlawful discrimination and that they treat everyone with dignity and respect; and,

Indirect discrimination
This is the form of discrimination most likely to apply to the work of enforcement agents. It occurs where an apparently neutral policy or practice is applied to everyone, but works to put certain groups with protected characteristics at particular disadvantage.[21] The subject will be discussed in detail later.

4.4.4 Duties of those performing public functions

Public bodies and those undertaking work on their behalf have two clear responsibilities under the Equality Act 2010. There is the duty to avoid discrimination in the exercise of those public functions. Secondly, public bodies (and those working with them) are under a duty to eliminate discrimination and to advance equality. This general responsibility under s.149 of the Act is called the "equality duty."

Public bodies have duties to act to ensure that their policies and services are appropriate and accessible to all. Public bodies must have "due regard" to:

· Eliminating unlawful discrimination and harassment;
· Advancing equality of opportunity by removing or minimising the disadvantages faced by people with protected characteristics and meeting the special needs of such individuals; and,
· Fostering good relations.

'Due regard' means consciously bearing the three above aims of the equality duty in mind when formulating policies and practices, planning service provision and facilities or appointing staff.

Implementing the equality duty will involve the following issues for public authorities:

· Training staff so that they understand their obligations;
· Timeliness when devising and implementing policies - i.e. the terms of the Act should be a priority consideration, not an afterthought;

- Integrating the duty into the decision making process;
- Gathering information about service users so that informed decisions can be made (i.e. what is the breakdown of protected characteristics amongst debtors visited?); and,
- Periodic reviews of performance, as this is a continuing duty.

Having said all this, readers should note that the duty needn't be applied in irrelevant situations nor where it would involve disproportionate expense - for example, whilst it may be appropriate to provide notices and letters with translations into a few key languages, it is not necessary to translate information into every conceivable language that might be encountered.

4.4.5 Avoiding illegal discrimination

As stated earlier, the Act prohibits discrimination in the exercise of a public function. Discrimination can arise in two ways:

- Treating someone in a worse manner because of a protected characteristic; or,
- Failing to make "reasonable adjustments" to policies, practices or facilities with the result that disabled people are put at "substantial disadvantage."

Indirect discrimination
As suggested earlier, the work of enforcement agents seems most vulnerable to complaints of indirect discrimination. This form of discrimination occurs when policies or working practices are applied equally to all, but result in extra disadvantage for people with protected characteristics. For our purposes, "disadvantage" can be defined as detriment giving rise to a sense of grievance. Indirect discrimination is unlawful even where, as will frequently be the case, it is unintentional. That said, a practice or policy can be justified if it can be demonstrated to be "a proportionate means of achieving a legitimate aim." Such a justification would need to be supported by evidence and it would be necessary to show that:

- The aim of the policy is legal and non-discriminatory. A legitimate aim will include the fair exercise of legal powers and reasonable business efficiency;
- It has a real and objective purpose; and,
- It is being achieved in a proportionate way - that is, in a manner that is appropriate and necessary in all the circumstances. It will be essential to show that the aim could not have been achieved by less discriminatory means.

The more serious the disadvantage caused to the person with a protected characteristic, the more convincing the justification will have to be. A public body or its agents will also need to show that the 'equality duty' was taken into account when devising the policy and practice in question.

Reasonable adjustments
Where disabled persons are involved, there is a duty to make "reasonable adjustments" to the delivery of public functions or services. Steps must be taken to ensure that policies do not cause "substantial disadvantage" to disabled people. This means suffering an "unreasonably adverse experience" as a result of the exercise of a function. The detriment caused must be significant rather than being just minor or trivial.

If the duty to make a reasonable adjustment arises, the failure to make it cannot be justified. Nevertheless, readers should bear in mind that:

· It is accepted that the exercise of some functions is bound to have a negative impact on a person (for instance, having goods distrained or being arrested). The point is to ensure that a disabled person does not suffer a substantially worse experience as a result;
· There is no need to make adjustments which would fundamentally alter the nature of the function (for example, ceasing altogether to seize goods from disabled persons); and,
· The duty to adjust is a duty to take reasonable steps, taking into account all the circumstances of a case. The costs of making adjustments and the size of the organisation involved will all be relevant factors.

As with the 'equality duty', the duty to make adjustments should be applied in an anticipatory manner- policies and procedures should be reviewed in advance for possible discrimination. Moreover, the duty is an ongoing and evolving one with a responsibility to conduct regular reviews of services and experiences.

4.4.6   Examples of the Act's impact

The implications of the Equality Act for the activities of enforcement agents might include the following practical issues:

· *Seizure of cars* - bailiffs may need to be more alert to the needs of disabled persons and their carers;
· *Household goods* - again, consideration of the greater impact of taking audio-visual equipment from a housebound, disabled person may be needed. The same might be said for the seizure of

companion animals (and obviously guide dogs);

· *Mothers of babies* - greater consideration should perhaps be given to the needs of mothers with young babies or those who are still nursing their infants. Items for washing clothes and nappies, for sterilising feeding equipment or for the safety of a small child should naturally be avoided in levies. Arguably too, it may be discriminatory not to allow more lenient payment terms to a woman in this category as she will inevitably have lower income (maternity pay or benefit) and higher expenses;

· *Religion & belief* - these issues have been discussed at some length in Practice Note 11 on the National Standard, to which readers are referred. In summary, bailiffs will need to be conscious of festivals and days of religious observance and should seek to avoid levying upon items of cultural significance; and,

· *Joint ownership of chattels* - giving equal treatment to civil partnerships will require alertness to claims of joint ownership of household goods. Equally, the not uncommon practice of treating all the property in a couple's home as jointly owned regardless - of the actual circumstances - might be argued to be a form of discrimination on the basis of marriage or civil partnership.

4.4.7 Conclusions on 2010 Act

The Equality Act 2010 makes considerable demands of all businesses, whatever they do. Public bodies and their agents have extra responsibilities because of the important roles they undertake for the public. These duties apply at all levels of an organisation - they must be applied by managers in devising practices and policies and by staff when putting these into practice.

The key point to recall may be this - the Equality Act does not mean that everyone has to be treated the same, but it does mean that agencies need to think about peoples' different needs and how they may be met.

4.4.8 Other provisions on discrimination

In addition to the 2010 Act, bailiffs will also be required to respect two other provisions prohibiting discrimination. The first of these is the European Convention on Human Rights. Article 14 of the ECHR reads "The enjoyment of the rights and freedoms set forth in this Convention shall be secured without discrimination on any ground such as sex, race, colour, language, religion, political or other opinion, national or social origin, association with a national minority, property, birth or other status." This provision applies to all public authorities (central and local government departments) and to all those performing functions on their behalf. This will therefore apply to all bailiffs except those levying distress for rent for private landlords (and even then, should a claim for wrongful distress be brought against the bailiff in the county court, the judge would be obliged to apply ECHR principles in reaching a decision).

Secondly, the National Standard for Enforcement Agents requires that "Agents must not discriminate unfairly on any grounds such as age, disability, race, gender, religion or sexual orientation." This, of course, applies to all agents, whatever debt they may be collecting, and to all local and central government creditors.

The key aspect of both of these provisions is that they are more open in their coverage than the 2010 Act. Various forms of discrimination are identified, but they are not exclusive: article 14 of the ECHR mentions the possibility of discriminating on the grounds of "other status"; the NSEA prohibits discrimination on "any grounds" before listing a few examples. This means that an aggrieved individual may feasibly be able to identify other forms of discriminatory behaviour in his or her case than those so far discussed- and has a reasonable chance of succeeding in that argument.

Examples of other possible forms of discrimination might be:

· Seizing motor vehicles from debtors in rural locations where alternative public transport is limited so that they are put at greater disadvantage than urban dwellers;
· When removing goods to pounds or to sale rooms, failing to take into account the accessibility of those locations in light of the health, mobility or other circumstances of the debtor. Once again, those dwelling in remote rural locations might be disadvantaged if long and difficult journeys by public transport are necessitated; or,
· Failing to have access to translators in order to be able to deal adequately with debtors whose first language is not English.

Footnotes
1 *R v Havering Magistrates Court ex. p. Molloy* [1994] COD 187; *R. v B'ham Justices ex p Bennett*; too complex - *R v Basildon Magistrates ex p Holding v Barnes* (1994) COD 378.
2 [2005] EWHC 1942 (Admin).
3 Complaints no.99/A/1151, 99/A/1792 & 99/A/3103.
4 96/B/451.
5 Respectively report 93/A/2097; *R v Bristol City Justices ex p Wilsman*; 98/C/4810.
6 Respectively 96/B/2122; 96/A/3626.
7 *Ricardo v Maidenhead Board of Health* (1857) 27 LJMC 73.
8 *K v Sweden* (1991) 71 DR 94.

9 *Cremieux v France* (1989) 59 DR 67; *Funke v France* (1993) 16 EHRR 297; *Miailhe v France* (1997) 23 EHRR 491.

10 *K v Sweden* (1991) 71 DR 94; see also *Västberga Taxi Aktiebolag & Vulic v. Sweden* (2002) para.53; *Janosevic v. Sweden* (2002) para.88; Jamil v. France (1995).

11 Application No. 43457/98.

12 *Newman t/a Mantella Publishing v Modern Bookbinders Ltd The Independent*, February 3rd, 2000.

13 *Smith v UK* (1995) 21 EHRR 74.

14 20 EHRR 403.

15 71 DR 94.

16 *Hentrich v. France* (1995); *De Buck & Koolen v Belgium* (1963); *Air Canada v UK* (1995).

17 *R. (on application of Hoverspeed & Andrews) v. C&E* [2002].

18 Section 29.

19 See www.equalities.gov.uk or www.equalityhumanrights.com.

20 Part 3, section 28(1).

21 Section 19.

Chapter 5

Insolvency and taking control of goods

Introduction

The 2007 Act simply states that "This Schedule is subject to sections 183, 184 and 346 of the Insolvency Act 1986."[1] Nothing in the latter Act has been amended or altered by the new statute other than to substitute the new terminology of 'taking control' for the previous terms. This is not done section by section but generally by an amendment to s.436 of the 1986 Act which merely states that "'distress' includes use of the procedure in Schedule 12 to the TCEA, and references to levying distress, seizing goods and related expressions shall be construed accordingly."[2] In light of this, the terms distress and execution are by and large retained throughout this chapter to reflect the form of the statute.

It may be thought highly regrettable that the opportunity was not taken to more radically reshape the Insolvency Act by harmonising the treatment of different forms of seizure under different forms of insolvency. The Insolvency Act 1986 itself merely combined pre-existing provisions without any effort to impose a logical or equitable treatment of insolvents. The result is that insolvent companies are often better treated than insolvent individuals.

Whilst it is not the purpose of this chapter to discuss insolvency law generally, the insolvency of the debtor individual or company can have a major impact on the ability of bailiffs to proceed with recovery. Like the public law provisions discussed in the preceding chapter, insolvency law provides an overall framework for dealing with cases of serious indebtedness which, from time to time, will inevitably impinge on the work of the bailiff. Insolvency procedure is laid down by four separate bodies of statute.

· For individuals and companies the Insolvency Act 1986 and Insolvency Rules 1986 apply.[3] These provide a code for the insolvency of firms and individuals and lay down procedures to be followed in administering their affairs. The legislation splits into two parts. The first part deals with the insolvency of firms, the second with that of individuals. Parliament created parallel forms of insolvency for both companies and individuals. TCEA has amended the latter - see below;
· The insolvency of partnerships is dealt with separately by the Insolvent Partnerships Order 1994 (IPO) which modifies the relevant provisions of the Insolvency Act as necessary. A partnership may be

wound up as an unregistered company (see below) under articles 7 & 9 IPO. Winding-up can occur concurrent with the bankruptcy of the partners[4] or partners can be bankrupted alone on their own petitions or a creditor's.[5] A Company Administration Order may be made under article 6. Article 4 applies the CVA procedure to partnerships with the relevant amendments though the partners may need personal IVAs too. Everything said about the individual procedures applies to the partnership forms.

· For deceased bankrupts the Insolvent Estates of Deceased Persons Order 1986 applies. This applies the Insolvency Act 1986 to the administration of deceased insolvents' estates with the adaptations contained in Sch.1 to the Order. Part I of the Schedule applies certain provisions, including s.285 which deals with restrictions on enforcement and ss.346 and 347 which deal with limitations on seizures of goods. Part III applies the IVA procedure.

· TCEA 2007 itself has extensively amended the treatment of insolvent individuals by creating new form of insolvency. These new procedures will be noticed later in so far as they have an impact upon taking control of goods, but these measures include a reform of the individual administration order procedure found in the County Courts Act 1984.

Bailiffs must treat claims by debtors to be insolvent seriously and should take reasonable time to investigate them. If a bailiff proceeds to sell goods after the insolvency has been confirmed, he may be in contempt of court, but without notice of bankruptcy the bailiff cannot be liable in trespass for any seizure.[6]

This chapter will examine the effects of the different forms of insolvency, rather than the forms themselves, as it will be assumed that readers will have some familiarity with the general structure of the insolvency legislation. Some bailiffs' actions, such as CRAR and civil court execution, must be singled out for special treatment as they are treated separately in law. All references will be to the Insolvency Act and Insolvency Rules unless otherwise stated.

Part one - General matters

5.1 Security

Certain creditors are given preferential treatment in insolvency. Those with security (e.g. a mortgage on property) are in the most favourable position, getting paid first from the assets before any other claim is dealt with and, as will be seen, being largely unaffected in enforcing their security.[7] This is of relevance to the process of taking control of goods because of the decision of the High Court in *Re: A Debtor (No 10 of 1992)* which held a bailiff's walking possession agreement to be security within the meaning of s.383 of the Act. Section 383 reads:

> "a debt is secured ...to the extent that the person to whom the debt is owed holds any security for the debt (whether mortgage, charge, lien or other security) over any property of the person by whom the debt is owed".

It is presumed that a controlled goods agreement will be found to have the same effect. This decision did not create any new legal principle but simply revived an established principle. It could have a profound effect on the rights of creditors in an insolvency, as a prompt levy before any order is made would put that creditor in a preferential, secured position. A right of seizure in itself is not a form of security - it must be followed through by an actual taking into control of goods. It also seems undisputed that a creditor who has both taken control and removed the seized goods will be regarded as secured. It would appear that this right of security will be affected where a petition is presented by the execution creditor in question and it will have to be surrendered in whole or in part. Surrender of the security which derives from a levy and a controlled goods agreement will also be deemed to have occurred where a creditor fails, without good reason, to mention the levy in any proof of debt submitted to a trustee, liquidator or the like.[8]

Creditors levying against bankrupts have broad powers, which are significantly enhanced by these provisions. Restrictions on enforcement do not apply to secured creditors.[9] Where any goods of a bankrupt are held by any person by way of any pledge, pawn or other security, the Official Receiver when acting as interim receiver or during the course of investigations into the bankrupt's affairs may, after written notice, inspect them with a view to redeeming the security.[10] The security cannot then be realised without permission of court and unless the trustee has had a reasonable opportunity to inspect the goods and redeem them.

Equally, after the trustee has been appointed, where any goods are similarly subject to some form of security, the trustee may again serve notice with a view to exercising the bankrupt's right of redemption.[11] The notice has the effect preventing realisation of the security without the court's permission. The trustee may give notice to redeem at the creditor's proved value.[12] The creditor then has twenty one days in which to revalue the security and call on the trustee to settle for that sum. If either valuation is disputed, the trustee can require sale. It seems that the effect of these latter provisions is that a creditor with a controlled goods agreement may be paid even sooner than their already preferential position might suggest. This may be compared with similar powers to dispose of goods subject to security and to clear the secured debt that apply to companies (for example, s.15 for administrators and s.43 for administrative receivers).

5.1.1 Personal insolvency

None of these rights of security would appear to be exercisable if goods have not been seized before a bankruptcy order, after which date the estate vests in the trustee. Probably seizure should be before the date of the petition's presentation, otherwise the taking into control of the goods might be challenged as a void disposition.

5.1.2 Company insolvencies

In CAOs no security may be enforced by the taking of any steps. As taking steps to enforce security covers more than court proceedings, it would appear to include removal under a controlled goods agreement. If seizure precedes a winding up, the creditor enforcing against gods will be treated as secured as in bankruptcy and thus will have priority to any preferential creditors. This is subject to any specific limitations such as the 'three month rule' (see next section).[13]

5.2 Three month rule

In both bankruptcy and compulsory winding up special provisions apply to bailiffs taking control of goods in respect of any debt immediately prior to the court making an order against the insolvent firm or individual. The section relating to firms is s.176 and that relating to bankrupt persons is s.347. What may be termed the 'three month rule' applies where any person takes control of a debtor's goods and that person or firm is subsequently declared bankrupt or is wound up within three months of the date of the levy.[14]

In the case of companies if the assets of the company are insufficient to cover preferential debts, the goods taken into control, or the proceeds of their sale, are charged with those preferential debts to the extent that they cannot be satisfied from the assets.[15] Any person who must surrender goods or money as a result of this will also rank as a preferential creditor for payment after the other creditors with priority. Their position relative to other creditors is determined by the proceeds of sale of the goods by the liquidator but they will not be entitled to payment from those proceeds.[16] The provisions do not effect the operation of section 128, which voids any post petition levy - see *5.10 later.*[17]

In the case of levies against bankrupts, any goods seized or proceeds of sale realised, other than any amount held by the landlord on trust for the bankrupt's estate under section 347(2) (that is, any rent arrears accrued more than six months before the bankruptcy or any later rent due), shall be charged with the amount of any preferential debts that cannot otherwise be met from the bankrupt's estate. If the bailiff hands over goods or cash to the trustee as a result of this provision, s/he ranks as a preferential creditor to the extent of the sum paid over or the proceeds of sale of the goods but not so as to receive any money from the sums realised from the seizure.

Part 2- Forms of personal insolvency and enforcement

5.3 Individual Voluntary Arrangements

The individual voluntary arrangement (IVA) enables those in debt or facing insolvency to agree with their creditors proposals for the reorganisation of their finances in order to be able to avoid bankruptcy. Creditors are offered a scheme of repayment that should leave them better off than if the person went bankrupt, and the debtor avoids all the stigma and restrictions of actually being an undischarged bankrupt. Enforcement can be effected at two stages in the process of making an IVA.

5.3.1 Interim orders

The initial stage of the procedure is for the debtor to formulate repayment proposals with an insolvency practitioner who acts as 'nominee' and draws up a detailed scheme for presentation to the creditors. To buy time for this work to be done, the debtor can apply to the court for an Interim Order.[18] The Interim Order lasts for fourteen days initially and allows the nominee time to prepare a report for the court on the IVA proposal.[19]

The effect of the 14 day interim order is to establish a moratorium during which no execution or other legal process may be commenced or continued and that no distress may be levied, except with permission of court.[20] Whilst an interim order application is pending the court may stay any action, execution or other legal process and may also forbid the levying of any distress on the debtor's property, or its subsequent sale, or both.[21] This provides comprehensive protection against enforcement for the debtor.

5.3.2 Creditors' meetings

Before the expiry of the Interim Order the nominee must report to the court whether a creditors' meeting should be summoned to consider the IVA. If the court is satisfied with the report the order is extended to permit the creditors to meet in order to vote upon the proposals. If seventy five per cent by value accept the scheme it comes into effect and all unsecured creditors are bound by it. This means that they must accept the repayments and cannot enforce their debts whilst the IVA is in force and the debtor is complying with his/her obligations under it. Enforcement could not then continue and, for instance, to proceed with the execution of a writ would be malicious and wrongful.[22] Note that the status of secured creditors is different (see 5.1).

5.4 Bankruptcy

A bankruptcy order will be made against a person if, either on the application of the debtor or of a creditor, the court is satisfied that a debt is due and that the debtor is unable to pay it. Note that the courts have decided that it is irrelevant to the question of inability to make payment that the debtor claims to be unable to pay because he has been the victim of an illegal or excessive seizure.[23]

The making of a bankruptcy order has a number of effects on the person's finances and property, largely taking away the person's control of their affairs and placing their administration in the hands of a trustee. However in return debtors are given substantial protection from enforcement by their creditors, as will be described. If confronted with a claim to be bankrupt, a bailiff should request to see a copy of the order, be told its date or the address of the Official Receiver or trustee responsible.

Considerable restrictions apply to enforcement according to the stage in the bankruptcy process and the creditor's remedy. These are found primarily at s.285 and have an extensive impact on the enforcement of debts, both current and future.

5.4.1 Pending petitions

Whilst a petition is pending the bankruptcy court may, on application from the debtor (or, presumably, any other interested party), stay any 'action, execution or other legal process' against the property or person of the debtor.[24] Equally the court where the case is taking place, for instance a magistrates' court dealing with a liability order application, may stay proceedings or allow them to continue on terms.[25] The term "other legal process" has been considered in a number of cases, most recently In Re: A Debtor (Nos 13A & 14A-IO-1995) [1995]. The judgment is a useful summary of the argument that has taken place on the interpretation of the phrases. In short, all court action may be prevented

- whether civil or criminal - but the court cannot inhibit the exercise of an enforcement power which involves no prior legal proceedings (such as CRAR or levies for income and indirect taxes), though these are likely to be effected by the 'three month rule' (see 5.2).[26] The definition of 'property' is discussed in the next paragraph. The purpose of these sections in respect of debtors facing a pending petition is to maintain the status quo and prevent one creditor gaining advantage until the bankruptcy is adjudicated.

5.4.2 Effect of Bankruptcy Order - general

Enforcement after a bankruptcy order has been made is dealt with primarily by s.285(3). No creditor whose debt is provable in the bankruptcy may take any steps against the person or property of the bankrupt to enforce that debt. Property includes goods, chattels and money.[27] The effect of this is to completely bar enforcement of an existing debt that is included in the bankruptcy. These restrictions on enforcement are however subject to special rules applying to CRAR and judgments - see below.

If new debts arise the situation is more complex. If there are no existing debts proved for in the bankruptcy then the creditor can proceed as normal save that enforcement could be stayed on application under either s.285(1) or (2). In most cases there may be little reason to bar enforcement as bankruptcy does not absolve the debtor of responsibility for ongoing or subsequent liabilities. However, if the creditor has already proved for a debt in the bankruptcy, permission of court will be required at any time before the person is discharged in order to pursue any debt arising after the Order. Note that there is one authority slightly at variance with this, the case of *R. v. Camberwell Justices ex. p. Gravesande* [1973] in which it was held that enforcement of rates liabilities which arose after the bankruptcy order (albeit within the duration of the bankruptcy) did not require permission of court. Note however that decision was reached under Bankruptcy Act 1914 s.7, the wording of which is very similar to the present Act, but not exactly the same.[28]

The restrictions on enforcement that are imposed by subsection (3) do not affect the right of a secured creditor of the bankrupt to enforce his security.[29] This may have implications for bailiffs with possession agreements as described at 5.1.

5.4.3 Effect of bankruptcy order - executions

Special provisions are made in both bankruptcy and all forms of winding up in respect of High Court enforcement officers and county court bailiffs levying execution for any debt, whether provable or not. The provisions for winding up and for bankruptcy closely mirror each other and will be dealt with together.[30] These provisions apply only to executions in the sense of the enforcement of a civil court order by seizure of goods. It is presumed that road traffic execution is included in this. However, distraint under a power granted by statute is not covered by ss.183-4 - instead *see 5.4.5 below.*[31]

Ongoing executions

Statute intervenes in certain executions to deprive the creditor of the proceeds. There must be an execution in progress for the relevant sections to apply - it must not have been withdrawn, completed or otherwise abandoned, for instance due to there being no available goods. Conversely, there being an execution in progress cannot prevent a bankruptcy order being made. There is also a question as to whether the following provisions apply to partnership goods seized from an insolvent partner. It was held in *Dibb v Brooke & Son* [1894] that the execution creditors were entitled to the proceeds of sale of such assets as there is nothing in the applicable sections to show that such joint assets vest in the trustee after seizure under a writ. If a bankruptcy is annulled the trustee loses his/ her right to the proceeds, which revert to the execution creditors. Equally if one petition is dismissed, and the bailiff pays the creditor, if a subsequent petition is presented the proceeds cannot be reclaimed by the trustee. It should also be noted that the fact that an execution may be inhibited by the insolvency does not mean that later levies by other bailiffs will be inhibited in the same way; a bailiff who has taken control of goods subsequently, for instance for a statutory debt, might then be able to remove and sell.[32]

Service of notice

The following rights and duties are triggered by the enforcement agent receiving notice of the insolvency. It will often be important for the debtor, in order to protect him/ herself, to ensure that proper notice is given. The notice must be served on the enforcement officer or his recognised agent, not on the bailiff in possession. Notice can be verbal and its service is not covered by the rules for service in the Insolvency Rules. The notice should be specific enough for the bailiff to be able to identify the bankrupt as the person against whom a levy has been made: in *Re: Smith ex p Spooner* [1874] the sheriff's officer had levied against a debtor who was not apparently a sole trader, but went into insolvency as such.[33]

In cases of county court execution, notice may be implied if the district judge is responsible both for issuing execution and for making a subsequent bankruptcy order, even though direct notice from the Official Receiver is not received until after the statutory period. The onus of proof lies on the execution creditor, not the trustee, to show that no notice was received. If there is insufficient evidence to prove notice was not received any sale under the execution will be invalid and the proceeds must be returned to the trustee.[34] If a bailiff seizes the goods of a bankrupt in execution, even though no notice has been given, s/he may be liable in conversion to the trustee.[35] Any damages that the trustee may recover may be reduced by the bailiff's legitimate expenses.

Incomplete executions
Where the execution was issued before the bankruptcy order was made but the process has not yet been completed by sale of goods (or by receipt of the proceeds)[36] the creditor must abandon the seizure and is not entitled to retain the 'benefit of that execution'- any title to goods seized, the proceeds of their sale or any sums paid to avoid the execution.[37] If the judgment creditor seeks to continue with execution it is wrongful and malicious. After the presentation of a petition, the court can intervene by way of injunction to restrain sale under an execution. The same applies if an execution creditor seeks to enforce a provable debt after discharge.[38]

If the execution is complete, the plaintiff may retain the money regardless of the bankruptcy. The onus is on the creditor to prove that the execution had been completed. An execution is not complete where:

- the bailiff has withdrawn upon agreeing instalment payments or has re-entered when such an arrangement has broken down.[39] Indeed, the trustee may be able to recover any payments received from the judgment creditor;[40]
- the High Court enforcement officer has withdrawn permanently with the creditor's consent on payment of a lump sum or at the order of the court on the appointment of a receiver;[41]
- the debtor pays all or part of the debt to the High Court enforcement officer or direct to the creditor. Cheques in payment of the debt given to the High Court enforcement officer are received as a result of the coercive nature of the writ and are proceeds of the execution still in the High Court enforcement officer's hands;[42]
- successive sales occur under the same execution, and although the first is complete and the proceeds have passed to the creditor, other goods remain to be sold to satisfy the full debt. The High Court enforcement officer's duty is to go on selling goods to settle the debt until it is cleared. The proceeds of sale in this context mean the whole proceeds of all sales, not just proceeds of a partial sale;[43]
- there has only been delivery of the writ or warrant to the bailiff. There must be an actual levy for the execution to have the possibility of being completed. Thus where a second writ or warrant is satisfied

from the proceeds of a sale made under a prior execution, those proceeds cannot be retained against the trustee unless there has been an actual seizure. Where, however, a prior writ is set aside, a subsequent executed writ may still be valid and entitle to the creditor to the proceeds;[44]

· the bailiff has simply seized and is in possession;[45]
· a sale occurs that is not a sale under the execution, which may be fraudulent or which is not a full sale of the goods. In *Ward v Dalton* [1849] the sheriff's officer sold some of the goods seized by auction of lotted parts. Deposits were taken on each lot but lots were only separated from the mass of goods and delivered to the buyers after the bankruptcy order had been made. It was held that this was an 'inchoate sale' that enabled the trustee to recover the whole of the proceeds;[46]
· the creditor has only begun to prepare for the sale;[47] or,
· proceeds are still held by the bailiff/ High Court enforcement officer.[48]

It does not matter that the execution has not been completed because sale has been delayed by an injunction under the Insolvency Rules. The trustee will be able to claim any proceeds of sale or possession of the goods from the High Court enforcement officer. If the trustee recovers the proceeds a claim against the execution creditor for conversion by seizing goods after the commencement of the bankruptcy will probably fail as the proceeds are a fairer measure of damages than the value of the goods at the time of seizure.[49]

Completed executions
An execution is treated as being complete if there has been:

· a sale before the presentation of any petition;[50]
· the execution has been settled by a payment of cash and sale of goods to the creditor well before the bankruptcy;[51]
· a return of no seizeable goods by the bailiff;[52]
· an auction sale or full payment;[53] or,
· disposal by the High Court enforcement officer by means of a bill of sale and the officer has received full payment.[54]

Effect of notices
If before the execution is completed, notice of the debtor's bankruptcy is received by the enforcement agent, any goods or money seized or recovered in part satisfaction of the judgment debt after that time must be surrendered, on request, to the trustee as the right to enforce the security given by seizure is lost and the money is a by-product of that security.[55] The provisions refer to the High Court enforcement officer receiving notice after goods have been "taken in execution":[56]

this has been held to mean that the High Court enforcement officer is in possession of them (i.e. has taken control of them by one of the four means specified in the Enforcement Act). As the statute refers to sums paid to avoid execution, we must conclude that 'money recovered' by the bailiff includes these sums.[57]

The costs of the bailiff, up until the time that notice of the bankruptcy was received, constitute a first charge upon the goods, to satisfy which they may be sold by the trustee.[58] These costs do not include either the costs of preparing for a sale that could not proceed because of the insolvency or the execution creditor's costs of issuing and serving the warrant or writ of control; neither can the High Court enforcement officer deduct and retain a third party's expenses.[59] Costs incurred in a levy commenced after the insolvency has begun are very unlikely to be allowed.[60]

Executions over £500
There are further restrictions on an officer levying execution in respect of any completed execution for a judgment of over £500 which leads to the realisation of money whether by sale or by payment to avoid sale. This total figure includes bailiff's charges so that an execution will be affected even though the judgment debt is below £500, if the costs take it over the limit.[61] A judgment is not affected if it has been reduced below the limit by the time bankruptcy occurs. Creditors may avoid this provision and retain the proceeds of sale against the trustee in a number of ways: by abandoning part of their claim; by issuing execution for less than the specified sum of £500; or by ordering sale for less than £500, even though execution was issued for more.[62]

If the High Court enforcement officer or bailiff is notified of a pending bankruptcy petition, and an order is later made upon that petition, the sums collected will vest in the bankrupt's estate. The proceeds of any execution therefore must be held by the bailiff for fourteen days after the notice, or whilst the petition is pending, in case they should be paid over to the trustee. The execution creditor's right to receive the proceeds has been described as a vested right, but one which is liable to be divested if insolvency supervenes within fourteen days. The High Court enforcement officer can deduct the costs of the execution, but this will not include fees incurred after the date of the bankruptcy.[63]

Sums paid to prevent sale include any payments made under a controlled goods agreement to the High Court enforcement officer and any payment made to the High Court enforcement officer when he called in order to levy. However, payments made by a third party to the bailiff to avoid seizure are not effected.[64] The trustee also has no claim to payments made by the debtor to the High Court enforcement officer without there being any seizure: such payments made under pressure to buy the forbearance of the High Court enforcement officer are not paid 'under an execution'.[65]

The fourteen day 'waiting period' imposed by the Insolvency Act begins with the day of payment or the day that sale takes place and not the day on which the High Court enforcement officer receives the proceeds. If notice is received after this period has expired, as payment to the High Court enforcement officer in such circumstances is vested in the creditor and held by the High Court enforcement officer on the creditor's behalf, the creditor is entitled to receive it. In county court execution, if the warrant is transferred to a 'foreign court' for enforcement, the fourteen day period is reckoned from the date that proceeds are received by the foreign court rather than the court of issue.[66] If bankruptcy does occur following notice of a petition, money will have to be repaid whether paid to the High Court enforcement officer, the solicitor or the execution creditor. If money is paid over to the creditor despite notice of the bankruptcy, the High Court enforcement officer may be sued by the trustee but the High Court enforcement officer may in turn sue the execution creditor. The fact that the High Court enforcement officer is holding a sum for fourteen days does not render it a debt, even a contingent debt, upon which a petition could also be issued by the execution creditor.[67]

In the county court, the Civil Procedure Rules require that the enforcement agent will, as soon as practicable after sale or the receipt of money in discharge of a warrant of control, send notice to the creditor and the court. Where an enforcement agent is responsible for the execution of a warrant of control notice must be sent to the creditor and the court where one of the following occurs:

· the agent receives notice that a bankruptcy order has been made against the judgment debtor;
· where the debtor is a company, the agent receives notice that a provisional liquidator has been appointed or that an order has been made or a resolution passed for the winding up of the company;
· the agent withdraws from possession of goods seized; or,
· the agent pays over to the official receiver or trustee in a bankruptcy or to the liquidator, of a company, the proceeds of sale of goods sold under the warrant or money paid in order to avoid a sale or seized or received in part satisfaction of the warrant.[68]

Setting aside

The court has the power to set aside the trustee's or liquidator's rights to such extent and on such terms as it thinks fit.[69] A very strong case for set aside will have to be made, the guiding principle being fair treatment of all creditors. However, in a case where the creditor failed to complete execution because the debtor firm was stalling it (and all other creditors) there was no reason for the court to exercise its discretion in favour of that creditor and allow the execution to continue.[70] Those who have purchased property in good faith from the High Court enforcement officer are protected.[71] Under s.346(8) it seems to be permissible to issue execution for a non-provable debt, provided that only property acquired since the bankruptcy order, and not claimed by the trustee, is seized. If after-acquired property is seized for a debt provable in the bankruptcy, the execution will be set aside by the court on application by the debtor or trustee.

5.4.4 Effect of bankruptcy orders - CRAR

During bankruptcy a commercial landlord is granted a limited right of recovery by means of CRAR. Such landlords are thus in a more favourable position than many other creditors of a failed business.[72]

Six month rule

Generally rent arrears are irrecoverable by taking control of goods and will have to be proved for like every other debt of the tenant. However, the landlord may employ CRAR for unpaid rent due, but only for the rent that accrued in the six months immediately prior to the beginning of the bankruptcy, which is the date when the order was made.[73]

Where CRAR follows the order, even by minutes, anything other than the six month's element must be proved for and cannot be the subject of seizure and sale. If the tenant goes bankrupt during a rental period, the Apportionment Act 1870 will apply to allocate the sums due before and after the commencement of the insolvency, and CRAR may be levied at the end of the period for any sum accrued and due before the bankruptcy. If the landlord neglects to exercise his power to levy CRAR and allows goods to be sold by the trustee, the only remedy will be to prove for the rent debt in the bankruptcy. For the same reason a landlord who fails to actually take control of goods cannot claim any priority over any creditor who has obtained some sort of security, such as a solicitor with a charge under the Solicitor's Act.[74]

If the landlord takes control of goods between the petition and order, any surplus over and above the six months' rent plus costs, or any sums in respect of rent due after the distress, shall be held by the landlord on trust as part of the bankrupt's estate.[75] The trustee may seek a court order to recover such sums. An agreement between landlord and bankrupt tenant not to levy on terms of the landlord taking the dead stock of the rented farm at a valuation, though this may be beneficial to the estate, could not enable the landlord to recover more rent than the six months recoverable under the Act.[76] If there are no seizeable goods, the only remedy for the landlord will be to prove for the rent as other remedies against the tenant are barred by the bankruptcy.

Special cases

If a rent claim is met by the supervisor of a voluntary arrangement for a debtor who later becomes bankrupt, the estate can reimburse the supervisor for the sums paid; see too Re: Humphreys ex p Kennard [1870] where the Official Receiver made a similar payment prior to the appointment of the trustee. The trustee later sought to impugn this arrangement but it was upheld by the court.[77] If the bankrupt wishes to assign the lease but has rent arrears, the arrears may be cleared from the purchase monies and could not then be reclaimed from the landlord by the trustee. This is because the estate has benefited by the payment and the landlord has waived the right to seize goods. Equally money paid by a trader after the commencement of bankruptcy to avert an imminent levy of CRAR by a landlord could not be recovered by the trustee as again the estate has benefited by retaining the goods that might have been seized and the landlord could not be deprived of his/ her legal rights.[78]

After discharge, the landlord cannot levy CRAR upon any of the goods that were comprised in the bankrupt's estate. If CRAR is issued before an insolvency commences it may be completed against the goods found on the bankrupt's premises if s/he is not the tenant). If a joint tenant has gone bankrupt the landlord may levy CRAR against the non-bankrupt joint tenant for the same arrears, provided no dividends have been paid in the insolvency. The landlord may take control of goods, even though they have been sold or assigned by the trustee, if they are not removed promptly from the premises but it seems that if they are sold to a person residing on the premises they are held to have been removed.[79]

Levies

It is lawful for a landlord to levy CRAR even though the property is vested in the trustee: such property is not in legal custody so as to be exempt from seizure. It is not possible for the trustee to obtain an order for repayment of sums raised. Injunctions to prevent such seizures of goods may be made, but only on terms that the landlord is paid the rent allowable, or that the sum is secured for him/ her.[80] The trustee may agree to make payment to the landlord to avert an imminent seizure: these generally give the landlord preference over the trustee's costs, as s/he would have had if a levy had actually been made. Permission will generally be given to permit distress begun before the petition to be concluded. If the landlord is in control of goods under a power of CRAR when the insolvency begins, and that possession later becomes wrongful, the trustee may recover damages in conversion but in deciding the measure of damages the landlord must be allowed what the trustee would have had to pay to obtain possession at the start of the bankruptcy- that is, the arrears claimed.[81]

Continued possession

If the bankrupt tenant continues to occupy the rented premises, s/he will still be liable to pay rent. As a result there seem to be no restrictions upon the landlord using CRAR to collect rent arrears accruing after the order.[82] The court will not be able to intervene under s.285(1) or (2) because, as described earlier, an extra-judicial taking control of goods cannot be described as a legal proceeding. Even if the lease has been disclaimed, if the bankrupt is still in occupation the landlord can enter and take control of goods up until the date of termination. If the tenancy is terminated by notice to quit by the landlord, the landlord may only use CRAR due up until the notice becomes effective.[83]

If the tenancy vests in the trustee in bankruptcy and s/he does not disclaim, s/he may become personally liable for the rent. Vesting occurs where the tenancy is not exempt from the effects of the Insolvency Act. Exempt tenancies include those which are assured, secure and protected. Thus it will be business, unprotected and agricultural tenancies and restricted contracts that are most likely to vest. Landlords may therefore prove (or use CRAR within the limits described) for the rent due before the insolvency, but their rights in respect of rent accruing after the date of commencement are unaffected and the trustee may be liable to CRAR under privity of estate.[84]

5.4.5 Effect of bankruptcy orders - seizures under statute

Section 347(8) makes it clear that none of the restrictions affecting landlords apply to other forms of taking control of goods. The effect of this clause is that most forms of taking control are uninhibited by bankruptcy, being exempt from s.285(3). Bailiffs may therefore proceed take control of a bankrupt's goods for local taxes, income taxes and indirect taxes. Subsection 347(9) emphasises this right by stating that property that is included in the estate may be taken into control, even though it is vested in the trustee.

Customs & Excise and Inland Revenue policy has been not to exercise their rights to levy unless, respectively, the debtor continues to trade and incurs further debts or if other creditors also continue to exercise their rights to levy, to the HMRC's possible detriment. For other creditors the question how to instruct the bailiffs is also purely a matter of policy.

5.4.6 Post-bankruptcy debts

If debts accrue after the bankruptcy order has been made, they are largely unaffected by it and can be collected in the normal fashion. The only possible restrictions are in ss.285(1) or (2). Subsection 1 gives the bankruptcy court the power to stay any action, execution or legal proceeding against the property or person of the bankrupt. The court in which an action is proceeding also has the power to stay those proceedings or allow them to continue on terms.[85] As earlier discussions indicate this will effect court remedies but not those rights to take control of goods which require no prior court order (*see 5.4.2*).

5.5 Individual Administration Orders

Part 5 chapter 1 TCEA substitutes a new Part 6 County Courts Act 1984 and wholly reforms the administration order procedure. If an administration order is made to consolidate a person's debts of up to £15,000, s.112G requires it to include a condition that no qualifying creditor of the debtor is to pursue any remedy for the recovery of a qualifying debt unless regulations provide otherwise, or the creditor has the permission of the proper county court (*for the meaning of 'qualifying debts' see 5.8 later*). The county court may give permission subject to such conditions as it thinks fit. The regulations specify classes of debt which are exempted (or exempted for specified purposes) from the restriction imposed by s.112G(2).

These restrictions will remain in place for the duration of the order and will clearly prevent all enforcement. A county court is required, at the time it makes an administration order, to specify a day on which the order will cease to have effect. If the court does not specify a day under this section, the order ceases to have effect at the end of the maximum permitted period, which is five years beginning with the day on which the order was made.[86]

The restriction contained in s.112G is sufficiently broad to cover all forms of taking control; county court proceedings will also be affected.[87] If an administration order is made and proceedings in a county court are pending against the debtor in respect of a qualifying debt, the creditor under the qualifying debt is not entitled to continue the proceedings in respect of the debt provided the other county court receives notice of the administration order but instead the county court must stay the proceedings.

The power also exists under s.115 of the County Courts Act for the court, at the request of a judgment creditor, to issue execution against the debtor subject to an administration order where it is believed that his/her property is worth more than £50. This procedure will be a normal county court execution.

5.6 Enforcement restriction orders

Section 102 TCEA further amends the County Courts Act 1984 by inserting after Part 6 on administration orders a new Part 6A dealing with enforcement restriction orders (EROs). This has yet to be brought into force, section 117A defines an enforcement restriction order as an order that imposes various specified restrictions on certain creditors. A county court may make an enforcement restriction order if certain conditions are met. The order must be made in respect of an individual who is a debtor under two or more qualifying debts; that individual must not be a debtor under any business debts and should not be bankrupt or subject to an IVA. The debtor must be unable to pay one or more of his qualifying debts as a result of a sudden and unforeseen deterioration in his financial circumstances. There must, nonetheless, be a realistic prospect that the debtor's financial circumstances will improve within the period of six months beginning when the order is made. Moreover it must be fair and equitable to make the ERO and the county court must have regard to any representations made by any person about why the order should not be made before making an enforcement restriction order.

If an enforcement restriction order is made it will prevent any qualifying creditor of the debtor pursuing any remedy for the recovery of a qualifying debt unless the creditor has the permission of the county court or the debt is one which is exempted (or exempted for specified purposes) from any requirement imposed by s.117D. A proper county court may give permission for the purposes of subject to such conditions as it thinks fit.

This restriction upon all forms of enforcement will last for the duration of the enforcement restriction order. A county court, at the time it makes an enforcement restriction order, should specify a day on which the order will cease to have effect. If the court does not specify a day under this section, the order ceases to have effect at the end of the maximum permitted period of 12 months beginning with the day on which the order was made. As is the case with administration orders, any existing county court proceedings will also be stayed.[88]

5.7   Debt management schemes

The TCEA creates a new procedure called debt management schemes (s.104). Although yet to be implemented, a debt management scheme is a scheme which must be open to some or all non-business debtors on request. The scheme must provide that, if such a request is made, a decision must be made about whether a debt repayment plan is to be arranged and if such a plan is arranged the scheme must be operated by a body of persons (whether a body corporate or not).

Under s.105 a debt repayment plan can be established. This is a plan that meets the conditions which specifies all of the debtor's qualifying debts and which requires the debtor to make payments in respect of each of those specified debts (though full repayment is not necessary).

Under s.111 no qualifying creditor of the debtor is to pursue any remedy for the recovery of a qualifying debt, unless the creditor has the permission of a county court (which the court may give subject to such conditions as it thinks fit) or of regulations provide otherwise. Existing county court proceedings against the debtor are also stayed by a debt management plan.[89]

5.8 Debt relief orders

Section 103 TCEA amends the Insolvency Act 1986 by inserting, before Part 8, a new Part 7A. The contents of this new part are set out in Schedule 17 TCEA; it creates a new procedure termed debt relief orders.

An individual who is unable to pay his debts may apply for an order under s.251A to be made in respect of his 'qualifying debts.' These debts are those which are for a liquidated sum payable either immediately or at some certain future time and are not 'excluded debts'. A debt is not a qualifying debt to the extent that it is secured and certain debts are prescribed and thereby excluded from debt relief orders.

A moratorium commences on the effective date for a debt relief order in relation to each qualifying debt specified in the order.[90] The effect of this moratorium, is that, whilst it lasts, the creditor to whom a specified qualifying debt is owed has no remedy in respect of the debt, and may not commence any action or other legal proceedings against the debtor for the debt, except with the permission of the court and on such terms as the court may impose. If on the effective date a creditor to whom a specified qualifying debt is owed has any such petition, action or other proceeding pending in any court, the court may stay the proceedings or allow them to continue on such terms as the court thinks fit. Nothing in this section affects the right of a secured creditor of the debtor to enforce his security. It will be interesting to see whether the courts will be prepared to treat pre-existing controlled goods agreements as a form of security, as was held to be the case for walking possession agreements under the former law.

The moratorium relating to the qualifying debts specified in a debt relief order continues for the period of one year beginning with the effective date for the order, unless the moratorium terminates early or the moratorium period is extended by the official receiver or by the court.[91] The Official Receiver may only extend the moratorium period for the purpose of carrying out or completing an investigation under section 251K, taking any action he considers necessary (whether as a result of an investigation or otherwise) in relation to the order or, in a case where he has decided to revoke the order, providing the debtor with the opportunity to make arrangements for making payments towards his debts. The official receiver may not extend the moratorium period beyond the end of the period of three months beginning after the end of the initial period of one year. The moratorium period may be extended more than once, but any extension (whether by the official receiver or by the court) must be made before the moratorium would otherwise end.

Part 3 - Forms of company insolvency & enforcement

5.9 Company Administration Orders

The rules on company administration orders and upon administrators in insolvency generally have been altered by the Enterprise Act 2002. This inserted into the Insolvency Act a new Schedule B1, which replaced the previous Part II of the 1986 Act dealing with Administration Orders.

A company in financial difficulty may protect itself from its creditors, and create a breathing space in which it may restructure, by applying to the court for an administration order.[92] The company usually petitions for this protection, though it is possible for a creditor (alone or in conjunction with other creditors of the company) to do so and the clerk of a magistrates' court may petition under s87A MCA where an attempt to take control of the goods of a company has failed because of insufficient goods. The petitioner is most likely to be a major creditor such as the firm's bank or main supplier. An administrator can also be appointed by a floating charge holder or by the company or its directors.[93]

When an application is presented, and until the order is made or dismissed, an interim moratorium is in effect. A moratorium also applies for 14 days when a notice of an intention to appoint an administrator is filed in court. The terms of the moratorium are as described below.[94]

If an order is made, an administrator (an insolvency practitioner) is appointed and must notify all creditors that, for the period that the order is in force, s/he will be managing the company's business and property. To facilitate this process the firm is comprehensively protected from enforcement.[95] For instance:

- No security may be enforced by the taking of any steps. As taking steps to enforce security covers more than court proceedings it would appear to include removal under a controlled goods agreement (*see 5.1*);[96]
- No legal process may be instituted or continued except with either the consent of the administrator or the permission of the court. Legal process is defined as including legal proceedings, execution and distress. All bailiffs' actions for any debt are therefore prevented by the making of a company administration order. If the court does give permission to proceed, it may impose conditions.[97]

5.10 Compulsory Winding Up

A creditor may apply to court for a company to be declared insolvent and be wound up. This known as compulsory liquidation or court winding up and is the company equivalent of bankruptcy. It is a remedy that may be used against a company as a form of debt enforcement. In this context it may be used by a magistrates court under s.87A(1) MCA if a levy has failed due to insufficient goods. It is also possible for the firm itself to petition in order to gain the protection of the court. A winding up petition may be presented if one of a number of grounds is satisfied but the most common is that the company is unable to pay its debts.

If a winding up order is made all creditors are affected. The Official Receiver will normally be appointed initially as an 'interim' liquidator and will call a meeting of creditors to appoint an insolvency practitioner as liquidator unless it is felt that the assets of the company are too small to justify it. The directors' duties and powers cease. The primary function of the liquidator is to ensure that all assets are got in, realised and distributed to the creditors.[98]

Enforcement is affected by different provisions at the successive stages in the process of winding up. An important general point to note is that the wording relating to enforcement against insolvent companies differs from that dealing with other debtors. Reference is made to any 'proceeding' against the company. It has been held that this word included distraint as well as execution. A number of decisions, culminating in *Re: Memco* [1986], have expressed discomfort that distraint should be regarded as an "action or proceeding" under ss.126 and 130, but the judges have felt bound by the long line of authority. To explain the difference between this and the effect of IVAs, bankruptcy and company administration orders it is perhaps worth noting that the word used is 'proceeding' not 'proceedings'. In *Re: International Pulp and Paper Co Ltd* [1876], Sir George Jessell MR stated that the term should be construed as generally as possible. This approach was followed in *Eastern Holdings Establishment of Valduz v Singer & Friedlander Ltd* [1967] and it has been held that winding up bars a range of more or less non-judicial procedures, including local tax recovery in the magistrates court as well as seizures for rent.[99]

5.10.1 Enforcement after petition

Under s.126(1), between the presentation of the petition and an order being made, any action or proceeding pending against the company in either the High Court or Court of Appeal can be stayed. Also any other pending action or proceeding may be restrained by the bankruptcy court. Clearly this will affect court actions for debt recovery and enforcement but also any exercise of any other enforcement power. That said, it has also been held that recovery on any warrant issued before the petition was filed may continue unless there are special circumstances such as fraud or unfair dealing which mean that it should be stayed. Thus it was decided that a levy for rates begun before the winding up commenced might proceed unless the liquidator paid the rates.[100] Remember also that if seizure precedes the winding up, the creditor will be treated as secured as in bankruptcy and thus will have priority to any preferential creditors. This is subject to any specific limitations such as the 'three month rule' (*see 5.1 & 5.2*).[101]

5.10.2 Enforcement after the winding up order

Sections 128 and 130 deal with the protection afforded a company during winding up by the court. Under s.128 any distress or execution is void if initiated after the winding up commenced - in other words, after the petition was presented. Three points need to be made. Firstly all enforcement is effected. There is no differentiation between that for pre-insolvency provable debts and post-insolvency non-provable debts unlike bankruptcy (*see 5.4.2*). Secondly, void means void to all intents so that the creditor retains no interest under an execution, even against third parties. The restriction includes seizures of goods to recover both rent and rates and, one may presume, all other forms of taking control under statutory powers. Lastly, though, this apparent bar on enforcement is subject to the powers contained in s.130(2) as described in the following section. It is also possible that a sale may be allowed to go ahead as it has been held that a sale is not putting an execution or distress in force as contemplated by s.128.[102]

5.10.3 Warrants issued before a winding up

The bar on enforcement during a winding up imposed by ss.128 and 130 is subject to the powers contained in s.130(2), as a consequence of which it has been held that a warrant issued before a winding up petition was filed may continue unless there are special circumstances such as fraud or unfair dealing which mean that it should be stayed.[103] Under s.130(2) no action or proceeding can be begun or continued after an order has been made, except with permission of court and on such terms as the court may impose. This supplements the impact of s.128. Levies may not be begun, nor may they be continued, as the term 'proceeding' has been held to refer to any stage in the levy process-from seizure to sale. All warrants and all action upon them are wholly ineffective except that, as stated, permission of court may be given on terms to allow enforcement to continue.[104] Execution or other forms of control issued without permission will be invalid against the trustee.[105]

Pre-insolvency enforcement
Where the enforcement began before the commencement of the winding up, and unless special reasons exist which render it inequitable (such as fraud or unfair dealing), distress will generally be allowed to continue.[106] The simple fact of the petition being presented is no ground in itself to restrain a writ or warrant. Appointment of a provisional liquidator prior to a winding up order is not a necessary bar to taking control. The crucial point is when seizure occurs, rather than the issue of the warrant, so if this follows the presentation of the petition, even by minutes, the levy must be stayed. Even where a warrant or writ is issued before or at the same time as the petition, if the liquidator takes possession before the bailiff, the bailiff should be restrained.[107]

Permission to continue a prior levy may be given:

- if the court feels that the creditor has acted properly and simply been prevented from levying before the petition by the resistance of the debtor;[108]
- where the bailiff is already in control of goods, so as not to deprive a priority creditor of the fruits of their diligence;[109]
- if there are sufficient assets to satisfy all creditors so that the issue is simply whether a creditor should be paid now or later, having otherwise acted correctly at all times;[110]
- if subsequent writs of control have been lodged with the High Court enforcement officer, even though they have not been levied, provided that he is already in possession under a prior writ. The court may in such cases restrain sale until the winding up order is made and then order delivery of the property to the liquidator for sale, reserving to the creditors the same priority against the proceeds as if it was a sale by the High Court enforcement officer;[111] or,
- if the levy is for an ongoing liability such as rates, which should still be payable and enforceable where the liquidator retains beneficial

occupation on the behalf of the company, particularly where the business is carried on, permission to distrain may be given. A levy for rates begun before the winding up commenced may proceed unless the liquidator pays the rates.[112]

Permission to continue with a levy may not be given, where, for instance:

· there are no special circumstances and seizure followed the start of the insolvency proceedings;[113]
· the court doubts that the warrant was properly issued before the order was made;[114]
· forced sale under the enforcement power would be injurious to the company and its other creditors;[115] or,
· the aim is to ensure fair treatment of all creditors as it is the court's duty to ensure that there is an 'equality of equities'.[116]

Terms may be imposed when granting permission, such as in *Re: Bastow* [1867] in which the court made an order restricting the levy to moveable property i.e. stock rather than plant. Where the value of goods seized before the petition greatly exceeds the debt due the court may order the liquidator to pay the enforcing creditor off. It is also possible that a sale may be allowed to go ahead as sale is not putting an execution or distress in force as contemplated by s.128.[117]

Post-insolvency enforcement
Where the enforcement is to begin after the winding up, it will only be allowed where special circumstances apply. In the absence of special circumstances the court has to stay or restrain the execution to ensure an equal distribution to all creditors of the same class.[118] Special circumstances that might justify giving permission to continue with enforcement might be where:

· the creditor delayed the enforcement due to representations for indulgence on the part of the company;[119]
· where the actions of the company inhibited the bailiff;[120]
· where the execution creditor has delayed enforcement proceedings due to other proceedings disputing the validity of the insolvency itself;[121] or,
· where the creditor is secured and is proceeding to recover their own property.[122]

Exceptional circumstances do not include the fact that the creditor may have no other way of recovering their money. Where part of the claim relates to before the winding up and part to after its commencement, then the latter debt may be enforced with permission whilst the former will have to be proved for.[123]

5.10.4 CRAR

Rent enforcement has attracted special treatment in windings up. If a seizure for rent arrears has been initiated before the winding up it may continue unless the liquidator pays any rent due.[124] If CRAR is put in at premises rented by a company now in liquidation it is illegal under s.128 if the premises are not retained for the purposes of the winding up. The lessor's only remedy would be to prove for the debt. The landlord can, however, issue a warrant to bailiffs if the property is retained for the purposes of better winding up the firm.[125]

As stated, the landlord may levy if the lease is continued for the purposes of winding up. Rent payments in such circumstances are regarded as a debt contracted for the purpose of the winding up and should be paid in full like any expense properly incurred by the liquidator. See also *In Re: South Kensington Co-operative Stores* [1881], a voluntary winding up case, in which it was held that rent due must be apportioned under the Apportionment Act 1870 - the landlord being entitled to prove for rent due up until the commencement of the winding up, and being entitled to levy distress for the full rent after that date, for which the firm remained liable as it remained in possession of the premises for the purpose of carrying on the business under the liquidator during the winding up. Enforcement may proceed as normal in the event of non-payment. See too *In Re: Brown Bayley & Dixon ex p Roberts & Wright* [1881], in which it was held that distress could be levied for sums due after winding up began where the liquidator remained in possession, as the terms of the lease will continue to apply.[126]

The definition of 'liquidation expenses' has been reviewed most recently in *Kahn v. Commissioners of Inland Revenue* [2002]. This was a case of a creditors' voluntary liquidation in which application was made to the court for directions as to whether corporation tax was a liquidation expense. It was held that whilst the court may have a discretion as to how a creditor may recover a liability, it has no discretion as to whether an item is to be treated as a liquidation expense: the Act and Rules lay down what liquidation expenses are and that these should be paid from the assets before paying the creditors. The House of Lords provided a useful summary of the development of the relevant case law on distraint, confirming that *Re: Exhall, Re: Progress Assurance, Re: Lundy* and *Re: Oak Pits* all remain good law. It was also affirmed that rent may be treated as a liquidation expense if possession is retained by the liquidator for the purposes of the winding up and that, on equitable grounds, liabilities incurred before the liquidation in respect of property retained by the liquidator may also be paid.[127]

5.10.5 Executions in windings up

Executions are subject to special provisions where they were issued before the winding up began.[128] These provisions closely resemble those in bankruptcy and the principles shared by the two are discussed at 5.4.3. As under s.346 in bankruptcy, any execution not completed by sale before the winding up begins will lapse and the creditor will lose any benefits (i.e. rights) under that enforcement and any title to goods or proceeds of their sale realised.[129] Proceeds still held by the High Court enforcement officer must be handed over because the execution has not been completed. The court may on application set aside the liquidator's rights in favour of the execution creditor to such extent and on such terms as it thinks fit. However where the creditor failed to complete an execution because the debtor firm was stalling it (and all other creditors) there was no reason for the court to exercise its discretion in favour of that creditor and allow the execution to continue.[130] Any purchaser of goods in good faith from the bailiff will in all cases gain good title.[131]

If the High Court enforcement officer or bailiff is notified that a winding up petition has been presented against a firm, and a compulsory winding up results from this, the sums collected will vest in the bankrupt's estate. The proceeds of any execution therefore must be held for fourteen days after the notice, or whilst the petition is pending, in case they should be paid over to the trustee. The costs of the execution can be deducted from these proceeds, but enforcement fees incurred after the date of the order could not be included. In voluntary windings up notice to the High Court enforcement officer of the meeting at which a resolution to go into voluntary winding up may be made is adequate notice under the Act. Contrast to this *Re: T. D. Walton* [1966] in which notice to the High Court enforcement officer of a meeting of creditors to consider the possibility of voluntary winding up was held insufficient notice, as the meeting would not consider an actual resolution to wind up.[132]

Incomplete executions

Under s.184(1) after a winding up order, resolution for voluntary winding up or the appointment of a provisional liquidator the High Court enforcement officer has duties imposed upon him. If an execution has not been completed by sale or by receipt or recovery of the full amount due including costs the bailiff will have to deliver to the liquidator the goods or money seized (or received) in part satisfaction, though the costs of the execution are a first charge upon this and the liquidator can sell items to pay the High Court enforcement officer.[133] Readers should note that this requirement to pass on goods or money must be read in light of the general voiding of incomplete executions under s.183(1). That subsection states that the benefit of an execution may not be retained. It has been established by the courts that the benefit is not monies paid to the bailiff to avoid sale. A number of cases have explored the meaning of the phrase "benefit of execution" and have explained that it refers not to the money received (which constitutes the 'fruits of the execution') but to the security of the charge on the debtor's goods obtained by the issue of execution (the 'binding power').[134] The charge enables the creditor to proceed to complete the execution and clear the balance of the judgment debt then due by removal and/or sale and it is this benefit that is lost. This charge subsists as long as the goods are unsold or the debt is not fully satisfied. The creditor issuing a warrant is protected by a priority right, which prevents any other dealings with the goods as long as the execution is in force. To have this priority it does not matter that the security has not been enforced by sale. As a consequence we must take the reference to monies in s.184 (2) to refer to money seized by, not paid to, the bailiff. The situation is different in bankruptcy. Payments already made cannot, subject to the next section, be claimed back from the creditor. Note that the goods only need to be delivered by the bailiff when asked to do so by the liquidator. In the absence of such a request, the bailiff's duty is to proceed to sale as usual.[135]

Furthermore in any completed execution on a judgment over £500 the High Court enforcement officer must hold any sale proceeds (and any money paid to avoid sale), less any costs incurred, for fourteen days. The period begins on the day that the company makes payment or on the day that sale takes place.[136] If within that time notice is served that a winding up petition has been presented against the firm or that a meeting has been called at which a resolution to enter voluntary winding up will be presented, and a compulsory or voluntary winding up results from this, the High Court enforcement officer must pay the retained balance over to any liquidator. These rights may again be set aside by the court as it thinks fit but a very strong case will have to be made, the guiding principle being fair treatment of all creditors.[137]

5.11 Voluntary winding up

There are two ways in which a company can enter into voluntary liquidation. One is where the company's members resolve upon it, the second is where the firm's creditors vote on a resolution to wind up. The member's voluntary liquidation usually arises if the company's term of life under its articles expires or if some similar event occurs which, under the articles, requires the company to be wound up. The company is not insolvent and will indeed make a declaration to that effect before passing a resolution to wind up. A firm that realises that it cannot pay its debts and thus cannot make a declaration of solvency may wind up without court involvement by means of the creditor's voluntary liquidation. In either case a liquidator is appointed and winds up the company's affairs, disposing of its property. The liquidator is affected by a number of enforcement related provisions that are common to all windings up, whether voluntary or compulsory. These include regulation of such matters as the preferential charge on distrained goods (s.176 - *see 5.1*) and the restrictions on execution (ss.183/4 - *see 5.4.3 and 5.10.5*).

As the court need not be involved at all in voluntary windings up, there is as a result no automatic stay on enforcement under ss.128 and 130 as there is in compulsory liquidations described earlier. However the liquidator may apply to the court under s.112 for such protection and the court may use the powers it would have in respect of a compulsory winding up. The earliest stage at which the court can intervene is after a petition has been presented. If the company plans a meeting of members and creditors to consider plans to deal with creditors, this does not justify the court intervening.[138] The impact of court orders on enforcement can be as follows:

· all enforcement action against the company will usually be stayed, unless the circumstances are exceptional, in order to ensure fair treatment for all creditors.[139] Where the company has been stalling all its creditors it is not just and reasonable to give one stalled creditor, who has not been able to complete a levy before the winding up began, preference over other stalled creditors, whether they had completed levies or not. The court will stay threatened as well as actual enforcement;[140]
· this general bar includes CRAR, seizures of goods under statute and execution. In such cases the costs of the enforcement action will have to be met by the creditor and not the liquidator.[141]
· distraint begun before the commencement of the insolvency may be treated differently. In such cases only if special reasons such as fraud or unfair dealing make it inequitable for enforcement to continue will it be restrained.[142]
· although permission to enforce may be given under s.130(2), terms may be imposed by the court, such as that part of the debt only may be enforced.[143]
· the kinds of exceptional circumstance that may lead the court to allow enforcement to continue include deception of the bailiff, use of winding up as a deliberate way of avoiding payment or a levy upon a company where all assets are subject to floating charges that exceed their value.[144]
· the court may, when staying enforcement commenced after the commencement of the winding up, impose terms, such as that the creditor be permitted to prove for the debt plus court costs.[145]

5.12 Company Voluntary Arrangements

It is possible for firms to set up company voluntary arrangements (CVAs) with their creditors, just like an individual under ss.1-7 Insolvency Act. As of January 1st 2003 the remainder of the provisions of the Insolvency Act 2000 came into force. CVAs have been brought into line with Individual Voluntary Arrangements in that the courts are now given the power to order a moratorium of 28 days' duration whilst the proposals for a CVA are formulated. The impact of such a moratorium is that:

"(g) no other steps may be taken to enforce any security over the company's property, or to repossess goods in the company's possession under any hire-purchase agreement, except with the permission of the court and subject to such terms as the court may impose, and

(h) no other proceedings and no execution or other legal process may be commenced or continued, and no distress may be levied, against the company or its property except with the permission of the court and subject to such terms as the court may impose."[146]

This seems to prevent all forms of enforcement against goods, for whatever liability.

5.13 Partnership insolvencies

Insolvent partnerships are dealt with by the Insolvent Partnerships Order 1994 which applies company and individual procedures to such firms, modifying the relevant provisions as necessary. A partnership may be wound up as an unregistered company (see below).[147] Winding up can occur concurrent with the bankruptcy of the partners [148] or partners can be bankrupted alone on their own petitions or a creditor's.[149] A Company Administration Order may be made under article 6. Article 4 applies the CVA procedure to partnerships with the relevant amendments though the partners may need personal IVAs too. Everything said already about the separate procedures will apply to the partnership forms.

Unregistered companies are those not registered under Companies Act 1985. Part V of the Act deals with their liquidation. The effect of such winding up on enforcement against the partnership is that, between the presentation of the petition and the making of the order, the court may stay any action or proceeding against the firm.[150] Under s.227 the same also applies to proceedings against any of its contributories if the application for a stay is made by a creditor. Also, under s.228 the making of the winding up order will restrict a creditor's rights to begin or continue enforcement against any contributory of the firm except with permission given on application to the bankruptcy court and on such terms as it might impose.[151]

Limited liability partnerships were created by the Limited Liability Partnership Act 2000. Section 14 of the Act allows for the making of regulations relating to such partnership's insolvency and Part IV s.5 of the Limited Liability Partnership Order 2001 applies Insolvency Act provisions on company insolvencies (CVAs, administration orders and windings up) to them with minor modifications.[152]

5.14 Administrative Receiverships

These are the commonest form of insolvency procedure for firms. An Administrative Receiver (AR) is a receiver and manager of the company's property appointed by and on behalf of those creditors holding 'debentures' over the firms assets, as described at 10.21. The nature and effect of floating charges and their effect on bailiffs' activities is described in detail in this section.

If the AR has taken possession most forms of taking control of goods are defeated. However if payments are made to the bailiff under threat of removal and sale, these may be retained as against the AR when s/he is appointed. It does not make any difference whether the agreement reached over payment is for instalments or for a lump sum. If there has been a change of occupation of the premises as a result of the AR's appointment, s/he will become liable for any rates and may be subject to distraint for them. Normally, though, the terms of the debenture will not make the AR an agent of the company and thus s/he is not liable for any rates due after the date of the appointment. The company will remain liable, though possessing few seizable assets.[153]

Footnotes
1 Sch.12 para.69.
2 Sch.13 para.75.
3 See Sources of bailiff law c.1 p.19.
4 articles 8 & 10.
5 article 11.
6 Investigation - *Ayshford v Murray* (1870) 23 LT 470; contempt - *Re: Bryant* [1876] 4 ChD 98; notice - *Bailey v. Hazen* (1847) 5 NBR 416 CA.
7 s.285(4).
8 Walking possession - [1995] *Times* Feb. 1st; seizure not security - In *Re: Russell* [1885] 29 Ch D 254; removal - *ex p Birmingham Gaslight & Coke Co*, In *Re: Adams* [1870] 11 Eq 204; petitioning creditor - see s269 IA '86 and In *Re: Chidley* and In *Re: Leonard* [1875] 1 Ch D 177; surrender of walking possession - *LCP Retail v Segal* [2006] EWHC 2087.
9 s285(4) - see for example In *Re: Longendale Cotton Spinning Co* [1878] 8 Ch D 150.

10 s.285(5).

11 s.311(5).

12 Insolvency Rules 1986 rules 6.117 to 6.119.

13 s.11(3)(c). See on taking steps - *Bristol Airport v Powdrill* [1990] Ch 744; preceding winding up - *Re: Printing & Numerical Registering Co* [1878] 8 ChD 535 and *Re: Blue Bird Mines* [1942] 44 WALR 85; priority in winding up - *Re: D S Paterson & Co Ltd* [1931] OR 777.

14 ss176(1) & 347(3).

15 s.176(2).

16 s.176(3).

17 s.176(1).

18 s.253.

19 s.255(6).

20 s.252(2).

21 s.254.

22 Impact of IVA - s260(2); *Phillips v General Omnibus Co* (1880) 50 LJQB 112; *Seaton v Lord Deerhurst* [1895] 1 QB 853.

23 *Leicester v Plumtree Farms* [2003] EWHC 206 (Ch); [2004] BPIR 296.

24 s.285(1).

25 s.285(2).

26 1 WLR 1127; it would seem that the initial liability order needed for local tax qualifies as 'legal process' and would need permission of court (see *Re: Smith* [1990] 2 AC 215). See too *ex p Hill, In Re: Roberts* [1877] 6 Ch D 63 in which a gas company levying distress under a justice's warrant was held to be enforcing a form of execution by way of legal process.

27 s.436.

28 s.285(3(b); RA 297.

29 s.285(4).

30 ss.183/4 & s.346 respectively.

31 *Brenner v. HM Revenue & Customs* [2005] EWHC 1611 (Ch); see also *Re: Modern Jet Support* [2005] 1 WLR 3880.

32 No goods - *Re: Godwin* [1935] Ch 213; making of order - *Rorke v Dayrell* (1791) 4 TR 402; [1894] 2 QB 338; annulment - *Diggles v Austin* (1868) 18 LT 890; reclaim - *Re: Condon ex p James* [1874] 9 Ch App 609; later levies - *Re: Toomer ex p Blaiberg* [1883] 23 Ch D 254.

33 Notice - *In Re: Holland ex p Warren* [1885] 15 QBD 48 and *Bellyse v M'Ginn* [1891] 2 QB 227; verbal - *Curtis v Wainbrook Iron Co* (1884) Cab & E 351; service - *Lole v Betteridge* [1898] 1 QB 256; [1874] 10 Ch App 168

34 Late notice - *In Re: Harris* [1931] 1 Ch 138; notice to HCEO - *Engineering Industry Training Board v Samuel Talbot (Engineers) Ltd* [1969] 2 QB 270; onus of proof - *In Re: Joy ex p Cartwright* (1881) 44 LT 883 and *Pearson v Graham* (1837) 6 A&E 899; invalid sale - *ex p Schulte In Re: Matanlé* [1874] 9 Ch App 409; see also *ex p Dawes In Re: Husband* [1875] 19 Eq 438.

35 *Price v Helyar* (1828) 4 Bing 597; *Balme v Hutton* (1833) 9 Bing 471.

36 *Figg v Moore* [1894] 2 QB 690.

37 Respectively s.183(1)/ s.346(1) for winding up & bankruptcy; see *Heathcote v. Livesey* [1887] 19 QBD 285 - though see *Galt v. Saskatchewan Coal Co* (1887) 14 Man LR 304 contra; *Re: Norton ex p Todhunter* [1870] 10 Eq 425.

38 Injunction - *Re: Tidey* (1870) 21 LT 685; after discharge - *Davis v Shapley* (1830) 1 B & Ad 54.

39 *Re: Ford* [1900] 1 QB 264; *Re: Brelsford* [1932] 1 Ch 24.

40 *Re: Bowman* (1931) 4 ABC 155; *Re: Maywald* (1933) 7 ABC 9; *Rae v Samuel Taylor Property Ltd* (1963) 110 CLR 517 and see later.

41 *Re: Evans* [1916] 2 HBR 111; *Mackay v Merritt* (1886) 34 WR 433.

42 Payment to HCEO - *Re: Pearson ex p West Cannock Colliery Co* (1886) 3 Morr 157; to creditor - *Re: Godding* [1914] 2 KB 70 and *Re: Pollock* (1902) 87 LT 238; cheques - *Koppers Co v. Dominion Foundries & Steel Ltd* (1965) 8 CBR(NS) 49.

43 *Jones v Parcell & Thomas* [1883] 11 QBD 430.

44 Delivery - *Philips v Thompson* (1684) 3 Lev 191, *Arminer v Spotwood* (1773) Loft 114 & Re: Davies ex p Williams [1872] 7 Ch App 314; actual seizure - *Johnson v Evans* (1844) 7 Man & G 240; set aside - *Goldschmidt v Hamlet* (1843) 1 Dow & L 501; *Graham v Witherby* [1845] 7 QB 491.

45 *Cole v Davies* (1699) 1 Ld Raym; *ex p Rayner In Re: Johnson* [1872] 7 Ch App 732; *In Re: Dickenson ex p Charrington & Co* [1888] 22 QBD 187.

46 Sale - *Heathcote v Livesley* [1887] 19 QBD 285; fraud - *Re: Townsend ex p Hall* [1880] 14 Ch D 132 - 'sale' to a third party with sheriff's officer's consent; [1849] 7 CB 643.

47 *In Re: Chinn* [1881] 17 Ch D 839 and compare *Re: Ideal Furnishing* (1908) 7 WLR 558 and *Re: Nink* (1955) 17 ABC 13.

48 *Bluston & Bramley Ltd v Leigh* [1950] 2 KB 554.

49 Injunction - *Re: Gwynn ex p Veness* [1870] 10 Eq 419; trustee's claim - *Re: Johnson ex p Rayner* [1872] 7 Ch App 325; conversion - *Whitmore v Black* (1844) 2 Pow & L 445.

50 *In Re: Love ex p Official Receiver v Kingston on Thames County Court Registrar* [1952] 1 Ch 138; *Higgins v M'Adam* (1829) 3 Y&J 1; *Young v Roebuck* (1863) 2 H&C 296.

51 *In Re: Jenkins* [1904] 90 LT 65.

52 *Re: Fairley* [1922] 2 Ch 791.

53 *Galt v Saskatchewan Coal Co* (1997) 4 Man LR 304.

54 Bill of sale - *Christie v Winnington* (1853) 8 Exch 287; payment - *Loader v Hiscock* (1858) 1 F&F 132 NP.

55 *Re: Quirk* (1951) 15 ABC 148; *McQuarrie v Jaques* (1954) 92 CLR 262.

56 s.346(2).

57 s.346(1).

58 Under s.346(2); see for example *Re: Penny Lumber Co* (1921) 2 CBR 113 and *Re: Oshawa Heat, Light & Power Co* (1906) 8 OWR 415.

59 Sale costs - *Searle v Blaise* (1863) 14 CBNS 856; *Rush v Baker* (1734) Cun 130; costs of writ - *In Re: Woods* [1931] 2 Ch 320.

60 See for instance *Re: Saw Bill Lake Gold Mining Co* (1903) 2 OWR 1143.

61 Charges - *ex p Lithgow In Re: Fenton* [1878] 10 Ch D 169; over limit - *ex p Liverpool Loan Co In Re: Bullen* [1872] 7 Ch App 732.

62 Below limit - *Mostyn v Stock* [1882] 9 QBD 432; abandoning claim - *Re: Salinger* [1877] 6 ChD 332 and *Turner v Bridgett* [1882] 8 QBD 392; part warrant - *Re: Hinks* [1878] 7 ChD 882; part sale - *Turner v Hinks* [1882] 8 QBD 392.

63 s346(3)&(4); holding proceeds - *In Re: Greer, Napper v. Fanshawe* [1895] 2 Ch 217; nature of right - *In Re: English & Ayling ex p Murray & Co* [1903] 1 KB 680.

64 Payments to HCEO - *Re: Walkden Metal Sheet Co. Ltd* [1960] 1 Ch 170; 3rd party payments - *Bower & Co v Hett* [1895] 2 QB 51.

65 Payment without seizure - *In Re: Hassall ex p Brooke* [1874] 9 Ch 301 - see also *Stock v Holland* [1874] 9 Exch 147 - this seems to include payments made to avoid a sale that the execution creditor has agreed to accept.

67 Start date - *Re: Cripps, Ross & Co* [1888] 21 QBD 472; late notice - *Marley Tile Co Ltd v Burrows* [1978] QB 241; county court - *D P Toomey v King* [1952] CLY 260.

68 Duty to repay - *Re: Ford* [1900] 1 QB 264 and *Re: Godding* [1914] 2 KB 70; trustee sues - *Notley v Buck* (1828) 8 B&C 160; HCEO sues - *Re: Husband* [1875] LR 19 Eq 438; nature of debt - *In Re: William Hockley Ltd* [1962] 1 WLR 555.

69 CPR 83.20.

70 Under s.346(6) & ss.183(2)(c) & 184(5) respectively for bankruptcy and windings up.

71 Discretion to continue - *Re: Redman Builders* [1964] 1 All ER 851; set aside - *Barrow v Poile* (1830) 1 B & Ad 629.

72 Respectively for bankruptcy & winding up s.346(7) & s.183(2)(b).

73 s.347.

74 s.347(1).

75 Over 6 months - *Re: Bumpus ex p White* [1908] 2 KB 330; apportionment - *Bishop of Rochester v Le Fanu* [1906] 2 Ch 513 and *In Re: Howell ex p Mandleberg* [1895] 1 QB 844; sale allowed - *Anon ex p Descharmes* 1 Atk 102; priority - *In Re: Suffield & Watts ex p Brown* [1888] 20 QBD 693.

76 s.347(2).

77 Court order.- *Re: Crook ex p Collins* [1891] 66 LT 29; levy agreement - *Re: Griffith ex p Official Receiver* (1897) 4 Mans 217.

78 *Re: Ayshford ex p Lovering* (1887) 4 Morr 164; (1870) 21 LT 684.

79 Right waived - *Mavor v Croome* (1823) 7 Bing 261; paid to avert - *Stevenson v Wood* (1805) 5 Esp 200.

80 s.347(5). Complete levy - *In Re: Exhall Mining Co Ltd* (1864) 33 LJ Ch NS 595; joint tenant - *Holmes v Watt* [1935] 2 KB 300; prompt removal - *ex p Plummer* (1739) 1 Atk 103; sold to occupier - *ex p Grove* (1747) 1 Atk 104.

81 Right to levy - subs 9 and *Re: Mead ex p Cochrane* [1875] 20 Eq 282; not exempt - *Re: Collins* [1888] 21 LR Ir 508; no order - *Re: Cliffe ex p Eatough & Co Ltd* (1880) 42 LT 95; injunction terms - per Bacon CJ in *ex p Till In Re: Mayhew* [1873] 16 Eq 97.

82 Preference - *Re: Chapman ex p Goodyear* (1894) 10 TLR 449; proving - *Thomas v Patent Lionite Co* [1881] 17 Ch D 250; damages - *Cox v Liddell* (1895) 2 Mans 212.

83 *Re: Binns* [1875] 1 ChD 285; *Re: Thomas* (1876) Diprose's Friendly Soc Cases 64; *In Re: Wells* [1929] 2 Ch 269.

84 Disclaimed - *Briggs v Sowry* (1841) 8 M&W 729; notice to quit - *Re: Wilson ex p Lord Hastings* [1893] 10 Morr 219.

85 Vesting - *Burrell v Jones* 3 B&A 47; trustee liable - *In Re: Solomon ex p Dressler* [1878] 9 Ch 252.

86 s.285(2).

87 Section 112K.

88 s.112O.

89 s.117L.

90 s.114.

91 s.251G.

92 s.251H.

93 Sch.B1 para.12.

94 para.s 14 & 22.

95 para.44.

96 para.43.

97 para.43(2); *Bristol Airport v Powdrill* [1990] Ch 744.

98 para.43(6) & para.43(7)).

99 s.143(1).

100 [1986] Ch 86; [1876] 3 ChD 594; [1967] 2 All ER 1192; *Re: The Flint, Coal & Cannel Co Ltd* (1887) 56 LJ Ch 232.

101 Prior warrants - *Re: Bellaglade* [1977] 1 All ER 319 or *Venners Electrical & Cooking Appliances v Thorpe* [1915] 2 Ch 404; rates paid - *In Re: Dry Docks Corporation of London* [1888] 39 Ch 306.

102 Secured - *Re: Printing & Numerical Registering Co* [1878] 8 ChD 535 and *Re: Blue Bird Mines* [1942] 44 WALR 85; priority - *Re: D S Paterson & Co Ltd* [1931] OR 777.

103 Void - *In Re: Artistic Colour Printing ex p Fourdrinie* [1882] 21 ChD 510; all levies - *Re: Traders' North Staffordshire Carrying Co ex p North Staffs Railway Co* [1874] LR 19 Eq 60; prior levy - *In Re: Exhall Mining Co Ltd* (1864) 33 LJ Ch NS 595; sale - *Re: Great Ship Co* (1863) 9 LT 432.

104 *Re: Bellaglade* [1977] 1 All ER 319; *Venners Electrical & Cooking Appliances v Thorpe* [1915] 2 Ch 404.

105 s.130(2); see *Heeles v Creditors' Trustee of Samson* (1880) UB&F(SC) 196.

106 *Re: Crown Reserve Consolidated Mines Ltd* (1933) 14 CBR 229.

107 *Re: David Lloyd* [1877] 6 Ch D 339; *Re: Herbert Berry* [1977] 1 WLR 617; *Re: Bellaglade* [1977] 1 All ER 319; *In Re: Exhall Mining Co Ltd* (1864) 33 LJ Ch NS 595.

108 Petition presented - *Ex p Millwood Colliery Co* (1876) 24 WR 898; provisional liquidator - *In Re: Dry Docks Corporation of London* [1888] 39 Ch 306; timing - *Re: London & Devon Biscuit Co* [1871] LR 12 Eq 190; liquidator in possession - *Re: Waterloo Life (No 2)* (1862) 32 LJ Ch 371.

109 *Re: London Cotton Co Ltd* [1866] LR 2 Eq 53.

110 *Re: Prescott Elevator Co* (1902) 1 OWR 161.

111 *Re: Bastow* [1867] LR 4 Eq 689.

112 In possession - *Re: Hille India Rubber* [1897] WN 20; order sale - *Re: Plas-yn-Mhowys Coal Co* [1867] LR 4 Eq 689 and *Re: Hill Pottery* [1866] LR 1 Eq 649.

113 Permission - *Re: International Marine Hydropathic* [1884] 8 ChD 470; rates - *In Re: Dry Docks Corporation of London* [1888] 39 Ch 306.

114 *In Re: Poverty Bay Farmers' Co-operative Association Ltd* (1898) 16 NZLR 695.

115 *Re: Perkins Beach Lead Mining Co* [1878] 7 Ch D 371.

116 *Re: Twentieth Century Equitable Friendly Society* (1910) WN 236.

117 *D Wilson (Birmingham) Ltd v Metropolitan Property Developments Ltd* [1975] 2 All ER 814; *In Re: Dimsons Estate Fire Clay Co* [1874] 19 Eq 202; to ensure *pari passu* payment of all debts - *Mitchell v Buckingham International plc* [1998] EWCA Civ 247/ 2 BCLC 369.

118 ([1867] LR 4 Eq ; pay debt - *Re: Withernsea Brickworks* [1880] 16 ChD 337; sale - *Re: Great Ship Co* (1863) 9 LT 432.

119 Special circumstances - *In Re: Lancashire Cotton Spinning Co* [1887] 35 Ch D 656 and *The Constellation* [1966] 1 WLR 272; stay - *Bowkett v Fullers United Electrical Works* [1923] 1 KB 160.

120 *Re: Taylor ex p Steel & Plant Co* [1878] 8 ChD 183 or *Re: Richards* [1879] 11 ChD 676.

121 *Re: London Cotton* [1866] LR 2 Eq 53.

122 *Re: Prior ex p Osenton* [1869] 4 Ch App 690.

123 *Re: Aro Co Ltd* [1980] 1 All ER 1067.

124 No other remedy - *Anglo-Baltic & Mediterranean Bank v Barber* [1924] 2 KB 410; splitting debt - *Re: North Yorkshire Iron Co* [1878] 7 Ch D 661.

125 Recovery continues - *Re: Roundwood Colliery Co* [1897] 1 Ch 373.

126 Illegal - *Re: Progress Assurance Co ex p Liverpool Exchange* [1870] LR 9 Eq 370; proving - *Re: Coal Consumers Association* [1876] 4 ChD 625; retained for winding up - *Re: North Yorkshire Iron Co* [1878] 7 ChD 661.

127 Right to levy - for example where the lease has not been surrendered, *In re: Lundy Granite Co ex p Heavan* [1871] LR 6 Ch 462 and see too *Re: North Yorkshire Iron Co* [1878] 7 ChD 661; rent as expense - *Re: Oak Pits Colliery* [1882] 21 ChD 322; [1881] 17 ChD 161; [1881] 18 Ch D 649.

128 UKHL 6.

129 ss.183/4.

130 s.183(1).

131 Setting aside - s.183(2)(c); incomplete execution - *Bluston & Bramley Ltd v Leigh* [1950] 2 KB 554; permission to continue - *Re: Redman Builders* [1964] 1 All ER 851.

132 s.183(2)(b).

133 s184(3) & (4); holding proceeds - *In Re: Greer, Napper v. Fanshawe* [1895] 2 Ch 217; nature of right - *In Re: English & Ayling ex p Murray & Co* [1903] 1 KB 680; [1966] 1 WLR 869;

134 s.184(2).

135 *In Re: Caribbean Products (Yam Importers)* [1966] Ch 331; *In Re: Andrew* [1937] 1 Ch 122.

136 Payments made - *Re: Samuels* [1935] Ch 341; request for return - *Woolford's Estate v Levy* [1892] 1 QB 772.

137 s.184(3); *Re: Cripps, Ross & Co* [1888] 21 QBD 472.

138 Sections 184(4) &184(5).

139 *Booth v Walkden Spinning & Manufacturing Co Ltd* [1909] 2 KB 368.

140 *Needham v Rivers Protection & Manure Co* [1875] 1 Ch D 253; *In Re: Thurso New Gas Co* [1889] 42 Ch 486.

141 Stalling - *Re: Redman Builders* [1964] 1 All ER 851; stay - *Re: Zoedone* (1884) 32 WR 312.

142 Rent - *In Re: South Rhondda Colliery Co* (1898) 60 LT 1260; rates - *In Re: Margot Bywaters Ltd* [1942] 1 Ch 121 (note that in this case the distraint was only begun after the resolution); execution - *Westbury v Twigg & Co* [1891] 1 QB 77; costs - *Montague v Davies Benachi & Co* [1911] 2 KB 595.

143 *In Re: Roundwood Colliery* [1897] 1 Ch 373; *Venners Electrical Cooking & Heating Appliances v Thorpe* [1915] 2 Ch 404.

144 E.g. *In Re: G Winterbottom Ltd* [1937] 2 All ER 232 where only part of several years' rent arrears were recoverable by distress.

145 Deception - *Armoduct Manufacturing Co Ltd v General Incandescent Co Ltd* [1911] 2 KB 143; avoiding payment - *In Re: Imperial Steamship & Household Coal Co Ltd* (1868) 32 LJCh 517; floating charges - *In Re: Harpur's Cycle Fittings* [1900] 2 Ch 731.

146 *In Re: Poole Firebrick & Blue Clay Co* [1873] LR 17 Eq 268; *In Re: Sabloniere Hotel Co* [1866] LR 3 Eq 74.

147 Sch.A1 Part III para.12 of the 2000 Act.

148 articles 7 & 9.

149 articles 8 & 10.

150 art.11.

151 s.221(1) applying s.126 etc. & s.227.

152 *Gray v Raper* [1866] 1 CP 694.

153 SI 1090.

154 Retention of payments - *Robinson v Burnell's Vienna Bakery Ltd* [1904] 2 KB 624; manner of payment - *Heaton v Dugard Ltd & Cutting Bros Ltd* [1925] 1 KB 655; change of occupation - *Richards v Overseers of Kidderminster* [1896] 2 Ch 212; non-liability - *Taggs Island Casino Hotel Ltd v Richmond upon Thames Borough Council* [1967] RA 70.

Chapter 6

Preventing and postponing seizure

This chapter examines the strategies open to an individual to avoid or prevent a levy by the bailiff actually taking place. Enforcement may have been threatened, a warrant may even have been issued, but it will be assumed in most cases that the bailiff will not have made great progress with the levy itself.

A few warrants or writs can be suspended or postponed by a court; most cannot. There are also ways of frustrating or inhibiting takings of control that are open to debtors- some are legal and some are criminal offences. All these strategies will be described in this chapter. Beyond these narrow concerns of enforcement action, there may be various appeals or challenges to liability which may remove the threat of debt recovery, but these are not addressed here.

Section one - Applications to suspend enforcement

It may be possible to persuade a creditor to voluntarily withdraw a warrant, but this will normally only be in a situation where terms of payment have been agreed. Otherwise, for just four debts is it possible to apply to court to have a warrant stayed.

6.1 Suspending High Court execution

When admitting a claim on form N9A the debtor is invited to provide financial details and to request time to pay by instalments. Terms of payment will be determined by the Court.[1] On default, execution against goods may issue and a stay would then be necessary. If judgment is entered in default - or perhaps on summary judgment[2] - or if a county court judgment is transferred to the High Court for enforcement, it is more likely to be on terms of payment in full forthwith. If payment is not made, execution may again issue and a stay will be required.

The 2007 Act grants the High Court a power to order stays under section 70. Application can be made at any time after the judgment is entered, but this will normally be after the High Court enforcement officer has visited the premises and levied. If, at any time, the High Court is satisfied that a party to proceedings is unable to pay a sum recovered against him (by way of satisfaction of the claim or counterclaim in the proceedings or by way of costs or otherwise), or any instalment of such a sum, the court may stay the execution of any writ of control issued in the proceedings, for whatever period and on whatever terms it thinks fit.[3] The court may continue to stay enforcement from time to time until it appears that the cause of the inability to pay has ceased. For these purposes, a party to proceedings includes every person, whether or not named as a party, who is served with notice of the proceedings or attends them.

These provisions in the Act are supplemented by the Civil Procedure Rules.[4] When a judgment or order for payment of money is made, or at any time thereafter, the debtor or any other party who is liable to execution of a writ of control may apply on form N244 to the Court for a stay of execution. The Court's power to stay execution of a writ of control may be exercised by a Master or District Judge. Where the application for a stay is made on the grounds of the applicant's inability to pay, the application notice must set out those grounds and must be accompanied by a witness statement disclosing the debtor's means. If the Court is satisfied that there are special circumstances which render it inexpedient to enforce the judgment or order; or that the applicant is unable from any reason to pay the money, then the Court may stay the execution of the judgment or order, either absolutely or for such period and subject to such conditions as it thinks fit. An application for a stay, if not made at the time of judgment, must be made in accordance with Part 23 and may be made even if the party liable to execution did not acknowledge service of the claim form or serve a defence or take any previous part in the proceedings.

The previous case authority indicates that the Court has a broad discretion to stay the execution but that this should be exercised in light of the consideration that the claimant should only be deprived of an immediate opportunity to enforce the judgment if there is good reason.[5] Orders staying execution that the Court may make include the following:

- a stay on terms of payment, whether by instalments or by a lump sum or sums;
- an indefinite stay with liberty to apply or for a set period with a review at the end thereof; or,
- a stay subject to a moratorium for a set period.

Readers should also note that under CPR 40.8A a party against whom a judgment has been given or an order made may apply to the Court for a stay of execution of the judgment or order (or other relief) on the ground of matters which have occurred since the date of the judgment or order. The Court may grant such relief, and on such terms, as it thinks just. This power is without prejudice to the powers just described to suspend because of financial difficulties. This may be done on whatever terms the Court thinks just. It has been held that the effect of this provision is to enable the court to consider matters which would have prevented the original order being made, or would have led to a stay if they had already occurred at the date of the order.[6] A predecessor rule spoke of "facts which have arisen too late to be pleaded"- which makes clear the real intention of this rule. Application should again be made by N244.

Execution may also be stayed where a judgment is being appealed. A stay is not automatic on appeal and special circumstances will have to be shown to persuade the Court of the need to deprive judgment creditors of their rights.[7] Such circumstances may include the possibility of enforcement ruining or precipitating the bankruptcy of the defendant or the likelihood that if the debt or damages were to be paid to the claimant, they would not be recoverable if the appeal was successful.[8] Such stays may be on terms such as a requirement that the creditor be paid without undue delay if the appeal fails or that the appellant's assets are preserved in the meantime, other than for satisfying essential liabilities.

The judgment debtor may of course seek to negotiate a hold on enforcement with the creditor, subject to payment of the judgment debt in instalments or otherwise. Such an agreement to allow time for payment and to postpone execution made by the judgment creditor's legal representative is not binding upon the creditor, who may still issue execution.[9]

6.2 Suspending county court execution

Under section 88 CCA the county court has a general power to stay any execution issued in proceedings, whether for the whole sum due or an instalment thereon, where the paying party is unable for any reason to satisfy the order. This stay may be on such terms and for such periods as the court thinks fit, and may be renewed periodically until the cause of the inability to pay has ceased.

6.2.1 Suspending warrants

In respect of county court warrants of control, the power to suspend the warrant is exercised under CPR 83.7. At the time that a judgment or order for payment of money is made or granted - or at any time thereafter - the debtor or any other party liable to execution of a warrant is entitled to apply to the court for a stay of execution. The power of the court to stay execution of a warrant of control may be exercised by a District Judge or a court officer.

The Rules make detailed provision about the form of the application and its contents, but in reality in the county court these are fixed by the form of the application form used, N245, which requires the applicant to provide details of his/ her personal circumstances, income, expenditure and all other liabilities and to make an offer of payment.

When the debtor submits the N245 to the county court, it will send the judgment creditor a copy and require the creditor, within 14 days of service of the notification, to state in writing whether or not the creditor objects to the application and giving reasons. If the creditor does not notify the court of any objection within the time stated, the court officer may make an order suspending the warrant on terms of payment. If the judgment creditor agrees to the application, or objects only to the payment terms proposed, the court officer may determine the date and rate of payment and make an order suspending the warrant on terms of payment. Any party affected by the resulting order may, within 14 days of service, apply on N244 with reasons asking for the order to be reconsidered. If a party applies for reconsideration, the court will arrange a day for the hearing of the application before the District Judge and give the parties not less than eight days' notice of the date fixed. On hearing the application the District Judge may confirm the order or set it aside and make such new order as the court thinks fit.

If a judgment creditor objects to suspension of the warrant and wishes the enforcement agent to proceed to execution, the court will fix a day for a hearing before the District Judge of the debtor's application and will give the parties not less than two days' notice of that date.

If any of the terms of the suspension are not complied with, the judgment creditor may apply for the warrant to be reissued. This actually rarely seems to happen, and generally once a warrant is suspended, one may regard it as effectively set aside or cancelled.

From time to time in the past problems were experienced by defendants wishing to submit an application on N245 where the bailiff has yet to either visit or enter the debtor's property. Some courts will refuse to accept the form until the bailiff has levied on the grounds that, unless the bailiff has thus secured the judgment creditor's position, if the debtor were to default on the terms of the suspension, it may be more difficult for the bailiff to enforce the reissued warrant. There is no statutory justification for this approach and the ministry has given clear guidance that applications must not be refused, regardless of when in proceedings they are submitted. If a refusal still do occurs, the court has jurisdiction to suspend on the basis that the application may be regarded as having been made at the time that the defendant tried to submit it to court - see *Islington Borough Council v Harridge* [1993] in which an application to stop an eviction was refused on the basis that there was no judge in the court available to hear it when the tenant's solicitor attended.[10]

6.2.2 Suspending judgments

The court also has powers under s.71(2) CCA to suspend or stay any judgment or order where the person cannot pay the whole sum or any instalment. This can be done for such time and on such terms as the court thinks fit, and can be renewed periodically. This is supplemented by CPR 40.8A, under which a party against whom a judgment has been given or an order has been made may apply to the Court for a stay of execution of the judgment or order (or other relief) on the ground of matters which have occurred since the date of the judgment or order. The Court may grant such relief, and on such terms, as it thinks just. This power is without prejudice to the powers just described to suspend because of financial difficulties.

This provision is slightly broader in its application than s.88 and CPR 83.7 and can be of particular help where the defendant cannot pay at all. This is particularly so because of the form that the HMCTS guidance to its staff on processing N245 applications. The instructions are that an application making an offer of no payment must be treated as no offer at all, and cannot be considered. Instead whatever terms are requested by the judgment creditor should form the order. An application under s.71(2), being an application on notice to district judge on N244, will not be treated in the same way and will not encounter the same administrative problem. As in the High Court, execution may be stayed on application where a judgment is being appealed either to Circuit Judge or to the Court of Appeal.[11]

6.2.3 Suspending part warrants

A county court warrant of control is issued for part of a sum of money and costs payable under a judgment or order (*see 7.4.2*). If such a 'part warrant' is subsequently suspended on payment of instalments then, unless the court otherwise directs, the judgment or order will be treated as suspended on those terms as respects the whole of the sum of money and costs then remaining unpaid.[12]

6.2.4 Voluntary suspensions

If the county court is requested by the creditor to suspend a warrant of control because an arrangement has been made with the debtor, the court will mark the warrant as suspended by request of the creditor and the creditor may subsequently apply to the court for it to be re-issued. Such an arrangement will not prejudice any right of a judgment creditor to apply for the issue of a fresh warrant.[13]

6.3 Suspending magistrates' court enforcement

When a criminal penalty is first imposed, it will be normal for the magistrates' court to allow time for repayment.[14] If instalments are allowed, the period for payment and the level of the instalments will be specified.[15] A defendant is entitled to apply to vary a fines order and to seek more time to pay.[16] If a person defaults the court may then issue a warrant. A magistrates' court may, if it thinks it 'expedient', postpone the issue of a warrant until such time and on such conditions as it thinks just.[17] Applications for postponement may be made as often as necessary.[18] This means that, at a hearing at which a decision is taken to issue a warrant to bailiffs, the court can further delay the enforcement provided certain terms - usually for instalment payment - are met.

There is, however, no specific power to suspend warrants after they have been issued, unlike in the civil courts. Nonetheless magistrates' courts do have discretionary powers to grant 'stays of execution' in very exceptional cases. Victorian authorities indicate that these exist. For example it has been held that the court may suspend, on terms, the enforcement of 'a sum of money claimed to be due and recoverable on complaint to a Court of Summary Jurisdiction'; more recent cases have confirmed this power to grant a stay.[19]

However these cases also show that magistrates have only a discretionary power, not a duty, to grant a stay and that this power is only likely to be exercised where there are exceptional circumstances. This may be, for example, where an appeal is pending or where the welfare of a minor might be affected. Equally it has been held that an appeal against a maintenance order is not grounds to stay its enforcement and that once the court has confirmed liability, it cannot suspend a warrant.[20] The magistrates' powers were fully reviewed in *Crossland v Crossland* [1993]. A distraint warrant was issued to collect unpaid arrears of maintenance and the husband applied by way of complaint for the magistrates to suspend the warrant and, on their refusal, appealed by way of case stated. Sir Stephen Brown P held that there was no inherent jurisdiction to suspend and "that once having issued (the warrant) ... the matter was out of the court's hands" and the justices were *'functus officio'* - they had discharged their duty.[21]

A modest relation of these rigid rules has been allowed by recent statute. Under the Legal Aid, Sentencing & Punishment of Offenders Act 2012 the rules on fines collection have been amended by allowing warrants to be withdrawn in limited circumstances.[22] The new provisions state that, if a fines officer has issued a warrant of control for the purpose of recovering the sum due, s/he may subsequently withdraw the warrant if -

· the defendant remains liable to pay any part of the sum due; and,
· the fines officer is satisfied that the warrant was issued by mistake, including in particular a mistake made in consequence of the non-disclosure or misrepresentation of a material fact (presumably by the defendant).

Additionally, if a warrant of control has been issued to recover a fine and the fines officer subsequently refers the defendant's case to the magistrates so that they may consider such matters as variation of the payment terms and discharge of the fine collection order,[23] the court may discharge the warrant if -

· the defendant remains liable to pay any part of the outstanding fine, and,
· the power conferred by section 142(1) of the Magistrates' Courts Act 1980 (to re-open cases to rectify mistakes) would have been exercisable by the court if the court had issued the warrant. The justices may rescind any sentence or order they have issued if it is felt to be "in the interests of justice". It has been argued by some poverty campaigners that this power extends to withdrawing warrants against those who ought to be treated as vulnerable as a result of ill-health, disability and/or low income. The court may also replace any decision it has made if it later appears to be invalid.

6.4 Suspending CRAR

Under section 78 of the Act the court may intervene in CRAR. Under subsection 1, if notice of enforcement is given in exercise (or purported exercise) of CRAR the High Court or county court may make either or both of these orders on the application of the tenant -

· either an order setting aside the notice and effectively cancelling it- for example, where the preconditions have not been met (see later); or,
· an order that no further step may be taken under CRAR, without further order, in relation to the rent claimed. CRAR is thereby suspended. This might be used, for instance, where there is a dispute about the sums due.

Under subs.2 it is stated that regulations may make provision about the further orders that may be made and grounds of which the court must be satisfied before making an order or further order. No such rules have in fact been made. It appears, then, that tenants will be able to apply on any reasonable grounds to the courts, using general application N244.

This provision is an innovation and truly marks the break between distress for rent - an entirely extra judicial means of self help for landlords - and takings of control which are subject to a high degree of regulation. The new provision enables a tenant to bring a disputed attempt to enforce arrears in front of a judicial tribunal for impartial adjudication, thus dealing with one of the major criticisms levelled at distress.

Section Two - Resistance to taking control

The Act replaces most of the previous rules about interferences with seized goods and rescues. It provides instead a new set of remedies for creditors for dealing with such resistance.[24]

6.5 Creditor's remedy

If a debtor wrongfully interferes with controlled goods and the creditor suffers loss as a result, the creditor may bring a claim against the debtor in respect of the loss.[25] The damages would presumably be the amount of the debt that the creditor could no longer recover by the taking and sale of goods (or that proportion of the liability which had been covered by the value of the items of which the bailiff had taken control). A creditor's successful claim will clearly depend upon evidence from the enforcement agent as to the value of the goods taken into control.

The 2007 Act does not repeal the offence of interference with seized goods under s.78 of the Magistrates' Court Act 1980. This is curious in light of s.57(2) of the same Act, which is discussed at 13.6 later. The offence certainly still applies to distress for fines on shipping, but as s.54(4) of the new Act renames all distress warrants as warrants of control, it seems that this provision should be read in this light and that therefore it remains an offence punishable by fine to interfere with goods seized in respect of any fine. A person guilty of interference can on conviction be fined up to level one on the standard scale.[26]

6.6 Debtors' offences

The new Act completely replaces the old common law offences of rescue and poundbreach and certain statutory rights to seek damages for these and substitutes a new wholly statutory regime of offences.

6.6.1 New offences

Two new offences may potentially be committed by debtors. Under Sch.12 para.68 a person is guilty of an offence if he intentionally obstructs a person lawfully acting as an enforcement agent. A person is also guilty of an offence if he intentionally interferes with controlled goods without lawful excuse. This replaces the previous common law and statutory offences of poundbreach. Both of these offences are considered in more detail in the following paragraphs.

A person guilty of either of these new offences is liable on summary conviction to either imprisonment for a term not exceeding 51 weeks or a fine not exceeding level 4 on the standard scale, or both. In relation to an offence committed before the commencement of section 281(5) of the Criminal Justice Act 2003, the reference in to 51 weeks is to be read as a reference to 6 months.

The former case law indicates that, in cases of alleged illegal resistance or interference, it is up to the prosecution to show that all the elements of the offence have been committed.[27]

6.6.2 Obstructing an enforcement agent

The new offence of obstructing an enforcement agent appears to be modelled upon the existing offence of resisting or obstructing a High Court enforcement officer. This continues in force, although the lack of reported case law on the provision indicates that it is seldom - if ever - prosecuted.[28]

Despite the apparent redundancy of the High Court offence, the idea has been extended by the 2007 Act to all bailiffs taking control of goods. Despite the lack of case authority for the comparable offence against HCEOs, we are still able to draw upon the judicial interpretation which has grown up around the offence of obstructing a police officer.[29] It is an offence, punishable (interestingly) by only a month in prison or a fine up to level 3, to wilfully obstruct a constable in the execution of his duty. There is a separate offence of assaulting a police officer, which indicates that obstruction involves something less than the contact or physical force necessary for an assault. A physical element may well be present, such as bodily getting in the way of the bailiff, but a range of other behaviours are also likely to be treated as obstructive. Broadly we are concerned with conduct which prevents or makes it difficult for an enforcement agent to perform his duties. This could include such actions as warning a debtor of the bailiff's arrival, abusiveness, hostility and unhelpfulness, encouraging a debtor to be awkward and obstructive, providing false or misleading information and lying, delaying a bailiff and, possibly, refusing entry when the bailiff has a right to use force. Both action and inaction can amount to obstruction.[30]

The new offence in the Act refers to a person acting "intentionally." The same adverb applies to the offence against HCEOs whilst an individual must act "wilfully" against a police officer. All these terms have the same meaning: the individual must act with the deliberate intention of making life difficult for the bailiff. Showing hostility is not necessary nor is the motive for the action relevant - it does not matter whether the person acted to help a friend or out of a principled objection to bailiffs or to a particular liability. What is key is the result- and if that is to inhibit the bailiff in his duties, the offence is committed. Conversely if a person sets out to assist, although his/her help actually prejudices the bailiff's success, the intention to obstruct was absent and no offence was committed.[31]

A couple of defences are available to a person charged with obstruction. The first is that the person was genuinely unaware of the bailiff's identity. Secondly, a person may plead that s/he reasonably believed that there was a lawful justification for their actions - for example, obstructing a bailiff in the belief that an illegal levy was being prevented.[32]

6.6.3 Protecting goods from unlawful taking

It was a principle of the common law that an individual might exercise self help to prevent a trespass against his or her goods. In the past therefore the debtor could resist any seizure that was unlawful by taking back the goods that were being seized. However, if used at the wrong time or in the wrong circumstances, such an action risked being an offence. Given the wording of the new provisions this still seems to be the case. Resistance to a taking in breach of the 2007 Act could provide the 'lawful excuse' permitted to the debtor by the clause.

The previous case authority was that it was legal for a person to simply seize back their own illegally seized goods, where:

· the taking was illegal in respect of place, goods being seized or because there was no debt due;[33]

- where seized chattels were being abused or neglected by the bailiff who had taken them out of the place where they were originally impounded for an illegal use;[34]
- where a valid tender had been refused;[35] or,
- the levy was on an order of which there was no record at court;[36] or,

The levy being resisted must have been illegal in its execution, and rescue could not be used to challenge some other aspect of the process- for example, an objection to being held liable to rates is a matter of appeal, and does not justify rescue. Both forcible recapture and forcible resistance to wrongful seizure have been held to be lawful, though the reasonable level of force permissible may be difficult to determine.[37] The more recent case of *Devoe v Long & Long* [1951] confirmed that the right of recaption may be exercised to recover goods wrongfully taken by using whatever force is reasonably necessary and even entering onto another's property to do so if necessary, provided that the entry can be made can be peaceably and without any breach of the peace. Recovery must be by the owner of the goods, or by his agent, but not by a stranger. Thus, if the goods of two persons are wrongfully taken, each must rescue his own.[38]

6.6.4 Concealing or removing goods

It is not illegal for the debtor to hide items of value on the property prior to the levy. Most bailiffs tend to make only a fairly cursory search, despite a common law duty to use "reasonable diligence" in a search, so this strategy may succeed. Removing items from the property prior to a levy is also legal, though armed with a court warrant the bailiff can search elsewhere in England and Wales and may even force entry to premises (*see chapter 8*).

The debtor is not obliged to say where any goods are - so in fact it is extremely unlikely that a bailiff will be able to discover their new location. The only factor operating in the bailiff's favour is that after a while the debtor is likely to tire of not having the use of goods, so that they will be retrieved. At this point if the levy has not been terminated it is possible for the bailiff to return and try again; agents now have the right to make repeat visits to premises under the 2007 Act.[39]

6.6.5 Interferences with controlled goods

Naturally in instances where an offence is alleged, arguments can arise as to whether an interference with controlled goods has indeed occurred. These will in turn involve questions as to whether controlled goods had been released from control or were properly taken into control in the first place.[40] From the previous case law it is possible to suggest that release from control will not have occurred:

- where the bailiff withdrew at the request of the debtor so that he could arrange payment, which was then not forthcoming. It was found not to be voluntary abandonment to give up possession under fraudulent misrepresentations;[41]
- if a bailiff interrupted a levy to seek advice on the debtor's claim not to be liable for a debt, there was no abandonment;[42]
- where a bailiff permitted the debtor to continue to use seized goods. In one case the bailiff allowed the debtor to drive two cars that had been distrained for rent. This was done of the understanding that the cars would be returned daily to the premises upon which they had been impounded and therefore there was no abandonment;[43]
- where the bailiff withdrew under an agreement with the debtor allowing time for him to sell a business operating from the demised premises at which rent was due in order to raise funds to clear the debt;[44]
- where there is a demonstrable intention to retain control. Under the former case law it was held that there would be no abandonment where possession was adequately retained or the bailiffs intended to retain it. See for example *Jones v Biernstein* [1900] in which a rent bailiff took an inventory and then remained in close possession until he left the house over the weekend. The tenant re-took the goods in his absence but was held guilty of poundbreach as abandonment had not occurred. Although the bailiff had abandoned actual possession of the goods for no necessary reason, as he intended to return (as shown by the inventory), the court held that the distress was not abandoned completely and that the bailiff had remained in 'constructive possession'.[45] These contentions might well still arise in the context of goods secured on the premises or subject to a controlled goods agreement (*see chapter 9*).

Some of the principles applied here are similar to those applicable in determining whether a second levy is possible (*see 11.5 later*). The older case law indicates that there was abandonment and therefore no interference with seized goods by the debtor:

- where someone else disturbed possession first. In *Lavell & Co v O'Leary* [1933] a tenant, Mr Wong Gee, signed a walking possession agreement with bailiffs who distrained for rent arrears on goods in his business premises, the 'Canton Cafe'. Wong then got a removals firm to take the goods away. The firm was found not guilty of poundbreach because they took the goods from the landing outside the property. Wong Gee was guilty as he had moved the goods there after they had been impounded within his premises;[46] or,

· where the removal was by an innocent third party unaware of any prior seizure. In *Abingdon RDC v O'Gorman* [1968] a landlord distrained for rent upon a hired television set. The tenant signed a walking possession agreement but later asked Mr O'Gorman from the television hire firm to remove the rented set. The firm were not informed of the levy when doing this. The bailiff began an action for treble damages. The Court of Appeal held that the hire firm was not guilty of poundbreach because the walking possession agreement did not validly impound the goods against strangers. A person could not be guilty of poundbreach unless s/he has a guilty mind, i.e. knows of the impounding. O'Gorman was not guilty as he was not covered by the agreement. If he had been, he should have been notified of the seizure so that he could serve notice on the landlord of a claim to the goods;[47] or,

· the creditor fails without good reason to take adequate steps to protect and maintain their levy. In *LCP Retail Ltd v Segal* [2006] Chancery Division felt that a landlord's failure to protest when impounded goods were sold by the debtor company, and later to notify the liquidator in the company's winding up of the existence of a walking possession agreement, amounted to an abandonment of their claim over the goods.[48]

6.6.5 Theft of controlled goods by debtors

Because of the problems with prosecuting poundbreach under the former law, there was a noticeable increase in the number of instances of debtors being threatened with prosecution for theft by agents. Theft is defined as the dishonest appropriation of property belonging to another- but goods 'belong' to anyone having possession or control of them. In *R v Turner (No.2)* [1971] Turner left his car at a garage for repair. After the work was done, he took the car from the street so as to avoid paying the mechanic. Turner's appeal against his conviction was dismissed as the garage owner had sufficient custody of the car at the time for the taking from him to be theft. A bailee has possession and a bailiff who has impounded goods acquires a special property in them and so will probably be able to claim that the goods have been stolen if they are taken out of legal custody.[49]

Of course, the bailiff only has possession if the levy is lawful. If a vehicle is wrongfully in a bailiff's possession, it does not seem that it can be stolen from him.[50] Finally, theft is a dishonest appropriation of property. It is a defence to claim that a person believed there was a legal right to appropriate the property. Such a belief may also provide a defence for the manner in which goods are recovered - for example, if force is used.[51]

To summarise, a bailiff who has conducted a lawful levy upon goods and chattels may well be able to raise an allegation of theft if the goods taken into control are subsequently rescued, but several strong defences may be available to the debtor. If the levy was illegal, there will be no foundation for any allegation of theft.

6.7 Assaults on bailiffs

As well as being offences under the new Act, the use of violence and threats of violence to eject a bailiff from premises which have been legally entered may lead to forced re-entry and penalties in the general law - possibly prosecution for assault or an action for trespass to person brought by the bailiff.[52] Note also that an action for false imprisonment or for trespass would lie for unlawfully imprisoning a person in order to compel restitution of property and in such a situation the bailiff could also use force to escape.[53]

As well as the offences created by Sch.12 para.68, resistance by a debtor to a levy may give rise to the commission of one of several offences by the debtor:

Obstruction
It is an offence at common law to obstruct the execution of powers granted by statute.[54] The person can be fined or imprisoned up to two years at the court's discretion. A good example of a case of assault is *Southam v. Smout* [1963] in which a county court bailiff entered legally by a closed but unlocked door in order to arrest the debtor. The son-in-law of the debtor objected to this entry of his house without his permission and assaulted the bailiff when he refused to leave. This was held to be an offence.[55]

Criminal contempt
A debtor may be guilty of criminal contempt if s/he obstructs a High Court enforcement officer or county court bailiff in the execution of their duty - for instance, by assaulting the officer or by ejecting or excluding officers from a property.[56] The court may commit or fine the offender. This will be so even if there are minor errors in the writ. In *R v Monkman* [1892] it was held unlawful to resist a High Court enforcement officer executing three writs of fi fa which were incorrect as to the date of judgment on each. The High Court enforcement officer is under a duty to enforce a writ that is on the face of it regular, and such errors were mere irregularities that could be amended.[57]

Resisting civil court officers
Under section 8(2) of the Sheriff's Act 1887 if a High Court enforcement officer is resisted, he may arrest and imprison the guilty parties. The

county court may, under s.14 CCA, may commit and/or fine any person who assaults an officer whilst in execution of his duty. The bailiff may arrest the offender without a warrant and take him/her before the judge. A recent example of the use of the provision is the two consecutive custodial sentences of three months given to a defendant who attempted to run down two county court bailiffs with his car.[58] If a person is committed, they can appeal and apply for release pending their appeal, no notice of which need be served on the bailiff.[59] The alternative remedy for an officer who is the victim of an assault would be to lay an information before a magistrates' court under the Offences Against the Person Act 1861. Although it has been held that the justices have no jurisdiction over assaults arising during execution the correct procedure for the court would be to treat the matter as one that is only triable on indictment and accordingly take depositions and commit it for trial at the Crown Court if there is a *prima facie* case to be made out.[60]

It would be a defence for the debtor to say that s/he honestly, but mistakenly, believed the victim was not a court officer or not acting in execution of his duty.[61] The prosecution must show not that the defendant knew that the complainant was an officer acting in execution of his duty but that there was an assault i.e. an intentional or reckless show or application of unlawful force. As the use of reasonable force is lawful in self defence, if such force is applied to an officer as would be reasonable had he not been an officer, in the belief that he was not an officer, then the defendant has a good plea of self defence, even if his belief was unreasonable. Thus if the defendant believed he was being attacked by persons who were not court officers, and only reasonable force necessary to repel the attack was used, the use of force was not assault and the prosecution must prove he did not act reasonably or honestly in self defence. The appears to replace the previous authorities, such as *R. v. Forbes & Webb* (1865) in which it was held that it was sufficient to support a charge of assault upon an officer if he was in execution of his duty. It was not necessary to show that the defendant was aware that the person was an officer.[62]

Equally if the court order is void or ultra vires resistance by the owner of the goods to their seizure under that order is not unlawful obstruction. It is not illegal obstruction if the High Court enforcement officer is resisted when seeking to enter third party premises when neither the person nor the goods of the debtor are present.[63]

The legal position of dogs on the premises should also be noted. The law is that it is an offence to set on or urge a dog to attack, worry or put any person in fear and that the keeper will be liable for any damage or injury caused. Even if the dog is kept to guard a property, the owner may be liable if the animal prevents access by or injures innocent visitors on lawful business. The person may sue if their entry is under a legal right.

Section Three - Preventing seizures by transfers to third parties

Transferring goods to relatives, children or friends puts them beyond the reach of bailiffs in many cases and in genuine cases, if a third party then removed his/her goods before the bailiff's visit, they could not be pursued.[64] That said, the context within which these strategies will operate in the future has been significantly altered by the introduction of the enforcement notice and its 'binding' effect (see 7.2 later). A principal of law formerly applicable only to execution in the civil courts has now been extended to all debts and it may require individuals to be considerably more cautious when undertaking the kinds of transaction described in this section - although they are not necessarily invalidated entirely by binding as will be considered in the next chapter.

The fact that the debtor has disposed of goods to a third party just prior to a levy in order to defeat the seizure does not necessarily void the disposition merely because of the circumstances in which it occurred. If the bargain was for good consideration with a genuine intention to pass property it will be valid. It is not necessary for both parties to act in good faith, so long as there is good faith on the part of the purchaser.[65] The same principles might be applied to bills of sale and purchase and lease back. The deal will not be invalidated by the purchaser's knowledge of the intended execution provided that proof of payment and change of possession can be shown. Of course, transfers by loan or gift after a seizure has occurred are too late to protect the goods or to give the recipient any right in them regardless of the circumstances in which they might have been transferred- for instance in discharge of a debt to that person.[66]

If items genuinely transferred to third parties are taken, the person generally has a remedy - an injunction and a claim for wrongful interference. A third party may prove ownership by making a statutory declaration (see 13.3). If a third party's goods are in the hands of the debtor through fraud or theft they may be recovered by the true owner.[67] If the debtor voluntarily submits to a consent judgment for and even agrees to execution being issued for the sums due, this will be accepted to be a bona fide judgment for good consideration which will be sufficient to defeat other levies.[68]

Various means of transfer have been tried. The most common are outlined below.

6.8 Gifts

A gift, properly undertaken, will put property beyond the reach of bailiffs. Gifts may be affected by several means- by deed, by declaration of trust or by delivery. It is likely that the last is the method most commonly tried by individuals, though trusts are discussed later.

To make (and prove) an effective gift, the debtor would have to demonstrate the following:

· that the transfer of property was made with no intention of its return; and,
· that there was clear and distinct act of gift.

All property, real and personal, corporeal and incorporeal, may be given. We are interested in personal property and the main means of giving personal chattels is by transfer and retention of possession. Without actual delivery a gift of chattels will not be effective, thus if the donor wishes to retain possession, a gift will have to be by bill of sale instead, for which see later. Actual manual delivery is not essential, though an oral gift without some act of delivery will be ineffective.[69] Examples of successful and failed gifts follow. They include where:

· The donee is put in constructive possession by the donor- for example by handing over the key to a warehouse where goods are stored, by touching and words or by delivery of part as representative of the whole.[70]
· The nature of the donee's possession is changed - for example in *Winter v Winter* [1861] a barge was given to the donor's employee who had previously been in possession of it as employee, but who subsequently used it as his own. In *Cain v Moon* [1896] it was held that prior delivery, such as for safe keeping, can be converted into delivery as a gift by changing the capacity in which the item is held.[71]
· The donee is put in possession by donor - in *Kilpin v Ratley* [1892] a father verbally gave furniture to his daughter. They were in a room in her home where some of the furniture was stored. There was no manual delivery and after the gift the furniture remained where it was. The court held that he had done all he could to complete the gift and there was no need to go through "the mere formality of handling furniture in order to complete the gift".[72]
· However, intention alone is not enough - in *Jones v Lock* [1865] a father put a cheque into his baby son's hand and declared it to be the son's. The father died soon after and the cheque was found

still to be in his possession. His declaration in favour of his son was never followed through by investment or the like and thus was not an effective gift.[73]

Gifts between family members can be problematic. There is no reason why a gift cannot be made to a child provided that it is effected properly.[74] Between husband and wife the situation is more complex. They may make each other gifts of chattels and so on, but the need for a clear and distinct gift and evidence of intention is even more important. Such a gift must be unequivocal; if the facts are consistent with both a gift and an intention to share use with a spouse, no gift has occurred. See, for example, *Re: Cole ex p Trustee of Bankrupt's Property* [1964] in which the husband told the wife that goods in a house were all hers, but they continued to live together and share the chattels. No delivery or change of possession could be shown, and as a result title remained vested in his trustee in bankruptcy. In *Bashall v Bashall* [1894] a husband allegedly gave a pony and trap to his wife. Again both continued to use it and the wife's claim was held unproved. Delivery is needed to effect a gift to a spouse who does not have existing possession. An act showing an intention to change ownership may be sufficient, even if chattels are still shared, but mere letters written and signed by one spouse, giving furniture to the other are not enough.[75]

6.9 Trusts

It is not unheard of for debtors, particularly small firms, to try to protect property by putting it in trust. A valid trust of personal property may be created in writing or by oral declaration of the trust.[76] If the trust is created in writing no particular form must be followed so long as all the material terms of the trust are contained - the parties, the property concerned and the objects of the trust. The written instrument will have the advantage of being proof that can be shown to any bailiff calling to seize.

The problem with this stratagem is that written assignments of chattels will tend to fall under the Bills of Sale Acts (*see 10.19*) unless they are covered by one of the statutory exemptions: for example, that they are for the benefit of creditors of the grantor, that they are marriage settlements or that they have been made in the ordinary course of business. As none of these exemptions are likely to apply, the trust may have to comply with the technicalities of the Acts. One way for a debtor to try to escape this problem- and still to have some written proof of the trust- is where the bargain is completed without writing, such as by delivery, and the document simply refers to or confirms this transaction. Such evidence of the declaration of trust can be prepared at a date later to the creation of the trust itself. Although at common law only an absolute interest in chattels could be created by a trust it is now possible to create limited interests in all chattels except those exhausted by personal use. This does not include a business' stock or farming stock.[77]

A trust is effective as most bailiffs cannot seize equitable interests in property (see 10.5). As against strangers, the trustee and beneficiary are viewed as one person in equity, so possession of the trust property by the beneficiary is regarded as possession by the trustee.[78] Thus the trustee may sue in conversion even if the trust property is retained and enjoyed by the beneficiary.[79] Note however that it was held that where the whole beneficial interest is vested in the debtor(s), the trust would not be allowed to defeat the creditor. Now, the 2007 Act only protects trust property from being taken into control if the debtor's (or co-owner's) interest is not vested in possession.[80]

Finally we must note that trusts which are created for an illegal purpose or against the public interest are void. We may speculate whether a trustee in the circumstances described, who is forced to sue or interplead to protect the alleged trust property, may meet with some scepticism on the part of the courts as to the validity of the trust they seek to defend.

6.10 Bills of Sale

Assignment of goods under bill of sale is a means of transferring the property in goods whilst retaining the possession of them. It can afford effective protection for them against bailiffs, whether the purpose is the benefit of another creditor by the provision of security for the credit extended or the debtor's own protection, where the bill of sale is made with a friend or relative. For instance, if attention is paid to the legal technicalities (for which see 10.17), it has been successfully used between husband and wife, in respect of household goods that both continue to use, and between father and child. It can also be used to deal with trade stock, even though this may change over time.[81] This strategy can face considerable problems. All the detailed rules covering bills of sale must be followed by the family members - for example there must be consideration and a clear change of possession of the property - which can be difficult to achieve with a cohabiting couple, between family members residing together or in the same vicinity or within a family run business.[82]

In all such cases the validity of a bill may be open to challenge by a bailiff through the courts. In Miller v Solomon [1906] it was observed that bills of sale could be used to try to defeat seizure but that:

"It could not be right that a bill of sale holder, whose security is for a small sum on goods of large value, should be allowed to put an execution creditor in this dilemma and permit goods to escape execution ..." Thus the court might not allow "the furtherance of a dishonest purpose".

See also the judgment in *Reed v Thoyts* [1840]: if a person purports to dispose of goods under a fraudulent bill of sale, although it may be valid as against the other party to the agreement, from the point of view of other creditors seeking to take control, the bill is void and the property in it remains in the debtor.[83]

6.11 Furniture Leases

Another quite common approach, especially amongst small firms, is for the debtor to transfer his/her assets to a friend or relative and then to lease the items back again. In most cases this may be effective protection against seizure. For example see *Withers v Berry* [1895] - a husband gave property to his wife by a deed of gift. After they separated the furniture was leased back to him - but it was held not to be in his possession and thus not seizeable in execution. As with bills of sale, a distinct and public change of possession is likely to be essential for the lease's success. All the same, the courts may regard these arrangements as simply stratagems to avoid legal enforcement and refuse to uphold them in any action brought by the debtor for wrongful interference following seizure.[84]

Footnotes
1 CPR Part 14.
2 under CPR Parts 12 & 24 respectively.
3 TCEA s.70(1).
4 CPR 83.7(1)-(6).
5 *Winchester Cigarette Machinery Ltd v Payne (No. 2)* (1993) *The Times,* 15/12/93.
6 *London Permanent Building Society v De Baer* [1969] 1 Ch 321 - under Rules of the Supreme Court 1965 O.45 r.11.
7 CPR Part 52.7.
8 On ruin see - *Linotype-Hell Finance Ltd v Baker* [1993] 1 WLR 321; on recovery see - *The Annot Lyle* [1886] 11 P 114.
9 *Lovegrove v. White* [1871] 6 CP 440
10 *Times* 30/6, 7 CL 191
11 CCA s.77.
12 CPR 83.28.
13 CPR 83.22(4) & (5).
14 Courts Act 2003 Sch.5 para.12.
15 Sch.5 para.14.
16 Sch.5 Part 6.
17 s77(1) MCA.
18 *Re: Wilson* [1985] AC 750
19 *R v Paget* [1881] 8 QBD 151; *Re S* (an infant) [1958] 1 All ER 783 and *B(BPM) v*

B(MM) [1969] 2 WLR 862.

20 *Minor- Smith v Smith* [1971] 115 Sol Jo 444; appeal - *Kendall v Wilkinson* (1855) 24 LJMC 89; liability confirmed - *Barons v Luscombe* (1835) 3 Ad & El 589.

21 1 FLR 175.

22 New paragraphs 40A & B are inserted into Courts Act 2003 Sch.5 by s.88 of the 2012 Act.

23 Under para.42 Sch.5, Courts Act 2003.

24 Sch.12 para.57(2)(d).

25 Sch.12 para.67.

26 MCA s.78(4).

27 *R v Harron* [1903] 6 OLR 666.

28 Criminal Law Act 1977 s.10 as amended by Courts Act 2003 Sch.8 para.189; on conviction the penalty is 6 months imprisonment or a fine up to level 5.

29 Police Act 1996 s.89(2).

30 *Hinchcliffe v Sheldon* [1955] 3 All ER 406; *Ricketts v Cox* [1981] QB 509; *Green v Moore* [1982] QB 1044; *Green v DPP* (1991) 155 JP 816; *Ledger v DPP* [1997] Crim LR 439. 'Resisting' has much the same meaning as obstructing and will comprise striving against, opposing or impeding an agent.

31 *Wilmott v Atack* [1977] QB 495; *Hills v Ellis* [1983] QB 680; *Lunt v DPP* [1993] Crim LR 534.

32 *Ostler v Elliott* [1980] Crim LR 584; *Liepins v Spearman* [1986] RTR 24.

33 *Cotsworth v Betison* (1696) 1 Ld Raym 104; *R v Pigott* [1851] 1 ICLR 471; *R v Walshe* [1876] IR 10 CL 511.

34 *Gomersall v Medgate* (1610) 80 ER 128.

35 *Bevils Case* 4 Co Rep 11b.

36 *R. v. Carroll* (1828) 2 Ir L Rec 53.

37 Appeal - *R v Higgins* [1851] 21 ICLR 213; force - *Blades v Higgs* (1861) 10 CBNS 713.

38 Force -1 DLR 203 & *Rich v Woolley* (1831) 7 Bing 651; joint goods - *Jennyngs v Playstowe* Cro Jac 568.

39 Reg.24 TCG Regs; see ???

40 *Dod v Monger* (1704) 6 Mod 215.

41 *Harpelle v. Carroll* (1896) 27 OR 240.

42 *Saivers v. Toronto (City)* (1901) 2 OLR 717.

43 *Bevir v. British Wagon Co Ltd* (1935) 80 L Jo 162.

44 *Dios Holdings Ltd v. Laing Property Corporation* (1992) 12 CBR 190.

45 1 QB 100.

46 2 KB 200.

47 3 All ER 79 CA - see *Sources of bailiff law* c.7 p.200.

48 [2006] EWHC 2087

49 [1971] 2 All ER 441 CA.

50 *R v Meredith* [1973] Crim LR 253.

51 *R v Robinson* [1977] Crim LR 173.

52 See *Gregory v. Hill* (1799) 8 TR 299.

53 *Harvey v. Mayne* [1872] Ir 6 CL 417.

54 *R. v. Smith* (1780) Doug KB 441.

55 3 All ER 104.

56 Assault - *Lewis v Owen* [1894] 1 QB 102; ejection - *R. v. Campbell* (1893) 14 NSWLR 532.

57 8 Man LR 509.

58 *Read v King* [1997] 1 CL 5.

59 *Brown v Crowley* [1963] 3 All ER 655.

60 Jurisdiction - *R v Briggs* (1883) 47 JP 615; trial - *R v Holsworthy Justices ex p*

Edwards [1952] 1 All ER 411.

61 *Blackburn v Bowering* [1994] 3 All ER 380 CA.

62 10 Cox CC 362.

63 Void order - *R v Finlay* [1901] 13 Man LR 383; 3rd party premises - *R v Gazikom Aba Dore* [1870] 7 Bom Cr Ca 83.

64 *Pool v Crawcour* (1884) 1 TLR 165.

65 Consideration - *Wood v Dixie* (1845) 7 QB 892; good faith - *Mackintosh v Pogose* [1895] 1 Ch 505.

66 Bill of sale - *Tower Finance & Furnishing Co v Brown* (1890) 6 TLR 192; knowledge of execution - *Hale v Saloon Omnibus Co* (1859) 4 Drew 492; after levy - *Lossing v. Jennings* (1852) 9 UCQB 406.

67 *Earl of Bristol v Wilsmore* (1823) 2 Dow & Ry 755.

68 *Meux v. Howell* (1803) 4 East 1.

69 *Smith v Smith* (1733) 2 Stra 953.

70 Key - *Rowles v Rowles* (1750) 1 Ves Sen 348; touching - *Rawlinson v Mort* (1905) 93 LT 555; part - *Lock v Heath* (1892) 8 TLR 295 - the gift of a chair.

71 4 LT 639; 2 QB 283.

72 1 QB 582.

73 1 Ch App 25.

74 *Shephard v Cartwright* [1955] AC 431.

75 Respectively 1 Ch 175; 11 TLR 152; *Hislop v Hislop* (1950) WN 124; *In Re: Bretton's Estate* [1881] 17 Ch D 416.

76 Written - *Gee v Liddell (No 1)*(1866) 35 Beav 621; oral - *M'Fadden v Jenkyns* (1842) 1 Ph 153.

77 *Myers v Washbrook* [1901] 1 KB 360; *Breton v Mockett* [1878] 9 Ch D 95.

78 See *White v Morris* (1852) 11 CB 1015.

79 *Barker v Furlong* [1891] 2 Ch 172.

80 *Stevens v Hince* (1914) WN 148; Sch.12 para.3(2).

81 Husband & wife - *French v Getling* [1922] 1 KB 236; *Re: Satterthwaite* (1895) 2 Mans 52; parent & child - *Butler v. Lewis* (1932) 7 VLR 62; *Official Assignee of Slattery v. Slattery* (1897) 16 NZLR 332; trade stock - *John Woods & Co v. Thompson* [1930] 48 WN(NSW) 111.

82 Couples - *Brown v. Pearce* [1897] 11 Man LR 409; *Re: Dale* (1924) 5 CBR 65; family members - *Straker v. North of Scotland Canadian Mortgage Co* [1932] 1 WWR 354; *Fitzgerald v. McMorrow* [1923] 4 DLR 619; family businesses - *Ranney v. Moody* (1857) 10 UCQB 471; *McMillan v. Jones* [1923] 3 DLR 821

83 2 KB 91; 6 M&W 410.

84 Husband & wife - 39 Sol Jo 559; change of possession - *Chamberlain v. Green* (1870) 20 UCCP 304; refusal by court - *Scarfe v Halifax* (1840) 7 M&W 288.

Chapter 7

Issuing seizure

7.1 Warrants

7.1.1 Form

The beginning of the process of recovery of debt by taking control is the instruction of the bailiff. This is typically done by the issue of a 'warrant', a written authority from the creditor or court to the enforcement agent. From the warrant the bailiff derives his powers and rights. Without a warrant the taking would be illegal. In *Symonds v Kurtz* (1889) a person other than that named on the warrant carried out the seizure. This was held to be trespass. If the bailiff holds more than one warrant against the same person, there is nothing irregular in seizing under more than one at once.[1]

The form of the warrant will vary from one type of taking to another but typically specifies the debt due and commands the bailiff to seize and sell goods and immediately pay over the proceeds to the creditor. It has been held that a trivial error that does not detract from the general sense of a warrant does not invalidate it,[2] but it will be invalid if some important detail, such as the address, is wrong. Damages cannot be claimed for a wrongly calculated sum.[3]

For CRAR, the content of the warrant is laid down.[4] Where a landlord gives authorisation to a person under section 73(8) of the Act to exercise CRAR on the landlord's behalf, that authorisation must only authorise an enforcement agent (that is, a person who is authorised to act under the 2007 Act)) must be in writing, signed by the landlord and must set out the following:

- the date of authorisation;
- the landlord's name and contact details;
- the name and contact details of the agent authorised to act on behalf of the landlord;
- sufficient detail to enable the authorised person to identify the commercial premises in respect of which CRAR is to be exercised on the landlord's behalf;
- the amount of rent owed; and,
- the period in relation to which the rent is owed.

In the civil courts, the forms of writs and warrants are also prescribed by Practice Directions and standard forms exist.[5]

It is worth noting that in the past many magistrates' courts neglected to correctly issue warrants because they only enter the name of a firm of bailiffs rather than named employees. However, section 78(1) MCA provides that a warrant is not void because of any defect so long as it states that the sum has been adjudged to be paid. It would therefore not be possible for the bailiff to be sued for trespass however the defendant can claim any special damages caused by the defect in the warrant.[6] The guidance in *Stones Justices Manual* is that a minor error that does no injustice should be disregarded. This provision is the sole surviving example of what was previously termed 'irregular distraint.'

7.1.2 Address on warrant

As stated in the previous section, the warrant is likely to be invalid if the address given upon it is incorrect; the defect in the warrant will also tend to indicate that much of the proceeding correspondence (assessment and demand letters, court orders etc) will also have been misdirected and may well not have been received by the liable person. As a matter of good practice, therefore, if it comes to the attention of the bailiff during the levy that the address of the debtor is different to that provided by the creditor, the bailiff should place the enforcement on hold and notify the creditor so that the initial documents and notices may be reissued, thereby ensuring that the debtor has been given due warning of the liability and a chance to pay.

Certainly, in the case of road traffic penalties, the local authority must be notified so that application may be made to the Traffic Enforcement Centre for the issue of a revised warrant showing the corrected address.[7] For a council and its bailiffs to fail to do this is likely to be treated as maladministration.[8]

7.1.3 Production of warrant

The new Act stipulates that an enforcement agent must - on request - show the debtor, and any person who appears to him to be in charge of the premises, evidence of his identity and of his authority to enter the premises. Such a request may be made before the enforcement agent enters the premises or while he is there.[9] There is however no general right for the debtor to see a warrant, unlike a police search warrant, and no duty for the bailiff to show it before s/he is entitled to enter. Nonetheless, in *Symonds v Kurtz* (1889) the court held that it is a general principle of law that every person whose home is entered is entitled to know the authority under which this is done and be able to see whether that authority is followed.[10]

The common law courts have elaborated a clear set of principles relating to the production and possession of warrants, which will still be applicable in addition to the duty that exists under the new Act. Briefly, the purpose of a warrant is two-fold. It serves to identify the bailiff to the debtor; secondly, it confirms that the bailiff has the proper legal authority to enter the premises and to demand payment or remove goods for sale. Case law has expanded on both these functions.

The basic common law position on warrants of distress was established long ago. In *Buller's Case* (1587) the court decided that "when a bailiff distrains he ought, if he be required, to show the cause of his distraint, but if he be not required, he is not tied to do it."[11] In other words, if the debtor asks to see the warrant, the bailiff should produce it; if no request is made, it doesn't have to be shown voluntarily. Nonetheless, it clearly should be available to be shown if need be. For most forms of distress and execution, this situation had not changed materially since the late sixteenth century.

Almost all the succeeding case authority has actually been concerned with constables executing warrants of arrest. This does not detract from the relevance of these cases: the execution of an arrest warrant for a fine is a civil matter, just like the execution of a warrant of control. This is why the law developed on constable's rights of entry are also directly applicable to bailiffs' law.

The fundamental principle applicable to a warrant is that it should be in the actual, ongoing possession of the person executing it. This has not altered since *Buller's Case* - it has simply been elaborated upon. A warrant that is in the hands of the bailiff company, held at the firm's office, rather than in the hands of the individual bailiff, is not in the bailiff's possession.[12] This is too remote a possession; nevertheless, possession does not have to be immediate, physical possession: a warrant left by the bailiff nearby in his van or car and readily accessible to show to the debtor will do.[13]

It does not matter in these cases that the person arrested never asked to see the warrant. The principle was the key thing - if such a request had been made, it could not have been complied with in the cases where the warrant was at the police station. The reasons underlying this principle are that the person is entitled to know why enforcement action is being taken against him/her and to see the authority for that. Secondly, as Roskill LJ explained in *R v Purdy* (1974) "it is essential he should be able to know for what he is being arrested and whether he is being arrested for a matter of non-payment of a fine, arrears of maintenance...; he can, if I may be forgiven the phrase, "buy" his freedom from arrest by instant payment of the sum stated on the warrant."[14] In cases of taking control, the debtor would be paying to release their goods from imminent seizure.

If goods are taken into control in a situation where the warrant is not in the possession of the bailiff, what is the consequence? The courts have been clear that the taking would be unlawful and the debtor would be entitled to resist, using reasonable force (but no more than that). A claim for damages, combined if necessary with an injunction, would be the most likely remedy, however. If excessive violence was employed, an offence could be committed to which the absence of the warrant would be no defence.[15] Of course, the fact that a levy had been invalidated by the absence of a warrant would not prevent a subsequent lawful levy being made.[16]

There is one exception to the common rule, which was made as a result of recommendations by the court in *De Costa Small v Kirkpatrick* (1979). Bailiffs executing magistrates' court warrants have been granted greater flexibility but also have additional duties. The person who executes a warrant must either show it to the defendant, if s/he has it, or arrange for the defendant to see it if a request is made to inspect it but the bailiff does not have it with him. This should be done as soon as is practicable.[17] Bailiffs executing warrants issued by magistrates' courts in respect of civil debts must also produce a copy of their warrant to a debtor.[18] In addition, agents enforcing fines have separate duties to produce their authorisation to a debtor- both voluntarily and on request.[19] Lastly, agents enforcing fines should give defendants a written statement of their authority under which any warrant is being executed.[20]

A few final observations may be made. The warrant should be in the correct prescribed form; otherwise any levy will be illegal.[21] Secondly, as the purpose of the warrant is partly to identify those executing it, it should name the bailiffs to whom it has been directed. Warrants endorsed with another bailiff's name will be illegal.[22] The only exception to this will be where the relevant statute treats such defects in warrants as mere irregularities.[23] Lastly, these considerations only arise if an actual levy occurs or is attempted. If the bailiff simply visits the property to deliver a letter, to verify the address or to inspect the premises, with no intention of levying, argument about possession of the warrant does not arise.[24]

This case law continues to be of relevance. As Roskill LJ warned in *R v Purdy* in 1974, "The courts must never appear to condone an unlawful arrest, however unhampered by merit the argument may seem to be in relation to the facts of any particular case."[25] The same will apply to taking control of goods; however unsympathetic the debtor's record, the correct procedures must be followed. That said, onerous demands are not made of the bailiff. Possession means "control coupled with some sort of physical proximity." As long as the warrant can be shown to the debtor within a reasonable time, that will do.

Enforcement agents acting in the magistrates' court should show the warrant to the defendant if it is their possession, otherwise they should state where it is and what arrangements may be made to inspect it. They are however entitled to enforce a warrant without having it in their physical possession.[26]

Finally, readers may also wish to note that the NSEA also insists enforcement agents should always produce identification on request, together with a warrant from the creditor.

7.1.4 Validity and limitations

The debtor may be able to challenge the validity of a warrant of the basis that enforcement of the debt is time barred, or that the warrant itself has expired.

As to the validity of the debt, the Limitation Act 1980 is, in fact, of limited assistance. The Act is applicable to all classes of action, which includes any proceeding in a court of law, which is defined as including any form of initiating process, such as the summons for a liability order for local taxes.[27] 'Action' does not refer to the issue of execution on a judgment, to which special rules apply, nor does it apply to the recovery of taxes and duties by the Crown.[28] We may accordingly summarise the limitations that apply as follows.

Civil court writs & warrants
In the civil courts it is necessary for the judgment creditor to obtain permission of court before issuing a writ or warrant of control in any case where six years or more have elapsed since the date of the judgment.[29] An application for permission may be made in accordance with CPR Part 23 on form N244; it may be made without notice being served on any other party unless the court directs otherwise. The application must identify the judgment or order to which the application relates, state the amount originally due on the judgment and, if different, the amount due at the date the application notice is filed, state the

reasons for the delay in enforcing the judgment or order and, lastly, give such other information as is necessary to satisfy the court that the applicant is entitled to proceed to execution on the judgment or order, and that the person against whom it is sought to issue execution is liable to execution on it.[30] Failure to apply for permission is an abuse of process and the execution may be set aside by the court on application by the debtor. The Limitation Act 1980 does not apply to applications for permission to issue execution as there is a distinction between the right to take an action and the procedural right or remedy to issue execution.[31] These same rules apply to local authority warrants of control issued for traffic management debts.[32]

Crown debts
Recovery action does not have to take place within the tax year.[33]

Magistrates' court orders
There is no limitation placed upon criminal proceedings by the Limitation Act.[34] There are limitations on the commencement of civil and criminal proceedings within the Magistrates Court Act 1980 section 127(1).

Local taxes
There should not be undue delay in pursuing a debt. In one Ombudsman case the council was criticised for a delay of five years in following up previous bailiff visits. The bailiffs' fees were reimbursed and £100 compensation was awarded;[35]

CRAR
There were limits on when distress for rent could be used. Distress had to be levied within six months of the end of the lease and this is reproduced in the new Act. The maximum time allowed for enforcement of rent arrears was six years after they had accrued. Up to six years' arrears were enforceable, even if more than that are due.[36]

As will be described at 7.5.1, the warrant, liability order or writ subsequently issued to enforce the debt lasts for twelve months after the enforcement notice and can be extended. A taking made upon a defective warrant will attract a remedy under Sch.12 para.66 - *see chapter 13* for details.

7.1.5 Endorsement

Certain officers are required to endorse a writ or warrant as soon as it is received:

- Magistrates' court - as soon as possible after receiving a warrant of control issued by a justice of the peace the person to whom it is directed must, on its reverse, endorse the date and time of receipt. No fee may be charged for this;[37]
- County court - any warrant of control (or warrant of delivery or possession which also includes a power to take control of goods) must be endorsed as soon as possible by the bailiff, on its reverse, with the date and time of receipt. No fee may be charged for this;[38]
- High Court - under the Courts Act 2003 writs of control should be endorsed on their reverse with the date and time of receipt as soon as possible after it is received. No fee may be charged for this. If the writ is directed to a single HCEO, s/he must endorse it; if it is directed to two or more collectively, the individual who allocates it to one officer will endorse it; if the writ is directed to a person who is not an HCEO but is under a duty to execute it, that person enters the endorsement.[39]

The reasons for requiring endorsement are spelled out in the next section.

7.2 Binding of property

The TCEA has applied to all forms of seizure of goods a power previously only applicable to executions, that is, the binding in debtors' hands of their rights over their property by the issue of the enforcement instrument or the enforcement notice. This applies to the property in all goods that belong to debtors, except for those goods that are exempt or are protected under any other enactment.[40]

7.2.1 Date of binding effect

Property is bound either from the date on which the writ or warrant is endorsed (see 7.1.5 above) or from the date of the enforcement notice (see 7.5.1 below). The detailed rules are as follows:

- where the power to take control is conferred by a writ issued from the High Court, the writ binds the property in the goods from the time when it is received by the person who is under a duty to endorse it (see 7.1.5);
- where the power is conferred by a warrant to which section 99 of the County Courts Act 1984 or section 125ZA of the Magistrates' Courts Act 1980 applies, the warrant binds the property in the goods from the time when it is received by the person who is under a duty to endorse it under that section. In the county court in respect of a

warrant of control, delivery or possession warrants binds property from the date on which the person to whom the warrant is directed endorses it (see 7.1.5); and,

· in all other cases, when notice of the issue of a warrant of control is given to the debtor, the notice binds the property in the goods from the time when the enforcement notice is given.[41]

7.2.2 Nature of binding effect

The effect of 'property in goods being bound' is that any form of assignment or transfer of any interest that a debtor has in his or her goods that is made while the property in them is bound for the purposes of an enforcement power will only take place subject to that power.[42] The transfer or assignment therefore does not affect the operation of the warrant or writ in relation to the goods, except as provided by paragraph 61 (see 7.2.4 below).

The binding power does not prejudice the title to any of the debtor's goods that a person acquires in good faith, for valuable consideration, and without notice that either a court warrant or writ of control had been issued or that an enforcement agent had served an enforcement notice. For the purposes of this provision, a thing is to be treated as done in good faith if it is in fact done honestly (whether it is done negligently or not).

7.2.3 Duration

Property in goods of the debtor ceases to be bound in four situations:

· when the goods are sold or, in the case of money used to pay any of the amount outstanding, when it is used;[43]
· when the amount outstanding is paid out of the proceeds of sale or otherwise;
· when the warrant, writ or order under which the power is exercisable ceases to have effect; or,
· when the power ceases to be exercisable for any other reason.

Because the binding effect persists until the recovery process terminates for one reason or another, it may be intended that it not only provides a short term protection for goods until they are taken into control but also grants long term protection comparable to the former legal custody that arose upon impounding (see 7.2.6, c.9 and 10.11 below).

7.2.4 Binding & owners' rights

Where an interest of the debtor's in goods is assigned or transferred while the property in the goods is bound for the purposes of an enforcement power, and the enforcement agent knows that the assignee or transferee has acquired an interest in the particular goods (or the agent would know of this if s/he made reasonable enquiries) the assignee or transferee must subsequently be treated as if s/he were a co-owner of those goods. This means that the person is entitled to receive an inventory under Sch.12 paragraph 34, a copy of the valuation under paragraph 36 and copies of sale notices under paragraphs 39 to 41. As a co-owner the assignee or transferee of the goods is also entitled to remedies after payment of amount outstanding in ine with paragraph 59(6).[44] *For these matters, see later, respectively, 10.5, 11.2 and 11.3.*

If the interest of the assignee or transferee was acquired in good faith, for valuable consideration and without notice, "co-owner" is understood to include that assignee or transferee and the enforcement agent must pay the person who acquired the goods a sum proportionate to their interest in the goods out of the proceeds before the debt and costs are discharged.[45] If the interest of the assignee or transferee was not acquired in good faith, for valuable consideration and without notice, the enforcement agent must pay any surplus left after settling the debt and costs to the assignee or transferee and to the debtor (if he retains an interest).[46] If the surplus is payable to two or more persons it must be paid in shares proportionate to their interests.

7.2.5 Former case authority

The binding power of writs is a longstanding feature of the common law rules on execution. Considerable case law was developed in this connection and the relevant authorities are cited here as guidance as to how the new, more general, power might be interpreted under the Act in the future.

Date and priority
The receipt of the writ is the important date, so a writ received by the High Court enforcement officer before a writ issued on an earlier judgment had priority.[47] If a warrant was issued in one county court but transferred to another for enforcement, the time of binding was when the warrant was issued by the second court.[48] If the creditor lost the right to seize goods because there was delay by the court between the application for the warrant and its issue by the court office, the binding was held to be effective from the time of issue, thus giving the execution creditor priority.[49] An earlier writ had priority over a writ issued later, so that if a High Court enforcement officer received

payment towards the later one, it had to be credited to the earlier writ.[50] Equally the debtor could not tell the High Court enforcement officer to which writ a payment had to be credited.[51]

Effect of binding

'Bound' meant that the High Court enforcement officer had acquired the legal right to seize the goods though, notwithstanding this binding effect, ownership continued with the judgment debtor until sale and did not vest in the High Court enforcement officer but the bailiff could follow the goods and seize them, regardless of whose hands they had come into.[52] As the property in the goods was not altered by the binding the debtor could legally deal with the goods until seizure.[53] However a charge upon the goods had been created for the creditors.[54] Note that this charge was not such as gave priority in bankruptcy if there had only been binding, but not actual seizure.[55] A High Court enforcement officer acquired a special property in the goods which enabled him to sell as officer of the court. Any transfer or assignment of the goods from the date of binding was subject to the High Court enforcement officer's right to follow and seize the goods.[56] The binding effect of the writ effected any transaction occurring on the same day - such as a deed of gift, which was rendered ineffective, even if it is *bona fide*, if it follows the binding.[57]

Binding is not seizure

The delivery of a writ was not a 'taking in execution' or seizure. Some positive action was required on the part of the enforcement agent to alter the debtor's rights in his/her goods.[58] From this it follows that certain subsequent events could override the binding effect.

Binding could be defeated

By another levy which took place sooner than the execution of the writ or warrant in question or by an intervening bankruptcy.[59] Binding was only concerned with the actions of the debtor, not third parties, and, as binding did not divest property out of the debtor, another seizure might still take place.

Binding could be abandoned

The effect of binding was to give a bailiff time to pursue the debtor's goods. If the bailiff did not act sufficiently quickly, or fails to follow through his rights, the binding power can be abandoned.[60]

Sale

The binding effect of the writ was only defeated if the goods had been purchased in good faith without notice of the fact that a writ had been issued and remained unexecuted by seizure.[61] Alternatively the High

Court enforcement officer could recover the value of the goods from the purported purchaser, rather than pursuing and seizing the items themselves.[62] Disposal of the goods other than by sale in market overt was void.[63] Binding only applied to goods and not to other property such as money, which were not affected until actual seizure.[64]

7.2.6 Priority of instructions

What is not entirely clear from the new Act is how priority of warrants and writs is determined. Rules are, however, laid down for civil court writs and warrants of control.

Irrespective of whether or not the writ or warrant has been extended for a further 12 months by court order (*see 7.5.1 below*) the priority of a writ is determined by the time it is originally received by the person under a duty to endorse it and the priority of a warrant is determined by reference to the date on which it was originally issued. Production of an extension order - or of the writ or warrant endorsed with a note of the extension[65] - is evidence that the writ or warrant has been extended. These same rules apply to local authority warrants of control for road traffic penalties.[66]

In respect of other warrants of control and liability orders, if the binding effect applies from the date of the enforcement notice, then we may probably assume that the creditor who issues first will have priority over subsequent creditors. Whether being the first to actually take control of goods then supersedes this is also not clear (see 10.11). Also uncertain is the order of priority between two warrants issued on the same day. Those enforcement agents required to endorse their warrants will record the time of doing so; others will not, although their computer systems will doubtless record this information should a dispute arise.

7.3 Death of parties

In the civil courts permission is necessary in order to issue writs or warrants of control where either the judgment creditor or debtor has died, or any assets of the deceased have come into the hands of his/her executors or administrators since the date of the judgment.[67] These same rules apply to local authority warrants of control for road traffic penalties.[68]

An application for permission will be made in accordance with CPR Part 23 on general application form N244 and must:

- give details of the death of one the parties entitled or liable to execution since the date of the judgment or order;
- where a deceased person's assets are now in the hands of an executor or administrator, state that a demand to satisfy the judgment or order was made on the person liable to satisfy it and that the person has refused or failed to do so; and,
- give such other information as is necessary to satisfy the court that the applicant is entitled to proceed to execution on the judgment or order, and that the person against whom it is sought to issue execution is liable to execution on it.[69]

An application for permission to enforce may be made without notice being served on any other party unless the court directs otherwise. If because of the death of either the judgment creditor or debtor, an applicant seeks permission to enforce more than one judgment or order, the applicant need only make one application for permission. However, a schedule must be attached to the application, specifying all the judgments or orders in respect of which the application for permission is made and, if the application notice is directed to be served on any person, setting out only such part of the application as affects that person.[70]

In distress for rent, it was held that if the tenant died, but his/her executor or administrator continued in possession of the property, the landlord might distrain on the deceased goods in the hands of the executor/ administrator.[71]

7.4 Sums leviable

Typically the sums for which the warrant may issue will be the debt plus any court costs incurred. Two cases require special mention.

7.4.1 CRAR

CRAR is not exercisable except to recover rent that meets certain conditions specified in s.77. Firstly, the rent must have become due and payable before notice of enforcement is given. These issues were examined in detail in the former law on distress for rent, so it is helpful to reproduce the case authorities. Two separate criteria had to be met within this overall condition:

- *rent had to be lawfully due.* This was determined by the true construction of the agreement; it might have been that the sum due could only be ascertained after the due date for payment.

Thus where the rent might have been subject to a review clause, any higher sum ascertained by this procedure would become payable retrospectively once it was determined.[72] If rent had been tendered (albeit late) then, unless time was made of the essence in the lease, it was no longer unpaid and was not lawfully due. In one such case the tendered rent was refused and was paid into court. The landlord was held liable for the costs of the proceedings. It was also held that permitting unpunctual payment of the rent in the past without protest did not justify the tenant assuming it would be permitted in the future, nor waive a right to levy for arrears.[73] Even if the landlord had accepted a reduced sum of rent for a period, on default the whole sum might be levied. If the rent was due, the landlord might then distrain on the day immediately after the rent has fallen due for all or part of the arrears. If the rent was due on a Sunday, the landlord could distrain on a Monday.[74]

· the rent had to be in arrears on a current tenancy.[75] There were no 'arrears' for which distress could be levied until the day after payment fell due, the tenant being able to pay the rent at any time during the day on which it fell due.[76] Thus a distress before midnight on the day upon which rent fell due was illegal. Longer might have been allowed if time to pay was given by the landlord.[77] This situation was not altered where the rent was payable in advance, if it was not paid on the day it was due. Payment of course terminated the right to enforce, though it was held that giving a cheque in payment did not suspend the landlord's remedy until it was cashed.[78]

Secondly, section 77 of the 2007 Act stipulates that the rent must be certain, or must be capable of being calculated with certainty. This section repeats the previous case authorities on this matter. It was held that rent payable had to be certain in the sense that its quantity, extent and time of payment should be known or be capable of being ascertained.[79] A rent that fluctuated was not uncertain and distress upon it was valid provided that it might be calculated, though based on factors that might vary. The essential factor was that the sum payable could be worked out.[80] If there was no agreed rent, distraint could not be levied and the landlord had to begin a court action instead. If the rent could not be ascertained, perhaps because an appeal was pending, the landlord could not levy - even for the possible difference between the agreed rent and the rent demanded.[81]

The amount of any rent recoverable by CRAR is reduced by any permitted deduction.[82] Permitted deductions may include sums allowed for damages for breach by the landlord of his obligations (such as a duty to repair or the covenant of quiet enjoyment) or in respect of compensation for improvements under Landlord & Tenant Act 1954 s.11(2). This clause repeats the rule previously established for distress for rent. It used to be held that there is no right of set off at all - even for repairs - but the Court of Appeal in *Eller v Grovecrest Investments Ltd* [1995] held that there was no difference between a claim for rent arrears by court action and a claim by distress. In both the respective rights of landlord and tenant should be considered. A cross claim for damages by the tenant could be used by way of set-off as a defence against a claim for rent by distress. An injunction was granted in the *Eller* case to restrain a levy where the damages claim exceeded the rent due. In *Fuller v Happy Shopper Markets Ltd* it was decided that a tenant with a genuine counterclaim in respect of rent may offset this against the sums claimed by way of a distress for rent. The tenant's business property had become partially unusable and after continuing payments for some time, he withheld rent. Distress was levied and the goods seized were sold. The court decided that the tenant was entitled to reduce the rent arrears by the overpayment before the proceeds of sale were applied. Set off can be excluded by the agreement, but it will have to be an explicit term and a covenant to pay "without deductions" is not sufficient.[83]

CRAR is exercisable only if the net unpaid rent is at least a minimum amount immediately before each of these times - when notice of enforcement is given and the first time that goods are taken control of after that notice. The minimum amount of net unpaid rent for which CRAR may issue is an amount equal to seven days' rent, which must be due on the date of the enforcement notice and on the date on which goods are taken into control.[84] This provision will give tenants the opportunity to reduce the arrears level below the 'trigger figure' and thereby to postpone or prevent enforcement. In addition, it was previously held that a landlord might recover part of the rent only in so far as rent for individual periods might be enforced for separately, and in any order. However one sum due on one date had to be levied in one levy.[85]

The net unpaid rent arrears comprise the amount of rent that is lawfully due after making allowance for any interest or value added tax included in that amount under section 76(1)(a) or (b), and any permitted deductions. Regulations may provide for these conditions not to apply in specified cases, but no such rules have yet to be made. Permitted deductions, against any rent, are any deduction, recoupment or set- off that the tenant would be entitled to claim (in law or equity) in an action by the landlord for that rent. In allowing these set-offs, tenants are favoured over landlords as it delays the date at which the minimum enforceable arrears will accrue.

Section 79 of the Act states when the lease ends, CRAR ceases to be exercisable - subject to certain exceptions. This repeats the established case law of distress for rent.[86] CRAR continues to be exercisable in relation to rent due before a lease ended in two situations - where either:

· the goods were taken into control before the lease ended; or,
· where the lease did not end by forfeiture;
· not more than six months has passed since the day when it ended;
· the rent was due from the person who was the tenant at the end of the lease;
· that person remains in possession of any part of the demised premises;
· any new lease under which that person remains in possession is a lease of commercial premises; and,
· the person who was the landlord at the end of the lease remains entitled to the immediate reversion.

In other words, the rent will be recoverable from tenants holding over in the premises or renewing their tenancy. When deciding whether a person remains in possession under a new lease, section 74(2)- which requires that a lease to be evidenced in writing- does not apply. It does not matter that the continuation tenancy is not set out in writing as the landlord is only entitled to recover the rent due under the expired (written) agreement. In the case of a tenancy by estoppel, the person who was the landlord remains "entitled to the immediate reversion" if the estoppel with regard to the tenancy continues. A lease ends when the tenant ceases to be entitled to possession of the demised premises under the lease together with any continuation of it by operation of an enactment or of a rule of law.

Section 80 deals with premises which are an agricultural holding as defined by s.1 Agricultural Holdings Act 1986. CRAR is not exercisable to recover rent that became due more than a year before notice of enforcement is given. For these purposes, deferred rent becomes due at the time to which payment is deferred. "Deferred rent" is defined as rent the payment of which has been deferred, according to the ordinary course of dealing between the landlord and the tenant, to the end of a quarter or half-year after it legally became due. The permitted deductions allowed to be set off at any time under section 77(7) include any compensation due to the tenant in respect of the holding, under the Agricultural Holdings Act 1986 or under any custom or agreement that has been ascertained at that time. This section reproduces the contents of sections 16 and 17 of the Agricultural Holdings Act 1986.

7.4.2 County court

Although an application for the issue of a warrant of control may be made without notice to a county court, in the request the judgment creditor must confirm -

- the amount remaining due under the judgment or order; and,
- where the order made was for payment by instalments, certify:
  - that the whole or part of any instalment due remains unpaid; and,
  - the amount for which the warrant is to be issued.

Unless an instalment order has been made and unless the following conditions apply, any warrant issued by the county court must be for the whole of the sum of judgment remaining unpaid. However, where the court made an instalment order and default has been made in payment of an instalment, a warrant of control may be issued for the whole of the sum of money and costs then remaining unpaid or for such part of that total amount as the judgment creditor may request, as long as it is not less than either £50 or the amount of one monthly instalment or four weekly instalments, whichever is the greater. Even so, no warrant will be issued unless at the time of issue the whole or part of an instalment which has already become due remains unpaid and any warrant previously issued for part of the sum of money and costs has expired, been satisfied or abandoned.[87]

Two or more warrants of control may be issued concurrently by a county court for execution by two or more different enforcement agents against the same individual. However, this is subject to two conditions:

- that no more may be levied under all the warrants together than is authorised to be levied under one of them; and,
- that, unless the court orders otherwise, costs for the enforcement of more than one warrant will not be allowed against the judgment debtor.[88]

7.4.3 Road traffic penalties

Execution must be issued separately on each unpaid penalty charge notice. It is not possible to consolidate several unpaid penalty charge notices into a single warrant of control. There is, though, no objection to an enforcement agent attending to levy multiple warrants on one occasion.

7.5 General preconditions and warnings

7.5.1 Notice of enforcement

In respect of all debts TCEA imposes a requirement that prior notice be given before an attempt to take control of goods may be made.[89] The minimum period of notice in all cases is seven days.[90] These are seven clear days which do not include the day on which the period begins or the day upon which any event takes place if the end of the period is defined by that event.[91] If the notice period includes a Sunday, bank holiday, Good Friday or Christmas Day, these also are not counted in calculating the minimum period.

On application, a court may order that a lesser period of notice is given, but this will only be done where the court is satisfied that the debtor's goods would otherwise be removed from the premises or otherwise disposed of in order to prevent their seizure.[92] Such an application will be on form N244 and may be made without notice to the debtor (for obvious reasons). It must be accompanied by evidence demonstrating that goods will be hidden or otherwise put beyond the bailiff's reach, thereby frustrating the levy, if the order is not made. At this very early stage of the enforcement process, enforcement agencies will be relying wholly upon creditors to supply this type of information.[93]

The regulations detail the form and contents of the notice.[94] It must be writing and must set out:

- the name and address of the debtor;
- any reference numbers assigned to the case by the enforcement agent or the agent's office;[95]
- the details of any judgment or court order upon which the enforcement depends and sufficient detail of the debt so that the debt in question may be identified by the debtor. Details of the sum due, any interest or costs accruing and any possible enforcement costs likely to fall due should also be specified;
- the date on which the notice is given and the date by which payment should be made to prevent further action and costs. The costs involved will be the enforcement fee in the short term and, possibly, a sale stage fee and associated disbursements (*see chapter 12*);
- how and where payment may be made; and,
- contact details for the enforcement agent.

The enforcement agent must keep a record of the time when the notice is given.

The notice may be served by one of several methods:[96]

- by post addressed to the debtor at one of the addresses at which s/he usually resides or trades;
- by fax or other electronic means;
- by hand delivery through a letter box at one of the addresses at which s/he usually resides or trades;
- personally to the debtor if s/he is an individual rather than a

company or partnership; or,

· where companies, corporations or firms are involved, by delivery to the registered office or one of the addresses at which the debtor usually carries on business.

It is notable that the Act makes no provision for failure of service of the enforcement notice. It is possible that a tenant could employ the application to set aside the notice on these grounds, but otherwise no mechanism exists for raising this issue. It is possible that prudent enforcement agencies might wish to re-serve a notice if there was a dispute about the validity of the notice and the subsequent period for taking control of goods, but in the absence of any mention of such an eventuality, it might equally be arguable that service by the enforcement agent is sufficient and that proof of receipt by the debtor is not essential. In doing so it will be possible to rely upon the Interpretation Act 1978, which grants the following concession -

"Where an Act authorises or requires any document to be served by post (whether the expression 'serve' or the expression 'give' or 'send' or any other expression is used) then, unless the contrary intention appears, the service is deemed to be effected by properly addressing, pre-paying and posting a letter containing the document and, unless the contrary is proved, to have been effected at the time at which the letter would be delivered in the ordinary course of the post."[97]

For guidance as to the 'ordinary course of the post' that might be allowed, an enforcement agency could also turn to an earlier part of the Civil Procedure Rules for guidance. Part 6 sets out the delivery periods that may anticipated- for example, with first class post a letter may be deemed to arrive the second day after posting on a business day or the next business day afterwards if delivery falls on a Saturday; personal or electronic service is assumed to deliver documents the same day if done before 4.30pm, or the next day if items are despatched after that time.[98]

The significance of the enforcement notice is not only that it provides the debtor with warning and a chance to make payment or take other steps and that the date of its service is the date from which the binding power runs for warrants under than those issued by the courts but also because from the date of service of the notice a limited period for enforcing the warrant starts to run. The basic period within which control of goods must be taken is 12 months, beginning with the date on which the notice was given.[99] However, if the debtor and agent enter into a repayment arrangement, the notice period is effectively suspended whilst the debtor maintains instalments. If the debtor breaches the terms of the repayment arrangement, the 12 month notice period will then begin to run from the date of the default.[100]

In addition, the regulations provide for the period to be extended by the court in certain cases. Application will be made by the enforcement agent or creditor but can only be made on one occasion. The court may allow a further 12 months under the notice if it is satisfied that there are reasonable grounds for the applicant not having taken goods into control within the initial 12 months period.[101]

The form of the enforcement notice is prescribed by regulations. The only change that may be made to this document by enforcement agencies is the addition of logo and contact information. The mandatory notice strangely makes no mention on the binding effect of the notice (*see 7.2*) and, as a result, it is anticipated that all bailiff companies will in addition send a covering letter warning of this and of the power to pursue goods fraudulently removed to other premises (see next chapter).

7.5.2 Other warning letters

Most bailiffs will send a variety of warning notices to the debtor of the fact of that a warrant has been issued, as this may provoke payment without the need to take any further steps. Whatever the situation, it is important to check the contents of such communications to be satisfied that no untoward or illegal threats are made. It is an offence under s40 Administration of Justice Act 1970 to harass a person whilst endeavouring to collect any debt due under contract (this will apply to rent arrears and, presumably, contractual debts being enforced by execution upon a judgment). A person will be guilty of the offence if s/he:

> "1a) harasses the other with demands for payment which, in respect of their frequency or the manner or occasion of making any such demand, or of any threat or publicity by which any demand is accompanied, are calculated to subject him or members of his family or household to alarm, distress or humiliation;
> b) falsely represents... that criminal proceedings lie for failure to pay..;
> c) falsely represents himself to be authorised in some official capacity to claim or enforce payment".

This section could cover a range of actions. Examples would include threats of imprisonment for failing to allow entry, claims of status as court officers when that is not the case or any threats of violence, racial or sexual abuse. Any harassment must be deliberate. It would be necessary to show that the bailiff was aware (or could not ignore) the fact that his actions were illegal. Neglect to make proper enquiries as to the legality of certain actions does not constitute knowledge that an offence is being committed. Both the person making such threats plus anyone who supported or assisted them (such as an office manager) may be prosecuted in the magistrates' court. On summary conviction the defendant may be fined up to £5000. Any one enforcing a debt by legal process is not affected by this provision so long as their actions are "reasonable (and otherwise permissible in law)".

Attention should also be paid to the Malicious Communications Act 1988. Under s1 it is an offence to send any letter or article which conveys a threat or "information which is false and known or believed to be false by the sender" and which it was known would be likely to cause distress or anxiety to the recipient. This may include threats to break in and remove goods whether or not the debtor is at home. Malicious communications are a criminal offence leading to a fine on summary conviction of up to £2500. The defendant may show that s/he used the threat to reinforce a demand s/he believed there were reasonable grounds for making and that it was believed that the use of the threat was a proper means of reinforcing the demand.

The NSEA stipulates that all notices, correspondence and documentation issued by an enforcement agency must be clear and unambiguous and, to the satisfaction of the creditor, must avoid unnecessary and unhelpful use of legal and technical language. Enforcement agents must not be deceitful by misrepresenting their powers, qualifications, capacities, experience or abilities. This includes but is not restricted to:

- falsely implying or stating that action can or will, be taken when legally it cannot be taken;
- falsely implying or stating that a particular course of action will ensue before it is possible to know whether such action would be permissible; or,
- falsely implying or stating that action has been taken when it has not.

7.6 Preconditions for certain debts

For many debts, in addition to the requirements of the Act, other conditions will have to be satisfied before the debt can be enforced by seizure of goods.

7.6.1 Magistrates' court orders

If instalments are in default, enforcement will be for all instalments still unpaid. A warrant will be issued in the following circumstances:

· *Fines* – on convicting a person a court can make a collection order regarding payment of the fine. This will specify the sum to be paid and the mode and rate of payment.[102] A fines officer will be allocated to oversee the fine's repayment. If the defendant defaults the fines officer can increase the fine by up to 50%.[103] If there is still no contact from the defendant, the fines officer can either refer the matter to the court or issue a 'further steps notice'.[104] A further steps notice can include the issue of a warrant of control. If the matter is referred to the court the magistrates can reduce the sum payable, vary the payment terms or order enforcement of the fine themselves, which could include the issue of a warrant of control.[105] Issue of a notice of default on the fine before enforcement by warrant of control is also still required by the Magistrates' Court Rules 1981;[106] or,

· *Maintenance* - a warrant will be issued by the magistrates after a hearing to consider whether there is good cause for the failure to pay.[107] The hearing will follow a complaint made by the spouse or collecting officer. A request for a complaint can only be made at least fifteen days after the date of the original maintenance order itself during which time it is normal to serve a copy of the order on the defendant.[108]

· *Civil debts* - a notice issued to the defendant by the court prior to enforcement by taking control of goods will be required.[109]

In respect of fines, the Queen's Bench Divisional Court has clarified the procedure that was to be followed by a magistrates' court in enforcing a fine by distress in *R. v. Hereford Magistrates Court ex p MacRae* [1998].[110] If no payment or response is made following a final demand, it is appropriate to issue a warrant without further proceedings. The court had no duty, and indeed no power, to hold a means enquiry hearing when considering whether to issue distress. Such a hearing is only necessary under ss82-84 MCA when the issue of a warrant of committal is being considered. Thus *R. v. Birmingham Justices ex p Bennet* [1983], which held that if the evidence reveals a 'reasonable likelihood' that there are distrainable assets, a warrant should be issued, must be understood to apply when the court is "considering committal as an alternative".[111] In *R. v. Norwich JJ ex p Trigger* [1987] it was held that the use of distraint as an option, and the availability of seizeable goods, should be considered before committal is threatened: though not cited in *MacRae* the decisions must now be read in light of that case. Nonetheless none of these decisions were an authority for the proposition that there had to be a means enquiry in every case, even if only a distress warrant was being considered. The decision in *R. v. German* [1891], which states that generally, before issue, the court may require positive evidence of the existence of distrainable goods and of the circumstances of the debtor, held no more than that the justices have a discretion in such circumstances.[112]

The decisions in *R. v. Guildford Justices ex parte Rich* [1996], that in every case the defendant should have an opportunity to make representations at a hearing before the warrant is issued and thus there is a chance for distraint to be further postponed (*see 6.3*) on varied terms of payment, must be distinguished.[113] In that case the defaulter had no notice of the possible issue of distress. In the *MacRae* case the final demand sent specific notice of distress. The decision in *Forrest v. Brighton JJ* [1981] that the only exception to the debtor's right to attend is where the person is in prison, though there should still be a hearing, must also now be understood in light of MacRae.[114]

MacRae also held that, as no hearing is necessary, it is acceptable for the justices to delegate the task of issuing warrants to a court officer. Whoever makes this decision must still consider the circumstances of the debtor. If the court is satisfied that there are no seizable goods, for instance the debtor's only asset is income, there is no need to attempt to levy, and alternative enforcement such as committal may be used instead. The finding of the magistrates of insufficient goods is a judicial finding that must be set out on the order by them.[115]

7.6.2 Income taxes

Taking control of goods may be used where tax has been demanded and there has been a neglect or refusal to pay. A taxpayer will be sent demand notes asking for payment. Non-payment after such a demand is evidence of refusal to pay. If the demands cannot be proved to have been received by the debtor, the warrant may be unlawful. The time lapse between the original demand and warrant is variable because in the absence of an actual refusal to pay, reasonable time must be allowed before refusal can be inferred. Taking control has been held to be unlawful, therefore, where the collector seizes goods immediately after demand and in the absence of the occupier.[116]

Footnotes
1 *Smith v Birmingham Gas Co* (1834) 1 Ad & El 526; (1889) 61 LT 559; *Robertson v Hooper* [1909] 12 WLR 5.
2 Though see IRC v Rossmeister [1980] AC 952.
3 Key detail - *R v Atkinson* [1976] Crim LR 307 CA; amount - *Bavin v Hutchinson*

(1862) 6 LT 504.

4 Reg.51 Taking Control of Goods Regulations.

5 CPR PD 4, forms 53-57.

6 *Price v Messenger* (1800) 2 Bos & Pull 158; s78(3) MCA.

7 CPR Part 75.7(7).

8 LGO decision 12 005 084, LB Redbridge.

9 Schedule 12 para.26.

10 61 LT 559; see too *Andrews v Bolton Borough Council* (2011), in *Sources of bailiff law*, c.7 p.230.

11 (1587) 1 Leonard 50.

12 *Galliard v Laxton* (1862) 2 B&S 363; *R v Chapman* (1870) 12 Cox CC 4; *Codd v Cabe* (1876) 1 Ex D 352; *Horsfield v Brown* [1932] 1 KB 355; *De Costa Small v Kirkpatrick* (1979) 68 Cr App R 186. See too *Rhodes v Hull* (1857) 26 LJ Ex 265.

13 *R v Purdy* [1974] 1 QB 288.

14 [1974] 1 QB 297A; see too *Hall v Roche* (1799) 8 TR 187.

15 *Codd v Cabe* (1876) 1 Ex D 352; *R v Purdy* [1974] 1 QB 288.

16 *Plomer v Ball* (1837) 5 A&E 823.

17 MCA s.125D(1) & (4); Criminal Procedure Rules Part 52.8(2).

18 Magistrates' Court Rules 1981 r.54(3B) as amended by Tribunals, Courts & Enforcement Act 2007 (Consequential, Transitional & Saving Provision) Order 2014 Sch.para.1(d).

19 Approval of Enforcement Agents Regulations 2000 reg.11(7)(b).

20 Magistrates' Courts Act 1980 s.125B(4).

21 *Horsfield v Brown* [1932] 1 KB 355.

22 *Symonds v Kurtz* (1889) 61 LT 559; *R v Whalley* (1835) 7 C&P 245; *R v Patience* (1837) 7 C&P 775; see also *Collins v Yewens* (1838) 10 A&E 570.

23 These are s.78 Magistrates Court Act & s.125 County Courts Act.

24 *Robins v Hender* 3 Dowl PC 543.

25 [1974] 1 QB 292F.

26 MCA s.125D(4) & Crim PR Pt.52.8(5); s125D(1).

27 *China v Harrow UDC* [1954] 1 QB 178.

28 ss.38(1) & 37(2).

29 CPR 83.2.

30 CPR 83.2(4) & (5).

31 Abuse - *LB Hackney v White* [1995] 28 HLR 219; limitations - *National Westminster Bank v Powney* [1990] 2 WLR 1084; claim/remedy - *Berliner Industriebank Aktiengesellschaft v Jost* [1971] 1 QB 278 and *W T Lamb & Sons v Rider* [1948] 2 KB 331.

32 CPR 75.6(c).

33 *Elliot v Yates* [1900] 2 QB 370.

34 See *AG v Bradlaugh* [1885] 14 QBD 667.

35 Local Government Ombudsman case 98/C/4810.

36 6 month limit - s71 TCEA (see later); 6 year limit - s19 Limitation Act 1980; *Doe d Davy v Oxenham* (1840) 7 M&W 131.

37 S.125ZA MCA inserted by s.68 TCEA 2007.

38 S.99 CCA inserted by s.68 TCEA 2007.

39 Courts Act 2007 Sch.7 para.7.

40 Schedule 12 para.4.

41 Sch.12 para.5(4) & (5).

42 Sch.12 para.5.

43 Paragraph 6.

44 Para.61(2).

45 Para.50(6).

---

46 Para.50(5).
47 *Guest v Cowbridge Railway Co* (1868) 6 Eq 619.
48 *Birstall Candle Co v Daniels* [1908] 2 KB 254.
49 *Murgatroyd v Wright* [1907] 2 KB 333.
50 *Bearnes v. Machattie* (1885) 1 WN(NSW) 159.
51 *Slack v. Winder* (1874) 5 AJR 72.
52 *Payne v Drew* [1804] 4 East 523; *Woodland v Fuller* (1840) 11 Ad & El 859.
53 *Lucas v Nockells* (1833) 10 Bing 157; *Lowthal v Tomkins* (1740) Barn C 39.
54 *Woodland v Fuller* (1840) 11 Ad & El 859.
55 *In re: Davies* [1872] LR 7 Ch 314.
56 *Ehlers, Seel & Co v Kauffman & Gates* (1883) 49 LT 806.
57 *Boucher v Wiseman* (1595) Cro Eliz 440.
58 *Smallcomb v Cross & Thompson* 1 Salk 320; *Lucas v Nockells* (1833) 7 Bligh NS 140; *Payne v Drew* [1804] 4 East 523; property is not finally altered until sale - *Samuel v Duke* (1838) 3 M & W 622.
59 *Payne v Drew* [1804] 4 East 523; *Samuel v Duke* (1838) 3 M & W 622; *Philips v Thompson* (1685) 3 Lev 191.
60 *Payne v Drew* [1804] 4 East 523; *Samuel v Duke* (1838) 3 M & W 622.
61 *Samuel v Duke* (1838) 3 M & W 622; *McPherson v Temiskaming Lumber Co Ltd* [1913] AC 145.
62 *Cockburn v Jeanette* [1942] 3 DLR 216.
63 *Giles v Grover* (1832) 6 Bligh NS 277.
64 *Johnson v Pickering* [1908] 1 KB 1.
65 CPR 84.5(3)(b).
66 CPR Part 75.6(ca).
67 CPR 83.2(3)(b) & (c).
68 CPR 75.6(c).
69 CPR 83.2(4) & (5).
70 CPR 83.2(6) & (7).
71 *Braithwaite v Cooksey & Another* 1 H Bl 465; *Bolton v Canham* (1670) Pollexfen 20.
72 Agreement - *C H Bailey v Memorial Enterprises* [1974] 1 All ER 1003; retrospective liability - *United Scientific v Burnley Council* [1978] AC 904.
73 *Bird v Hildage* [1948] 1 KB 91.
74 Whole sum - *Re: Smith & Hartogs* (1895) 73 LT 221; day - *Child v Edwards* [1909] 2 KB 753.
75 *Regnart v Porter* (1831) 7 Bing 451.
76 *Dibble v Bowater* (1853) 2 E&B 564; *Duppa v Mayo* 1 Saund 287.
77 Midnight - *Albert v. Storey* [1925] 52 NBR 495; time to pay - *Clun's Case* (1613) 10 Co Rep 127a.
78 Rent in advance - *Lee v Smith* (1854) 9 Exch 662; cheque - see *Harris v Shipway* (1744) Bull NP 182a.
79 *Parker v Harris* 1 Salk 262; *GLC v Connolly* [1970] 2 QB 100.
80 Fluctuating - *In Re: Knight ex p Voisey* [1882] 21 Ch D 442; calculable - *Daniel v Gracie* (1844) 6 QB 145.
81 Court action - *Dunk v Hunter* (1822) 5 B & Ald 322; appeal - *Eren v. Tranmac* [1994] 138 Sol. Jo. 524.
82 s.77(5)(b) & (7).
83 2 WLR 278; 14/2/2001 ChD; excluded - *Electricity Supply Nominees v IAF Group* [1993] 2 EGLR 95.
84 Regulation 52 Taking Control of Goods Regulations.
85 Part rent - *Tutthill v Roberts* (1673) 89 ER 256; any order - *Palmer v Stanage* (1661) 1 Lev 43; one sum only - *Bagge v Mawby* (1853) 8 Exch 641.

86 The landlord could not levy if a tenancy had been terminated by forfeiture (*Grimwood v Moss* [1872] 7 CP 360; *Serjeant v Nash Field & Co* [1903] 2 KB 304) or by a notice to quit (*Murgatroyd v Dodworth & Silkstone Coal & Iron Co.*[1895] 65 LJ Ch 111). Distress could not be employed where the tenancy had been surrendered by the tenant - for example in *North Bay TV & Audio Ltd v. Nova Electronics Ltd* [1983] 44 OR 342 the tenant abandoned the property, the landlord retook possession and then purported to levy distraint on the goods left behind. This was illegal. Acceptance of rent- or levying distress - after the issue of a notice to quit did not act as a waiver of any breach of the tenancy unless the clear intention was to create a new tenancy (*Clarke v Grant* [1950] 1 KB 104 but see *Zouch v Willingdale* 1 H Bl 311). If the old tenancy had ended, and a new tenant had entered the premises, distress could not be levied even though a few goods of the old tenant remained behind (*Taylerson v Peters* (1837) 7 A&E 110).

87 CPR 83.15.

88 CPR 83.29.

89 Para.7(1).

90 Reg.6 TCG Regs.

91 Reg.2(a).

92 Reg.6(3) & (4) TCG Regs.

93 CPR 84.4.

94 Reg.7 TCG Regs.

95 Reg.2.

96 Reg.8 TCG Regs.

97 Interpretation Act 1978 s.7.

98 CPR Part 6.26; see also Practice Direction 6A paras.10.1 to 10.7 for examples of deemed service.

99 Sch.12 para.8; reg.9(1) TCG Regs; CPR 83.4 for writs and warrants of control.

100 Reg.9(2) TCG Regs; CPR 83.4 for writs and warrants of control.

101 Reg.9(3) TCG Regs; CPR 83.4 for writs and warrants of control.

102 Courts Act 2003 Sch.5 Part 4.

103 Sch.5 part 7.

104 Sch.5 para.37(6)

105 Sch.5 Part 9 para.39.

106 1981 Rules r.46 as amended by Tribunals, Courts & Enforcement Act 2007 (Consequential, Transitional & Saving Provision) Order 2014 Sch. para.1(b).

107 s.59 MCA.

108 s93 MCA.

109 Magistrates' Courts Rules 1981 r.53 as amended by Tribunals, Courts & Enforcement Act 2007 (Consequential, Transitional & Saving Provision) Order 2014 Sch. para.1(c).

110 *Times* December 31st.

111 147 JP 82; see too *R. v. Clacton JJ ex p Commissioners of the Customs & Excise* (1987) 152 JP 120.

112 Respectively 151 JP 465; 66 LT 264.

113 *Times* May 17th 1996; and see too *Harper v. Carr* (1797) 7 TR 270.

114 2 All ER 711.

115 No goods - *R. v. Mortimer* (1906) 70 JP 542; form of order - *R. v. Tyrone JJ ex. p. Patterson* (1915) 49 ILTR 25

116 Taxes Management Act 1970 s.61(1) distraint & s.60 - demand; refusal - *Lumsden v Burnett* [1898] 2 LR QB 177; no demands - *Berry v Farrow* [1914] 1 KB 632; unlawful - *Gibbs v Stead* (1828) 8 B & C 528.

PART FOUR - INITIATING SEIZURE

Chapter 8

Initial visits

Section One - Persons, place and time

If the debtor fails to pay in full or to make an instalment arrangement upon receipt of the enforcement notice, visits to premises in an effort to take goods into control will inevitably follow. It is worth observing that, for the purposes of fees, the 'enforcement stage' begins with the first visit to premises (*see chapter 12*). No mandatory notice need be delivered if an attendance is made but there is no contact with a debtor, but it is recommended that this should be done for reasons of clarity and good practice.

8.1 Liable persons

8.1.1 Exempt persons

A bailiff is entitled to take control of the goods of the liable person, the debtor, whether that person is an individual or a company. Special rules apply to partnership property (*see 10.13*), but a debt due from a partnership maybe pursued against any partner, even if s/he is the only surviving member of a firm.[1] If the debt in question is a joint debt it may be enforced against the debtors' sole or joint property. The property of any one of the liable individuals may be seized and the others need not be chased.[2] The warrant or writ which issued must follow the judgment or order, so a joint judgment must be enforced by a warrant issued against all defendants. This point was confirmed also in Penoyer v Bruce (1697), which further held that if one of joint debtors has died, enforcement may continue unabated against the other (*see also 7.3*).[3] Special rules also apply to property jointly owned by the debtor.

Some individuals are specially privileged from enforcement:

- *Diplomatic staff* may not have execution levied on them, their family members or their employees. The privilege extends to the furnishings of diplomatic missions, other property thereon and to vehicles owned by the mission for the transport of the diplomatic staff. However this is not a blanket protection - see *Novello v. Toogood* (1823) in which it was decided that the goods of an ambassador's servant were not protected where he did not reside with the ambassador and where none of the items seized could be said to have been necessary for the convenience of the ambassador.[4]

· *armed forces*: the goods of those volunteering or called up for service in the armed forces cannot be taken into control without permission of court.[5] This is sought by application to the High Court or county court on application notice N244, setting out the details of the judgment and of the circumstances of the judgment debtor.[6] This does not apply to judgments for damages in tort, to orders for costs, to judgments for debts incurred after the military service began or to orders in criminal proceedings. Furthermore any military equipment, instruments or clothing supplied to a person in the armed forces may not be seized in execution.[7]

· *the Crown*: although TCEA s.88 abolishes crown preference, s.89(2) provides that the procedure for taking control of goods may not be used either to recover debts due from the Crown or to take control of or sell goods of the Crown. This protection includes goods owned by the Crown jointly or in common with another person.

If a judgment is executed against the goods of a privileged person, or in a privileged place (see later), the process can be set aside, but no claim for trespass lies against those acting in disobedience of a lawful writ or order, even if malice is alleged.[8]

8.1.2 Vulnerable persons

Goods should not be taken into control where:

· The debtor is a child (i.e. under 16 years of age);
· A child or vulnerable person (whether more than one of each or a combination of both) are the only persons found to be present on the premises where the goods are located; or,
· The goods that the enforcement agent wishes to take into control are also premises and a child or vulnerable person (whether more than one of each or a combination of both) are the only persons found to be present there.[9]

These new rules give the former NSEA guidance statutory form. However, the regulations fail to provide a definition of 'vulnerability' or even guidance on its interpretation, so that it will be necessary for practitioners to revert still to non-statutory materials.

The NSEA still requires that both enforcement agents and creditor organisations should protect the vulnerable and socially excluded and should have procedures in place to deal with such cases when they were identified. The Standard suggests that those who might be potentially vulnerable will include:

- elderly people;
- people with disabilities or suffering from serious illness;
- those recently bereaved;
- single parent families & pregnant women;
- unemployed people;
- those who have obvious difficulty in understanding, speaking or reading English. Agents should if possible be able to rapidly access translation services & provide on request information in large print or in Braille.

This is not intended to be an exhaustive or exclusive list. Enforcement agents are now under a duty to be proactive in identifying and protecting possibly vulnerable individuals.

As well as identifying potentially vulnerable groups, the revised NSEA repeatedly stresses the various duties of creditors and enforcement agents to vulnerable persons. Creditors must consider the appropriateness of referring debtors to enforcement agents at all if they are in potentially vulnerable situations and, if they decide to proceed, must alert the enforcement agent to this. Creditors should ensure there are clear protocols agreed with their enforcement agents governing the approach that should be taken when a debtor has been identified as vulnerable. Should a potentially vulnerable individual be identified, creditors should be prepared at any time to take over control of the case from the bailiff, if necessary. Where enforcement agents have identified vulnerable debtors or situations, they should alert the creditor and ensure they act in accordance with all relevant legislation.

Agents should be trained to recognise vulnerable debtors, to alert creditors where they have identified such debtors and when to withdraw from such a situation. A debtor may be considered vulnerable if, for reasons of age, health, disability or severe financial insecurity, they are unable to safeguard their personal welfare or the personal welfare of other members of the household.

Bailiffs are also reminded by NSEA that they need to be aware that vulnerability may not be immediately obvious. Combined with the duties to avoid discriminatory behaviour imposed by the ECHR and the Equality Act (see later), these provisions are clear directions to enforcement agencies as to conduct.

If a public authority is aware that a person is potentially vulnerable, or has sufficient facts indicating this drawn to its attention, it will be maladministration for the body to fail to act upon this information. Such a failure could be the subject of a complaint to an ombudsman.10 However we define vulnerability, it will be essential for bailiffs to make the necessary enquiries about any individuals found on premises before any attempt is made to enter, to inspect goods or to take them into control.

8.1.3 Discrimination

The NSEA also imposes duties similar to those found in article 14 ECHR upon enforcement agents. It states that agents must not discriminate unfairly on any grounds such as age, disability, race, gender, religion or sexual orientation. Further it is required by NSEA that enforcement agents should respect the religion and culture of others at all times. They should be aware of dates for religious festivals & carefully consider the appropriateness of enforcement on any day of religious or cultural observance or during any major religious or cultural festival.

The majority of enforcement agencies will also be subject directly to ECHR article 14 where they are acting on behalf of a public body (*see 4.3 above*). It will also be necessary for agencies and creditors to bear in mind the Equality Act 2010 (*see 4.4*). The NSEA repeats this guidance.

8.2 Time

The Act states that "The enforcement agent may enter and remain on the premises only within prescribed times of day."[11] A detailed set of rules on the timing of various forms of entry to premises are laid out in the regulations.

8.2.1 Day of week

The new Act applies a simple rule across all forms of enforcement: an enforcement agent may make initial entries (under Sch.12 para.14 or 15) to search for and take control of goods on any day of the week.[12] The same is the case for re-entries for the purposes of inspecting or removing controlled goods under Sch.12 para.16 (*see 11.2 below*).

8.2.2 Hour of day

In general, initial entry for the purposes of taking control of goods and re-entry for the purposes of removing controlled goods should only take place between 6am and 9pm.[13] However, these limits do not apply in three situations:[14]

- where the goods to be taken into control are located on premises which are used (whether wholly or partly) for the purposes of carrying on a business and those premises are open for business during the 'prohibited hours' of 9pm to 6am the bailiff may enter and remain on the premises during any of the business's opening hours;
- where an enforcement agent made initial entry or re-entry within the permitted hours or in either of the above situations and needs to conclude the levy. The bailiff may remain on the premises during prohibited hours if it is "reasonably necessary" to continue to search for goods, take control of goods, inspect controlled goods or remove goods taken into control (provided that the bailiff does not remain on the premises an unreasonable time in order to accomplish this); or,
- because the court, on specific application from an enforcement agent, has made an order authorising an entry or re-entry to take place outside the permitted hours. An application by an enforcement agent for such an order may be made without notice (on form N244) but must be accompanied by evidence demonstrating that if the order is not made, it is likely that the debtor's goods will be moved, or otherwise disposed of, in order to avoid the enforcement agent taking control of them.[15]

8.3 Place

The Act has introduced a complete code as to the premises which may be entered for the purposes of taking control of goods. The basic rules are that an enforcement agent may enter:

- any premises which s/he reasonably believes to be the place, or one of the places, where the debtor usually lives;
- any premises which s/he reasonably believes to be the place, or one of the places, where the debtor carries on a trade or business. This will naturally include factories, shops and cafes, but may also apply to a home if an individual trades from that address; and,
- vehicles on a highway- whether to seize the vehicle itself or goods being transported within it. The meaning of 'highway' is discussed at 9.4. In certain circumstances, force may be used to effect an entry to a vehicle (see 8.7).

For the purposes of these rules, premises are defined as "any place", though it is clarified that this in particular includes a vehicle, vessel, aircraft or hovercraft as well as a tent or movable structure.[16] Where there are different relevant premises agents are authorised to enter to each of them. Repeated entry to the same premises is also authorised, subject to any restriction in regulations (see 8.11).[17]

Within these broad general rules, certain further restrictions are imposed by the new Act as are set out below. In addition, for fines enforcement, a broader rule remains in force: agents are permitted to execute warrants anywhere in England and Wales.[18]

8.3.1 CRAR

If an enforcement agent is acting under section 64(1) of the Act (collecting rent arrears) the only relevant premises are the demised premises.[19] This provision preserves the common law rule that distress for rent could only be levied at the premises where the rent was due.

8.3.2 National insurance contributions

If an enforcement agent is acting under section 121A of the Social Security Administration Act 1992 and is seeking to take control of goods to recover unpaid NICs, then the relevant premises where seizure may take place are the place, or one of the places, where the debtor carries on a trade or business.[20] As described in the introductory paragraph, this would seem to include domestic premises if a person trades from their home.

8.3.3 Other premises

Schedule 12 para.15 authorises enforcement agents to enter other "specified" premises in order to search for a debtor's goods, subject to certain conditions. The enforcement agent must apply to the court for the issue of a warrant authorising him to enter specified third party premises to search for and take control of goods. Before issuing the warrant the court must be satisfied that all the following conditions are met- that an enforcement power has become exercisable, that there is reason to believe that there are goods that might be taken into control on the premises and that it is reasonable in all the circumstances to issue the warrant. As part of the application on N244, the enforcement agent must provide the court with sufficient evidence and information to satisfy the court that the conditions specified are met.[21] Such a warrant authorises repeated entry to the same premises, subject to any restriction in regulations (see below).

These other premises that may be specified in a warrant are likely to be either third parties' premises or separate premises used by the debtor but not for residential or trade purposes (for example, a rented garage). Earlier case authority determined that third party premises did not include any property where the debtor's goods were ordinarily deposited, or where the debtor was ordinarily resident, though s/he may not be classed as the occupier.[22]

8.3.4 Crown premises

Section 81(2)(c) of the Act states that the procedure in Schedule 12 may not be used to enter premises occupied by the Crown. This seems to expand the rule previously applicable to executions that writs could not be levied at royal residences[23] although this did not include the Palace of Westminster.[24] Nonetheless, the new Act may provide a broader exemption, though the term 'occupied by the crown' may require definition by the courts.

8.3.5 Highways

The Act replaces the confused and uncertain former law relating to levies on highways (*this term is discussed in 9.4 below*). If an enforcement agent applies to the court it may issue a warrant which authorises him to use, if necessary, reasonable force to take control of goods on a highway.[25] However, the court may not issue a warrant unless it is satisfied that prescribed conditions are met (*see 8.7.2 later for details*). If such a warrant issued by the court, it may also require any constable to assist the enforcement agent in executing it.

The Act makes it clear that the enforcement agent may not seize goods on a highway except within the prescribed times of day, though regulations may give the court power in prescribed circumstances to authorise him to exercise a power at other times, further to which this authorisation may be subject to conditions (*see earlier 8.2*).[26]

If the enforcement agent takes control of goods on a highway or enters a vehicle on a highway with the intention of taking control of goods, he must provide a copy of the prescribed notices of entry and taking control to the debtor giving information about what he is doing.[27] If the debtor is present when the enforcement agent is there, the enforcement agent must give him the notice there and then. Otherwise the enforcement agent must deliver the notice to any relevant premises (as defined by Sch.12 paragraph 14) in a sealed envelope addressed to the debtor (*see 8.9 below*).

8.3.6 Special locations

Under the former law it was held that special rules applied in respect of the following locations:

Flats, maisonettes and bedsits
A common problem confronted during entry into a block of flats or house in multiple occupation is determining which is the outer door -

the common entrance or the door to the premises solely and exclusively occupied by the debtor. The often quoted English case under the old law was *Lee v Gansel* (1774).28 General Gansel was arrested by a bailiff who entered the property where he lodged by means of an open outer door but then broke into the General's bedroom. Gansel rented rooms in his landlord's home - two rooms on the first floor, with doors opening onto the landing, two rooms on the second floor, with separate doors. He shared the kitchen with his landlord and both used the outer door. It was held not to be logical for Gansel to have four outer doors to his premises, therefore the bedroom was legally broken open, for as was held in *Astley v Pinder* (1760) 'an inner door has no protection at all'. This case seems to favour the case for occupiers of flats and HMOs. A more definitive answer is given in *Welch v Kracovsky* (1919). In this it was held that a door connecting a suite of rooms occupied exclusively by a tenant in an apartment block with a hallway used by all tenants and leading to the main entrance is an outer door and therefore could not be forced.[29]

Hotels and lodgings
If the debtor is resident in a hotel or lodgings house, it may be that the debtor would have no protection from forcible entry to the premises in order to seize their goods, and the levy would be valid, though the actual owner of the premises may have a cause of action against the bailiff.[30]

Diplomatic premises or the private residences of ambassadors
Executions could not be levied under articles 22 & 30 Sch.1 Diplomatic Privileges Act 1971. This has not been amended by the 2007 Act.

8.3.7 Changes of address

Where an enforcement agent discovers on visiting an address that the debtor no longer resides or trades there, having perhaps moved home or deliberately absconded, it will usually be necessary to return the instruction to the creditor. The current warrant may therefore be cancelled and, after the debtor has been traced to a new address, a new instruction may be issued and a new enforcement served at the correct address. This has the particular advantage to bailiff and creditor of restarting the twelve month deadline for taking control of goods.

For road traffic penalties special provisions are made. Civil Procedure Rules Part 75 requires that, where the address of the respondent (the liable person) has changed since the issue of the warrant, the authority may request the reissue of the warrant by filing in court a request specifying the new address of the respondent and providing evidence that this address is that used by the debtor named in the order and against whom enforcement is sought. If the court is satisfied that the new address given in the request for the reissue of the warrant relates to the respondent named in the order, it will seal the request and return it to the authority. The council must then prepare the reissued warrant in the appropriate form within seven days of the court sealing the request to reissue. A reissued warrant will only be valid for the remainder of the 12 month period beginning with the date it was originally issued.[31]

Section Two - Rights of entry

One of the most significant aspects of the new Act is its remodelling of bailiffs' rights of entry to premises. The new provisions have sought to change substantially some fundamental principles of English common law rights of entry in order to improve the effectiveness of enforcement action. The following sections will discuss initial entries to premises for the purposes of taking control of goods.

The Act and the regulations distinguish between two entries at two stages in the process - initial entries (Schedule 12 para.14 and 15) and re-entries (para.16). Re-entries made for the purposes of inspecting or removing goods seized on a previous occasion are discussed later (*see 11.2*). The new rules also regulate the bailiff's right to remain on premises after an entry (*see 8.10 below*) and also the bailiff's right to make repeat entries (*see 8.11*).

Initial entries are in turn subdivided into those which require a warrant to use force for the purposes of gaining access and those which do not. These complex new rules are examined here after a discussion of some broader issues of access to premises and trespass.

8.4 General right of entry

It has been accepted for centuries that a bailiff acting on a lawful warrant has a right of entry to a debtor's premises. This right of entry has always been understood to be subject to two very significant qualifications - that it had to be peaceable (in most cases) and it had to be with the permission of the debtor or occupier. The new Act reaffirms this established right in terms. Schedule 12 para.14(1) states that an enforcement agent "may enter" relevant premises to search for and take control of goods.

As has already been discussed, the new legislation sets out clear rules on the circumstances in which initial entry and re-entry to premises may take place. These deal with the legitimate days, hours, premises and the situations that may be encountered: initial entry or re-entry should not be made (nor should a bailiff remain on premises) if:

- The debtor is found to be a child under 16 years of age; or,
- The only persons present on the premises the bailiff wishes to enter are found to be either a child or vulnerable person (whether more than one of each or a combination of both).[32]

This new provision gives statutory effect to what was previously merely guidance contained in the National Standard. It must be repeated that 'vulnerable' is not defined at this point in the Regulations, as a consequence of which it will almost inevitably be necessary to continue to refer to codes of practice and other materials for guidance as to its interpretation. Nevertheless, it is a fundamental part of the bailiff's duties to conduct the necessary checks before attempting to enter or to remain on premises to establish whether or not a child or vulnerable individual might be present.

Additionally, detailed rules are made to prescribe access routes and when force may be used to enter premises (see 8.5, 8.6 and 11.2). What is not entirely clear is whether the general statement of the bailiffs' right of entry in Schedule 12 para.14(1) is intended to override the established common law principle that permission from the occupier must be obtained. Because the paragraph does not explicitly remove the need to enter with consent, and because the right to use force is very highly circumscribed - as will be described later - it is assumed in the discussion that follows that the law has not been altered in respect of the need for permission.

8.4.1 Entry with permission

English law has laid great emphasis on the concept of the licence to enter. As Lord Camden held in *Entick v Carrington* (1765):

> "Our law holds the property of everyman so sacred that no man can set foot upon his neighbour's close without leave. If he does, he is a trespasser, though he does no damage at all. If he will tread upon his neighbour's ground, he must justify it by law."

In *Morris v Beardmore* [1980] Lord Scarman emphasised the continuing relevance of these principles, both under the common law and under the ECHR. The licence has therefore been a fundamental aspect of bailiff's entry rights. The new Act asserts the general right of the bailiff to enter, and to do so as often as s/he requires. What is not fully clear is whether this provision is intended to replace the common law rule on licences nor whether, even if it is, the courts will choose to understand it this way. There is no explicit statement to this effect, which might be anticipated in the circumstances. Given this element of uncertainty before the Act is fully in operation, the following paragraphs examine the established law in licences in detail, as it is not well understood by enforcement agents.[33]

If the debtor expressly invites or permits the bailiff to enter, whether by standing back to allow him in or by issuing an invitation, there can be no doubt about the legality of the entry. It is in the concept of an implied licence that the difficulties arise. A number of situations have been identified where an implied licence may be inferred.

Persons on lawful business
This concept underlies many of the modes of entry described in the previous section. The courts have held that there is an implied right for an officer on lawful business to enter an individual's house.[34] However, if there is no legal right to enter (for example because there is no warrant or no liability) then no licence can be implied.[35]

This right of entry for lawful visitors has been extended to include means of access to premises. In other words the bailiff has a right of entry onto gardens paths and driveways and, in blocks of flats and maisonettes, the common stairs and hallways.[36] It has recently been confirmed that a garden is private property, and therefore subject to the rules on consent, however small it may be.[37]

Business premises
These are a special case because, by their nature, they are frequently open to free public access. The courts have emphasised that the same principle of an implied licence extends to bailiffs and other officers making entry on lawful business to a shop, a café or a garage.[38]

Grant of licence
The licence may be imputed by the circumstances - for example, the bailiff has a warrant and there is no contrary indication (see below) or it may be implied by conduct. In *Faulkner v Willets* [1982] a police officer attended the defendant's home.[39] The door was opened by his wife who was told that the officer was investigating a road traffic accident. She fully opened the door and walked back into the house, giving the officer the impression that he had an implied licence to enter. He did so and arrested Willets. The court held that it could imply a licence to

enter as this action was coupled with a lack of a subsequent request to leave. This case also raises the question of who may grant a licence. A spouse, partner or adult may do so, as may (probably) a member of the household such as a lodger or co-resident relative. In *Jones & Jones v Lloyd* [1981], it was questioned whether a guest at a party could invite a police office into premises.[40] The court was prepared to assume in this case that the owner would have allowed a guest to invite in persons on lawful business. That said, the courts have been reluctant to give too wide a scope to the right to imply a licence. In *R v Landry* [1981] a constable attended premises whilst investigating certain offences. Two persons matching descriptions given were seen in a ground floor flat, the door to which was open. Landry (one of the two) was asked if he lived there, but made no reply. The officer therefore entered to arrest him and a scuffle developed. The court found that entry without objection did not necessarily mean that a licence had been granted. There had been no request for permission to enter. One of the three judges dissented, feeling that he had entered on lawful business, but felt that the assault could be interpreted as a revocation of the licence.[41]

If a child opens the door either in the absence of the parent or whilst the parent is elsewhere in the house, is the entry legal? Very probably this is not a legal mode of entry. The National Standard advised that agents must withdraw if the only person present is, or appears to be, under the age of 18 although it would be permissible for them to ask when the debtor will be home - if this is felt to be appropriate. Enforcement agents must withdraw without making enquiries if the only persons present are children who appear to be under the age of 12.

Third party premises
Another question which has arisen in a few cases is the extent to which a licence may be inferred when third parties' premises are entered for the purpose of lawful business involving a person who is not resident or employed there. Thus in *Brunner v Williams* [1975] a trading standards officer followed men delivering coke onto premises, believing that they were committing a weights and measures offence. The court held that a licence could cover a person entering on lawful business not with the occupier, but express permission was required to continue with that purpose after entry. In *Morris v Beardmore* [1980] Lord Diplock in the House of Lords queried whether it would be trespass on third party premises where a police officer is acting on lawful business; in *Nevill v Halliday* [1983] Bailey J echoed this, doubting whether an arrest of third party premises was invalidated even in the absence of a third party's implied licence to enter.[42]

Notices

As already discussed, there is a right to enter on the assumption of an implied licence unless the occupier has taken steps to make it clear that such a right is denied. It seems then that it would be perfectly lawful for a person to display notices refusing a right of entry to bailiffs and police officers. In *Lambert v Roberts* [1981] Donaldson LJ said "there can be no doubt that, in the absence of a locked gate or some notice such as 'police keep out' police officers, like all other citizens, have an implied licence to enter the driveway and approach the door of a dwelling house if they have, or reasonably think they have, legitimate business with the occupier."[43] The Australian case of *Nevill v Halliday* repeated this; Brooking J stated that the question of the existence of a licence is one of fact, but the law implies one unless the occupier has "in some way manifested an intention to exclude" such as locking a gate or displaying a notice.[44]

Revocation

As the High Court held in *Halliday v Nevill* (1984), the existence of an implied licence is a question of fact, but it will exist unless there is evidence that such a tacit licence has been negated or revoked. The notices described in the previous paragraph may prevent such a notice being created. Express revocation will terminate it. On revocation the bailiff or other officer has a duty to leave and will become a trespasser if he remains. If he becomes a trespasser, the bailiff's actions will be invalidated.[45]

The key issue therefore, is how the licence may be revoked.

- *revocation clear* If the debtor simply refuses entry before the bailiff is over the threshold the bailiff may not proceed.[46] Equally, if shortly after entry the bailiffs are told specifically to leave and are told that they remain as trespassers, the licence will clearly be revoked.[47] For example in *Lambert v Roberts* [1981] the police officer was told he was on private property- this was considered a clear enough revocation of his licence to be there.[48] Even if obscenity and abuse accompany the revocation, it still can still be effective, as in *Davis v Lisle* [1936] when obscene and abusive instructions to "get outside" were found to be sufficient to revoke a licence and in *Bailey v Wilson* [1968] the appellant "intimated" police officers should leave by saying "You bastard copper, you leave my house." On refusing to leave, they trespassed.[49]

- *revocation unclear* In some cases the revocation may not be sufficiently clear for its purpose to be unequivocal. In *Pamplin v Fraser* [1981], the defendant locked himself in his car parked on his property and refused to get out. As the police did not know the land was his and as there was no unequivocal revocation of the licence, they acted lawfully in remaining. In *Snook v Manion* [1982] the appellant' declaration that he was on his own property and that the police should "fuck off" was found not to be a sufficiently clear revocation of the licence. His words might have been mistaken for mere vulgar expression rather than an express termination of the implied licence. The same conclusion was reached in *R (application of Fullard & Roalfe) v Woking Magistrates Court* [2005]. It was decided that "fuck off you cunt" addressed to a police officer could have been understood to be simply abusive, whereas "fucking get out of my house" was a sufficiently clear revocation of the licence with which the police officer would have had immediately to comply.[50]

The right of revocation applies as much to business premises as to domestic premises. In *Macky v Abrahams* [1916] a police officer entered a shop to investigate an alleged illegal sale made by an employee there. After a discussion with the shopkeeper, he was asked to leave and was then physically escorted from the premises. The court held that, although the keeping of a shop, "implied an invitation or licence to any to enter that shop on the business of the shop," that licence was revocable "at any moment, for any reason or for no reason." A shop keeper can refuse to do business with any customer, and when he orders person to go, the licence is ended.[51] A further issue is who is entitled to revoke the licence. In *McArdle v Wallace* [1964] the question was raised as to whether the son of a café owner was entitled to revoke a police officer's implied licence to enter.[52]

Once the bailiff has commenced the process for which he has entered (that is, the actual selection and listing of goods and placing them under control) time should be given to complete this task before he can reasonably be expected to leave. Reasonable force can be used to resist a premature ejection.[53]

Forcible expulsion
If a licence is revoked, and the bailiff remains, he may be ejected with force.[54] Force should only be used once the person has first been asked to leave.[55] Secondly, force may only be employed once the bailiff has been given a reasonable chance to depart - though he in turn should depart with "all reasonable speed."[56] As to the degree of force that is deemed reasonable, hitting a trespassing police officer has been condoned, as (indeed) has attacking police officers with a car.[57] Repeated blows may well constitute excessive force and an unprovoked attack is not acceptable.[58]

Under false pretences

The NSEA is clear on this situation: "Enforcement agents should not seek to gain peaceable entry to premises under false pretences - for example by asking to use the toilet or to use the telephone. They should be clear as to why they are seeking entry to the premises." In general it appears from the older case law that entry gained under false pretences will not render a levy illegal. The authorities on this are not explicit, but the conclusion may be inferred, particularly from *R v Backhouse* (1771). In the course of executing an arrest warrant an officer gained access by pretending he had a note for the attention of the defendant. When the officer was let in and revealed his true purpose, he was assaulted by Backhouse. At the trial the actual circumstances of the assault were disputed, but Backhouse was held culpable and was fined. The means by which the officer entered initially were neither examined nor criticised, from which it may be implied that they were neither thought wrongful nor a mitigating factor in Backhouse's defence.[59]

Deliberate deception was not considered to make an entry and seizure wrongful, which may explain why mistaken deception was similarly not treated as wrongful. In *Cresswell v Jeffreys* [1912] a bailiff instructed to distrain for rent arrears told the tenant that he could not legally seize his livestock. The tenant had intended to remove them from the property but then did not. The bailiff later seized some of the cattle and was then sued for wrongful distress. It was held that the bailiff's remarks were either a misstatement of law or a declaration of an intention to abandon a legal right, but in neither case could they create an estoppel preventing seizure. A misstatement of law cannot create an estoppel and a representation can only do so if it is regarding existing facts, not an intention. The right to distrain was not waived either, as there was no consideration for the waiver.[60]

It seems that entry under false pretences was only felt to be wrongful if a court was misled by the bailiff as part of the procedure. In one eighteenth century case a sheriff procured a search warrant by pretending stolen goods were on premises so that he could enter with the real aim of arresting the occupant. No search was made for any goods. The court regarded the means used to gain entry as 'undue' or improper.[61] From this we may deduce that a county court bailiff misleading a district judge in seeking permission to force re-entry, might render the levy illegal.

However it should be observed that these cases were all decided before the concept of the licence to enter was elaborated. It has more recently been suggested that any licence to enter is invalidated where the enforcement agent has gained access under false pretences - whether as to the bailiff's identity or purpose.[62] This is because the occupant will have granted permission to enter to one person or for one purpose only. As a consequence entry by someone else or any subsequent attempt to carry through another purpose will be an abuse of that licence and will be trespass.[63] The law on entry by false pretences for the purposes of seizure of goods is thus left rather uncertain. The best course of action is undoubtedly for an enforcement agent not to conceal his/ her identity or purpose - especially as identification and the warrant will have to be produced if requested.

Conclusions: Doubts about the extent of bailiffs' rights of entry under the Act and about the continuing relevance of the wider principles of licences to enter and trespass will doubtless be the source of dispute and litigation. It is likely that enforcement agencies will wish to benefit from the most generous reading of the new legislation and that, backing this up with a threat of prosecution for obstruction (*see 6.6*), may have a powerful tool for gaining entry. Nevertheless, the construction of the Act overall and the lack of explicit abolition of householders' rights must give grounds for an assumption that the fundamental English law has not been altered.

8.4.2 Forced re-entry

As stated earlier, the Act endorses re-entry to premises with a reasonable use of force in order to inspect or remove goods. The former case law suggests two other situations in which it may be appropriate to forcibly re-enter in the context of initial visits for the purposes of taking control of goods.

- *after forcible ejection*: if the bailiff is obliged to leave premises because of threats or the use of force immediately after a lawful first entry or later during the process of seizure and impounding, he may use force to regain entry. Examples include after peaceable entry and during seizure.[64] Force may be employed in such cases even after a considerable delay - in the case of *Eldridge v Stacy* (1863) the bailiff returned three weeks after forcible expulsion. However the bailiff must have made a full entry initially, not just a foot in the door.[65]
- *after forcible exclusion*: If the bailiff leaves temporarily, and returns to find his way barred, he may again use force to get back in.[66] It was argued in this case that force is justified as being kept out by force is equivalent to being turned out by force. This right to re-enter will only apply if the bailiff voluntarily leaves for a short time (and on return only goods previously seized may be taken). The bailiff should not re-enter after a long delay because the goods will

have been abandoned. In one case the bailiff left in a state of 'high excitement, bordering on insanity'. The creditor broke in six days later to remove the goods and was found to have trespassed.[67]

No demand need be made before forcing re-entry.[68] This is because, in the circumstances under discussion, the debtor is taken to know the purpose for which the bailiffs entered and have returned and to be unlawfully obstructing them by preventing entry. Lastly, note that writer David Feldman also proposed that, in light of the judgment in *Southam v Smout* (*see later*), it may also be held lawful for a bailiff to use force to open a door in order to summon help.

8.4.3 Manner of visits

There is guidance as to how a bailiff should conduct him/herself at a person's premises. The NSEA provides variously that agents should not discuss a case with anyone except the debtor if possible, that agents must withdraw if the only person present is, or appears to be, under the age of 18 (though enquiries may be made as to when the debtor will be home) and that they must withdraw without making enquiries if the only persons present are children who appear to be under the age of 12. All information obtained during the administration and enforcement of warrants must be treated as confidential. Where the debtor is not met with, the relevant documents must be left at the address in a sealed envelope addressed to the liable person. Enforcement agents must not act in a way likely to be publicly embarrassing to the debtor, either deliberately or negligently (that is to say through lack of care). Over and above respecting confidentiality, agents must not act in a threatening manner when visiting the debtor by making gestures or taking actions which could reasonably be construed as suggesting harm or risk of harm to debtors.

8.5 Manner of entry - general

The 2007 Act lays down clear rules on the conduct of entries to properties. Certain access routes are sanctioned and the use of force is prohibited except in specific cases (*see 8.6 and 8.7*).

8.5.1 Entry route

The Act has tried deliberately to simplify the confused and illogical law on the routes by which a bailiff may enter premises. The regulations stipulate that entry or re-entry to premises may only be made by:

- Any door or other usual means of entry (such as a loading bay at business premises); or,
- Any usual means of entry to premises other than a building (that is, the normal access routes to an aircraft, ship, hovercraft, tent or other moveable structure).[69]

The purpose of the new guidance is to do away with many of the more exotic routes of entry that case law had come to allow under the older law. These included windows and skylights. It was also accepted that bailiffs could climb over a wall or fence to gain access to premises.[70] Given that the new regulations only allow entry by doors or 'any usual means,' we must assume that climbing over boundaries is no longer permissible. Moreover, the form of the new wording would also appear to prohibit a bailiff climbing over a locked gate in the perimeter of premises, however low that barrier might be.

8.5.2 Usual entry points

The older case authorities dealt with the problem of which doors were protected from forcible entry and may provide helpful guidance in the future. The rule was that all buildings within the boundary of a property were likewise protected. Even if an entrance was within the property boundary but could only be reached by passing through other gates or doors, if it was still treated as the entrance to a dwelling it could not be forced. A door leading to a garden or yard within a property was not an outer door, though.[71] On this, see *Munroe & Munroe v Woodspring District Council* (1979): bailiffs forced entry to a garage in the plaintiffs' garden. The court awarded damages for trespass, for the value and loss of use of the car and for the damage to the garage door.[72]

8.5.3 Usual means of entry

Whilst it is simple enough to insist that only 'usual' means of access are employed, in practice a variety of complications are likely to arise. It was previously held that use of a landlord's pass key is illegal as entering by such means is not "the ordinary way in which visitors gain access".[73] It seems that this will still be the case under the new rules. It does not matter whether the bailiff found the key or it was provided by a landlord.[74] If the key is left in the lock it seems it may be permissible to turn it like a door handle to open the door if it has been left in the lock so as to make the premises accessible to all with a legitimate reason to enter, though whether such a general authority from the householder to enter in such situations can now be assumed seems to be questioned in the judgment in *Southam v Smout* [1963].[75]

If the door is already broken open, it would seem that the bailiff may enter. Such an entry would also act as a justification for subsequent forced entry of an internal door, it seems.[76] It was decided in one case that, regardless of whether a prior bailiff's entry had been trespass, a subsequent bailiff who took advantage of this and entered did not act wrongfully. However, if the bailiff claiming to make a peaceful entry was an associate or colleague accompanying the one who had forced a prior entry, he could not take advantage of the property being accessible and enter without it being trespass: the whole entry is rendered trespass ab initio by the use of force.[77] In *Whalley v Williamson* (1836) a levy was conducted at premises that were only part built. The bailiff entered through a hole in the wall and then forced a boarded over window. It was held that this was trespass because the hole was not intended to have a door or window fitted later, therefore it had to be considered that the 'outer fence' of the house was the boarded window, which was illegally entered by force.[78]

Except where it is sanctioned, it is implicit in the new legislation that no measure of force may be applied to gain access to any premises. The former caselaw may provide some helpful parameters here. The bailiff could enter by an open door; he could also open and enter an unlocked door on the grounds that he had legal authority under the warrant to use the door in the ordinary way just as other visitors to the premises might.[79] It was permissible to apply light pressure to a door to see if it was locked and to open it if not.[80] Breaking open a door or gate in a wall was trespass.[81] The use of a locksmith to open a door was illegal and otherwise removing or damaging locks and chains was likewise wrongful.[82] On this point see *Beaver Steel Inc v Skylark Ventures Ltd* [1984] in which it was held that picking and then changing a lock was a forced entry by a bailiff for which he and the landlord were both liable; the landlord had queried the legality of the procedure but had failed to get advice.[83] If an obstruction had been placed against the door by a person but s/he then permitted the bailiff to remove this to enter the door, the entry was legal provided that no force was used.[84] If a door was nailed shut, it was illegal to force it open.[85]

8.5.4 Unusual cases

The legality of entry in a couple of special circumstances might still need to be considered:

Assistance
in *Nash v Lucas* (1867) the court dealt with a question not addressed in the new Act: may a bailiff be let in by a third party already on the premises? In *Nash* the bailiff encouraged a workman employed by the

landlord to let himself into the house by opening a shut window so that he could then open the locked front door to admit the bailiff. As he acted at the behest of the bailiff the whole entry was held to be illegal. However reference was made to *Sandon v Jarvis* (1859) where a bailiff arrested a man by touching him through an already broken window. This action was held to be legal and the principle could be extended to 'assisted entry'.[86]

To escape
It was an established principle of the former law, which presumably should be considered to be preserved under the new statute, that a bailiff might use force to escape from premises if he is locked in and is unable to continue the levy.[87] It is not certain whether any demand for release should be made before force is employed in such cases. In the case cited no-one remained in the property to assist, but it might be reasonable in other cases for the bailiff to exercise this precaution.

8.6 Manner of entry - by force without warrant

Force may be used to make an initial entry to enforce two debts, fines and judgments against businesses. The NSEA nonetheless supplements this statutory right to force re-entry, advising agents that the power should only be used to the extent that it is reasonably required and only after the debtor has been warned that the power exists and the consequences of a wilful refusal to co-operate.

Certain debts may also be enforced using forced re-entry to premises by the bailiff without any need for any sanction from the court or creditor.[88] Finally note that the enforcement agent is required to leave the premises as effectively secured as he finds them.[89]

8.6.1 Forced entry to collect fines

More specifically the Act states that where the enforcement agent has a right to enter the premises (whether under the general right, as a re-entry to remove previously seized goods or under a warrant to third party premises) and where that bailiff is acting under an enforcement power conferred by a warrant of control under section 76(1) of the Magistrates' Courts Act 1980 for the recovery of a sum adjudged to be paid by a conviction, 'reasonable force' may be used if the bailiff considers it to be 'necessary.'[90]

This wording reproduces the form of Domestic Violence, Crime & Victims Act 2004 which amended the Magistrates Court Act 1980 and granted a right to force entry in fines recovery a decade ago.[91] There has been no judicial interpretation of the terms and they must be presumed to have their normal, everyday meaning. The degree of force that is reasonable must judged by the circumstances and should be proportionate to the resistance or obstruction that is met.

8.6.2 Judgments against businesses

If an enforcement agent reasonably believes that a debtor carries on a trade or business from premises, reasonable force may also be used to gain entry in order to execute a writ or warrant issued for the enforcement of a county court or High Court judgment. This power does not apply to warrants of control issued for road traffic penalties under the Traffic Management Act 2004.[92]

This provision reproduces the former common law rule applicable to executions.[93] The right to use force did not apply if the non-domestic premises were connected to a dwelling, even though they might have had separate entrances and no communicating doors - for instance a flat over a shop.[94] Further, the courts' guidance was that, before using force, the bailiff should make enquiry as to the presence of goods first.[95] These rules will probably still be good practice for enforcement agents.

8.7 Manner of entry - by force with a warrant

In certain cases it may be possible for an enforcement agent to force initial entry to premises provided that a court warrant has first been obtained.[96] This applies if an enforcement agent has power to effect an initial entry to premises either under paragraph 14 (the general right) or under a warrant under paragraph 15 (to specified premises) and if certain debts are being enforced. If the enforcement agent applies to the court it may issue a warrant which authorises him to use, if necessary, reasonable force to enter the premises or to do anything for which entry is authorised. The question of the degree of forced deemed 'reasonable' is discussed in the previous section.

Warrants may be sought by enforcement agents to enter either premises or vehicles. In either case, a warrant issued by a court under paragraph 20 or provision included under paragraph 21 may also require any constable to assist the enforcement agent to execute the warrant.[97]

8.7.1 Warrants to enter premises

If an enforcement agent is applying under paragraph 15 for a warrant to enter specified premises at which the debtor neither lives nor trades the court may include in the warrant provision authorising him to use, if necessary, reasonable force to enter the premises or to do anything for which entry is authorised.[98]

The court may not issue a warrant including a provision under paragraph 21 permitting the use of reasonable force unless it is satisfied that prescribed conditions are met. The conditions of which the court must be satisfied before it issues a warrant under paragraph 20(2) of Schedule 12, or includes a provision permitting force in a warrant under paragraph 21(2), are as follows:[99]

- the enforcement agent is entering premises under either paragraph 14 or 15 of Schedule 12 (initial entry to the debtor's home or business premises or to other specified premises with a court warrant); and,
- either the enforcement agent is attempting to recover a tax debt enforceable under section 127 of the Finance Act 2008 or the premises are premises to which the goods have been deliberately removed in order to avoid them being taken into control; and,
- there are, or are likely to be, goods of the debtor on the premises of which control can be taken; and,
- the enforcement agent has explained to the court-
    - the likely means of entry, and the type and amount of force that will be required to make the entry successfully;
    - how, after entry, the enforcement agent proposes to leave the premises in a secure state; and,
    - in all the circumstances an authorisation ought to be given, having regard (among other matters) to the sum outstanding and the nature of the debt.

As part of the application to court on N244, the enforcement agent must provide the court with sufficient evidence and information to satisfy the court that the conditions specified are met.[100] Given that, in many cases, an forced entry to a third party's premises will be proposed, it is reasonable to suspect that courts may require a high degree of proof of the presence and value of goods before granting a warrant.

8.7.2 Warrants to enter vehicles

Where the enforcement agent wishes to take control of goods on a highway (*see 9.4 below for definition of this term*), the conditions of which the court must be satisfied before it issues a warrant allowing the use of force are:[101]

- the enforcement agent is attempting to recover a debt enforceable by virtue of a writ or warrant as described below, or to collect taxes due under section 127 of the Finance Act 2008;
- the enforcement agent has explained to the court the type and amount of force that will be required to take control of the goods; and,
- in all the circumstances an authorisation ought to be given, having regard to (among other matters) the sum outstanding and the nature of the debt.

As part of the application on N244, the enforcement agent must provide the court with sufficient evidence and information to satisfy the court that the conditions specified are met.[102]

The writs and warrants which would justify the grant of a warrant allowing forced entry on the highway are:

- High Court writs of control which confer a power to recover a sum of money;
- High Court writs of delivery which confer a power to take control of goods and sell them to recover a sum of money;
- High Court writs of possession which confer a power to take control of goods and sell them to recover a sum of money;
- county court warrants of control issued under to section 85 of the County Courts Act 1984 but not those that are issued by Traffic Enforcement Centre to recover a traffic contravention debts as defined by section 82 of the Traffic Management Act 2004;
- county court warrants of delivery which also confer a power to take control of goods and sell them to recover a sum of money;
- county court warrants of possession which also contain a power to take control of goods and sell them to recover a sum of money; and,
- a magistrates' court warrant of control issued under section 76 of the Magistrates' Courts Act 1980.

It is assumed here that an application to use force will be made in circumstances where it is known (or strongly suspected) that valuable assets are contained within a lorry or van located on the highway. Given the degree of uncertainty over this - and the mobility of vehicles and assets- such applications may actually prove to be quite rare.

8.8 Personnel

An enforcement agent may take other people onto the premises who may assist him in exercising any power, including a power to use force.[103] Those persons must not remain on the premises without the enforcement agent, however. In addition the enforcement agent may take any necessary equipment onto the premises (for removing large and/or heavy chattels, for example). The agent may leave equipment on the premises if s/he leaves controlled goods secured there. This will not be construed as a trespass on the debtors' premises.

8.9 Identification & notice

The enforcement agent must on request show the debtor and any person who appears to him to be in charge of the premises evidence of his identity, and his authority to enter the premises. Such a request may be made before the enforcement agent enters the premises or while he is there.[104]

Further, after entering premises or a vehicle on the highway the enforcement agent must provide a notice for the debtor giving information about what the enforcement agent has done.[105] The regulations state that the notice must be in writing and must contain the following information:[106]

· The debtor's name and address;
· The enforcement agent's name and reference numbers and the date of the notice;
· Confirmation that the agent has entered the premises - and their address;
· The sum outstanding on the date of the notice;
· Details of any goods taken into control (see chapter 9). If goods are 'seized' a single document serves to give notice of both the entry and the taking. Even if no levy takes place, though, a notice will still be required; and,
· Details of how payment may be made to prevent further action and the time limits for doing this.

This notice provided after entry (as distinct from seizure) is an innovation. Its purpose must be to ensure that debtors understand exactly what steps have been taken, why and by whom at every point in the enforcement process - and more particularly, what charges have been made for these.

If the debtor is on the premises when the enforcement agent is there, the enforcement agent must give him the notice then. If the debtor is not there, the enforcement agent must leave the notice in a conspicuous place on the premises. If the enforcement agent knows that there is someone else there or that there are other occupiers, a notice he leaves behind on the premises must be in a sealed envelope addressed to the debtor. If the premises are occupied by any person apart from the debtor, the enforcement agent must leave at the premises a list of any goods he takes away.

In magistrates' courts additional rules apply. There is a duty to provide identification as follows. Each authorised individual shall be issued by the approved enforcement agency with an identity card bearing their photograph and a photographic reproduction of the authorisation from the court, and this should be carried at all times and shown to the person against whom the warrant is being executed - otherwise it should be produced on demand from any other individual when executing warrants.[107] Having executed any warrant a CEO or enforcement agent has a duty to produce identification on demand from the defendant. This should be done as soon as is practicable. The identification should be a written statement giving the person's name, employment details and, if they are a CEO or employee of an approved enforcement agency, their certificate of authorisation.[108] There is now a statutory duty to state the reasons for the issue of the warrant that is being executed.[109] It is also provided that the contract between the MCC and the enforcement agency should require the bailiff to hand to the defendant a leaflet providing the following information:

· the purpose of the visit by the bailiff;
· the powers vested in the enforcement agency;
· how any sum due, in respect of which the warrant being executed was issued, may be paid;
· where advice about the effect of the warrant and related matters may be obtained (presumably it will be sufficient for the enforcement agency to direct the defendant to a local CAB or solicitor);
· the charges that may be made in respect of the warrant;
· details of the complaints procedures operated by the MCC and the agency.[110]

These new rules confirm the existing common law duty to give reasons.

8.10 The right to remain

The entry to premises is for a sole purpose, of course- to search for goods that may be taken into control - and the Regulations make clear that the right of entry carries with it a right for an enforcement agent to remain on premises in order to search for and take control of sufficient goods.[111] However, as noted earlier, reg.22(4) supplements this possibly broad power by emphasising that bailiffs should not remain longer than is reasonably necessary to complete their task.

These new regulations supplement the former case law, the principles of which are still worth remembering. Hitherto, the courts ruled that, once goods had been taken into control, the bailiff should not remain an unreasonable time.[112] For example in one case a bailiff stayed fifteen days on the premises and was held to be a trespasser for remaining too long and disturbing the plaintiff's possession. Indeed, unreasonable possession by a sheriff was held to render the execution trespass ab initio. The sheriff had entered into the property on April 10th and remained twelve hours. This was repeated on diverse days over the next month. Sale of the seized goods was held on the premises, without the debtor's consent, on April 26th, but the sheriff remained constantly on the premises for a further ten days even though the goods could have been sold and removed in only a few hours. This major disturbance of the debtor's possession was held to have been wholly illegal.[113] Similarly a sheriff remaining in possession for nearly six months was found to be trespass.[114]

In addition, it is stipulated that an enforcement agent should not attempt to remain on premises after initial entry if:

· The debtor is found to be a child under 16 years of age; or,
· The only persons present are found to be either a child or vulnerable person (whether more than one of each or a combination of both).[115]

8.11 Repeat entries

There will inevitably be situations when, for whatever reason (deliberate or accidental) the debtor has no seizeable assets on the premises at the time of the bailiff's first visit. Regulation 24 of the Taking Control of Goods Regulations makes provision for those occasions when no or insufficient goods to cover the debt are found at the time of the initial entry.

The enforcement agent is entitled to re-enter the premises on a second or subsequent occasion to search for goods in two specific circumstances. Firstly a repeat visit may be made if there is a genuine reason to believe that goods have been brought onto the premises since the bailiff's last visit and that these are items worth taking into control. An agent should be able to demonstrate good grounds for any decision to make a return visit. The kinds of situation in which it might be appropriate to re-enter to take control of further goods might include:

· Where it is believed that goods which were removed to other premises to avoid seizure have been returned to the debtor's home

or workplace;
· Where a business may have brought new stock onto its premises; or,
· Where new assets may have been acquired- for example, at gifts or perhaps as a result of inheritance.

As the regulation refers to items "brought" onto premises it appears that the natural increase in value of items already present at the time of the bailiff's first attendance - such as growing crops or maturing livestock - are not covered.

Secondly, a repeat visit may be made where a previous attempt to take control was prevented by the fact that the goods in question were in use at the time and the agent feared that an attempt to seize them could have precipitated a breach of the peace (*see 10.4.2 below*). In such circumstances, the agent may only take control of the goods which were being used on the earlier occasion (unless it is also discovered that wholly new chattels have been brought onto the premises by the debtor).[116]

Creditors should potentially benefit from these changes as it establishes an explicit right to keep endeavouring to enforce a warrant, which may be particularly significant when combined with the fact that a warrant remains valid for a year after the issue of the enforcement notice.[117] It will be good practice to provide a debtor with some kind of notice or statement at the conclusion of the first levy that it is considered insufficient and may be topped up. Whilst it could be self-defeating to be too specific in this, an individual is still entitled to know what is likely to follow next- further visits to take control of goods or a removal for sale. Once removal for sale has begun, the right to add to the inventory will have been terminated (*see too 11.2.7 below*).

8.12 Police presence

In addition to the new duties of constables to assist in certain forced entries and re-entries (subject to the issue of a court warrant), and the existing duty of constables to assist HCEOs in the execution of writs that is preserved by Courts Act 2003,[118] a police officer may be called by a bailiff to attend a levy or forced entry if a threat of violence can be shown.[119] The officer's presence would be to prevent a breach of the peace and not to assist in the seizure. A breach of the peace may be defined as a situation when and where:

· harm is actually done or is likely to be done to a person whether by the conduct of the person against whom the breach is alleged or by

someone provoking that breach;
· harm is actually done or is likely to be done to a person's property in his presence, provided that the natural consequences of such harm is likely to be a violent retaliation; or,
· a person is genuinely in fear of harm to him/herself or property in their presence as a result of an assault.

The police can arrest the person who commits, or who they reasonably believe will commit, a breach of the peace.

A request for police attendance can only be justified by a bailiff if it can be shown that it was necessary because of threats of resistance or violence or similar circumstances met on a previous visit.[120] Conversely, for the occupier of premises, if a person enters and makes a noise or disturbs the peace it is lawful for the occupier to eject him if he refuses to leave or for the police to be called.[121]

A number of other cases have elaborated on the nature of breaches of the peace and how the police should respond. If a breach of the peace occurs within an officer's sight he is bound to intervene immediately.[122] What constitutes a breach can include refusing to leave a property and resisting expulsion when causing a disturbance.[123] Also wrongful would be an attempt at forcible entry to premises, despite resistance.[124] However, mere trespass is not a breach of the peace, so that simply refusing to leave a property and creating a disturbance does not justify an arrest[125] - nor does ringing on a door bell and making a noise in order to gain entry.[126] It is clear from these cases that the common threat in correspondence to attend with police is at least misleading and should not be made as a matter of course. Both parties are entitled to have the police present if there is a genuine threat of violence. Other attendance or threats of police attendance are inappropriate and should be taken up with the local constabulary as well as with the bailiffs' firm, even if no action is taken for illegal taking of goods.

Guidance given to the Metropolitan Police is that officers asked to attend levies should first check that the warrant is valid; that their entry to the premises should only be by invitation of the occupier or in order to prevent a breach of the peace; that officers should remain impartial and only become involved if an offence is occurring or possible; that they should not assist the bailiff in any way, such as advising the occupier to open the door. However they should prevent the bailiff committing any criminal offence. This advice is tempered by the recommendation that the constables' duty is to ensure that the bailiff is not hindered or resisted in any way. There is a concern about the police becoming liable to the creditor for unreasonably preventing the bailiff enforcing a warrant. Also the guidance appears to assume that only a debtor might commit a breach of the peace.

Given the above, it is useful to examine a recent case on this issue. In *Bibby v Chief Constable of Essex* [2000] the Court of Appeal reconsidered these issues.[127] Bibby was arrested after he sought to remove goods under a lawful possession agreement and was met with resistance. He claimed for assault and wrongful imprisonment. The Court of Appeal set out a list of conditions which must be satisfied in order to justify the arrest of a bailiff for breach of the peace:

· there must be the clearest of circumstances and a sufficiently real and present threat to the peace to justify arresting a person who is not acting unlawfully;
· the threat to the peace must be coming from the person who is arrested, who must be acting unreasonably;
· that conduct must interfere with the rights of others, and the natural and not wholly unreasonable response to that conduct must be violence.

The Court the elaborated the principles of breach of the peace as applicable to cases of taking control of goods:

· neither a lawful taking by a bailiff nor a refusal to leave a building lawfully entered could justify a breach of the peace by an occupier;
· exercising the rights and duties of a bailiff is not a breach of the peace;
· a bailiff is entitled to call for police assistance if there is a genuine fear that violence will be employed. To do this would not be unreasonable behaviour and does not interfere with the rights of others (the Court emphasised that removal for the purposes of sale does not interfere with any right the debtor has in goods subject to a controlled goods agreement);
· If the debtor in such a situation uses violence it will be wholly unreasonable.

Bibby's arrest was unjustified and the use of handcuffs was particularly unnecessary. However, the Court did not go so far as to say that a bailiff could never be arrested. Whilst it felt that in this case the arresting officer had wrongly analysed who was potentially liable to cause the breach of the peace, and that there was nothing in the evidence to suggest that Bibby had acted unreasonably or was likely to initiate violence, Pill LJ stated:

"I do not of course exclude the possibility that a bailiff, or someone in a similar position, might behave so outrageously, short of violence, that he is likely to provoke a not wholly unreasonable violent reaction from others, thereby justifying his arrest."

The rights of bailiffs and police in these situations have also been considered in light of the ECHR.[128] A complaint was brought under article 8 (*see above*) after police entered a house in the company of an ex-husband who wished to remove his possessions. The European Court considered the common law powers of the police to prevent breaches of the peace. Their right to enter and remain on premises and to arrest an offending person were felt to be 'in accordance with law', for a 'legitimate aim' (that is the pressing social need to prevent disorder and crime) and 'necessary in a democratic society' if there was a risk of physical harm to a person or their property. However, in the case in question the police's entry the house was 'disproportionate'. With only an elderly woman at home, there was no risk of a breach of the peace taking place. It was immaterial that there had been a genuine concern that there would have been a breach if the ex-wife had been there. The police failed to strike a fair balance between respect for the home and the prevention of crime and disorder, and had failed to show that their actions were proportionate to the degree of risk existing at the time. In the absence of a significant and indisputable threat to persons or property their interference could not be justified.

To conclude, police attending levies need to be satisfied of the bailiff's right or need to enter the premises. Additionally there is no right for the police to enter property if the debtor is absent or there is otherwise no likelihood of a breach of the peace.

8.13 Failed entry

If the bailiff fails to gain entry or find any adequate goods on a first visit s/he will not immediately give up on the levy. S/he will try once or twice again, very likely at different times (something which is now explicitly sanctioned in the rules - *see 8.11 above*) and may make also discrete local enquiries in the neighbourhood as to whether the debtor still trades or lives at the address. If they still do not meet with success a return of 'no goods' or 'no sufficient goods' may be made to the creditor. The case law on this matter is discussed later.

8.14 Criminal sanctions for unlawful entries

There is no reason why a bailiff acting under a warrant may not commit, or be accused of, a criminal offence.[129] Experience suggests that the police are often reluctant to become involved in anything that may be classed a 'civil matter' and, other than a warning against a breach of the peace, they are unlikely to take criminal proceedings.

8.14.1 Forced entry

Under section 6 of the Criminal Law Act 1977 it is an offence for any person to use or threaten violence, without lawful authority, in order to secure entry into any premises. On summary conviction a person can be fined up to level five and/or be sentenced to up to 6 months in prison. For the entry to be treated as a criminal offence there must be someone on the premises opposed to the entry and the bailiff seeking to enter must know this. It is immaterial whether the violence was directed against the premises or person. If such an entry is in progress the police may be called by the debtor and under subsection 6, a uniformed constable is empowered to arrest, without warrant, anyone with reasonable cause suspected of committing such an offence. Despite its age, there has been no reported use of this provision.

Note also that a criminal entry may also involve criminal damage under Criminal Damage Act 1971. This offence arises wherever another's property is intentionally or recklessly destroyed or damaged without lawful excuse, or threats to that effect are made. The offence is triable on indictment and on conviction the penalty is imprisonment for up to ten years. Self defence- or defence of another - are lawful excuses for the offence but it is doubtful if the existence of a warrant per se would assist the bailiff. There is no power of arrest by constable at the time the offence is being committed, as with forced entry.

8.14.2 Unlawful wounding

Unlawful wounding or other bodily harm can be prosecuted if a bailiff's actions cause any malicious injury. For example, in ex p. Smith (1890) a bailiff broke open a door with excessive force whilst trying to levy execution. The bailiff was convicted by the magistrates.[130] The offence is imprisonable. Assault is also an offence for which the court may fine or imprison a person.

8.14.3 Criminal contempt

It is a misdemeanour and contempt for a civil court bailiff to commit certain offences when in execution of their duty.[131] The High Court may fine or commit the offender.

8.15 Claims for trespass

The impact of Sch.12 para.66 of the Act, combined with the entry provisions, is to remove most of the scope for initiating claims for trespass against enforcement agents. In most cases the remedy for a disputed entry will arise under the Act alone (*see 13.6 below*). A claim for trespass will in future only be possible where the bailiff acts wholly without authority. Possible instances might be:

 · Where the premises entered were those of a third party entirely unconnected with the liable person; or,
 · Where the debt had been cleared before the levy took place, so that the validity of the warrant had ceased.

In these cases claims for damages and injunctions, and a reliance on the principle of void ab initio, may still be possible.

8.16 Previous areas of concern

Advisers have encountered the following problems with rights of entry under the former law:

Deception
Bailiffs being misleading as to their identity or the reason for their visit in order to gain access;

Calling the police
In order to add further psychological pressure to encourage the debtor to allow entry. In most such cases no breach of the place was taking place, nor was any threatened. Not infrequently the door was closed and the debtor was inside the property, so that a breach of the peace was a remote possibility.

Placing a foot in the door
It appears to have been the belief of many firms and their staff that placing a foot in the door in order to prevent the person exercising their legal right to close it against the bailiff was a lawful act. Given

such confusion over what should have been a very clear matter of basic principle, there is clearly reason for concern over the use of the new powers - or their simple avoidance.

Footnotes

1 *Eddowes v Argentine Loan & Mercantile Agency Co Ltd* (1890) 62 LT 602.

2 *Herries v Jamieson* (1794) 5 TR 553.

3 *Abbot v Smith* (1774) 2 Wm Bl 947; *Clarke v Clement & English* (1796) 6 TR 525; 1 Ld Raym 244.

4 Respectively articles 31(3), 37 (1) & (2) & 22(3) Sch 1, Diplomatic Privileges Act 1971; 1 B&C 554.

5 s1(2) & (3) Reserve & Auxiliary Forces (Protection of Civil Interests) Act 1951 respectively as amended by TCEA Sch13 para.26; *Stepney BC v Woolf* [1943] KB 202.

6 CPR 83.2(4) & 8).

7 s185 Army Act 1955; s185 Air Force Act 1955 and s102 Naval Discipline Act 1957.

8 *Magnay v Burt* (1843) 5 QB 381.

9 Regulations 10 Taking Control of Goods Regs 2013 - nor should premises be entered - reg.23.

10 LGO decision against Torbay BC, 10 002 564.

11 Schedule 12 para.25.

12 Taking Control of Goods Regulations 2013 reg.21.

13 Regulation 22 Taking Control of Goods Regulations 2013.

14 Reg.22(3)-(5).

15 CPR 84.7.

16 Sch.12 para.14.

17 Sch.12 para.14(2) & (3).

18 MCA s.125 & 125B(1).

19 Sch.12 para 14(4).

20 Sch.12 para14(5).

21 CPR 84.9.

22 See for example *Cooke v Birt* (1814) 5 Taunt 765 or *Sheers v Brooks* (1792) 2 H Bl 120.

23 *Winter v Miles* [1809] 10 East 578; *AG v Dakin* [1820] 4 HL 338.

24 *Combe v De La Bere* [1882] 22 Ch D 316.

25 Schedule 12 para 31(1).

26 Paragraph 32(1).

27 Sch.12 para.33.

28 1 Cowp 1.

29 3 WWR 361.

30 See the discussion in *Kirkpatrick v Kelly* (1781) 3 Doug KB 30 and *Piggot v Wilkes* (1820) 3 B & Ald 502.

31 CPR 75.7(7)-(10).

32 Reg.23 TCG Regs.

33 Respectively All ER 41 & 2 All ER 753.

34 *Lambert v Roberts* [1981] 2 All ER 15; *Schoenau v Brymer* [1990] 89 Sask R 30; *Dobie v Parker* [1983] WAR 48; *Transport Ministry v Payn* [1977] 2 NZLR 50 CA.

35 *Great Central Railway v Bates* [1921] 3 KB 578.

36 *Lambert v Roberts* above; *R v Roberts* [2003] EWCA Crim 2753; *Bailey v Wilson* [1968] Crim LR 617; *Halliday v Nevill* [1984] 155 CLR 1; *Robson v Hallett* [1967] 2 QB 939 (see *Sources of bailiff law* c.2 p.46); in flats see *Knox v Anderton* [1983] Crim LR 115.

37 *R v Leroy Lloyd Roberts* [2003] EWCA 2753.

38 Shop - *Mackay v Abrahams* [1916] VLR 681; café - *McArdle v Wallace* [1964] Crim LR 467; garage - *Davis v Lisle* [1936] 2 KB 434.

39 Crim LR 453.

40 Crim LR 340.

41 128 DLR 726.

42 Crim LR 250; 2 All ER 753; 2 VR 553.

43 2 All ER 15 at p.19.

44 2 VR 553 at 556; see too *Bailey v Wilson* [1968] Crim LR 617 on an unlocked gate as an implied licence to enter; also *Snook v Manion* [1982] Crim LR 601 and *Robson v Hallett* [1967] 2 QB 939 (see *Sources of bailiff law* c.2 p.46).

45 155 CLR 1; duty to leave - *Dobie v Pinker* [1983] WAR 48; *Bailey v Wilson* [1968] Crim LR 618; *Morris v Beardmore* [1980]; *R v Allen* [1981] Crim LR 326.

46 *Semaynes Case* (1604) Yelv 29; *Vaughan v McKenzie* [1968] 1 All ER 154 - see *Sources of bailiff law* c.2 p.54.

47 See cases already cited - *Transport Ministry v Payn*; *R v Allen* [1981]; *Robson v Hallett* [1967] - see *Sources of bailiff law* c.2. p.46; *Morris v Beardmore* [1980].

48 2 All ER 15.

49 See too *R (Wayne & Ryan Roalfe) v Woking Magistrates Court* [2005] EWHC 2922 (Admin).

50 Respectively RTR 494; Crim LR 601; EWHC 2922 (Admin).

51 VLR 681.

52 Crim LR 467.

53 Reasonable time - *Mathews v Dwan* [1949] NZLR 1037 and *Kay v Hibbert* [1977] Crim LR 226; reasonable force - *Schoenau v Brymer* [1990] 89 Sask R 30.

54 *Green v Bartram* (1830) 4 C&P 308.

55 *Green v Goddard* 2 Salk 641; *Polkinhorn v Wright* (1845) 8 QB 195.

56 *Lambert v Roberts* [1981]; *Robson v Hallett* [1967] - see *Sources of bailiff law* c.2 p.46; *R (Wayne & Ryan Roalfe) v Woking Magistrates Court* [2005] EWHC 2922 (Admin).

57 Punching - *March v Jones* (1991) 91 Nfld & PEIR 307; car - *McLorie v Oxford* [1982] 1 QB 1290.

58 *Gregory v Hall* (1799) 8 TR 299; *Simpson v Morris* (1813) 4 Taunt 821.

59 Lofft 61.

60 28 TLR 413.

61 *Anon* [1758] 2 Keny 372/ 96 ER 1214.

62 See David Feldman, *Law regarding entry, search & seizure*, Butterworths, 1986, para.s 2.09- 2.10 for an analogous situation.

63 *Cundy & Bevington v Lindsay* [1878] 3 App Cas 459.

64 *Eagleton v Gutteridge* (1843) 11 M&W 465; *Francome v Pinche* (1766) Esp NP (3rd Edn) 382.

65 (1863) 15 CBNS 458; *Boyd v Profaze* (1867) 16 LT 431.

66 *Bannister v Hyde* (1860) 2 E&E 627.

67 *Russell v Rider* (1834) 6 C&P 416.

68 *Aga Kurboolie Mahomed v R* [1843] 4 Moo PCC 239.

69 Reg.20 TCG Regs.

70 For the cases see *Law of seizure of goods*, 2nd edition, 7.4.3 or *Sources of bailiff law* c.2.

71 *American Concentrated Must Co v Hendry* (1893) 57 JP 521; *Hopkins v Nightingale* (1794) 1 Esp 99.

72 (1979) CLY 2226.

73 *Miller v Curry* [1893] 25 NSR 537.

---

74 See *Welch v Krakovsky* [1919] WWR 361.

75 *Ryan v Shilcock* (1851) 7 Exch 72 (see *Sources of bailiff law* c.2 p.28); [1963] 3 All ER 104 (see *Sources of bailiff law* c.2 p.35).

76 See the case of *Levitt v. Dymoke* (1868) 3 Ir CL 1.

77 *Henderson v. McGuigan & Thompson* [1933] 3 WWR 230.

78 (1836) 7 C&P 294.

79 *Budd v Pyle* (1846) 10 JP 203; *Ryan v Shilcock* (1851) 7 Exch 72.

80 *McKinnon v McKinley* [1856] 1 PEI 113.

81 *Long v Clarke* [1893] 1 QB 119.

82 Hardwick CJ (1735) cited in *Viner's Abridgment.*

83 [1984] 47 BCLR 99.

84 *McKay v Douglas* [1919] 44 DLR 570.

85 *Russell v Buckley* [1885] 25 NBR 264.

86 (1867) 2 QB 590 (see *Sources of bailiff law* c.2 p.30) ; (1859) EB & E 935.

87 *Pugh v Griffith* (1838) 7 Ad & El 827.

88 Sch.12 paras 17 & 19; see 11.2 later.

89 Sch.12 paragraph 30.

90 Sch.12 para.18.

91 s.125BA(3) &125BA(5) MCA.

92 Sch.12 para.18A.

93 Force could be used to enter a workshop (*Hodder v Williams* [1895] 2 QB 663) or a barn (*Penton v Browne* (1664) 1 Keb 698).

94 *Hudson v Fletcher* [1909] 2 Sask LR 489.

95 *Hobson v Thelluson* [1867] 2 QB 642.

96 Sch.12 para.20.

97 Sch.12 para.22.

98 Sch.12 para.21.

99 Reg.28 TCG Regs.

100 CPR 84.9.

101 Sch.12 para.31(1) & reg.29 TCG Regs.

102 CPR 84.10.

103 Sch.12 para.27.

104 Schedule 12 para.26 and see discussion at 7.1.3.

105 Sch.12 para.28.

106 Reg.30 TCG Regs.

107 Reg.11(6) & (7)(b).

108 ss125A(4) & 125B(4) MCA; Pt 18.11(2) & 52.8 Crim PR.

109 Ss125(A)(4) & 125(B)(4) MCA; Pt 18.11(2) & 52.8 Crim PR.

110 Reg.6(12) Approval of Enforcement Agencies Regulations 2000.

111 Reg.21(1)(a) TCG Regs.

112 *Cartwright v Comber* 2 Ld Raym 1427; *Cooke v Birt* (1814) 5 Taunt 765; *Winterbourne v Morgan* (1774) 11 East 395.

113 5 Taunt 198; see also *Ash v Dawnay* (1852) 8 Exch 237; *Lee v Dangar & Co* [1892] 1 QB 231 and *Chase v. Scripture* (1857) 14 UCQB 598 - trespass by the landlord remaining 9 days and assuming control of the house and business.

114 *Reed v Harrison* (1778) 2 Wm Bl 1218.

115 Reg.23 Taking Control of Goods Regulations.

116 Reg.24(2)(b) & (3) TCG Regs.

117 See next chapter and reg.9(1) TCG Regs.

118 Sch.7 para.5.

119 *Skidmore v Booth* (1854) 6 C&P 777 - see *Sources of bailiff law* c.2 p.56.

120 *Skidmore v Booth* as above.

121 *Green v Bartram* (1830) 4C&P 308; *Shaw v Chairitie* (1850) 3 C&K 21.
122 *Anon* (1593) Poph 12.
123 *Howell v Jackson* (1834) 6 C&P 723.
124 *Ingle v Bell* (1836) 1 M&W 516.
125 *Green v Bartram* (1830) 4 C&P 308; *Jordan v Gibbon* (1863) 8 LT 391.
126 *R v Bright* (1830) 4 C&P 387; *Grant v Moser* (1843) 5 M&G 123.
127 (2000) Casetrack, April 6th - see *Sources of bailiff law* c.2 p.58.
128 *McLeod v UK* (1998) application no. 72/1997/856/1065; [1999] 1 EHRLR 125.
129 *R v Beacontree JJ ex p Mercer* [1970] Crim LR 103.
130 7 TLR 42.
131 s.29 Sheriff's Act 1887.

Chapter 9

Taking control of goods

The second major feature of the new Act (after rights of entry) is its reshaping of the procedure for levying upon goods. The complex former law on seizure and impounding is replaced with a simpler, harmonised process, termed 'taking control of goods.' This new regime has a number of significant aspects:

- · Enforcement agents are provided with a wider range of means of taking control of goods; but,
- · These means of taking control are formalised in statute and therefore must be conducted correctly in the manner prescribed.

The effects of this may be two-fold: doubts about the legality of clamping and other practices are removed, but the obligation upon the bailiff to adhere strictly to the rules will be considerably greater.

We must consider briefly the effect of taking control. Under the former law, it was said that seized goods were impounded by the bailiff 'in the custody of the law.' Securing goods in legal custody gave them protection from interference by the debtor (termed 'poundbreach') and gave the bailiff the right to force re-entry and sell them. Although the new Act does not use this term, we may infer that taking control will have an analogous effect. The Act creates self-contained enforcement powers permitting a bailiff to seize and sell goods for certain debts. Goods taken into control for this purpose remain 'controlled goods' until they are either sold or abandoned. Title is passed only by sale under the Act; if abandoned, the goods cease to be subject to the enforcement power. Whilst controlled, they are protected against interference by the debtor. All these provisions operate to give controlled goods a special status which is likely to be recognised in subsequent judgments interpreting the Act. This impact of taking into control is certainly reinforced by the binding effect of the issue of an instruction or enforcement (*see 7.2 above*) - if it is not in fact entirely replaced by it (*see also 10.11 later on previous levies*).

9.1 Time for taking control of goods

The new regulations distinguish between entry to premises and seizure of goods as two separate stages for which it is necessary separately to specify permissible times for enforcement. This has been done, we must infer, partly for the purposes of complete clarity and partly to deal with situations in which an entry might be made but which does not lead (for whatever reason) to goods being taken into control.

9.1.1 Deadline for taking control

Readers should recall (*see 7.5 above*) that generally goods should be taken into control within 12 months after the notice of enforcement was served.[1] This deadline may be extended by agreeing a repayment scheme with the debtor by application to court by the bailiff for a further twelve months.

The application to extend the deadline must be made on form N244 supported by:

- · a witness statement from the person making the application confirming that no previous application has been made to extend that period; and,
- · the applicant's grounds for not taking control of goods of the debtor during the initial period allowed.

If the bailiff submits the application before the first twelve month period has expired and the court subsequently orders the period of extension requested, it shall start on the day after the expiry of the initial period - or on such later day as the court may order.

If the court orders the period of extension the applicant must serve a copy of the extension order on the debtor - and on the creditor, enforcement agent or enforcement officer as appropriate - and if the goods are to be taken into control by virtue of a warrant or writ of control, or of any other writ or warrant conferring the power to use the Sch.12 procedure, the court will endorse on the warrant or writ a note of the extension.[2]

9.1.2 Day of week

Under the new Act, an enforcement agent may take control of goods on any day of the week.[3] Nonetheless, the NSEA requires that enforcement agents should be respectful of the religion and culture of others at all times and should carefully consider the appropriateness of undertaking enforcement on any day of religious or cultural observance or during any major religious or cultural festival. This will not, of course, prevent goods being taken into control but may necessitate visits and entries being postponed.

9.1.3 Hour of day

In general, control of goods may be taken between 6am and 9pm.[4] However, these limits do not apply in three situations:[5]

- where the goods to be taken into control are located on premises which are used (whether wholly or partly) for the purposes of carrying on a business and those premises are open for business during the 'prohibited hours' of 9pm to 6am;
- where an enforcement agent began the process of taking goods into control within the permitted hours (or at a time allowed by either of the above paragraphs) and it is necessary to complete that process during prohibited hours (provided that the bailiff does not remain on the premises an unreasonable time in order to do this); or,
- because the court, on application from an enforcement agent, has made an order permitting a seizure to take place outside the permitted hours. Such an application is made to the court on form N244; it may be made without notice but must be accompanied by evidence demonstrating that if the order is not made, it is likely that goods of the debtor will be moved, or otherwise disposed of, in order to prevent the enforcement agent taking control of them.[6]

9.2 Taking control - general issues

Rather than the previous common law procedure of seizure and impounding which had grown up piecemeal over centuries and was, as a result, complex but flexible, the new statutory procedure is highly defined. We shall review first some general principles of application to all forms of taking control of goods.

9.2.1 Ways of taking control

Schedule 12 paragraph 13 lays out the new procedure to be followed by enforcement agents once they have effected initial entry to premises. To take control of goods an enforcement agent will have to do one of the following:

- secure the goods on the premises on which he finds them;
- secure the goods on a highway. The regulations make a distinction between vehicles and other goods found on a road, *as described later in sections 9.4 and 9.5*;
- remove them and secure them elsewhere; or,
- enter into a controlled goods agreement with the debtor.

Each of the new ways of taking control will be examined in detail in later sections, after consideration of some general issues.

The regulations make detailed provision about taking control in the ways listed above, including provisions for determining the time when control is taken and prohibiting use of any of those ways for goods by description or circumstances or both. These are examined in the following sections. It is worth repeating again for emphasis the fact that one of these four means of taking control must be used and that the detailed rules given in the regulations must be followed. For a bailiff to fail to take goods into control by one of the prescribed ways would mean that the goods had not been taken into control at all; to fail to stick to the prescribed procedure could lead to a breach of the Act giving rise to damages under Sch.12 para.66 as well as to an invalid levy.

Paragraph 3 of Schedule 12 provides definitions for the new procedure and explains that "controlled goods" means goods taken into control which have not been sold or abandoned, which (if they have been removed) have not been returned to the debtor (unless subject to a controlled goods agreement), or which, if they are goods of another person, have not been returned to that person.

9.2.2 Securing goods

Wherever seized goods are secured, the place chosen must be suitable. The new regulations make specific provision for the care of goods removed from premises or from the highway for secure storage,[7] but the common law established a number of principles in this respect. It was held that a definite place must be chosen and must be fit, as the bailiff is responsible for taking care of seized goods and can be sued for any damages caused by the pound's unfitness. The place chosen must not only generally be fit, but must be fit at the particular time in question- in other words, it should be checked beforehand and regularly during the course of the impounding. If it becomes unfit the distrainor must find an alternative location.[8]

9.2.3 Place of taking control

It is worth repeating that the rules on entry and those on taking control are harmonised for obvious reasons. Timing has already been discussed; location parallels the rules on entry. Goods may normally only be taken into control:

· At premises where the debtor resides;
· At premises where the debtor conducts his or her business; or,
· On the highway.

On application to a court, an enforcement agent may be able to enter other premises if it is possible to demonstrate the strong possibility of goods worth taking onto control being found.

9.2.4 Exempted individuals

Readers should recall that the regulations prohibit attempts to take control of goods where the debtor is a child (that is, under 16) and/or where a vulnerable person is involved.[9] It will be an essential preliminary of every levy for enforcement agents to make these basic checks as to the age and health of persons found on premises.

9.2.5 Successive takings

It may be permissible for successive takings to take place in individual cases. This is expressly sanctioned for takings on the highway, where clamping may be followed by a removal of the vehicle (see 9.5) and it is possible to envisage other situations where such a possibility would be useful to an agent.

In instances of securing goods on business premises (see 9.3) a bailiff in possession of the goods during the day could lock up the entire property at the end of the working day when employees had departed. Increasing degrees of security might also be achieved. If assets were initially secured by a controlled goods agreement (see 9.7) but repeat visits to check on the items gave rise to concern about their safety, the bailiff could respond firstly by locking them in a convenient room and then, if necessary, by removing them.

The major legal issue that may arise from such practices would be establishing the date of taking control from which the deadline for conducting sale must be calculated (see 11.3.3). The best and most correct course of action is probably to choose the first date upon which goods were taken into control. Whilst substituting one form of taking for another may be allowed, a succession of postponements of the terminal date for sale would very likely be illegal unless the debtor consented in writing to this being done (see too 11.3.3).

9.3 Securing on premises

This procedure replicates but extends the right to impound on premises previously created for distress for rent by the Distress for Rent Act 1737 s.10. However, it applies now to all forms of taking control of goods, thereby overcoming the fundamental (if little understood or appreciated) problem that, at common law, impounding of goods on premises is unlawful.

The regulations provide detailed guidance on the manner of securing goods on a debtor's premises.[10] As a general rule they may be secured:

- In a cupboard, room, garage or outbuilding It is to be presumed that this wording will be regarded as broad enough to include cellars and attics);
- By fitting an immobilisation device. In such cases a warning in the prescribed form must at the same time be fixed in a prominent position to warn the debtor that clamping has taken place. The notice should be signed by the enforcement agent and must state that goods have been immobilised, the date and time upon which this was done, the reason for the doing this (i.e. because of the debt outstanding) and any reference numbers. A twenty four hour contact telephone number must be provided. The enforcement agent must supply the clamp himself. The reason for this provision is to prevent enforcement agencies from employing separate contractors to supply (and possibly fit) clamps and then claiming the cost of this as a disbursement. This could be a way of circumventing the cap on the fee for enforcement action, but has been excluded by this regulation;
- On premises used solely business purposes, by leaving a bailiff to guard the goods taken into control. This is, of course, a continuation of the idea of the possession man in close possession of goods, though whether the new fees schedule makes this means of securing goods anymore feasible now than under the scales applicable heretofore remains to be seen. Under the former law it was held that a bailiff should not remain in possession an unreasonable period or without the debtor's consent: see for example *Re: Finch* (1891), where possession for a period of ten days months was felt more reasonable than five months.[11] The circumstances of the possession should also not be unreasonable: for example in the case of *Griffin v Scott* (1726) leaving eight bailiffs in possession for six days led to an award of damages for trespass;[12] or,
- By locking up the whole of any business premises or that part of any premises used for business where there is mixed business and residential use. In other words, where premises comprise a shop and flat above, the shop might be secured.

The first three means of securing goods may not be employed where their use would mean that any persons in occupation would be deprived of adequate access to essential facilities (such as a kitchen or bathroom) and goods which are exempted from seizure. Entry and exit to the premises should not be restricted in any way and fire escapes in particular should not be barred.[13] Careful consideration by the bailiff may be required if this means of taking control is seriously being contemplated. It should be clear which entrance and exit routes must not be obstructed, but preserving access to exempted goods (see next chapter) will need more thought. It ought to be obvious that items required for cooking, cleaning and sleeping will still have to be accessible to the debtor and household; equally, if items needed for medical or personal care are treated as exempted, for example, their availability to the debtor will have to be ensured as well.

Where an enforcement agent is contemplating securing the goods by locking up trade premises entirely, it is still necessary to consider first whether any other means of taking control is practicable. Other means of securing on the premises (such as selecting a room or outbuilding or clamping) or immediate removal to a place of storage (*see 9.6*) should always be preferred. In other words, locking up the whole business and excluding the debtor from his/her trade should always be a last resort.[14]

The earlier case law on this practice may provide some guidance on this latter practice, although the manner and extent of impounding on the premises under the Distress for Rent Act 1737 generated some conflicting opinions in the case authorities. An impounding that involves the selection and securing of a part of the premises (a room, cupboard or outbuilding) will probably not be susceptible to challenge, unless the occupier was deprived of essential facilities on the premises such as exclusion from the kitchen or main bedroom. What is less certain is whether the whole of the premises may be secured. It seems that use of the entire property may be lawful in a number of defined circumstances. This might have been done because:

· *To secure the goods, not to exclude the occupier* - in *Cox v Painter* (1837) the distraining landlord locked up the tenant's cottage in order to impound the entire contents. There was some dispute at trial as to whether, in fact, the tenant had surrendered possession of the property, but the court found in trespass against the landlord for excluding the tenant for a period of three weeks from his home. Even so, the court implied that using the entire premises for impounding could be lawful, as long as the purpose was genuinely to impound the goods and not to exclude the occupier.[15]
· *It was the most fit & convenient place* - in *Woods v Durrant* (1846) goods were impounded in the whole house by locking and bolting the doors and windows and expelling the plaintiff. This lasted until the sale twenty one days later, excluding the tenant from his home and disrupting the business he carried on there. It was held that for the landlord to justify his procedure he should have shown that either the whole house, or that part the doors of which were locked, was the fittest and most convenient place for securing the distress - otherwise the tenant was improperly excluded when there was no necessity for it.[16]
· *The nature of the premises and/ or goods justified it* - in *Smith v Ashforth* (1860) a silk weaving workshop was locked up in order

to impound the looms. The defendant landlord relied on *Woods v Durrant* to justify his actions - as the premises comprised only one room, he had no choice but to secure it and exclude the tenant. The court doubted the need to lock out the tenant - as the machines were too large and heavy for the landlord to remove them to his own pound, it was equally unlikely that the tenant would have committed poundbreach in removing them.[17]

In conclusion, it would seem that impounding the goods on the entire premises, thereby excluding the occupier from their enjoyment, may in limited circumstances be permitted, but the enforcement agent will have to justify his/her actions by showing that removal was inappropriate, that no other location were available and that use of the whole of the premises was necessary because of the nature of those premises or the quantity or type of goods involved. In other cases, locking out the occupier will be a wrongful act.[18] It is trespass to expel the occupant after entry. Similarly in *Rawlins v. Monsour* (1978) impounding goods by closing up the debtor's sports goods shop and thus effectively exercising a right of re-entry was an illegal levy of distress for rent and trespass ab initio. Conversely, it amounts to trespass for the debtor to exclude the bailiff.[19] It has been held that excluding the tenant in this way can be treated as surrender by operation of law by the courts. This of course would terminate the tenant's liability for rent and the right to continue any use of CRAR, but it seems a double edged sword with advantages and disadvantages for both parties.[20]

As was suggested earlier, it is possible that a combination of means of taking control might be a permissible and useful facility, especially at business premises: for example, an enforcement agent might spend the day of business premises in control of goods but, at the end of the working day, might secure the premises by locking them up for the night. Whatever method of taking control is used, once goods have been secured on the premises, notice that they have been taken into control will be provided, incorporating an inventory. This prescribed form is a combined notice of entry and notice of taking control. The notice will be handed to the debtor if s/he is present or otherwise will be left on the premises in a conspicuous place, sealed in an envelope if confidentiality may be an issue.

9.4 Securing goods on a highway

An enforcement agent may secure goods found on a highway where they are discovered or nearby.[21] 'Highway' is not defined in the Act and should be understood as having its wider common law meaning.

Taking Control of Goods

A highway is a way over which there exists a public right of passage on foot, riding, with a beast of burden or with vehicles or cattle; members of the public are entitled to pass and re-pass without hindrance. It is a wide enough term to embrace public footpaths, bridleways and carriageways. The boundary of the highway is defined by the buildings or fences along its route, so that grass verges are generally to be regarded as being part of the highway.[22] It follows from this definition that car parks on private land and driveways on the property of persons other than the debtor are not highways and goods may not be taken into control in such places. Any liability of an enforcement agent (including criminal liability) arising out of his securing goods on a highway under this paragraph is excluded to the extent that he acted with reasonable care.[23]

The regulations make further detailed provision on the taking into control of goods found on the highway. These restrictions appear to be related to the fact that many of the items identified should only be transported by qualified individuals with the correct equipment, training and licences. Accordingly, an agent should not attempt to secure:[24]

· Animals or livestock (which includes cattle, sheep, pigs, horses and poultry); or,
· Any goods or materials believed to be perishable or hazardous. The latter category includes nuclear materials, radioactive waste or any other radioactive or contaminated substance;
· Where, in either case, there is a perceived to be a risk to human health if the items were taken into control. This provision only applies if the agent is, or ought to be, aware of the potential risk.

These provisions might, for example, apply where contagious livestock diseases are involved, but how often a bailiff without specialist knowledge is likely to be aware of any risk or telltale symptoms is debatable. If there are grounds for concern neither the animals or items nor the vehicle in which they are contained (horse box, livestock transporters etc) should be taken into control.

There are clearly several problems with this provision. Whilst in cases where livestock are being seized it is more likely that specialist assistance will be employed so that the chances of spotting any illness should be substantially raised, it is difficult to imagine how bailiffs will detect dangerous materials unless they habitually conduct at least Geiger counter checks on every item or vehicle identified on the highway.

Goods taken into control on the highway may be secured by the use of an immobilisation device. The bailiff will have to supply this clamp.

The reason for this provision is to prevent enforcement agencies from employing separate contractors to supply (and possibly fit) clamps and then claiming the cost of this as a disbursement. This could be a way of circumventing the cap on the fee for enforcement action, but has been excluded by this regulation.

The bailiff must prominently fix a warning of the immobilisation to the goods. This notice will be in the prescribed form and should be signed by the enforcement agent and must state that goods have been immobilised, the date and time upon which this was done, the reason for the doing this (i.e. because of the debt outstanding) and any reference numbers. A twenty four hour contact telephone number must be provided.[25] In addition notice that goods have been taken into control, which incorporates an inventory, will be supplied.

9.5 Securing vehicles on a highway

The agent may secure vehicles where he finds them on a highway or within a reasonable distance of that location. This presumably means that if a car is found parked on double yellow lines or where it may cause a hazard, it may be moved to a better location. What is not clear is whether the goods must be moved to another part of the highway. As they have been taken into control by the agent by the act of moving them, it may be that the new location simply has to be a suitable place (*see 9.6*) - perhaps a local authority owned car park where the bailiff is enforcing a PCN and the council endorses the action.

When the enforcement agent secures a vehicle on the highway (*defined in 9.4*) that vehicle must be secured by an immobilisation device (which is to be supplied by the bailiff see above), unless the debtor voluntarily surrenders the keys to the vehicle to the enforcement agent instead.[26] At the time of immobilising the goods, the enforcement agent must provide a written warning to the debtor (see previous section) as well as a notice that goods have been taken into control, which incorporates an inventory.[27] This will be fixed prominently to the vehicle in question - on the windscreen or driver's door.

The clamped vehicle must remain immobilised where it was found for a period of not less than two hours from the time of immobilisation unless the sum outstanding is paid or an agreement to release the vehicle, on part payment of the sum outstanding, is made between the enforcement agent and the debtor. Curiously, the prescribed form of warning does not mention this minimum period of immobilisation. After this minimum period has expired, the bailiff may remove the vehicle to storage, ensuring that the vehicle is then properly cared for (*see 11.2 below*).[28]

9.6 Immediate removal

Immediate removal to secure premises has always been a lawful means of impounding goods. The right is continued by the new Act. It is important for readers to note that there are, strictly, two separate forms of removal envisaged by the Act. The first is that considered here- removal as a form of taking control. The second is removal for the purpose of sale, which it is anticipated will occur appreciably later in the process, goods having previously been taken into control on premises by another means. Despite this key distinction, rules of procedure are shared between the two processes. The greatest significance in this dichotomy is that removal as a form of taking control will fall into the 'enforcement stage' of the fee scale (*see chapter 12*) whilst removal for sale is treated as part of the 'sale' stage. In fact, except against businesses, this method of levying is rarely used because of the expense and trouble involved (when the goods are impounded off the premises the bailiff is liable for them).[29]

Other than in exceptional circumstances, the goods should only be removed to a secure location within a "reasonable distance" of the place where they were taken into control initially.[30] What is meant by this phrase is not elaborated upon: presumably it will vary according to a number of factors. The question may depend upon whether or not a rural or urban debtor is involved, taking into account the availability of public transport if the debtor lacks his or her own vehicle and bearing in mind also the person's personal and family circumstances. Distinctions may also be made between individual and corporate debtors: the latter might be expected to be able to travel further to recover their goods. Consideration might also be given to the auction house which will be used for disposal of the goods - if they are of a specialist nature, a longer removal distance may be justified in the circumstances.

A notice in prescribed form will be left on the premises setting out the standard information (parties, debt outstanding, payment options). It includes an inventory of the goods removed and warns of the storage costs which will accrue daily or weekly (these are recoverable as a disbursement from the debtor - *see chapter 12*).

9.7 Controlled goods agreements

This procedure is the replacement for the former 'walking possession agreement'. A controlled goods agreement is defined as an agreement under which the debtor is permitted to retain custody of the goods, acknowledges that the enforcement agent is taking control of them, and agrees not to remove or dispose of them, nor to permit anyone else to do so, before the debt is paid.[31] Central to the purpose of the controlled goods agreement is a payment arrangement: this is why considerable emphasis is placed upon defining lawful signatories. In addition, enforcement of the agreement hinges upon the existence of a repayment scheme (*see 11.2*).

Although the controlled goods agreement replaces walking possession, it is not the former process renamed. As will be described, the issue of who may sign has been revised by the new statute and the resulting agreement is clearly a contract between debtor and bailiff. This underlines the necessity of strictly observing the statutory form, ensuring that all terms are included and that the correct signature is obtained.

9.7.1 Signatories

Regulation 14 of the Taking Control of Goods Regulations 2013 stipulates in detail who may enter into a controlled goods agreement. To a degree this gives statutory form to the case law formerly applicable; it also clarifies various areas of uncertainty that afflicted walking possession agreements. An agreement may only be made by:

- A debtor aged 16 years or over. Plainly the bailiff will need to check age before accepting a debtor's signature;
- A person aged over 18 who has been authorised by the debtor to enter into an agreement on his/her behalf. What form that authority should take is regrettably not explained in the regulations: and,
- A person who is found to be in 'apparent authority' on premises used wholly or partly for trade or business purposes. This might be an employee of a business as well as the partner in a firm or company officer. Again, the meaning of this phrase is not provided by the regulations but it seems clear that enforcement agents will have to undertake some interrogation of any individual found to be present to establish whether or not that person can be regarded as being imbued with the necessary authority and,
- Finally, the same regulation continues by adding that controlled goods agreements must not be made with either the debtor or another person if it appears (or ought to appear) to the bailiff that the person does not understand the effect of the agreement and

would not be capable of entering into it. This may be because of language difficulties, mental disability or mental illness and should be more readily apparent to an agent after even a relatively brief discussion with a person.[32] NSEA repeats this guidance, explicitly relating it to the issue of vulnerability: "The enforcement agent must be sure that the debtor or the person with whom they are entering into a controlled goods agreement understands the agreement and the consequences if the agreement is not complied with."

It will be clear that entering into a controlled goods agreement will not just be a matter of accepting a signature from any available person. Their personal fitness and legal status as a signatory will have to be established by the enforcement agent first, by means of a reasonable degree of investigation.

9.7.2 Authority to sign

The provisions of reg.14(1) as to who has authority to sign a controlled goods agreement will probably prove to be regrettable. No clarification of the terminology used is supplied by the Regulations, sadly, and this will have to be derived from guidance and from case law which will, doubtless, be developed upon the foundations of the well established definitions of 'authority' found in agency law. It may also be worth noting, in passing, that the new law reverses the former position. Previously, the bailiff appointed a possession man to act as his agent under a close or walking possession agreement. With controlled goods agreements, the concern is with identifying who has been appointed agent of the debtor.

Matters may not be helped by a rather loose use in the Regulations of phrases which have precise meaning in agency law. At business premises an agreement may be made with a person found to be in "apparent authority." Properly, the concept of apparent or ostensible authority denotes individuals whom a principal has led others to believe acts in his/her name. This will seldom apply in enforcement cases, but might conceivably arise because of previous contacts between debtor and enforcement agency- for example, a conversation which indicates that the debtor is happy for another person on the premises to deal with the bailiff. Luckily, perhaps, in the context of the regulations we are interested not in those "with apparent authority" but those discovered to be "in apparent authority". It may be permissible therefore for the bailiff to rely wholly on the circumstances s/he encounters at the address.

It seems, then, that we will be concerned with those who properly may be said to have 'actual' or 'presumed' authority to make controlled goods agreements.[33] 'Authority' may be defined as approving, permitting or sanctioning an action carried out on a person's behalf; it can be granted in writing or verbally. One spouse or partner might be assumed to have the authority of the other to enter into agreements. There may be occasions where authority to sign an agreement has been expressly given- by letter to the bailiff company or in some document left with the person found on the premises, perhaps- but this will probably be the exception. In most cases it seems likely that the bailiff conducting the levy will have to make a presumption that authority exists, based on the situation discovered at the property and the information gathered from the individual found in occupation. Of course, this presumption may be rebutted by the debtor on the evidence, which is the major weakness of this situation. Equally, though, the debtor may ratify the agreement by making payments to the bailiff in recognition of the fact that the goods are subject to control and/or by explicitly confirming that the signatory acted with authority.

Before accepting a person's signature on a controlled goods agreement, it will be necessary for a bailiff to make some quite detailed enquiries. It will be essential to know a person's identity, their relationship to the debtor or other status within the household or business and whether the debtor has expressly delegated to them the legal power to act on their behalf. These enquiries may be time consuming, it is recognised, but they will avoid challenges to agreements subsequently which are likely to be more time consuming and much more costly.

9.7.3 Form of agreements

The regulations specify the form of the controlled goods agreement. Agreements should be in writing and signed by both the enforcement agent and the person entitled to sign under the provisions just discussed - the debtor, a person authorised by the debtor or a person in apparent authority on the premises.[34]

The agreement must set out:[35]

- · The debtor's name and address;
- · The reference number and date of the agreement;
- · The bailiff's contact details and the times at which the office may be contacted;
- · A list of the goods taken into control providing sufficient details to enable the debtor to identify them, such as their model, make, serial or registration number, colour, usage or other identifying feature. Such a list can be omitted if one is also included in any notice of entry or levy or if an inventory has been provided (always

assuming that the goods taken into control are identical to those covered by the signed controlled goods agreement); and,

· The terms of the repayment arrangement made with the debtor. As stated before, discharge of the outstanding debt is central to the purpose and functions of the controlled goods agreement and must be agreed at the same time. The elements of such payment scheme should include the amount of the payments, their frequency and their effect (*see 11.1.1*). A controlled goods agreement that does not incorporate these terms is, essentially, no agreement at all. If not invalid, it will - at the least - be very difficult to enforce (*see 11.2*).

Copies of the signed agreement should be provided to the signatory and, if that person is not the debtor, to the debtor personally. This can be done by leaving the copy agreement in a conspicuous place on the premises where the goods were taken into control or by delivering it to any relevant premises where goods have been taken into control on a highway. In the latter case, and wherever the debtor is known to share the premises with other occupiers, the copy agreement should be delivered in a sealed and addressed envelope. These provisions particularly embody the duties of clarity and openness is that is fundamental to the new law.[36]

9.7.4 Trading businesses

The former law made special provision for possession agreements made with trading businesses. Where distress was levied upon a business that continued to trade, the stock and materials that were seized and subject to walking possession had to be sold by the firm if the business were to continue to function. In theory this would have been a breach of the possession agreement by the debtor and to allow it would have been abandonment by the bailiff. At the same time, to permit a firm to trade is likely to raise income to satisfy the debt. The bailiff had therefore to find a means of taking possession that was both apparent and yet permits the business to continue to operate.

A solution was allowing the trader to dispose of seized items so long as they were replaced immediately. The bailiff had to make any such arrangement very carefully or else he risked abandonment of the goods. Upon initial seizure a detailed inventory was taken and the fact that stock would change was noted on it. Limits on the amounts of stock that may be sold over a given period were imposed. Regular repeat visits were made to the premises to check on the goods. On such occasions it was necessary for the bailiff to either up date the inventory by seizing more goods or to receive the proceeds of sale of the items that had been sold by the trader. If sold stock was not being replaced by the trader, it would be necessary for the bailiff to consider removal if no funds were available to make payment to cover the value of the missing goods. that the procedure could be legal in distress for rent.

This kind of approach was sanctioned by the courts in *Re: Dalton ex p Herrington & Carmichael v Trustee* [1963]. See also *Re: Hunter* [1912] in which the sheriff, instead of seizing and selling the assets of a liquor business, placed a bailiff in possession to receive the daily receipts of the business as a going concern. Where the receipts were handed over on a daily basis, the court was prepared to place on this the legal construction that each taking was a levy of execution. However where the debtor was allowed to trade with no indication of any alteration in possession, and no accounting for proceeds to the man in possession, the seizure was voided and the goods were abandoned.[37]

See also *Toussaint v Hartop* (1816) in which the sheriff was in possession but the seizure and possession were both "concealed from the world" by the fact that the debtor was allowed to keep trading with the seized goods over an extended period of five months. When the trader went bankrupt the trustee's claim to the goods defeated that of the sheriff. A similar conclusion was reached in *Jackson v Irvin* (1809) the debtor's employee acted as possession man of his stock and carried on the business as normal. When the debtor went bankrupt the trustee's claim to the goods defeated that of the execution creditor. In *Edwards v Edwards* [1876] a receiver failed to take effective possession of a business when trade was continued ostensibly by the debtor and the change of possession was not publicised. Such a 'mere nominal possession' was not enough to defeat a later execution. These cases suggest that controlled goods agreement will not operate to remove the goods from the "order and disposition" of the debtor.[38] In contrast bills of sale cases show that publicly apparent possession of business assets will be effective seizure.[39] Numerous commonwealth cases give the same impression. It seems that such apparent possession is not necessary in respect of domestic assets.[40] It was held that a person with claims to the property of a business could lose priority in those claims if the trader is allowed to continue to act as if s/he is entitled to them for all purposes and may sell or borrow against them, but such no such inference about absolute ownership can be drawn from continued possession of household effects as they are being properly employed for their normal purpose if they are permitted to remain in the home.

9.7.5 Ineffective agreements

Under the previous law, the courts held that, to be valid, a possession agreement had to accord with certain minimum requirements. If it did not, the bailiff had failed to retain possession and had 'abandoned' the goods (*see below*). There are three main ways in which an agreement could be invalid and it is worth noting these in case similar practices are carried over into the new regime of 'taking control.' Ineffective forms of agreement included those that were:

Posted to the debtor
An agreement had to follow a legal entry and paperwork dropped through the door for signature and return by the debtor was unacceptable and ineffective.[41] It was clear, therefore that the mere posting of documents by bailiffs had no effect whatsoever on the debtor's goods. A person could not retrospectively make an agreement transferring rights over their property. A 'walking possession' agreement signed by the bailiff alone and posted to the debtor could not create an agreement binding on the debtor. Even if s/he subsequently signed and returned the document, as was normally requested, the debtor did not thereby waive any irregularity in the manner of levy or adopt the agreement. Signing the agreement retrospectively would not bar a debtor from any subsequent objection to its legality. If the agreement was invalid, or if there had been abandonment, the goods were not effectively seized. The debtor might thus continue to deal with goods as s/he wished as they were not in the custody of the law and could not be until the bailiff had at least entered the property;

Made off the debtor's premises
Agreements signed at an office (or any other location) without any entry or even visits to premises were void; and,

Bearing the wrong signature
Although under the former law courts were prepared to accept that, if a suitable person could not or would not sign, the goods might still be impounded constructively - the agreement with the 'third party' being evidence of the bailiff's intention to remain in possession and not to abandon the impounded goods - the form of the new controlled goods agreement probably precludes this.[42] This is because the statute now prescribes who may be a signatory (*see above*). Agreements made with those not authorised to sign will probably be treated as invalid as they are in breach of the Act.

9.8 Seizure - general principles

A number of established principles of the former law may continue to apply to the new procedure of taking control of goods. They concern issues not discussed in the Act which still remain fundamental to the bailiffs' successful conduct of his duties.

9.8.1 General conduct

In *Evans v South Ribble Borough Council* [1992] Simon Brown J made clear that the seizure of household goods depended upon a three stage process, the first stage of which was the entry into the premises. Entry clearly must remain fundamental to the process of taking control of items inside premises. There is no reason to suppose that a bailiff is any more likely to be able to take control of goods by the sort of 'remote' techniques employed in Evans (looking through a window, listing goods and posting an 'agreement' for the debtor to sign subsequently) than was possible in levies of distraint.[43]

It remains to be seen how strict the courts will be about the process of taking control and whether they will give bailiffs a measure of leeway, as was the case under the former law. Hitherto, actions amounting to, and indicative of an intention to conduct, a seizure were accepted what was called 'constructive seizure.' A number of cases sought to define this process. The bailiff's intentions might be inferred from his actions, which may include looking through a window, walking round premises, making and presenting an inventory of the goods seized or by some means preventing the removal of goods. The process was summarised by Chisholm J in *Noseworthy v Campbell* [1929]: "to constitute seizure it is not necessary that there should be physical contact with the goods seized [but] some act must be done to intimate that seizure has been made." A good example of this is *Cramer & Co v Mott* [1870]. The lodger in the defendant's house hired a piano from Cramers. He failed to pay the hire charges therefore two men were sent to collect the instrument. They were met by Mrs. Mott who said, in the lodger's presence, that the piano should not be removed until her rent was paid. It was held that there might be a distress without actual seizure and what occurred amounted to distress as it was enough for the landlord to prevent removal: if the firm had ignored her words, Mrs Mott was at the door of her lodger's room and could have barred the way, i.e. her words could have been carried into action. A similar case, cited by counsel for the defendant in *Cramer*, is *Cotton v Bull* (1857), in which a lodging house keeper prevented a tenant in arrears removing personal items from the premises, which detention was held to amount to a distress. The ability to carry an intention into deed if necessary is the key matter, underlining the need for an entry if household goods in particular are to be effectively secured.[44]

With the much more prescriptive rules for taking control found in the new Act, it is probable that the sorts of practice just described will no longer be admissible, although arguments might conceivably arise in respect of goods secured on premises or by controlled goods agreements.

Lastly, it previously was accepted that a bailiff could seize one item or part of the goods in the name of all, but the whole had to be in his power: he had to know what had been distrained and had to have power to take possession of them.[45] At least one item had to be taken nto actual possession, it seems: in *Re: Henley ex p Fletcher* [1877] Mellish J. stated that "it may be by construction of law that his taking of one of the things in deed will amount to possession of all" but that there had to be actual possession by the bailiff before it could be said that there was formal possession of the rest.[46] Given the emphasis placed on the completion of a full and detailed inventory by the new legislation, it is probable that the courts will be as generous in cases of taking onto control.

9.8.2 Reasonable search

It was an established common law principle of distress and execution that a bailiff must make adequate efforts to enter and must conduct a reasonably diligent and thorough search of property. One reason for this was to protect the interests of the creditor as principal. If the bailiff failed to find any adequate goods, a return of 'no goods' or 'no sufficient distress' might be made to the creditor and other enforcement might then be attempted by them (*see below*). It seems reasonable to expect that these principles will still be applicable to taking into control.

Case law makes it clear that the bailiff must have made reasonable efforts to actually enter or search for goods to be able lawfully to make a nil return. Such returns could be made in the following cases:

 · if the goods were hidden;[47]
 · if entry was obstructed or refused;[48]
 · if the value of the goods was fully exhausted by prior charges- but it was essential for the bailiff to investigate the validity and value of these charges and if possible supply documentary proof of these charges to the creditor;[49] or,
 · if goods were already subject to seizure (*see below and 10.11*).[50]

Over and above this duty, which was linked to further recovery of the debt, a bailiff had a further duty to the creditor arising from his/her role as an enforcement agent. In order to perform the function of securing the principal's debt on goods, the bailiff had a duty to conduct a reasonable inspection of the premises.[51] He could only say that there were no goods where they were not visible upon reasonable inspection of the property. It seems it was possible for a debtor successfully to hide goods as the court in *Doe d. Haverson v Franks* (1847) did not require an absolutely exhaustive search to be made. However in *Rees d. Powell v King & Morris* (1800) it was indicated that the whole of the property should have been inspected. The case was a claim for forfeiture based upon there being insufficient distress. The claim failed because it was proved at trial that the bailiff had not gone into every part of the premises. Indeed, in this case, the main part of the tenement was a cottage, which had not been entered at all. The court rejected the landlord's statement that no distress was 'visible' and insisted that it was necessary to "examine every private place where the tenant may have concealed his goods."[52] Certainly, it seems that the bailiff should have attempted to see the goods or should have had an assurance that goods were not present.[53] The exercise of due diligence in making a levy was said to include situations where, with reasonable exertion, the bailiff would have had notice of the goods' presence. If the bailiff failed to take such steps, he would be unable to make a return of no goods and would be liable in negligence.[54] There was no negligence on the bailiff's part where he made repeated visits to the premises and, short of standing permanent guard there, failed to get entry.[55] He was not required to use extraordinary exertion or try to provide against unexpected or unforeseen contingencies.[56]

As part of the search process the common law accepted that a bailiff might break open any inner door, cupboard or other receptacle both to find goods.[57] In one case it was held that legal entry through an outer door then justified not only the breaking of internal doors, but also windows inside the property. Because of the huge inconvenience it could cause to bailiffs, no demand need be made before forcing each inner door, though this precludes the unnecessary use of force where a door is broken despite the debtor's offer to open it. If force were used despite an offer to open the door, damages would probably be recoverable.[58] Force may also be used against inner doors if they are locked and the debtor or occupier refuses to open them.[59] This situation is not discussed in the new Act, but the old rules may be anticipated still to apply.

The duty to make a careful search is inevitably likely to involve the enforcement agent in some process of choice and selection. A bailiff is not necessarily entitled to all the goods on the premises and has to select sufficient to cover the debt and costs whilst ensuring this is not excessive. Thus in the unreported case of *Rai & Rai v Birmingham City Council* (1993), a deputy stipendiary magistrate held that bailiffs have a duty of care to exercise when seizing goods: they must act with discernment and judgment as the power of distraint is not " a dragnet trawling all within it". If they are put on notice that certain goods did not allegedly belong to the debtor, the bailiffs must then act with appropriate 'caution and circumspection'. The goods seized must be available for seizure, that is, not exempt in some way.[60]

As the process of taking control of goods must involve some process of selection before seizure, where this completely fails to happen the purported levy may be challenged. For example, the court held in *Brintons v Wyre Forest D.C.* [1976] that no valid seizure occurred when, calling at the plaintiffs' offices, the bailiff simply demanded payment of the rates and costs. He never said that all or any of the goods were seized, no effort was made to inspect or select suitable assets and nothing amounting to the taking of possession was done, for example there were no threats to leave a possession man on the premises.[61] Seizure also failed where the levying bailiff failed to make his intention to seize clear. Thus in *Nash v Dickinson* [1867] the sheriff went to the debtor's house with a warrant and without saying or doing anything more produced the warrant and demanded the debt and costs. It was held that this did not amount to a levy because the bailiff did nothing such as leaving a notice or a possession man to indicate seizure had occurred. Equally in *Re: Williams ex p Jones* [1880] a sheriff went to Williams' house and effected an alleged seizure of a horse and cart. It was held there was no seizure as no warrant was produced, there was no inventory that identified what had been seized and it was insufficient to touch items without informing the debtor that they were being seized by bailiffs.[62] These were cases of execution, but similar principles applied outside the courts. For example in *Whimsell v Giffard* [1883] the landlord made two visits to the house, declaring he had seized everything. He touched nothing and made no inventory, so it was found that there was no valid seizure. The judgment in *Central Printing Works v Walter* [1907] confirmed that if all the bailiff did was wait on the premises whilst the debtor sought to arrange payment of the sum due, without any indication of any seizure having been made, there would be no levy; see also *Ancona v Rogers* [1876] in which a mere demand for possession after default on a bill of sale failed to alter actual possession.[63] Given the strictures placed upon bailiffs when taking control of goods it is fair to assume that the courts will take a similar view of such cases under the 2007 Act.

9.9 Selecting sufficient goods and 'no goods' levies

An important concept of the former law which is likely to retain its validity under the new regime (given the ongoing duty to avoid excessive levies and the obligation to value all goods removed for sale) is the idea of the nulla bona or no goods levy. It is even fixed in statute as in the recovery of local taxes, in which a return of no goods is a necessary preliminary to the local authority initiating committal proceedings. A similar provision applies to the further enforcement of road traffic penalties.[64] The issue is not directly addressed in the new legislation, but the possibility of finding no or insufficient goods to take into control is acknowledged in the new rules permitting repeat visits.[65]

9.9.1 No goods returns in executions

Where, following a failed execution by a HCEO or county court bailiff, the judgment creditor may enforce the debt by petitioning for bankruptcy on the basis that execution has been returned unsatisfied in whole or in part. This was examined in *Re: A Debtor* (No 340 of 1992)[1994] in which the court held that the failure of the sheriff to gain access on un-stated occasions at un-stated hours did not justify a return of the writ as 'unsatisfied'. The court made a distinction between an unexecuted and an unsatisfied writ and stated in this case that the return that the writ was unsatisfied was merely the bailiff's opinion on the effect of what he has done (or failed to do) - the court is not bound by this.[66] A return of no goods would be false where there was simply no levy at all. However, where goods were seized and it later transpired that these were all subject to a bill of sale and in the possession of the bill's holder, the enforcement officer was entitled to say that no goods were found.[67] A writ orders goods to be seized: where this has not been done at all the return in question was at least irregular as it could not be justified by what the bailiff had actually done.

A return of *nulla bona* was also one of the common law returns which an officer could make on a writ of *fieri facias*. Whilst the case law on the exact interpretation of the phrase 'no goods' was extremely limited for distraint, there was ample authority for levies of execution by High Court enforcement (sheriff's) officers. Over the centuries, the courts provided the following guidance. It was permissible for an officer to advise a judgment creditor that there were no goods available to put towards the debt and costs where:

- All available goods had been seized under earlier writs and warrants;[68]
- All goods available were the property of third parties;[69]
- The judgment debtor was bankrupt and all goods were in the hands of the receiver;[70]
- The debtor had barricaded his premises and denied the officer access to any goods;[71] or,
- The costs of execution would absorb the proceeds of any sale.[72]

Making a return of no goods was evidence that there were no goods available which were applicable to the writ. However, if some goods were available or if a levy was made (albeit partial), it was inappropriate for the officer to later on state that no goods were available for seizure.[73]

In most of the situations outlined above, goods were present at the premises but claims of ownership or debts that had chronological or legal precedence prevented the officer from being able to levy. Of most interest is the last situation - unencumbered goods were available for seizure, but their value was too low to justify it. In the case of *Dennis v Whetham* from 1874 Archbald J. stated in his judgment that if rent was due and exceeded the value of the goods available, the officer was excused from levying and could make a return of nulla bona. He continued by saying that, if the fees and expenses of the levy absorbed the proceeds of sale, the officer might also return *nulla bona*. Presumably, though, if the officer judged that the value of the goods was too low, he might - as in rent cases - be excused from levying and might simply make a return of no goods without the need for a seizure and sale.[74]

9.9.2 No goods in CRAR

In the case of CRAR the landlord might turn to consider other remedies such as possession proceedings or forfeiture. For example the inability to enter to distrain founded a claim in forfeiture: in *Doe d. Chippendale v Dyson* (1827) Lord Tenterden held that 'no sufficient distress' was to be understood to mean 'no distress which could be got at.' In the case in question the house was locked up so that the landlord could not enter to levy. By refusing entry the tenants permitted the landlord to clam ejectment on the basis that there was no distress available at all. In *Doe d. Cox v Roe* (1847) it was accepted that a sworn statement by the bailiff that he believed there to be insufficient distress on the premises would be adequate grounds to found ejectment. Several prolonged attempts had been made to gain access to the premises, but these had failed. The court accepted this as evidence that there were no seizable goods.[75]

Note in this connection the case of *Rahman v Benwell Properties Ltd* [1997]- the Court of Appeal refused leave to appeal the decision of a recorder in a county court. Mr Rahman was arguing that a levy of distress for rent the day after a purported forfeiture of the lease waived the preceding breaches of the lease. The Court upheld the decision of the recorder that even though the bailiff had issued a notice of seizure, drawn up an inventory and, apparently, entered into walking possession with Mr Rahman's wife, he was still at this stage entitled to conclude that there were insufficient goods to justify the costs of the seizure and sale and to withdraw from the levy, thus not prejudicing the landlord's position in respect of the forfeiture.

9.9.3 Remedies for levying on insufficient goods

If an officer or bailiff proceeded needlessly with a levy when there were no goods of any value available, a debtor might have several remedies. Some form of public law challenge might be available on the basis that the levy was disproportionate. As a recent case concerning Slough Borough Council has shown, a complaint of maladministration to the Local Government Ombudsman would certainly be possible.[76] Additionally, it may be possible to challenge such a levy as 'excessive'.

In chapter 13 there is discussion of the concept of an 'excessive' levy, one in which far more is seized than is required to cover the debt and costs.[77] Levying in such a manner is wrongful at common law and, also, under chapter 4 of the Statute of Marlborough 1267. The second clause of chapter 4 states that "Distraints are, moreover, to be reasonable and not too severe [78] and, if anyone makes unreasonable or undue[79] distraints, he is to be heavily amerced on account of the excessive nature of those distraints." As will be seen, an unreasonable distraint is one that is "severe (or harsh)" and is "undue (or improper)." These terms, it seems, may be as applicable to a levy which is excessive in the sense that it could not be justified by the value of the goods taken as to one in which too much was taken.

9.9.4 Consequences of a failed levy

As already stressed, the link between a failed levy and further enforcement is important because various regulations specify the conditions that must be satisfied by the bailiff to enable other steps to be taken. In local tax recovery the billing authority may seek to have the debtor committed to prison where the bailiff reports that "he was unable (for whatever reason) to find any or sufficient goods of the debtor on which to levy the amount".[80] If the bailiff fails to make any proper levy at all, then a nil return is not correct and an application for committal cannot be based upon it. In *R. v. Bradford Justices ex. p. Delaney* (1994) an application for committal failed when it transpired that the bailiff had merely visited the property and had withdrawn on being shown proof of payment by the debtor. It has recently been stressed in *R.(on the application of Nwankwo) v. Hendon Magistrates Court* [2003] how important it is for the local authority to supply evidence that distress was sought, or that there were insufficient goods, in order to be able to justify an application for a committal order.[81]

In the case of road traffic debts, a local authority may make an application for an attachment of earnings order, an order to obtain information from a debtor, a third party debt order or a charging order in those cases where bailiff action does not manage to clear the debt.

However, where the authority has not attempted to enforce by taking control of goods, it must give the reason why no such attempt was made or else it must certify in its application that there has been no 'relevant return' to the warrant of control. 'No relevant return' means that an enforcement agent has been unable to seize goods for one of three reasons - because:

· access to premises occupied by the defendant was denied or because goods had been removed from those premises;
· any goods taken into control under the warrant of control were insufficient to satisfy the debt and the costs; or,
· the goods were insufficient to cover the cost of their removal and sale.[82]

9.10 Abandonment

It was an accepted principle of the former law of distress and execution that, if the bailiff failed to retain adequate control over the goods he had seized or purported to seize, then any rights established over them, and any security obtained for the recovery of the debt due would be lost- the goods were said to be 'abandoned'. The new Act gives a new meaning to this term, which is discussed at 11.6. Abandonment in the former common law sense of the word can no longer be used, but there may still be situations where it is possible to allege that a bailiff has failed properly to retain control of goods- perhaps by neglecting to secure them adequately on the debtor's premises or by neglecting to clamp them on the highway. It may therefore be worth summarising the previous case law.

The former common law principles of abandonment may provide guidance on situations in which it may be possible to argue that the control over goods has been lost or has lapsed. Abandonment occurred when the bailiff failed to remain adequately in possession, or delayed his return too long after agreed payments had been missed, and thereby altogether lost any right to return and remove goods seized. For example there was abandonment where a creditor failed without good reason to take adequate steps to protect and maintain a levy. In *LCP Retail Ltd v Segal* [2006], Chancery Division felt that a landlord's failure to protest when impounded goods were sold by the debtor company, and later to notify the liquidator in the company's winding up of the existence of a walking possession agreement, amounted to an abandonment of their claim over the goods. Any abandonment, however urgent and necessary, had to be satisfactorily accounted for if the bailiff was to retain his rights. Any sort of agreement or arrangement with the debtor was likely to be evidence of seizure which would contradict a claim of abandonment.[83] If a valid seizure had been made but had not been followed through, or if a payment arrangement had been made but had lapsed without the bailiff promptly following this up, any claim to the goods was eventually lost, even though a signed controlled goods agreement might exist.[84]

There are five situations which have been held by the courts clearly not to be abandonment:

- *withdrawal under false representation by the debtor* to the bailiff did not amount to abandonment;[85]
- *temporary withdrawal*: it was not abandonment for the bailiff to go out of possession briefly with the intention of returning: for example, where he went out to get a drink of beer. The bailiff was held to have retained a 'constructive possession' during his brief absence from the premises. Another example of such an absence is *Coffin v Dyke* (1884) - Coffin was left as a 'possession man' in premises under a warrant of execution. No refreshment was provided for him therefore he went to a pub one mile away taking the warrant with him. His absence was only temporary. On return he was assaulted by Dyke to prevent re-entry. The court found that Coffin was in execution of his duty in re-entering and Dyke could be convicted for assault on a court officer.[86]
- *walking possession*: the courts were prepared to treat walking possession, whether by agreement or not, as a form of ongoing constructive possession that survived the bailiff's absence from the premises, even though that may be prolonged. However in one case where the bailiff withdrew simply on receiving from the debtor a letter (rather than signed agreement) acknowledging the possession and permitting him to re-enter as and when he wished it was held that the bailiff went out of possession and did not retake it, so that the goods were abandoned. Being formally sanctioned by statute, a controlled goods agreement will doubtless contradict claims of abandonment, but questions might still arise over anything less than a full, formal agreement in the proper form;[87] or,
- *payment*: there might be no abandonment where there was an arrangement to pay, such as by instalments. If the bailiff then withdrew from control such abandonment at the debtor's request was not voluntary;[88] and,
- *allowing temporary removal of goods:* allowing temporary removal on terms agreed with the debtor need not be abandonment. Where a bailiff permitted a person to take seized goods off the premises for a temporary purpose, with the intention on the part of the bailiff that they should be returned (which was done) it was held that there was no abandonment if the plaintiff restored goods

to the bailiff voluntarily.[89] Generally, though, enforcement agents must heed the warning that permitting sale or removal of goods by the debtor was usually regarded by the courts as abandonment. In *Bagshawes v Deacon* [1898] the sheriff seized goods from Bagshawes but was persuaded to withdraw from possession on learning that the business's goods were to be sold to a limited company. He received part payment and a written promise from Bagshawes to allow him to re-enter. The sale took place and then eight days later the sheriff once more seized the goods. The limited company which had purchased the goods initiated interpleader. The court held that as the sheriff withdrew to enable the goods in the custody of the law to be sold, without being able to demonstrate any urgent necessity to do this, he had abandoned the goods. Secondly in *Re: Dalton* [1963]: a sheriff levied on the stock of a shop and took walking possession but gave limited permission to allow the trader to sell goods as long as they were replaced. The court held that the goods sold under that agreement were abandoned and the value of the execution thus reduced. It went on to make recommendations as to how such levies should be conducted.[90]

To conclude, whether goods have been abandoned is a question of fact, and depends on the court deciding whether firstly goods have been secured and secondly whether there has been an intention to remain in possession of them.[91] Finally, remember that arguments over abandonment are linked to questions as to whether an offence of interference may have occurred (*see 6.6*).

9.11 Notice

The enforcement agent must provide a notice for the debtor giving information about what the enforcement agent is doing after he has entered premises.[92] A similar notice should be presented after taking control of goods or after entering a vehicle on the highway in order to take control of goods. The notice must be in writing and must contain the following information:[93]

· The debtor's name and address;
· The enforcement agent's name and reference numbers and the date of the notice;
· Confirmation that the agent has taken control of goods on a highway or entered a vehicle on a highway with the intention of taking it into control.
· The location of the goods on the highway which were taken into control or the vehicle which was entered

- The make, model, colour and registration number of any vehicle on the highway entered with the intention of taking it into control;
- Whether goods have been taken into control and if so, the date and time of doing this along with a list and description of those goods- that is, their make, model, serial or registration number or other identifying features. This will generally be satisfied by the list provided with the controlled goods agreement (*see 9.7*) or the inventory required under reg.33 (*see next section*) provided that identical goods are concerned;
- The sum outstanding ion the date of the notice;
- Details of how and when payment should be made to prevent further action and the time limits for doing this;
- Confirmation that, if payment is made, the goods will be released from control.

If goods are immobilised on the highway or on the debtor's premises, a written warning after immobilisation will also be required (*see 9.4 above*).[94] If a vehicle on the highway is involved, the notice must also provide the information required by reg.18(4) of the 2013 Regulations (*see 9.5 above*).

If goods are taken into control by removal for storage at a secure location, the notice should also explain:

- That the agent has on a specified date removed the goods to store them securely at another location;
- List the goods removed if they are different from the total of those taken into control. If the goods in question are identical with those listed on the inventory, the latter will be sufficient;
- Provide details of any charge made for storage; and,
- Details of how the goods may be released on payment and collected.

If the details required in these cases are not known at the time of removal, it should be provided as soon as reasonably practicable.[95]

If the debtor is on the premises when the enforcement agent is there, the enforcement agent must give him the notice then. If the debtor is not present at that time, the enforcement agent must leave the notice in a conspicuous place on the premises. If the enforcement agent knows that there is someone else there or that there are other occupiers, any notice left must be placed in a sealed envelope addressed to the debtor. If the premises are occupied by any person apart from the debtor, the enforcement agent must leave at the premises a list of any goods he takes away.

Note that under the former common law provisions it was held that a seizure or could not be invalidated just because the debtor refused to accept the notice or inventory. Moreover, the courts held that a notice should correctly state the person to whom the debt is due- an error in this is a material fault.[96] It was also held that, where a notice is mandatory, failure to provide one or provision of an inadequate notice will not make a seizure invalid or void.[97] Certain errors on notices will not invalidate them- in the name of the debtor, in the date the debt fell due or in not including the date at all.[98] Generally minor mistakes that neither prejudice nor mislead the debtor will be ignored. The fact that exempt items are included in the list does not give an aggrieved person a right to sue as an intention to sell is not a cause of action.[99]

9.12 Inventory

If an enforcement agent takes control of goods he must provide the debtor with an inventory of them as soon as reasonably practicable.[100] Furthermore, if there are co-owners of any of the goods, the enforcement agent must instead provide the debtor as soon as reasonably practicable with separate inventories of goods owned by the debtor and each co-owner and an inventory of the goods without a co-owner. The regulations provide a separate form of inventory, but inventories are also combined with the other key notices (of taking, removal and so on) and will generally be provided in this way.

The regulations must state that the inventory must be in writing, must be signed by the enforcement agent and must contain:[101]

- The debtor's name and address;
- The agent's name, reference numbers and the date of the inventory;
- The name and address of any co-owner of the goods;
- Confirmation that the goods listed on the inventory have been taken into control;
- A list of the goods providing sufficient details to enable the debtor or co-owner to identify them, such as their model, make, serial or registration number, colour, usage or other identifying feature. The reference to usage of goods seems to be a clear allusion to the categories of exempt household and business assets as well as to considerations of the degree of use of an item - its age, condition and value. This provision seems to underline the fact that there is an onus on the bailiff to make enquiries about goods in order to try to elicit such information from debtors. The bailiff should be pro-active in this respect.

The inventory may be combined with a controlled goods agreement or with any notice given under the regulations provided that the inventory is provided at the same time as the agreement/notice and that the goods taken into control are the same as those listed.[102]

These new rules on inventories give statutory form to the previous case law on the matter.[103] The courts repeatedly explained that the purpose of an inventory was to advise all concerned parties, clearly and unambiguously, exactly what items had been seized. With their emphasis upon precise descriptions of the goods taken into control, even down to colour and usage, the new regulations give explicit expression to this. Vague lists, catch all categories and reference to unnumbered collections of items will no longer be acceptable. This is of course reinforced by the provision of mandatory contents for inventories which agents will be obliged to use.

Note that in *Ward v Haydon* (1797) it was held that the mere act of making an inventory or completing a notice is not, on its own, such an "intermeddling" with goods as to make a person liable to trespass. Removal or sale, or payment under the duress of a threatened sale, would be different matters.[104]

9.13 Prior claims

Under the previous law certain creditors had rights to assert prior claims over certain seizures by enforcement agents; most of these have been abolished. The rights of landlords in executions under s.1 Landlord & Tenant Act 1709 and under County Courts Act 1984 s.102 have been repealed. In addition section 80 of the new Act abolishes Crown preference for the purposes of execution against goods.

A further common law principle that previously applied was that goods already seized could not be seized again because the goods levied were in legal custody. It is not clear if a similar principle will be found to apply to the process of taking control of goods, but as discussed in the introduction, on the assumption that this will be the case, the existing law is here outlined (*see also 10.11*). The basic principle was that goods already seized and in the custody of the law could not be seized again by a bailiff. Properly, each bailiff had to wait for the one with a prior levy to complete that levy before proceeding (note that an agreement with the creditor whereby the bailiff will not enforce on terms of payment is equivalent to withdrawing a warrant, so that later levies will gain priority).[105] An alternative approach to this situation which fits within the provisions of the Act is to bring together the binding provisions (see 7.2) and the offence of interfering with goods taken into control to provide similar protection for goods against wrongful dealings with them by debtors. Binding does not, however, address the problem of subsequent attempts to take control by other bailiffs.

9.14 Recent problems with levies

Under the former law various improper means of trying to seize and impound goods were employed by certain bailiffs and firms. These included:

'Remote levies'
Bailiffs would claim to have seized goods without ever having entered premises. This might be done by trying to get a debtor to sign a walking possession agreement at some other location such as his/her place of work or at the bailiff's office. Other specific variants of this procedure:

'Drive-by levies'
Seizures of motor vehicles would be claimed to have taken place by bailiffs who only drove past the premises, stopping briefly to take a note of a car registration number and leaving no notice of the seizure for the debtor;

Levies without entry
Levies have been purported to have been made following a conversation with a debtor on the doorstep (or over an intercom in a block of flats) or by means of looking through the debtor's windows;

Levies without formal documentation
Hitherto it was accepted that, if a bailiff made clear his intention to seize goods and took sufficient steps to follow this up (such as regular and frequent repeat visits to the property) it could constitute a valid levy. Given the far more prescriptive and detailed provisions in the new law, it is unlikely that this will any longer be acceptable.[106]

The mandatory nature of the new forms of taking control should exclude all of these practices in the future. Nonetheless, habit may lead to their mistaken use, at least to begin with.

Footnotes
1 Reg.9(1) TCG Regs.
2 CPR 84.5 & regulation 9(4) TCG Regs.
3 Reg.12 TCG Regs.

4 Regulation 13 TCG Regulations.

5 Reg.13(2).

6 CPR 84.6; reg.13(2)(a) TCG Regs.

7 Reg.34 TCG Regs and see c.12.

8 *Wilder v Speer* (1838) 8 Ad & El 547; *Bignell v Clarke* (1860) 5 H&N 485.

9 Reg.10(1) TCG Regs; see 8.1.2 earlier.

10 Reg.16 TCG regs.

11 65 LT 466.

12 1 Barn KB 3- see also 8.10.

13 Reg.16(2) TCG Regs.

14 Reg.16(4).

15 (1837) 7 C&P 767.

16 6 M & W 149.

17 (1860) 29 LJ Ex 259

18 See *Watson v Murray* [1955] 1 All ER 350 - a case of execution in which the sheriff's officers trespassed by locking up a clothes shop and excluding the trader for a number of days. See also *Saunderson v. Baker & Martin* (1772) 3 Wils 309 - a case of trespass where a sheriff locked premises and took the key after removing goods.

19 *Bissett v Caldwell* (1791) Peake 50; (1978) 88 DLR(3d) 601.

20 Surrender - *Planned Properties v Ramsdens Commercials* (1984) *Times* March 2nd.

21 Sch.12 para.13(1)(b).

22 See R. Card & J. English, *Police law*, Oxford, 13th edition, 2013, p.343; *Suffolk County Council v Mason* [1979] AC 705.

23 Sch.12 para.13(2).

24 Reg.11 Taking Control of Goods Regulations 2013.

25 Regs.17 & 16(3) TCG Regs.

26 Regulation 18 Taking Control of Goods Regulations 2013.

27 Regulation 16(3).

28 Reg.18(5) & (6).

29 See *Wilder v Speer* (1838) 8 Ad & El 547.

30 Regulation 19 Taking Control of Goods Regulations 2013.

31 Para.13(4).

32 Reg.14(2).

33 Again, the term 'implied authority' may appear apt but should be avoided as it refers to powers arising from or implicit in the duties of an agent.

34 Reg.15 TCG Regs.

35 Reg.15(2).

36 Regs15(5) & (6).

37 [1966] Ch 336; [1912] 8 DLR 102; *Paget v Perchard* (1794) 1 Esp 205.

38 (1816) Holt NP 335; (1809) 2 Camp 48; [1876] 2 Ch 291.

39 For example *Re: Basham* (1881) WN 161; *Gibbons v Hickson* (1885) 55 LJQB 119.

40 *Meggy v Imperial Discount Co Ltd* [1878] 3 QBD 711.

41 *Evans v South Ribble Borough Council* [1992] 2 All ER 695 - see *Sources of bailiff law* c.3 p.86.

42 *Lumsden v Burnett* [1898] 2 QB 177 - see *Sources of bailiff law* c.3 p.70.

43 2 All ER 695

44 Respectively 1 DLR 964; LR 5 QB 357

45 *Cole v Davies* (1698) 1 Ld Raym 624; *Re: Meehan* [1879] 6 Nfld LR 172.

46 5 Ch D 809.

47 *Doe d Haverson v Franks* (1847) 2 Car & Kir 678.

48 *Doe d Cox v Roe* (1847) 5 Dow & L 272; *R v Dudley Justices ex p Blatchford* [1992] RVR 63.

49 *Massey Manufacturing v. Clement* (1893) 9 Man LR 359.

50 *Grove v Aldridge* (1832) 9 Bing 428: this includes goods arrested by the Admiralty marshal - *Williamson v. Bank of Montreal* (1899) 6 BCR 486.

51 *Mullet v Challis* (1851) 16 QB 239.

52 (1847) 2 Car & Kir 678; (1800) Forrest 19.

53 *R. v. Vroom* (1975) 58 DLR 565.

54 *Yourrell v. Proby* (1868) 2 CL 460.

55 *Finnigan v. Jarvis* (1851) 8 UCQB 210.

56 *Hodgson v. Lynch* Ir 5 CL 353.

57 *White v Wiltshire* (1619) 79 ER 476 ; *Browning v Dann* (1735) Bullers NP 81c.

58 Locked chests - P.18 Ed.IV fo.4 pl.19 - see *Sources of bailiff law* c.2 p.23; windows - *Lloyd v Sandilands* (1818) 8 Taunt 250; offer to open - *Hutchison v Birch* (1812) 4 Taunt 619.

59 *Ex p Smith* (1890) *The Times* Nov.8th 15b (QBD) & *The Times* Nov.20th 1899 p.17.

60 *Legal Action* April 1994, pp.17 & 18 - see *Sources of bailiff law* c.4 p.112.

61 3 WLR 749; see *Sources of bailiff law* c.3 p.82.

62 Respectively 2 CP 252 ; 42 LT 157.

63 Respectively 3 OR 1 CAN ; 24 LT 88; 1 Ex D 285.

64 For example, Council Tax (Administration & Enforcement) Regulations 1992 reg.47(1); CPR Part 75.10.

65 Reg.24; see 8.11.

66 s268(1)(a) Insolvency Act 1986; [1994] 3 All ER 269 CA; see also *Re: Worsley ex p Gill* [1957] 19 ABC 105.

67 No levy - *Dennis v. Whetham* [1874] 9 QB 345; bill of sale - *Stimson v. Farnham* [1871] 7 QB 175.

68 *Chambers v Coleman* (1841) 9 Dowl 588; *Dennis v Whetham* [1874] 9 QB 345.

69 *Crosley v Arkwright* (1788) 2 TR 603; *Remmet v Lawrence & Nicol* (1850) 15 QB 1004; *Milner v Rawlings* [1867] 2 Exch 249.

70 *Smallcombe v Olivier* (1844) 13 M&W 77; *Milner v Rawlings* [1867] 2 Exch 249.

71 *Munk v Cass* (1841) 9 Dowl 332.

72 *Dennis v Whetham* [1874] 9 QB 345.

73 *Avril v Mordant* (1834) 3 N&M 871; *Molsons Bank v McMeekin ex. p. Sloan* (1888) 15 AR 535; *Slade v Hawley* (1845) 13 M&W 758.

74 *Dennis v Whetham* [1874] 9 QB 345.

75 (1827) 1 Mood & M 77; (1847) 5 D&L 272; *Hammond v Mather* (1862) 3 F&F 151 - another case of ejectment because the tenant locked the house & prevented the landlord distraining.

76 Complaint 10 007 469.

77 See my discussion in *A lawful trespass* chapter 6.

78 *"non nimis graves"*.

79 *"indebitas"*.

80 Reg 47(1) CT(A&E) Regs; reg 16(1) NDR(C&E) Regs.

81 Respectively *R v Burnley JJ ex p Ashworth* [1992] 32 RVR 27; *Legal Action* May 1994 p.22; EWHC 1659.

82 CPR Part 75.10 & 75.1(2)(b); see too Enforcement of Road Traffic Debts Order 1993 article 3 as amended by Tribunals, Courts & Enforcement Act 2007 (Consequential, Transitional & Saving Provision) Order 2014 Sch.para.5(c).

83 [2006] EWHC 2087; must explain - *Ackland v Paynter* (1820) 8 Price 95; agreement - *Anderson v Henry* [1898] 29 OR 719; *Black v Coleman* (1878) 29 CP 507.

84 *Lovick v Crowder* (1828) 8 B&C 132.

85 *Wollaston v Stafford* (1854) 15 CB 278.

86 *Bannister v Hyde* (1860) 2 E & E 627; [1884] 48 JP 757.

87 *Bower v Hett* [1895] 2 QB 337.

88 *Thwaites v Wilding* [1883] 12 QBD 4.

89 *Kerby v Harding* (1851) 6 Exch 234.

90 2 QB 173; [1966] Ch 336.

91 *Eldridge v Stacey* (1863)15 CB NS 458; *Jones v Biernstein* [1900] 1 QB 100- see *Sources of bailiff law* c.3 p.70.

92 Sch 12 para.28.

93 Reg.30 TCG Regs.

94 Regulation 31Taking Control of Goods Regulations 2013.

95 Reg.32 TCG Regs.

96 *R v Butterfield* (1893) 17 Cox CC 598; *Ireland v Johnson* (1834) 4 M&S 706.

97 See *Re: George Castle Ltd* [1928] NZLR 1079.

98 *Wootley v Gregory* (1828) Y&J 536; *Gambrell v Earl of Falmouth* (1835) 4 Ad & El 73; *Moss v Gallimore* (1779) 1 Doug KB 279.

99 *Rutherford v Lord Advocate* [1931] 16 Tax Cases 145; *Beck v Denbigh* (1860) 29 LJCP 273.

100 Schedule 12 para 34.

101 Reg.33 TCG Regs.

102 Reg.33(2).

103 See *Law of seizure of goods*, 2nd edition, 10.2.2 and *Sources of bailiff law* c.4.

104 (1797) 2 Esp 552.

105 *Hunt v Hooper* (1844) 12 M&W 664.

106 *Lloyds & Scottish Finance Ltd v Modern Car & Caravans (Kingston) Ltd* [1964] 2 All ER 732 - see *Sources of bailiff law* c.3 p.72.

Chapter 10

Goods

10.1 Introduction

The Act lays down a number of general principles determining which goods may be seized. It also introduces certain new restrictions upon the personal property that may be taken into control, but most of the established principles upon seizable goods - and therefore the associated case law - will be inherited unamended from the former law.

Broadly it may be said that four categories of property are identified by the new legislation:

- That which can never be taken into control because it is not the property of the debtor;
- That which could potentially be taken into control but which is exempted because it is deemed essential for domestic or trade purposes;
- That which can be taken into control but, because it is subject to claims of co-ownership, has to be given preferential treatment; and,
- That which can always be taken into control and sold because it is the sole property of the debtor. Even this latter category is subject to qualification, though, as the goods must be of sufficient value to justify the taking and associated costs.

There has been a tendency in the past for agents to confuse or overlook these categories and to list items on inventories merely as a means of putting debtors under duress to pay, even though the goods themselves should never have been the subject of a levy. It is to be hoped that with the clearer statutory rules and the simpler procedure for taking control, such incidents will not be repeated in the future.

10.1.1 Location

An enforcement agent may take control of goods only if:

- they are on premises which he has the power to enter under Schedule 12. This refers to premises at which the debtor lives, at which s/he trades, or in respect of which an entry warrant has been issued by a court; or,

·   they are situated on a highway. This may include vehicles, animals found straying or items which have recently been delivered to or are awaiting collection from the debtor's premises.[1]

Subject to these conditions an enforcement agent may take control of goods anywhere in England and Wales (*see chapter 9*).

10.1.2 Debtor's property

An enforcement agent may take control of goods only if they are the sole or joint property of the debtor.[2] Jointly owned goods are discussed in detail later (*see 10.7*). Goods which are the sole property of any third party are now clearly exempt - for example, goods that are hired or leased as well as the property of relatives and friends; their remedies at examined at 13.6.

The Act defines ownership: references to the goods of the debtor or another person are references to goods in which the debtor or that other person has a beneficial interest- in other words, any interest of value in the worth or use of the goods.[3] Also, references to goods of the debtor do not include references to trust property in which either the debtor or a co-owner has an interest not vested in possession (*see 6.9 above*). These definitions seem principally to be concerned with establishing that jointly owned goods are liable to being taken into control (and, as mentioned, specific detailed provision is made regulating the treatment of co-owners- see 10.7), but they have wider implications. It seems that for an enforcement agent to be able to take an interest in goods into control, it will have to be saleable. This may well exclude from seizure third party goods found in a debtor's possession subject to a hire purchase agreement. If the contract is of such a nature that the debtor has no saleable interest or if the interest is determined by the seizure, the bailiff cannot legally take control.[4]

The paragraph specifies that only the debtor's goods may be seized. Under the previous law case authority was developed in respect of bailiff's rights to seize chattels. It is to be presumed for the time being that these rules will still apply. The term 'chattel' covers more than just tangible property and can include such items as:

·   leases (but not interests in leases [5]);
·   rights under contracts; and,
·   such items as the negatives of copyright photographs.[6]

These items and similar forms of property should not be liable to seizure under the new Act.

It will be important for enforcement agents to establish the actual ownership of goods. This will involve enquiries on the premises. If motor vehicles are to be taken into control, then there should at least be "reasonable cause" to assume that a car or van is the property of the debtor and is not needed for business purposes (*see next section*). The mere fact of the vehicle being parked in the street outside the debtor's home is not sufficient; but regular use by the debtor or its regular presence on a driveway may be adequate evidence of its ownership.[7] If any dispute over ownership arises, proof in some form will be required. This might be a statutory declaration (*see 13.3*) and if any claim is resisted a remedy is provided (*see 13.5*).[8]

10.1.3 Exempt & non-exempt goods

An enforcement agent may only take control of any goods that are not exempt.[9] Exempt goods are defined in regulations (*see 10.2-10.4 for full discussion*). The Act also states that the regulations may authorise an enforcement agent to take control of exempt goods in prescribed circumstances, if he provides the debtor with replacements in accordance with the regulations; no such provision has been included in the Taking Control of Goods Regulations 2013.[10] As described later, the new legislation has expanded the categories of exempted goods somewhat, notwithstanding which most of the rules as to what may or may not be taken into control by enforcement agents will derive from the former law. If disputes arise to the exempt status of goods, a remedy exists in the courts - *see 13.12*.

Although not a formal exemption as such, readers should recall that regulation 11 of the Taking Control of Goods Regulations effectively exempts from taking into control various hazardous or diseased goods found on the highway. See the discussion earlier at *9.4*. Likewise, it will be remembered that goods may not be taken into control where only a child and/or a vulnerable person is found on the premises (*see 8.1.2 above*).[11] In both of these instances, some careful investigation of circumstances will be required for an enforcement agent to be satisfied that goods do not fall into either category.

10.1.4 Value of goods relative to debt

An enforcement agent may not take control of goods whose aggregate value is more than the amount outstanding and an amount in respect of future costs, calculated in accordance with regulations.[12] In other words, a seizure must be reasonable and not excessive (see c.13 for remedies). The 'amount outstanding' is defined as the sum of the amount of the debt which remains unpaid (or an amount that the creditor agrees to accept in full satisfaction of the debt) and any amounts recoverable out of proceeds in accordance with regulations under paragraph 62 (costs).[13]

All the same, an enforcement agent may take control of goods of higher value but only to the extent necessary, if there are not enough goods of a lower value within a reasonable distance on a highway or in premises which there is a power to enter under Schedule 12, either initial entry under paragraph 14 or under an existing warrant.

Goods are treated as being above a given value only if it is or ought to be clear to the enforcement agent that they are.[14] Presumably 'more' means significantly more and enforcement agents are allowed some margin for error. These provisions do not affect the power to keep control of goods if they rise in value once they have been taken.

Section One - Exempt goods

The Act defines exempt goods as those which the regulations exclude from being taken into control either on the grounds of description, or circumstances, or both.[15] The meaning of this is that some items may not be seized because of their nature or identity, whereas some may not be seized because of the identity of their owner (the debtor).

The new Act exempts from seizure certain basic and 'necessary' household and business items. This provision repeats protection that has been extended to most forms of seizure since the early 1990s. However, despite that fact that this protection has been in force in English law generally since the mid-1980s, there is surprising little case law authority upon its interpretation. This chapter will therefore draw in part upon Commonwealth authorities upon similar exemptions in force in those jurisdictions and upon informal guidance produced in England and Wales.

It is worth emphasising at the outset the highly subjective nature of the exemptions. The clauses are phrased in such a way as to oblige enforcement agents to enter into a dialogue with the debtor during the levy. Decisions as to the necessity of retaining various chattels cannot be imposed. The debtor's circumstances and needs must be investigated to enable an informed conclusion to be reached. This will inevitably tend to lengthen the levy process, but it is the unavoidable consequence of the form of the provisions on exempt goods.

Taking Control of Goods

If goods are taken into control which a debtor feels should have been treated as exempt, a procedure exists to challenge the seizure through the court. This is described later at *13.12*.

10.2 Statutory exemptions: basic trade items

10.2.1 Form of statutory exemption

The exemption for trade items is as follows:

> "items of equipment (for example tools, books, vehicles, telephones, computer equipment and vehicles) which are necessary for use personally by the debtor in the debtor's employment, business, trade, vocation, study or education, except that in any case the aggregate value of the items or equipment to which this exemption applies shall not exceed £1350."[16]

The meaning of 'tools' was defined in one older judgment: tools of a workman's trade are protected so that he might not be prevented from earning a living, and the term does not extend to items that are not implements, such as documents, patents, address books and references.[17]

It is notable that the new regulation extends protection to students by protecting items needed for study or education (whether full or part time and whether advanced or not). It may also prove to be significant that the text speaks of items (plural) and then proceeds to give plural examples, indicating perhaps that a business could reasonably expect to be left with more than one telephone, PC or van. As for the ceiling for protection of £1350, this will probably require further clarification as the basis upon which this figure is assessed is not clear - is it purchase or resale value?

However, tools are not protected from being taken into control in cases where the bailiff is levying for one of the following debts:[18]

- business rates due under the Local Government Finance Act 1988; and,
- drainage rates due under the Land Drainage Act 1991 and special drainage charges due to the Environment Agency under the Water Resources Act 1991; and,
- taxes due under s.127 of the Finance Act 2008.

We can analyse the elements of this exemption in some detail.

10.2.2 Necessary trade items

The exemptions apply to those chattels which are 'necessary'. This is the key phrase and it is important to define its meaning. Cases have elaborated a number of points:

· *Necessary is not the same as convenient*: In *York v Flatekval* [1971] a Canadian court held (in respect of a car) that the word meant indispensable and essential and related to a tool without which the person could not trade. Nevertheless it had to be construed in light of the relevant facts and circumstances of each case. In the Ontario case *Langdon v. Traders Finance Corporation* (1966) it was repeated that necessity implies that an item or tool is not just a convenience, in the absence of which a person's activities would be restricted, but something in the absence of which the physical ability or capacity to perform some essential qualification or function of his/her business would be inhibited. Again it is a question of fact in each case. Thus, whilst it may be 'beneficial' or 'convenient' to have a car, and its loss might curtail a person's activities, but such questions are not the concern of the creditor and unless it is inconceivable that a person could carry on without it, the vehicle is not to be defined as 'necessary'.[19] Consequently, for example, whilst a van is very useful to a baker for the purposes of deliveries, it is not central to performing the task of baking. Likewise, it was decided that a costermonger (a market seller of fruit and vegetables) did not have to have a barrow in order to continue his trade. It was useful for transporting and displaying wares, but it was not the only method, as (for example) baskets and panniers could be substituted. Finally, a very recent claim by a university lecturer to require a vehicle to get to college was rejected by the High Court as he taught sociology, not motorcycle maintenance.[20]
· *Necessary does not mean the same as cheaper*: another argument made by the claimant in the case just mentioned was that it was cheaper for him to get to work by bike than by other means, such as public transport. True as this may have been - and despite the fact that the available funds might have helped clear the debt - it was not relevant to the question of the need for the bike for performing his teaching duties.[21]
· *Necessary does not mean beneficial to a business* - in *Palmer v Meux* (1857) it was argued that a billiard table and fittings were needed for the purposes of trade as a public house. The Court of Exchequer, however, disagreed: it was not an implement of trade but a mere addition to the furniture of the pub for the purposes of attracting customers. This was especially the case because it was used by the clientele of the pub, not by the publican himself. A similar case is

Addison v Sheppard [1908]. A commercial traveller, employed to sell typewriters on commission, was distrained for rent arrears and the sample machine he carried with him was seized. He claimed this as a tool of his trade but the High Court refused his appeal, doubting that he had any tools or implements of his trade at all. The typewriter was not felt to be essential to his work - it was merely a sample of an implement rather than being an actual implement of his trade as such.[22]

· *Necessary does not imply irreplaceable*: it was argued by the defendants in the case of *Lavell v Richings* in 1906 that a cab driver's cab was not an essential implement of his trade as he could always hire a replacement (the seized cab in question being a hired vehicle). The Lord Chief Justice did not accept this suggestion- if the cab was essential to trade and should be treated as exempted - and that was an end to the argument.[23]

In modern practice in comparable cases it is often argued that if the Public Carriage Office licence is left with the debtor, s/he can always transfer it to another vehicle and carry on trading as a taxi or minicab driver. This argument does not seem to be sustainable. The licence itself is not an asset that may be taken into control and sold, being a merely personal permit (see 10.6.3 later), therefore it is irrelevant to the decision as to what should be exempted. In consequence, this still leaves the vehicle itself as the indisputable trade asset which must be protected.

10.2.3 Aggregate value

Before the 1990s the exemptions of essential tools were capped at a maximum value. The new regulation 4(1)(a) has reverted to this approach. The intention was to prevent businesses claiming all assets as essential items, leaving the bailiff with nothing leviable. It will now be necessary for traders to choose a limited number of the most vital pieces of equipment that fall within the £1350 ceiling and this will unavoidably involve the bailiff in some negotiation and discussion.

10.2.4 Personal exemption

The specification that goods should only be for personal use means that the protection may only be claimed by an individual. There is Canadian authority that the wording is likely to exclude partnerships.[24] From an unreported 1993 Court of Appeal decision in *Sheriff of Bedford & Toseland Building Supplies Ltd v Bishop* it we learn that if a tool was occasionally used by another, it was not protected.[25]

10.2.5 Actual use of tools

The Taking Control of Goods Regulations 2013 make provision for the general protection from taking into control of items in active use by the debtor.[26] It is stated that if an item belonging to the debtor is in use at the time that the agent seeks to take control of it, seizure will not be possible if, in all the circumstances of the case, it is likely to give rise to a breach of the peace. 'In use' is defined as meaning an item in the hands of a person or being operated by him/her. It is notable that the tool or machine in question must be the debtor's property but does not have to be operated by the debtor personally to fall within the exemption. Employees and subcontractors using equipment will qualify for protection.

This specific new provision is, however, complemented by a body of case law relating to tools of the trade, which it may be helpful to review. An item claimed as vital to the continuance of trade does not have to be in use by the debtor every second that s/he is trading for it to be covered by the exemption. Thus, where a woman claimed a sewing machine as a tool of her trade as a seamstress, the fact that at the time of both the levy and of the court hearing she was actually caring for a recently born child did not detract from the validity of her claim; similarly, in another case, even when the possession man told the court that a typewriter had been found covered in dust, it was still treated as an "indispensable" tool of a woman's profession.[27] Comparable is the case of the DJ's record collection mentioned earlier. Some thousands of records were claimed as exempted and clearly only one could be played at a time or only a few could be selected for any particular radio broadcast. Nonetheless, the collection as a whole was exempted from seizure by the High Court.[28]

Many of the earlier cases on usage arose in the context of levies of distress for rent. Before November 1888 tools of the trade were only exempted from seizure if there were sufficient other distrainable goods available or if they were in actual use at the time of the levy. This last common law exemption is still relevant to all forms of seizure of goods and deserves a little more examination.

The point of the exemption of items in use (whether tools or personal apparel such as clothing or jewellery) is that an attempt to seize an item in actual manual possession and employment will give rise to a danger of personal violence and a breach of the peace. The common law has always been careful to avoid any such risk and this potential is as real today as it was a century or longer ago. This caution will particularly apply to tools because of their inherent danger, whether hand or power operated.

What exactly is meant by the phrase "in actual use"? The courts have examined a number of scenarios and have determined that an item is in use if it is in the debtor's hands or is about to be used (or is placed in such a position that it could be used at any moment). For example, tools laid down before a workman, which he might pick up at any second, are covered just as much as an implement actively being worked by an individual (such as a sewing machine or mangle actually in operation at the point of levy).[29] In contrast, though, if the debtor is merely nearby an item- or has even left the room in which it is situated, s/he will not be able convincingly to argue that it was in actual use at the time of the levy, even though it may have been in use minutes previously.[30]

This discussion brings us to the matter of motor vehicles in use. It appears from the cases just examined that if a car or van were to be stopped on the highway, with the debtor at the wheel, the vehicle would be 'in use' and would not be susceptible to being taken. This will probably be the case whether or not the engine is still running. If the driver is in a position where s/he may set off at any minute, any attempt to obtain the keys or to prevent further movement would clearly give rise to the potential for personal injury or damage to property and so would violate the basic common law principle.[31] Of course, if the driver has got out of the vehicle to discuss the matter with the bailiff or officer, it would seem that the vehicle could then lawfully be taken.[32]

Means of transport are therefore, without doubt, lawfully seizeable (*see below*), but most of the older case law features situations in which they are not actively in use at the time of seizure. The only apparent exception to this (and a modern one too) is the case of *Quinlan v LB Hammersmith & Fulham* [1989].[33] In this case a motor car was distrained for rates arrears in the street outside an underground station. What is not clear from the case report is whether Mr Quinlan had parked his car or was driving it at the time. He was certainly inside it, as he was asked to get out and remove his possessions before it was driven away by a bailiff, but whether the engine was running and whether he was about to move is unfortunately unknown to us. Mr Quinlan unsuccessfully argued that a vehicle on the highway could not be taken in any form of seizure under statute - which the Court of Appeal rejected- but he did not advance any argument about the car being in actual use. Perhaps we can infer, therefore, that it was not. Leaving this inconclusive case aside, it seems preferable to assume that persons actively going about their lawful business in motor vehicles should not be impeded by attempts to levy as bad feeling, if not outright hostility, is very likely to be the result and will therefore put the action in breach of the common law rule and so render the levy illegal.

10.2.6 Continuing need

The person must, at the time of the seizure, actually be involved in whatever employment or trade they claim makes the item a necessity. Thus in *McLeod v Girvin Central Telephone Association* (1926) the plaintiff claimed his car as necessary to his work as a telephone line repair man. However as he had been dismissed by the defendants some time previously and now worked as a farmer the car was not exempt.[34] Though a seizure of an exempt item is a nullity, if the debtor's circumstances change after seizure, a vehicle will lose its exempt status and may be seized a second time by the same or another creditor- though a separate, new seizure will be required.[35] Equally if a trade is abandoned before seizure, the exemption could not be claimed, nor may a seizure become illegal because the debtor's business changes after seizure has taken place.[36]

10.2.7 Nature of business

How may 'employment, business or vocation' be defined? It seems that the definition should be a lot broader than that attached to the previous term 'trade', which tended to be regarded only as manual employment and not as encompassing one who acts as a contractor, merchant or service provider.[37] That said, it was held that a piano used by a music teacher was her tool of the trade and accordingly exempt.[38] It will become apparent that a much broader range of jobs, including the 'professions' and company directors and executives, may be included in the phrase, and it seems that even a politician could be included: a member of a legislative assembly with a rural constituency successfully claimed his car as exempt.[39] Vocation has been defined as a person's ordinary occupation or business.[40] Nonetheless there seem to be limits on the application of the term. In *Hayoz v. Patrick* (1961) the court analysed the meaning of the relevant Canadian phrase- "trade, calling or profession" and found that a calling (or vocation in the English equivalent) is more general than a trade or profession but must mean something analogous to the less general words. Neither trade nor calling are synonymous with 'business', so that running a restaurant or café business were found not to be practicing a calling. On the basis of this strict interpretation of this narrowly constructed phrase, it was concluded that it was a lawful to seize tables, chairs, cooking and storage equipment and air conditioning units. Similarly it was held in *Rodi &. Weinberger AG v. Kay* [1959] that any occupation of a business or commercial nature does not fall within the term trade- which implies an artisan, mechanic or craftsman.[41]

10.2.8 Employed or self employed?

A distinction may be made between debtors who are employed and those who are self employed, though similar considerations apply to each. Where the debtor is in paid employment a vehicle can only be regarded as exempt where the possession and use of a car is a condition of employment. If a person is required to have a car in order to perform their duties, and could not keep their job without the use of a car, the vehicle is a necessity and is exempt.[42] Thus the exemption will apply to an estate agent where a car is necessary in order to travel considerable distances between properties and show them to prospective purchasers and would also apply to a salesman where a car is a condition of employment and without which doing the job would be nearly impossible.[43] The person's individual degree of success in actually carrying out the job with the car is irrelevant.[44] A pharmacist who was principal and shareholder in his business and required the vehicle to pick up stock, deliver prescriptions to elderly or housebound customers and to work as a relief chemist in different locations was found to be able to claim the exemption.[45] If the debtor's contract of employment neither requires the employee to have a car nor defines the person's duties as involving the use of one, the vehicle is unlikely to be necessary. See *Goldsmith v Harris* [1928]: the claimant was a manager in a house building firm, and used his car to travel from site to site within the city where he supervised the construction work. The vehicle was claimed as a necessary, but it was not required by the terms of his contract, nor was it essential because of the nature of his occupation. Denniston JA held that:

> "A saw, a plough, an anvil, a fishing net, a truck are necessary to a carpenter, farmer, blacksmith, fisherman or carter if he is to follow his occupation at all. A vehicle for a country doctor, books of account for a business man... are recognised as necessaries as soon as mentioned, for without them pursuit of their respective occupations is impossible. The mere statement that a person is a manager of a building company does not import that a private motor car is necessary; it is only after special evidence is given to show special circumstances relating to a particular position, which involves special duties, that one may say that the work cannot be done without a motor car."

In this particular case there was no such evidence that the person would be unable to hold his position or performing his duties. The debtor may have suffered inconvenience (*see 10.2.2*), and may have had to curtail his activities, but that was a matter for arrangement between him and his employer and was not the concern of the judgment creditors.[46]

In summary, then, for an employee possessing a car is not essential but is simply convenient - for example, in order to get to work - that vehicle will not be exempt. Some other examples include *MacLachlan v Trans Canada Credit Corporation* (1992) - the debtor was a PE teacher and army officer and could not show that the car was essential; Stewart - *Schnurr v Royal Bank* [1993] - employees were allowed to rent cars as and when it was necessary in order to take business trips so that owning a car was not a requirement of the job; *Royal Bank v Smith* (1982) and *Canadian Acceptance Corporation v Laviolette* (1981) - labourers using a truck to get to work did not need it for their jobs; *Langdon v Traders Finance Corporation* (1966) - the debtor was a salesman but there was no evidence that he had to supply a car or carry stock: it was not needed for actually selling goods, just for getting about; *Davies & Davies v Avco Financial Services Canada Ltd* (1966) - a car was not needed in the plaintiff's actual employment and was therefore not exempt, even though the journey to work was 16 miles each way.[47] Finally, a car used in order to transport the debtor's spouse or partner to his/ her job is not exempt because it is not used for the purposes of the defendant's own work. However if the spouse drives the car for this purpose s/he may be able to recover damages for loss of use of the vehicle.[48]

With self employed persons the important question for consideration by the bailiff and the court must be whether the person can continue their trade without the vehicle. Is it so necessary as to be indispensable? In some cases the question will have only one answer: thus a haulier operating with only one lorry or a taxi driver using his only vehicle as a cab should be able easily to prove that their vehicle is exempt, as without it they could not trade.[49] In many other situations the self employed person's business will demand a vehicle for them to be able to trade effectively. Examples include a musical technician using a van to transport equipment; a musician requiring a car to carry instruments and equipment to and from engagements; a floorer who used his car to transport tools and materials (even though it was also used as a family 'pleasure car' for weekend trips); a fisherman who used his car to haul his catch to market; a pedlar who travels round selling goods- even though the vehicle was acquired for use in another business which had by then ceased trading; a manufacturer of neon signs using a van to deliver completed signs- even though there were alternative means of transport available to the defendant, the van was exempt as it was his preferred means of transport, and an accountant working in a rural area who visited clients over a large area and had to transport bulky equipment and materials.[50] These decisions should be compared with the case of a lawyer who partly worked from home and used his car to visit clients around Quebec: when the car was seized in execution it was held not to be specialised equipment essential to his profession.[51]

In respect of the self employed it should also be noted that using a vehicle to seek business is not sufficiently vital to the conduct of the business to make it exempt. Equally, whilst a vehicle itself may be exempt, items used with it, such as a trucker's tarpaulin and blocks, may not be treated as exempt, although they may be convenient and even desirable.[52]

Whilst it is no doubt true that more vehicles will be liable to exemption under the amended rules than before (witness for example the reluctance in Canada to regard a car as a 'tool')[53] it is by no means a blanket exemption. The necessity of an item must be construed in light of both personal and social factors. Because of the nature of the exemption (i.e. that it is necessary to them for personal use) the onus of proof will be on the debtor and a bare assertion of right will not be enough. The fundamental test of the need for the vehicle will be whether the business will cease trading without it. It is a long established principle of enforcement that the purpose of a levy should **not** be to close a business down. The evaluation of the evidence will inevitably fall on the bailiff in the first instance and the bailiff's endeavours to do this may attract the court's sympathy, as it clearly did that of Buchanan CJDC in *Rodi & Wienenberger AG v Kay* [1959] in which he remarked that, in interpreting and applying the provisions on exemptions, the legislature required that bailiffs "will necessarily be persons of outstanding talent".[54]

10.2.9 Examples of exempt & non-exempt trade assets

From the case law it is possible to distil the following further guidance as to what items may be regarded as necessary to a business, or not. Goods that are necessities include:

- Sawmill equipment was felt to be necessary to a mill owner.[55]
- Pool hall equipment such as tables and cues are 'necessary' to such a business.[56]
- The exemption of tools of the trade extended to record books and ledgers. The authority in question was an appeal which proceeded on the basis that the exemption was accepted by the parties and by the earlier judge and jury - an assumption that was questioned but not overturned in the judgment.[57]
- The exemption of tools was also extended to materials.[58]
- Craftsmen's tools - this has included such individuals as joiners, surgical instrument makers and carpenters;[59]
- Lawyers' papers;[60]
- Vehicles integral to a business- such as those used by cab drivers;[61]
- A seamstress' sewing machine;[62]

- A music teacher's instrument;[63] and,
- A laundress' mangle.[64]

Items which may not be regarded as exempt as necessities include:

- *Stock of a business* - as a trader's stock includes all goods and utensils on the premises - the safe, cash register and counter of the business as well as the merchandise actually sold, these items are not exempt from seizure.[65]
- *Samples held by a commercial traveller or representative.*[66] As described earlier, having these is helpful to the individual but not essential to their business, so they are not exempt.
- *An adding machine and typewriter* are not 'necessary tools' for the purposes of a wholesale jewellery business;[67] and,
- *Office equipment* - In the case of a lawyer who partly worked from home, items of office equipment such as a computer, fax, desk and filing cabinets it was held that these items, however useful to him, were not specialised equipment essential to his profession - unlike his law books. (Note also that the court stressed that seizure gave no rights over the personal records kept in files or on the computer).[68]

With all of these examples, the determining factor was that trade could not continue without the continued availability of the items in question. This is the key test which must be applied. It is also notable that direct, physical use of most of the items was another key aspect in their employment.

10.2.10 Claiming the exemption

Claims that items of equipment fall within the exemption may be made by the debtor who uses them or (it seems) by the spouse upon whose behalf the debtor has provided them for his/her business use.[69] On this latter point there has been some difference of opinion. In one English case the county court judge was of the opinion that an item which provided income for an entire household should be exempted, whoever might have acquired it or used it. By contrast, in an Australian decision the court felt that a tool was only protected if it was used in the same trade as that of the debtor: where a wife claimed a sewing machine as exempt in a levy against her stonemason husband, the claim accordingly failed.[70] The stricter interpretation might be only to protect items needed for income earning by the debtor, but protection of the income of the entire household- and therefore the ability to raise funds to clear the debt- might be the more pragmatic as well as 'socially acceptable' approach.

If a claim is to be made, it should be made promptly and in an honest and straightforward manner. For example, in the case of *Moffatt v Lemkin* (1993), a claim to photographic equipment was made by a photographer. In itself, as will be appreciated from what has already been said, this would have been a well-founded claim, with a very good chance of success. However, it was not made until over a year had passed since the levy; a large part of the reason for this was that the debtor had previously sought to claim that the items in question were the property of a third party. The High Court rejected the application because the debtor had not acted with either expedition or honesty.[71]

Initially the claim should be raised with the enforcement agency and/ or the instructing creditor, along with whatever supporting documentation there might be available. Over the last century and a quarter, the courts have formulated guidance for bailiffs when assessing the validity of claims to exemption. These principles have been forgotten of late, but they are worthwhile restating for the twenty first century. In one case the judge warned that the bailiff's duty is to consider the interests of the debtor as well as those of the creditor so that, although no claim for exemption might be made during the levy, the bailiff ought to take care to make "reasonable and proper enquiry" as to tools of the trade on the premises. Any such claims have to be properly dealt with- they cannot simply be ignored because they are inconvenient or may inhibit a levy.[72] If any doubts existed, erring on the side of the debtor will always be the bailiff's best course of action. Any item which might supplement family income potentially falls within the exemption and the agent should be proactive in seeking to establish the exempt status of goods. The judiciary have warned that failure to make enquiries about exempt items could also endanger a bailiff's certificate. In *Atkinson v Lyons* (1905) the court advised against seizing tools of the trade unless (at least) the debtor signed the inventory to confirm that an item was not an essential tool and that s/he consented to its seizure. In *Singer Manufacturing Co v Butterfield* (1902) the judge even suggested that the debtor be invited to select the items to be treated as exempt.[73]

10.2.11 Challenging seizures

If representations to the bailiff company are not accepted, the debtor may initiate a formal claims procedure under the new legislation. This is similar to that used by third party claimants to goods and ultimately can lead to an application to court for a determination (*see 13.12 below*). It may be noted that, although this remedy is provided by the Civil Procedure Rules, debtors are not alerted to it by any of the notices that must be served upon them.

10.3 Statutory exemptions: basic household goods

The regulations state that an enforcement officer may not seize the following basic household items:[74]

"such clothing, bedding, furniture, household equipment and provisions as are reasonably required to satisfy the basic domestic needs of the debtor and every member of the debtor's household, including but not restricted to" the following examples. A quite comprehensive list is then provided:

- either a cooker or a microwave - but not both cooking appliances;
- a refrigerator;
- a washing machine;
- a dining table large enough, and sufficient dining chairs, to seat the debtor and every member of the debtor's household;
- beds and bedding sufficient for the debtor and every member of the debtor's household;
- one landline telephone, or if there is no landline telephone at the premises, a mobile or internet telephone which may be used by the debtor or a member of the debtor's household;
- any item or equipment reasonably required for —
  - the medical care of the debtor or any member of the debtor's household;
  - safety in the dwelling-house (presumably items such as safety gates and fire blankets); or
  - the security of the dwelling-house (for example, an alarm system) or for security in the dwelling-house (perhaps items such as safes and personal alarms);
- sufficient lamps or stoves, or other appliance designed to provide lighting or heating facilities, to satisfy the basic heating and lighting needs of the debtor's household; and,
- any item or equipment reasonably required for the care of-
  - a person under the age of 18;
  - a disabled person; or
  - an older person."

Several observations may be made on this newly expanded set of exemptions. It is notable, firstly, that 'provisions' are included alongside items of equipment and furnishings. This must refer to food and other consumable supplies such as cleaning products. Secondly, as items needed for the care of children and disabled persons are exempted, it will be necessary for the bailiff to make enquiries with the debtor as to the ages and needs of individuals in a household before making any decisions as to what should be taken into control and what should be treated as exempt. Readers must bear in mind the definition of disability contained in regulation 2 of the Taking Control of Goods Regulations (*see 2.2*). The NSEA repeats some of these exemptions, for example advising that enforcement agents should not remove items clearly identifiable as required for the care and treatment of the disabled, elderly and seriously ill.

The regulation also exempts certain dogs from seizure (regardless of value).[75] This category includes guide dogs, hearing dogs and dogs for disabled persons, sheep dogs, guard dogs and domestic pets. It is to be observed that more than purely 'domestic' or companion animals are included: 'assistance' dogs for persons with disabilities are protected, as are working dogs on farms. This latter mention is one of the few direct references to the needs of farming businesses (*see 10.12.1 below*). One point of uncertainty in this regulation is the reference at the end to "domestic pets." It is unclear whether this a general exemption regardless of species, or whether it refers only to dogs in line with the rest of the sentence.

There are also exemptions for certain motor vehicles (for which see later). These new categories of exemption are far more generous than those they replace, both in the scope of items listed and also in the fact that the regulations take the trouble to stipulate that each member of a household should be provided with adequate seating, bedding and the like.

Unlike trade vehicles and tools, there is no limit placed on the value of household goods which might be treated as exempt. There is no reason in principle why assets of considerable value might not be protected by the above categories. See, for example, the pre-reform case of *Brookes v Harris* [1995] in which the defendant successfully argued that, as a presenter of musical programmes on television and radio, his collection of records, cassettes and compact discs was exempt from seizure because it was a tool of his trade. The High Court accepted this, irrespective of the fact that the total collection was valued by the defendant at between £10,000 and £20,000.[76]

10.4 Other Statutory exemptions

10.4.1 Homes

An innovation in the new regulations is to specifically exempt from seizure goods that also constitute the debtor's only or principal home. Hitherto, there was no specific protection for tents, caravans and mobile homes.[77]

10.4.2 Items in use

As already described, the new Regulations have partly confirmed a longstanding common law rule that items in use should not be seized. Any chattel belonging to a debtor should not be taken into control if it is in use at the time of the attempted taking and the bailiff's attempted seizure could provoke a breach of the peace.[78] 'In use' is defined as meaning that the item is in the hands of or is being operated by the person;[79] this clearly relates to tools and other such manual implements rather than large machines operating without human supervision or, for that matter, items of clothing or jewellery. Although the common law rules on distraint on wearing apparel in use have probably been abolished, it may still be useful to observe their guidance as breaches of the peace are just as likely to be provoked by attempts to take control of watches and coats as tools of the trade.

Part Two - Taking control of specific goods

10.5 Saleable goods

The purpose of taking control of goods and chattels is their eventual sale, if the debt cannot otherwise be cleared. It follows inevitably from this that the goods taken into control must be capable of sale. The issue of third parties' property is discussed later. Here the saleability (and therefore liability to be taken into control) of the debtor's personal property is discussed.

10.5.1 Goods with value

The bailiff could previously only seize such things "where the valuable property is in somebody" and that could be sold.[80] As a consequence items that could not be sold, such as deeds and other personal papers, or personal photographs, should not have been the subject of a levy.[81] Equally personal effects of minimal worth (and very likely not attractive at public auction, as is the case with much jewellery) should not have been taken. A further relevant principle that was applicable in execution is that where the only goods available were of insufficient value to even cover the costs of the process, the proper course of action for the bailiff was to notify the creditor of this and to return the warrant unexecuted.[82] Where inexpensive jewellery or other personal items are taken, they will very likely not even cover the standard visit and levy fees, and a return of no goods is the still appropriate response by the bailiff.

The sorts of goods typically worth seizing are office furniture, cars, high quality domestic furniture, garden equipment and antique and 'art' items. These will be seized based on a valuation of their sale price at auction. Only enough to cover the execution can be seized.[83] However it is difficult to sell many second hand goods by auction because of controls, such as Consumer Protection Act 1987, over the electrical safety of audio visual and white goods, the fireproofing of furniture and safety of children's items. The effect of this is that it may often not really be worth removing any items from the average home.

The NSEA explicitly addresses the issue of levies made upon goods of negligible value - largely for the purposes of securing a bailiff's costs. It states that "Enforcement agents should be aware of circumstances where a 'no goods' valuation may be appropriate– for example where no goods of sufficient value have been identified; or where the removal of goods would lead to severe hardship for the debtor. In such instances the enforcement agent should make the creditor aware of this situation." This guidance helpfully supplements the passing acknowledgement of such situations made by regulation 24 of the 2013 Regulations.

10.5.2 *Equitable interests*

As they cannot be sold, equitable interests should not be seized.[84] In *Schott v Scholey* (1807) the court reasoned that whilst a legal interest in property such as a lease could be seized and sold, the same could not apply to equitable interest through simple practical considerations of inconvenience- for example the difficulty of valuation and the impossibility of delivery of possession.[85] Although the court in Schott did question if the case might be different for equitable interests in goods rather than land, the case law is that any equitable interests, whether under an equitable mortgage, under a bill of sale or otherwise are protected from seizure and may be protected by a claim to third party ownership.[86] For the treatment of trust property *see 6.9 above*.

10.6 Financial assets

It is not only personal property such as goods and chattels that may be taken into control. The new Act has expanded the range of financial assets liable to seizure by enforcement agents.

10.6.1 *Money*

It seems that bailiffs may no longer seize money, in the sense of cash; the statutory powers permitting this have been repealed and there is no explicit mention of the right within the new Act. In a couple of places there are allusions to the apparent possibility of taking money into control,[87] but otherwise the legislation speaks only in terms of 'goods.' There is a possibility that taking control of notes may be possible under the provisions relating to securities (see next section), as strictly a bank note is a promissory note, but the situation is unclear.

The only exception to this rule seems to be magistrates' courts, in the enforcement of civil debts. Bailiffs enforcing warrants of control for these liabilities are still permitted to seize money as well as goods under much older provisions which have not been repealed.[88]

10.6.2 Bills of exchange and other securities

It is made clear that "securities" includes bills of exchange, promissory notes, bonds, specialties and securities for money. These items are seizeable under the provisions of the 2007 Act, though special rules are made regarding their disposal (*see Chapter 11*).[89]

Bills of exchange and the like partake of the nature of money, but have the character of chattels and choses in action as well. It is as chattels that they may be seized by bailiffs. It is as choses in action that they may be converted in to the proceeds of execution. At common law negotiable instruments and cash were not seizeable, and it is only by statute that this situation has been changed. This was done originally for sheriffs by means of s.12 Judgments Act 1838. This section provided a model for the later civil court provisions (e.g. s.91 CCA) and, it is suggested, for the procedure to be followed by other bailiffs in this position.

The instruments (or sufficient as are necessary to cover the judgment debt) may be seized and held as security by the bailiff. When the time for payment on the bill, bond etc arrives, the bailiff may sue upon it in his/ her name to recover the sums due (and may even issue execution upon such a judgment). The sums raised are paid over to the original creditor. Any surplus after the expenses of the execution shall be returned to the debtor. Note however that the High Court enforcement officer is not bound to sue on the instruments unless indemnified for all the costs of the action by the execution creditor.

10.6.3 Other assets

A life assurance policy was held not to be security for money and thus not seizeable, nor was any money payable under it.[90] The common law principle that choses in action could not be taken has not been altered by statute other than in respect of bills of exchange,[91] so it seems that it will not be possible to seize the following:

- the debtor's debts;[92]
- a liquor licence, as it is a non-assignable personal right;[93]
- an interest from year to year after the expiry of the term;[94]
- stocks and shares;[95]
- dividends;[96]
- patents;[97] or,
- trade marks and copyright.[98] In similar fashion it was observed that pensions could not be seized as, like patents and copyrights, they are personal privileges given to a person as a compensation or reward for the public advantage gained from that person's work.[99]

Goods held on pawn by the debtor could not be seized, but the debtor's interest in them could. The bailiff could then receive monies paid to redeem pledges or sell the pawned items when the time for redemption was passed.[100]

10.7 Jointly owned goods

A "co-owner" in relation to goods of the debtor is defined as a person other than the debtor who has an interest in the goods, but only if the enforcement agent knows that the person has an interest in the particular goods or would know - if he made reasonable enquiries.101

If goods that are jointly owned by the debtor and another person are seized, that person is entitled to a copy of the inventory taken under para.34(3) (*see 9.12*), to a copy of the valuation conducted preparatory to sale (*see Chapter 11*)[102] and to notice of any sale that is arranged. The duty on the enforcement agent to supply this succession of notices indicates that there is a clear obligation to make enquiries about ownership. Once again, as with the exempt status of items, the bailiff is possessed of the information on parties' legal rights and should be pro-active in making enquiries to discover the necessary information. The bailiff should not be passive and assume that the co-owner will make a claim if s/he feels that they have an interest which should be protected; it cannot be taken for granted that a person will have the confidence to do so or will realise that their rights are still respected even in cases of seizure and sale.

On a practical note at the stage of taking an list of goods, it may be noted that the stand alone inventory prescribed by the Certification Regulations includes space for recording the details of joint owners. However, the inventories incorporated into the controlled goods agreement, removal notice and notice of taking control do not make the same provision. It seems that agents who discover that co-owners exist will be obliged to complete both forms in order to capture the necessary information.

If a sale takes place, the Act provides that the enforcement agent must first pay the co-owner a share of the proceeds of those goods proportionate to his interest before dealing with the rest of the proceeds of the sale.[103] This interest will be cleared in full from the proceeds (along with the auctioneer's fees) before anything else is paid.[104] If a dispute arises over a third party's claim to goods, it may be resolved by application to a court (see *13.5 below*).

These provisions of the new Act confirm the previous common law position,[105] but in the past most bailiffs took little care to ensure that joint owners received their due share of any proceeds of sale. Placing this duty on a statutory basis will considerably enhance the position of co-owners and may alter bailiffs' attitudes to seizures in properties shared by spouses, civil partners and co-habiting couples (see *10.17 below*).

10.8 Fixtures

This section will describe the old case law on fixtures in levies of execution and assumes that these rules are likely to be adapted to cases of taking control.

10.8.1 Basic rules

The basic principle was that as execution could not be levied on real property, fixtures which were attached to the property had ceased to be chattels and as a result could not be taken.[106] In *Boyd v Shorrock* [1867] the court defined fixtures as "things ordinarily affixed to the freehold for the convenience of the occupier, and which may be removed without material injury to the freehold", for example machinery and cupboards.[107] Chattels actually built into the structure of a property become part of it, such as doors, windows, hearths and chimney pieces.[108]

Help may also be derived from the definition found in *Hellawell v Eastwood* (1851).[109] Whether an item is a fixture is a question of fact: the court must firstly consider the mode of annexation and the extent of annexation - whether an item can be removed easily, safely and without damage to itself or the building; secondly the court must examine the object and purpose of the annexation and the intention of the person fixing them - whether it was for the permanent and substantial improvement of the property or for a temporary purpose.

These elements may be examined in detail:

- *degree of annexation*: articles simply resting on the ground by their own weight are not normally regarded as fixtures. This is so even though the ground may be specially prepared to receive them or though a base is built and even though they may sink into the ground by their own weight.110 If items can be removed without great damage, even though they may be well attached and the process of removal may involve digging, they are not fixtures.111 Items screwed, bolted or nailed down are generally fixtures, but the purpose can be a very important factor. Consequently even if the chattel is cemented in, it will not be a fixture if the purpose is not permanent.112 The importance of degree as a factor will vary also with the size of the item in question, so that a house, though not fixed, will probably be a fixture. Unfixed articles essential for the use of the property may be treated as fixtures, such as keys.113 Items simply plugged into a power supply aren't fixtures but light fittings wired in probably are.114
- *purpose of annexation*: increasingly in modern cases degree has been replaced by purpose as the important factor in determining the nature of a chattel.115 If the purpose of the annexation of a chattel is its better enjoyment as a chattel, it is not a fixture. An item affixed for permanent improvement of a property is a fixture.116 Thus items such as paintings, tapestries and antique panels are not fixtures, but a wall, though simply resting by its own weight, is a fixture if the intention is to make it part of the realty.117 The purpose of annexation is to be ascertained not from the motives of the person fixing the chattels but from the circumstances of the case.118 The circumstances can include current tastes and fashions as well as the property interest of the person.119 Direct evidence of intention is inadmissible; instead the court's test should be objective.

This analysis was adopted in the modern case *TSB ex p. Botham* [1996] in which the Court of Appeal repeated that the two main factors to be considered when determining whether items were fixtures were method and degree of annexation, and object and purpose of annexation. On this basis it was concluded that fitted carpets, curtains, gas fires and white goods were not fixtures, whilst, on the facts of the case in question, light fittings, bathroom fittings and fitted kitchen units had become fixtures.120 The existence of a hire purchase agreement in respect of a chattel or an agreement that it will not become a fixture, does not prevent it becoming one.

Most recently the subject of fixtures has been examined in *Peel Land & Property (Ports No.3) Ltd v TS Sheerness Steel Ltd* [2013].121 The case was concerned specifically with 'tenant's fixtures' (for which see later) but it provides a very clear modern exposition of the basic principles of the law on fixtures, a valuable summary of the key cases and confirmation of the continued relevance of this learning to modern practice. As a preliminary to his analysis of the individual pieces of machinery and plant which were the subject of the dispute, Morgan J surveyed the law on the treatment of fixtures and examined the means of distinguishing classes of goods. He emphasised that, to differentiate between chattels and fixtures, the test is the degree and object of annexation to the property. If they are attached for the permanent and substantial improvement of the premises, they are fixtures; if they are attached on a temporary basis, and for the purposes of improved enjoyment and use of the goods themselves, they are chattels. A further distinction is made between fixtures which must be left by a tenant and those which may be taken away at the end of a lease. Tenant's fixtures are items annexed to a property for reasons of trade, or for "mere ornament and convenience" and which may be removed without causing substantial damage to the property and without destroying or seriously impairing the item itself. The size and weight of an item is not especially relevant here- a large prefabricated building could be disassembled and taken away for rebuilding elsewhere without damage to itself or the land; a concrete base upon which it stood could not be removed - nor could a more conventional brick structure.

We may therefore identify the following as classes of fixtures:

- *barns, sheds & greenhouses*: these are not fixtures even if they are bolted down.[122] A conservatory however will be a fixture;
- *machines*: engines and parts fitted to them are fixtures. Looms nailed to the floor are affixed as are beer machines in a pub, but a printing machine simply standing on a floor remains a chattel. Freestanding equipment does not become a fixture solely because another machine supplying power to it is affixed;[123]
- *other business equipment*: fixtures may include stills set in brickwork, fixed ladders, swimming pool equipment, an alarm and video door entry system and a lift; a cinema screen fixed to a wall, advertising boards and tip up seats fixed to the floor, all equipping a cinema; millstones; a skating rink floor especially installed by the tenant; items, such as an emulsifier, cream separator and ice chopper used in a dairy ice cream business; an inn signboard; post office fittings such as lockable letter boxes, and railway tracks.[124] By contrast chairs lent on hire for a limited period but screwed to the floor for safety reasons, a machine fixed by brickwork to a factory floor and a railway laid on piles are not fixtures- nor are horses, and by extension motor vehicles, used by a firm off their premises.[125]

- *fuel meters and fittings* are fixtures; light bulbs are not;[126]
- *shop fittings*: a counter and rack lightly screwed to a wall are not fixtures;[127] and,
- *domestic fittings*: kitchen units are fixtures, but appliances within them such as fridges and gas cookers are not. However items such as ranges and ovens are fixtures. Bathroom fittings in a fitted bathroom are fixtures as are fitted wardrobes and cupboards, mirrors, shelves and towel rails; the same case also indicates that parquet floors and linoleum or vinyl flooring are also likely to be treated as fixtures.[128]

In summary, items simply resting on the premises or lightly attached to it are unlikely to be fixtures but once an item is a fixture, any other article which is an integral part of it also becomes annexed, even if not attached to the fixed item (such as the drive belt on a machine) and the whole assemblage then remains a fixture permanently and cannot be seized. A bailiff could be sued for trespass to land for removing fixtures, although mere constructive seizure without severance or removal was not enough to found claim.[129]

10.8.2 Other examples

The above examples can be supplemented by case law looking at various situations in which claims were made to property affixed to the freehold by the owner - for example, between mortgagor and mortgagee or tenant for life and remainderman.[130]

The principle in mortgage case law is that items annexed by the mortgagor pass as fixtures with the freehold to the mortgagee.[131] This seems to apply even when partnership property is annexed to the premises of one partner.[132] Thus from mortgage cases we gather that if machines are fixtures which pass automatically with the land, so is every part of them, such as drive belts; that the degree of annexation is an important factor to consider- so even an item on HP secured by bolts to prevent rocking ceases to be a chattel and becomes a fixture;[133] that even if fixtures are intended only as temporary improvement, they can still become part of the land but the onus of arguing this lies with the person seeking to protect them; that items set into, but not attached to property, are not fixtures - nor are spares for machines that are not actually attached to them;[134] that all machinery affixed in a 'quasi-permanent' manner becomes part of the property (i.e. the items are intended to remain on the premises for their better use and enjoyment), even though the purpose of annexation was steadying the items and that they could be removed without injury to them or to the freehold; and that even if goods are simply annexed for their more convenient use, not to improve the property, and may be removed without any appreciable damage to the freehold, they are fixtures.[135]

Note that items do not need to be separately mentioned to pass as fixtures with a mortgage. If they are separately described, it will not make the mortgage a bill of sale - nor will the right of a mortgagee of a leasehold to remove fixtures as against the lessor (for which see below).[136] However if the mortgage allows the mortgagee to sever and sell fixtures apart from the land, it is a bill of sale- for which see 10.19.[137]

The above rules were complicated by the further principle that, in execution against a tenant, whatever the tenant could sever, as between landlord and tenant, could be seized by the bailiff.[138] Therefore, having determined that an item was a fixture, in some cases it was necessary to move onto consideration of the separate issue of whether it was a fixture removable by a tenant (see next section).

10.8.3 Tenant's fixtures

Generally tenants are permitted to remove those chattels that they have affixed for the purposes of trade, and those put up for ornament or domestic use, and which are physically capable of removal without substantial damage to the land or to the chattel.[139] All such items could be seized in execution.[140] However these rights may be modified by the lease, in which case the High Court enforcement officer could not remove if the tenant could not.[141] The rules on tenant's fixtures apply to licencees just as much as tenants.[142]

The authorities on landlord and tenant fixtures give a contrasting picture of what can be removed from premises, but the case law may be summarised as follows. Trade fixtures include:

- *business equipment* such as machines, plant, vats and utensils but not chemical plant; engines for collieries; petrol pumps- though bolted down and linked to underground petrol tanks; pub fittings and brewing equipment;[143]
- *small buildings* such as sheds built on brickwork in the ground, glasshouses in a market garden and pre-fabricated buildings;[144]
- *electrical & gas fittings* including fluorescent light boxes screwed to a ceiling;[145]
- *shrubs & trees* which are the stock of a market garden,[146] but not fruit bearing trees in an orchard or trees which would be destroyed by removal;

The purpose of this right of removal is the protection of trade. Accordingly it has been held that locks, keys, bolts and bars to secure premises are not fixtures that can be taken by a tenant.

There is also a right to remove fixtures installed for ornamental purposes or for the domestic convenience and utility of the tenant. In determining whether the fixture is removable a number of considerations should be taken into account. Has the method of fixing made it permanent, as a more secure method of annexation may indicate that purpose of affixing was improvement of the premises? Would the chattel still be usable after removal? Would removal do serious damage to the structure of the property, rather than just the decoration? Ornamental items should be specifically ornamental and not an ordinary accessory of the property. Thus a conservatory was not a removable fixture.[147] This class of fixtures includes such items as: panelling, suspended ceilings and chimney pieces installed by a tenant in a flat; bookcases and ornamental fireplaces; pictures and frames screwed to walls; blinds; cupboards; bookshelves; cornices, wainscotting and stoves, ranges ovens and boilers.[148]

The High Court enforcement officer could also seize any interest that the tenant had in fixtures which were included in the lease. All fixtures removable by a tenant might be taken - whatever their description - unless they were simply too unwieldy to remove. Upon seizure fixtures had to be separated from the rented property and sold.[149] The High Court enforcement officer could not seize fixtures unlawfully severed by the tenant.[150]

Lastly, a tenant's right to remove items as against the landlord ceases on termination of the lease and on disclaimer by the tenant's trustee in bankruptcy[151] - though it has been held that the tenant (and his/ her trustee) has a reasonable time to remove after termination.[152] At the time of termination of the lease, property in the tenant's fixtures vests in the landlord. The tenant may still remove fixtures if s/he is holding over at the end of the term.[153]

10.8.4 Agricultural fixtures

One class of tenant's fixtures requires separate consideration - that of chattels affixed to premises by tenants of agricultural holdings. At common law such fixtures were not removable, but statute intervened to alter this, with the consequence that these items were seizeable in execution. Two statutory codes apply, depending on the nature of the tenancy.

If the tenancy is of an agricultural holding regulated by Agricultural Holdings Act 1986, the rights of tenants to remove fixtures are controlled by s.10. The basic rule is that a tenant farmer may remove:

- any engine, machinery, fencing, or other fixture of any description fixed to the holding by the tenant, whether for agricultural purposes or not; and,
- any building erected by him on the holding.[154]

These rights apply to any fixture or building acquired by the tenant as well as erected by him/ her, but do not apply to any buildings or fixtures put in place as a result of an obligation; any fixture or building replacing one belonging to the landlord; a building in respect of which the tenant is entitled to compensation under the Act or a building or fixture dating to before 1884. The tenant's common law right to remove trade or ornamental fixtures is unaffected.[155]

If the tenancy is a farm business tenancy regulated by Agricultural Tenancies Act 1995, the Act provides a complete code relating to all tenant farmers' fixtures. The basic right to remove applies to:

- any fixture of whatever description affixed to the holding by the tenant, whether for agricultural purposes or not; and,
- any building erected by him on the holding.[156]

As under the 1986 Act these rights to remove do not apply to certain fixtures - specifically any buildings or fixtures put in place as a result of an obligation; any fixture or building replacing one belonging to the landlord; a building in respect of which the tenant is entitled to compensation under the Act or a building or fixture to which the landlord gave consent on the condition that it was not removed by the tenant. These provisions apply to any buildings or fixtures acquired by the tenant as they apply to items fixed by him/ her. Tenants of farm business tenancies are deprived of their common law rights regarding fixtures.[157]

There is also a common law right for tenants of agricultural properties to remove certain items which may at first glance appear to be fixed buildings. These are Dutch barns; barns resting on the soil and barns resting on staddles.[158] These structures are not regarded as fixtures as normally soil is not displaced in their erection, nor is there any cementing or fastening of them to existing structures in the soil. Readers should however note that the Court of Appeal felt it could derive little assistance from these cases because of their age when determining the issues that were in dispute *Elitestone v Morris* in 1997 (see 10.8.1 earlier).[159]

10.9 Personal items

Over and above the exemption of basic clothing described earlier, wearing apparel in use, in the sense of clothing, may not be seized.160 Whether this exemption extends to items such as jewellery and watches is unknown. Nevertheless the courts may be prepared to extend these authorities as their primary purpose was not to protect specified items but to avoid levies which would almost necessitate an assault and breach of the peace in order to realise them. However if the clothes have been removed, for instance in getting ready for bed or for the purpose of washing them, they may be seized.[161]

10.10 Assets of deceased debtors and their personal representatives

10.10.1 Introduction

If the debtor dies a number of extra rights and liabilities come into effect. In the execution of court judgments, if the debtor dies after the judgment, but before issue of a writ or warrant, permission of court is needed to issue (see 7.3 above). If the judgment debtor dies after the writ is issued the bailiff may proceed and seize the debtor's goods, whoever may be holding them. Goods of a testator in the hands of an executor or administrator could be taken in execution against that person as executor/ administrator.[162]

10.10.2 Trustees

Execution against a trustee for a personal debt could not be levied on the trust estate. Note also the judgment in *Duncan v Cashin* [1875]- the settlee had replaced some of the items left in trust for her by her father: it was suggested that these were bought by her with her own money as agent for the trustees and also could not be seized.[163] If a trustee ran up debts whilst administering the business of the assignor, the trust property could not be seized.[164] However the trustee had a right and interest in the goods and so had a right of indemnity in the nature of a lien. A creditor of the trustee could in turn demand an indemnity for trade debts out of the business estate held on trust.[165]

10.10.3 Personal Representatives

Where execution was levied against a debtor acting as personal representative for a deceased third party, the bailiff could not seize the deceased's goods in the debtor's hands.[166] In the latter case, the fact that the executor carried on the deceased's business as his own was held not to entitle the judgment creditor to seize the deceased's assets. However, it was stressed that lapse of time and enjoyment of assets in a manner inconsistent with the trusts in the will, coupled with the consent of the beneficiaries, might raise an inference of a gift of assets to the executor by them, thus entitling the judgment creditor to seize them. If the business was carried on in line with trusts in the will, the lapse of time was not relevant.[167] If the business was continued for the benefit of the estate, but debts were accrued, it appeared that creditors of the business might enforce against the assets of the estate.[168] If the personal representative and spouse treated the testator's goods are if they were their own, they might be seized in execution against the spouse.[169] If the executor incurred debts in the course of such trading, these were his/ her personal debts, and enforcement had to be against his/ her own property.[170] Creditors were regarded as having a lien on the personal representative's interest in the estate, so as s/he was entitled to be indemnified out of the estate, they might also claim the benefit of that right.[171] Creditors were also entitled to an indemnity if the assets of the testator were used for the benefit of the executor.[172] Goods in the hands of an agent of the executor could not be seized.[173] Where a receiver or manager was appointed in an administration action to carry on the business in succession to the executor, the same principles applied.[174]

10.10.4 Heirlooms

Heirlooms require special mention apart from fixtures, *for which see 10.8*. They are chattels which are so associated with real property that they are regarded as an essential feature of its ordinary enjoyment and use, and they were accordingly treated as inseparable from the land in any settlement. A settlement may thus annex furniture and household chattels, goods and effects to a house as heirlooms and give them a heritable character which they would not otherwise possess. Because of this nature as real property, heirlooms could not be seized.

10.11 Goods subject to prior levies

The new Act is not entirely clear on the status of goods taken into control and whether they may subsequently be taken again by a later creditor. The binding effect of a warrant or enforcement notice was described earlier at *7.2*; this may give precedence throughout the entire process. It is not explained whether the security created by taking into control is additional to the effect of binding (*see the introduction to chapter 9*). If this is so, reference to former case authority may be beneficial.

The principle applied under the former common law was that those items already seized could not normally be seized again as an interest in the goods has been vested in a third party by the prior seizure;[175] it was said, though, that a creditor could consent to waive his rights.[176] It is assumed that the courts will decide that a similar consequence flows from goods being taken into control.

There was an exception in respect of execution, as later writs bind earlier (*see 7.2*), even though the goods are already seized and in the custody of the law under a prior writ.[177] Otherwise, the courts held that goods already distrained could not be seized in execution whether for rent or for taxes;[178] equally, goods already seized in execution can't be seized unless the execution had been abandoned, the levy was irregular or the execution had been satisfied.[179] An illegal seizure did not disturb the debtor's possession so the goods might still be seized in subsequent levies.[180] If goods already subject to a levy were seized again it was treated as the offence of poundbreach, for which *see 6.6*.[181]

10.12 Motor vehicles

Motor vehicles are available for seizure like any other asset, and are obviously the most valuable and easily accessible of most debtors' possessions. There is almost no legal guidance as to the procedure to be followed in seizing vehicles.

10.12.1 Statutory exemptions

Vehicles are exempt if they are needed personally for trade (see earlier) but also if they fall into certain essential classes:[182]

- a vehicle on which a valid disabled person's badge is displayed because it is used for, or in relation to which there are reasonable grounds for believing that it is used for, the carriage of a disabled person. Careful enquiries will have to be made; readers must bear in mind the definition of disability contained in regulation 2 of the Taking Control of Goods Regulations (*see 2.2*);
- a vehicle (whether in public ownership or not) which is being used for, or in relation to which there are reasonable grounds for believing that it is used for, police, fire or ambulance purposes; and
- a vehicle displaying a valid British Medical Association badge or other health emergency badge because it is being used for, or in relation to which there are reasonable grounds for believing that it is used for, health emergency purposes.

Readers should observe the subtle difference in language between the different exemptions. There seems to be a contrast between vehicles needed by disabled persons and those used for emergency purposes. The latter must be "being used" - seemingly in active use at the time of the levy - whilst cars displaying blue badges do not seem to have to be being driven by the disabled person at the time - nor even to have to be displaying the blue badge - for the exemption to apply. However, possession of the blue badge is essential to the exemption. If the bailiff could tell from observing the vehicle that it was used by a disabled individual - for example, because of adaptations made to it - this could still furnish sufficient grounds to protect it from taking into control.

10.12.2 Ownership: third party claims

Issues of ownership are very likely to arise in respect of cars as they may be subject either to HP or leasing agreements. Before removal therefore the bailiff will check ownership with HPI and DVLA and if the results of this are satisfactory is then likely to remove promptly. One issue to note in respect of road traffic penalties is the difference between who may be held liable for such a penalty, and ownership of a vehicle. Under the Traffic Management Act 2004 the registered keeper of the vehicle can be regarded as the owner for the purposes of imposing a penalty.[183] It is proposed that these provisions apply solely to liability for the penalty and could not be held to alter the rights of a person with legal title to a vehicle. In this latter connection note the Canadian case of *Director of Maintenance Enforcement (Prince Edward Island) v. MacConnell* (1992).[184] The sheriff seized a car in respect of a judgment for arrears of child support. The debtor claimed that he had transferred the vehicle to his father in return for him settling a debt for his son. The car had been damaged in an accident and was then stored at the father's home, but it was not registered in his name. The court found that the son's debt had been settled by the father to protect himself as guarantor. The car had not effectively been transferred to him under any form of bill of sale. Storing it for six months at the fathers' property was not a visible or continued change of possession and where possession was doubtful, the rule should be that it stays with the person with legal title. Failing to reregister the car in the father's name equally failed to divest ownership from the son. As a consequence the car had been lawfully seized.

10.12.3 Ownership: evidence

As mentioned earlier, the bailiff must have satisfactory evidence of ownership by the debtor before seizing a vehicle. A presumption based upon mere proximity to the debtor's address will not be sufficient-there will have to be something more to indicate a connection to the liable individual to justify a seizure.[185]

10.12.4 Removal of vehicle

When removing a vehicle any personal contents in the vehicle should be either returned to the debtor or listed in the presence of a witness. If possible the registration documents and keys will be obtained from the debtor or another responsible person. Forced entry may be possible in order to remove the vehicle, but the use of force is probably not justifiable as other means exist for transporting cars and vans - i.e. by towing or loading on transporter. The only English case law on the subject of cars relates to this matter. It indicates that the bailiffs should use reasonable care when arranging a contractor to move the vehicle, but, provided this is done, they are not liable generally for any negligence on the part of the contractor. Arranging removal by a reputable garage or haulage firm should be seen as discharge of the duty of care.[186]

10.13 Partnership assets

The rule in the civil courts is that execution under a judgment against a firm can be levied against any property of the firm, against the property of any person who admitted to being a partner or was held by the judgment to be a partner, and against the property of any person who was served with the claim and who failed to respond to it or to attend hearings.[187] The fact that membership of a partnership has changed is no bar to enforcement. Retirement will not prevent execution, nor will death of a partner after issue of the originating process.[188] Each individual partner can be separately pursued by execution but a claim against a firm must lead to a judgment against the firm, not just one partner.[189] In this case an action for wrongful execution and detention of goods was successfully taken. Similarly if judgment is obtained against several named individuals, the warrant must also be issued against them all.[190] That said, it does not have to be levied on all or any one or more of those joint judgment debtors.[191] If execution against one partner clears the debt, the others may not of course be pursued. There is no requirement that partnership property be seized before the private property of partners, or *vice versa*.

Execution may not be issued against a person who was out of the country when the claim was issued unless s/he was served within England & Wales; who with leave was served outside the jurisdiction, or (High Court only) who responded to the claim as a partner. Partners who were out of England & Wales when the action commenced are not otherwise affected. Permission can be sought from the court to issue execution against a person claimed to be a partner.[192] This gives the alleged partner an opportunity to contest the claim of liability, and the dispute may be tried as the court directs. Leave cannot be given to issue execution against a person who leaves the firm before an action begins. Leave may be given where a person has 'held themselves out' to be a partner.[193]

Execution may not be made against partnership property for the separate debt of a partner under section 23(1) of the Partnership Act 1890. If this were to happen the partners could jointly sue or make a claim to the goods - see chapter 13.[194] Note that in *Flude Ltd v Goldberg* [1916] a person interpleaded over goods claimed as his sole property. On hearing the case it was decided that the goods were in fact partnership property of the claimant and the defendant, but as the claimant had not claimed on this basis the claim was barred.[195] In road traffic enforcement, CPR 75.6 applies CPR 83.2 dealing with enforcement against partnerships.

10.14 Business assets

The protection for certain business assets has been significantly reduced in the transition to the new Act, although some of the former statutory and common law protections survive. These provisions are in addition to the exemptions for tools of the trade by statute (*see 10.2*), for motor vehicles used in trade (*see 10.2*) and for items subject to third party interests such as debentures and reservation of title clauses (*see respectively 10.20 and 10.21*).

10.14.1 Railway rolling stock

A limited protection for railway assets has been retained under s.4 of the Railway Companies Act 1867 which states that the "engines, tenders, carriages, trucks, machinery, tools, fittings, materials and effects constituting the rolling stock and plant" used by a company on its railway for the purposes of public traffic cannot be taken in execution (though the judgment creditor may obtain the appointment of a receiver). If a dispute arises as to whether items are covered by this exemption, application may be made on summons for summary determination in the county court or to a Judge in the High Court under s.5 of the Act. As will be observed, the 1867 Act only refers to executions on court judgments. The Railway Rolling Stock Protection Act 1872, which referred to distresses for rent, has been repealed and the surviving statute has not been amended to accommodate taking control of goods.

10.14.2 Farming stock

The Sale of Farming Stock Act 1816 has been repealed. This means that the only specific protection for agricultural assets derives from common law principles.[196] Generally the officer levying execution can seize any 'fructus industriales' - that is, any crops which are reaped at maturity. This includes such crops as corn and similar produce such as potatoes.[197] It does not include trees, grass, seeds unsprouted in the soil or fruit on trees.[198] Standing crops are bound by the issue of a writ though they cannot be sold until they have been harvested.[199]

Part Three - Third parties' goods

Other than jointly owned and partnership property, goods only wholly by third parties cannot be taken into control (see the express prohibition in Sch.12 para.10 of the Act). The clear rule making such takings unlawful is supplemented by the NSEA which advises that "enforcement agents should not take control or remove goods clearly belonging to a third party not responsible for the debt. Where a claim [of ownership] is made, the third party should be given clear instructions on the process required to recover their goods."

However, the third party may be estopped from recovering damages for a wrongful levy if s/he intentionally induced the bailiff to seize the goods, either by expressly or impliedly representing that the goods were the debtor's.[200] There must have been something equivalent to a licence from him/ her.[201] Howbeit, once notice of the true situation is given, even though the bailiff may have been justified in seizing the wrong goods if he was misinformed or mislead as to their ownership, once the true situation is know he will be liable for any subsequent wrongful acts such as failing to release them from custody or proceeding to sell.[202] Goods owned by the Crown (including those owned jointly or in common with another person) cannot be taken into control exercising the enforcement powers under the 2007 Act.[203]

The duty of the enforcement agent to deal properly with a claim to ownership from a third party was explored in some detail in the case of *Huntress Search v Canapeum Ltd & DSI Foods* [2010].[204] This was an appeal by HCEOs against a decision made in interpleader proceedings in which they sought to overturn an order of the High Court permitting DSI Foods to bring a claim for substantial damages against them.

Huntress Search had obtained a county court judgment for £4872 against Canapeum. This was transferred to the High Court for enforcement and a writ was issued for execution at Canapeum's business premises. In the meantime, Canapeum went into administration. An officer was directed to levy at Unit 8, Victoria Industrial Estate, Acton. He called instead at Units 5/6, the premises of DSI Foods, who had purchased from the administrators various assets of Canapeum, such as the lease for the units, all business equipment and even the business name. DSI did not however assume liability for the company's debts.

When the HCEO called to levy, he refused to consider any evidence of the sale and acted in a 'heavy handed manner' by starting to remove goods from the premises, seriously disrupting DSI's business. The High Court master agreed with the claimant that the HCEO had acted in a high handed and unprofessional manner. On appeal Mr Justice Eady was not prepared to reverse that decision or to protect the HCEO from court action. The officers argued that DSI's proper conduct on the day would have been to initiate an immediate interpleader claim on the basis that the goods were not the property of the judgment debtor.

As was discussed in chapter 9, the bailiff levying is under a duty to act with care, caution and common sense. Plausible claims to goods must be considered. Whilst it may be the legally correct procedure, insisting on formal proceedings and refusing to inspect any evidence made available, may seem inflexible and may serve only to aggravate a situation. Ultimately, if a claim to ownership of goods by a third party cannot be resolved by negotiation, a court procedure for determination of the dispute exists (see 13.6). It may be noted that, although this remedy is provided by the Civil Procedure Rules, debtors are not alerted to it by any of the notices that must be served upon them.

10.15 Utility fittings

There are statutory exemptions from seizure for fixtures and other property belonging to utility suppliers. The details are as follows:

- *Gas Act 1986* Sch.2B, para.29(1)(a): any gas meter connected to a service pipe and any gas fitting in a consumer's premises which is owned by a gas transporter or gas supplier and is sufficiently marked with an indication of ownership shall not be subject to being taken into control. Fittings for gas include hired cookers.[205] It is also an offence under para.10 Sch 2B to injure, or allow to be injured, any gas fitting or service pipe, whether intentionally or by culpable negligence;

- *Electricity Act 1989* Sch.6 para.9: any electrical plant, line or meter owned or hired by a supplier to a customer and marked with a sufficient indication of their ownership shall not be deemed to be landlord's fixtures, notwithstanding that they may be affixed to any part of the premises in which they are situated and shall not be taken into control. As with gas fittings, it is an offence to damage electrical fixtures (para.4); and,
- *Water Industry Act 1991*: s179(4) provides that any water fittings let for hire by a water undertaker shall, if they are properly marked, continue to be the property of the undertaker even if they are fixed to some part of the premises and shall not be taken into control. Water fittings are defined by s93 as including pipes, taps, cocks, valves, ferrules, meters, cisterns, baths and toilets.

10.16 Children's goods

Children may be given personal property in any manner- for instance by will or by gift: thus:

"if property be put up on a boy, this is a gift in the law, for the boy hath capacity to take it".[206]

Whenever property is given to a child, it becomes the child's as soon as the gift is made.[207] At common law there is a presumption in favour of the validity of a gift by a parent or grandparent to a child provided that the gift is complete, such as by delivery.[208] Purchase of property by a child is valid and effectual. Children can deal with property in the same manner as adults, whether disposing of it by gift or by sale of goods in the normal fashion.[209]

In consequence, therefore, items bought by children, or for children, and presents to them, should not be taken into control unless the bailiff can successfully challenge any of the above principles or show a particular transaction to be invalid. Subject to special procedural provisions,[210] the child may take court proceedings to protect their property.

It is worth noting that the NSEA takes this protection even further by also requiring bailiffs to exclude from levies property "for the exclusive use of a child." Unlike the Act, a child is classed as being under 18 years of age in the Standard.

10.17 Spouses' goods

It is not unusual for bailiffs to seek to seize the property of one spouse to satisfy the debts of the other. The existing case law relates to the rights of a married woman, but the general principles will apply to cohabitees as well.

A married woman is capable of acquiring, holding and disposing of any property in all respects as if she is a single woman.[211] All property belonging to woman at marriage, or acquired by or devolving upon her after that date, belongs to her as if she is a single woman. Clearly such goods cannot be seized. However none of the above stops couples jointly owning goods, which could be seized (*see 10.1 above*).

In respect of gifts from one spouse to another, it used to be a presumption that a gift had been made where the husband bought property in his wife's name. This is not now presumed. It will be assumed to be owned jointly if bought with joint money. If the wife buys property in her husband's or joint names, there is no presumption of a gift if it is acquired with her money. If the items are bought by the husband for the wife's own personal use (e.g. for birthdays, anniversaries or Christmas), they will be gifts. Note however the arrangement made by the spouses in *Rondeau Le Grand & Co v Marks* [1918] where execution creditors against a wife were unable to seize her personal effects because she had made a valid agreement with her husband that he would purchase items for her in his own name and simply lend them. Jewellery and such like given to the wife by relatives and friends are her property. Wedding presents from the wife's family are hers, and those from the husband's family are his, unless there is evidence of the donor's intentions. Gifts to the couple give each a separate share. If the one spouse makes a gift to the other, the items become the other's absolute property. In *French v Gething* [1922] the gift was by means of a post nuptial deed. Although the chattels transferred were furniture in the marital home which both continued to use, the goods were the wife's.[212]

If one spouse purchases chattels from the other there is no reason not to treat this as a valid transfer that would defeat an execution creditor. In *Ramsay v Margrett* [1894] the husband sold furniture and personal chattels to his wife. She received a receipt for them, though there was no formal delivery of the goods as they remained in the marital home. The wife succeeded in an interpleader claim against an execution as the court held that the intention of the deal had been to pass her absolute title which was demonstrated by her separate dealings with the goods (some were removed prior to the execution) and which was combined with sufficient possession.

The above principles don't just apply to married couples but could apply to any parties living together or sharing accommodation. See for example *Koppel v Koppel* [1966] in which the court upheld an interpleader claim by Mrs Wide the housekeeper to the contents of Koppel's house. They had been made over to her in return for her coming to live in the property to care for his two children and to replace items of her own that she disposed of before moving in. In this case the court held that there was no need for delivery to be demonstrated as the transfer was not a gift but was for money or money's worth.[213]

The real problems arise in respect of items bought by the couple after marriage (or after beginning to live together). The courts generally assume an intention to share any property acquired, and allocate interests in it equally. Housekeeping money or property acquired with that will be treated as shared equally unless it is clearly intended to be shared otherwise.[214] Where there is a joint bank account or other common pool of income, the wages of one spouse are generally seen as being earned on behalf of both and to be joint property, and the sums paid in or withdrawn by each are irrelevant . For instance see *Jones v Maynard* [1951] - the husband withdrew sums from a joint account to buy investments in his sole name. The court held the wife to be entitled to half their value. By way of contrast see *Re: Bishop deceased* [1965] in which a husband and wife opened a joint account to which each contributed in unequal amounts.[215] Money was withdrawn for housekeeping purposes and for investment, in both their sole and joint names. On his death the trustees sought to determine the wife's interest and it was held that as the account had been opened on terms that either could withdraw from it, with no evidence of any specific or limited purpose, then any item bought in sole name was for that person alone. Items bought from such an account therefore would be regarded as jointly owned and seizeable. This is not the case where one spouse provides all the income in a joint account, which is simply used as a matter of administrative convenience. The money (and thus the acquisitions) belongs to the person providing it.[216]

10.18 Goods subject to pledges and liens

For many centuries it was settled law that goods subject to pledges and charges might be seized in execution, albeit subject to those claims. Thus goods subject to a lien for work done upon them were seizeable, subject to that lien.[217] he lien had priority over both the debt and the bailiff's fees. If such goods were sold, the bailiff was liable for the amount of the lien and could be sued if he failed to settle it from the proceeds.[218] A lien could not have any effect if it had not yet come into effect. In *Byford v. Russell* [1907] it was agreed between builder and client that if work was not completed quickly enough notice would be served and a lien would be created on the builder's plant. The sheriff levied on the plant before the notice was served and the court held the client had no lien or interest and couldn't defeat the judgment creditor. Goods held by a debtor subject to a lien that s/he claimed against a third party could not be seized in execution.[219]

In execution it was also lawful to seize goods subject to mortgages. The bailiff was permitted to dispose of the judgment debtor's equity of redemption. If there was any doubt as to the validity of the security, the bailiff was permitted to request evidence of the charges so as to be able to seek instructions from the execution creditor or seek an indemnity - such diligence protected him/her from any charge of negligence. An equity of redemption, as well as being an estate in land, might also be sold in execution.[220]

Goods given in pledge by the debtor to a third party could not be seized in execution against the debtor, and the pawnbroker could sue the bailiff in conversion. Mather however speculated that pawn tickets, though not seizeable or saleable as such, could be taken in execution in order that the bailiff could redeem the goods and sell them.[221] If execution was levied against a pawnbroker, pledged goods could be seized. The High Court enforcement officer had a right of possession in the pledges arising from the pawnbroker's qualified property, and when the redemption period had passed the officer's interest permitted him to sell. If the pledgees redeemed their goods the officer could receive the redemption monies: if the pledges were not redeemed, the High Court enforcement officer could sell the goods.[222]

10.19 Bills of sale

Bills of sale are unlikely to be encountered as commercial arrangements very frequently. This is because the technicalities of the procedure mean that they are not a widely used form of security, and conditional sale or HP will be a preferred arrangement. Bills of sale may still be encountered in respect of loans on motor vehicles as a way of avoiding some aspects of Consumer Credit Act regulation. As discussed in chapter 6, they may also be encountered as a way of trying to avoid the impact of seizure.

Bills of sale are regulated by the Bills of Sale Acts 1878 and 1882 and numerous formalities and procedures must be followed for them to be effective against bailiffs. The following outlines the key elements to which attention should be paid. The bills of sale legislation is concerned with documents rather than transactions. Thus any transfer of property, if put into writing, can be liable to be treated as a bill of sale and will have to comply with the following requirements.[223] Gifts by deed or by declaration of trust can be included if the property remains with the donor and no effective transfer to another can be shown. Mortgages and charges of goods by companies are in the main outside the Acts, but instead *see 10.21* on debentures. The statutory requirements which must be complied with are described below.

10.19.1 Documents

A bill of sale document must exist in the correct form. The 1882 Act contains a standard form in its schedule which must be closely, though not exactly, followed. The statutory form identifies the parties, the loan and the terms of its repayment and allows the goods to remain in the possession of the owner unless s/he is in breach of the bill under section 7 of the 1882 Act, for instance by default, by becoming bankrupt or by allowing the goods to be taken into control in exercise of the powers in the 2007 Act.[224]

If two or more individuals grant a bill of sale over their goods, their shares should be identified if they are unequal, otherwise the bill will be void. Repayments of the loan do not have to be in equal amounts nor do the instalments have to comprise equal amounts of interest. Bills will be void where the times of payment are unspecified or the interest rate is not stated. A bill failing to comply with the statutory requirements is wholly void.[225]

Witnesses should attest the making of the bill.[226] Failure to do this renders the bill void. An affidavit should accompany the bill detailing its proper execution and attestation, the true date of execution and the residence and actual occupation of the grantor (the debtor) and every witness. Again failure to comply with these provisions avoids the bill.[227]

10.19.2 Inventory

An inventory of mortgaged goods must be attached. The bill of sale document itself does not describe the goods and chattels mortgaged, therefore an inventory must be attached (s.4 1882 Act). This must specifically describe the goods concerned and too vague an inventory will render the bill ineffective in respect of any personal chattels not properly described. If there could be no problem identifying the items concerned, more general words may be permissible. However, where there are large quantities of goods such as a shop's stock, a detailed inventory rather than a general statement of the goods' location or description should be prepared.[228]

A bill of sale may be made in respect of most goods and chattels, including furniture, growing crops and fixtures. Trade machinery are for the purposes of the Acts treated as personal chattels rather than fixtures (s.5 1878 Act), so all machines, plant and equipment in factories and workshops may be assigned, but the bill must be registered- see below. Trade machinery does not however include machines supplying power or gas, water or steam: any assignment of such items does not require registration. Even if a bill is void in respect of personal chattels, it will not prejudice the status of other items included in it, such as fixtures or excluded trade machinery. If the bill includes an assignment of real chattels as well as personal chattels, it is void.[229] The grantor of the bill must be owner of the personal chattels comprised in the bill otherwise it will be void (s.5 1882 Act) - this includes after acquired property, but not fixtures, plant and trade machinery acquired to replace items mentioned in the schedule to the bill (s.6 1882 Act).

10.19.3 Consideration

Consideration must have been given and must be stated in the document. A minimum advance of £30 is prescribed; anything less than this renders the bill void (s.12 1882 Act). The loan should have been made at the same time as the bill, unless it is to be made by instalments, in which case this should be disclosed in the bill. If the consideration is not truly stated, the bill is not wholly void, but is void only in respect of any personal chattels comprised in it.[230]

10.19.4 Registration

Registration of the bill must take place to make it valid.[231] The bill and inventory, a copy of these and the affidavit must be presented within seven days to Queens Bench Division of the High Court,[232] otherwise it will be void in respect of any personal chattels assigned. Registration must be renewed every five years (s.11 1878 Act) and failure to do this makes the bill wholly void, as a result of which it will be ineffective against a bona fide execution creditor.[233]

10.19.5 Enforcement

Enforcement of the bill of sale is by the bill holder or mortgagee (the secured lender) taking of possession of the goods given as security. This has to be such a taking of possession that it is obvious, visible to the public, physical and continuous and which thereby prevents any allegation that 'apparent possession' either remains with the debtor or has been restored to him/her after a brief period of possession by the mortgagee.[234] This can be the stumbling point for those endeavouring to protect domestic goods by some form of transfer within a household.

Thus in *Sanders v. Crossley* [1919] the husband voluntarily assigned all his furniture to his wife. As it remained in place in a property in which she had no title or interest and which he continued to occupy, the claim to protect the goods against execution failed. The same problem can apply to business stock and plant if there is not a clear and public change of control or management of the business. A symbolic transfer of control (such as the transfer of a key) may however suffice where the debtor ceases either to reside or trade at the premises where the goods are located whereas merely moving goods on site without clearly separating them from other stock or equipment will not be sufficient.[235]

A valid seizure was held to put the goods beyond the reach of the bailiff just like seizure by another bailiff.[236] If goods subject to a bill were seized before the debt secured by the bill had been called in by the creditor, that creditor would have no right to possession of the goods and could not sue the bailiff for conversion. A bill dated after the date of a levy was certainly ineffective and it seemed also that a last minute bill of sale might fail because of the 'binding effect' of a warrant which gives the warrant priority.[237] However this statement needs to be qualified as the effectiveness of a bill differed according to the debt being enforced:

- execution could not be levied on mortgaged goods and the execution creditor may be liable to the grantee of a bill for a levy on assigned goods.[238]
- under s.14 of 1882 Act - this amended section provides that a bill is of no protection against goods being taken into control for taxes or rates (for which we must read council tax and business rates).

If a taking and sale were to occur, it seems that there would be no duty to account to the grantee for any surplus. The grantee may pay off the debt being enforced and then issue a claim against the grantor.[239]

10.20 Reservation of title clauses

There are a number of modes in which title to goods being sold may be subject to provisions reserving title in the seller. For instance, if goods are supplied to a prospective buyer on approval or on 'sale or return', the property only passes to the buyer when s/he signifies approval or acceptance to the seller, or does any other act adopting the transaction- this may be by retaining the goods for a reasonable period of time.[240] The most common means of reserving title are the so called 'Romalpa clauses'.

The rule regarding sale of goods is that title of the goods passes only when the parties want it to. Consequently, by agreement, title is reserved until certain conditions are satisfied, typically that the goods (and sometimes others) are fully paid for, rather than passing when the contract is made or when the goods are delivered. Such agreements are often called 'Romalpa clauses' but such clauses are sanctioned by s.19 of the Sale of Goods Act 1979.[241]

In any of these situations if property in the goods had not passed to the purchaser who was then subject to a levy, the relevant goods were not seizeable. In reality it is often difficult for the sellers to claiming under retention of title clauses to identify which specific items are covered. When a firm is supplied with stock in the course of business invoices rarely specify serial numbers or even models. Furthermore where the goods being supplied subject to the reservation of title clause are materials rather than finished items, successfully asserting any claim may be even more difficult for the seller as the goods to which they claim title may no longer have any identifiable separate existence. In all cases the exact terms of the sales contract will need careful scrutiny to see if it does in fact protect the vendor against the enforcement being levied against the customer.[242]

10.21 Floating charges

Bailiffs may, in the course of levies against limited companies, endeavour to levy on goods subject to floating charges. Such a charge is created by a debenture- a document acknowledging the company's indebtedness and giving security over some or all of the present and future assets of the firm. The assets will change over time as the company trades in the normal fashion but the charge will apply to the changing plant and goods in stock. If the firm defaults in payment of its debt, an administrative receiver can be appointed and the floating charge 'crystallises' and becomes fixed, giving the creditors the power to recover their money. This is because effectively the firm loses any interest in the goods and they cease to be the firm's assets.[243]

The effectiveness of a floating charge in protecting goods against being taken into control depended on the stage that has been reached in the process of making and enforcing the charge when enforcement began. The debenture was regarded as valid and would defeat execution even if it was issued without authority.[244] If the property charged was far less in value than the sum charged, it could mean that property lost the protection of the debenture and could be taken.

10.21.1 Contract to issue

Where a firm had contracted to issue debentures but, before this is done, goods were seized, the intended debenture holder was in the same position as if the debenture had been issued: the goods were seized subject to all equities upon them.[245]

10.21.2 Before crystallisation

Prior to crystallisation of the charge execution or distraint on the charged goods could not be prevented as they were still the company's property.[246] If goods were charged to a value far in excess of their worth, the rights of the debenture holders defeated those of the execution creditors if the debentures were valid, even though the charge had not crystallised. The debenture holder could then interplead to safeguard the security.[247] If a debenture holder feared that their goods were in jeopardy (for example because a judgment creditor is in a position to issue execution), they might appoint a receiver.[248] This intervention had to be in such a way as to crystallise the whole security: a particular asset could not be claimed from the enforcing creditor whilst the security remained a floating charge against the other assets.[249] If goods were seized in execution prior to crystallisation, the debenture holder could interplead if the High Court enforcement officer disputed the validity of the charge.[250] If the bailiff levied and completed execution by sale the debenture holders could not compel the creditors to restore the money.[251] If the company paid the bailiff to get rid of a man in possession - or under threat of removal and sale - but, before the money was passed to the creditors, the debenture holders appointed a receiver, as the company had an implied power to settle its debts the creditors might receive the money from the bailiff.[252] It did not make any difference whether the agreement reached over payment was for instalments or for a lump sum.[253]

10.21.3 After crystallisation

Where a floating charge had crystallised on the appointment of a receiver, the goods were no longer the company's goods and were not available for seizure.[254] There is one case at variance with this established principle - *Cunliffe Engineering v English Industrial Estates* [1994]. Here a landlord was held to be entitled to seize goods from a receiver partly because the debenture holder was found to have an interest in the tenancy. It seems that seizures for criminal penalties might not be prevented by the charge's crystallisation.[255]

Generally, after crystallisation the bailiff was not able to levy and if he did, for instance, in ignorance of the receiver's appointment, he had to withdraw.[256] In *Re: ELS* it was explained that a ruling that a rates distraint could proceed after a receiver had been appointed as manager by debenture holders was distinguishable because there had been no change of occupation for rating purposes and no assignment of the chattels under the deed creating the equitable charge. The firm's creditors had a right to action, not a right to possession of any of the goods. See also *Re: Adolphe Crosby Ltd* (1910) in which it was held that debentures not secured by a trust deed operated only as an equitable charge on the company's property and could not prevent a levy of distraint.[257] Normally, though, as in Re: ELS, the charge crystallising resulted in transfer of the goods to the debenture holders' receiver, thus preventing most distraint. A creditor might appoint a receiver and begin winding up proceedings after seizure and before sale by a bailiff and thus assert priority over that bailiff against the proceeds of sale of the goods by the liquidator.

If there had been a change of occupation of the premises as a result of the AR's appointment, s/he became liable for any rates and may be subject to distraint for them.[258] Normally, though, the terms of the debenture will not make the AR an agent of the company and thus s/he would not be liable for any rates due after the date of the appointment. The company remains liable, though possessing few seizable assets. In *Re: British Fuller's Earth Ltd* (1901) the receiver and manager appointed by the debenture holders sold the company's property. The rating authority sought an order that they be paid out of the proceeds in his hands. This was refused. The receiver's duty was to sell the goods and the rating authority could not claim against the proceeds or follow the goods.[259]

Most recently this area has been examined in *Beck Foods Ltd v Richard Rees* [2001]. It was held that the actions of a receiver and manager do not amount to the rateable occupation of a company's premises and could not found a claim for rateable occupation by a local authority. Thus there is no basis for a liability order against a receiver and s/he should not face a levy.[260]

10.21.4 Agricultural charges

Assets on farms may be subject to charges that may be either fixed or floating created by banks with tenant or owner farmers, charging all the livestock, crops, machinery, seeds and manures, fixtures and other produce of the farm as security for short term credit, under the Agricultural Credits Act 1928. Such charges, whether crystallised or not, do not prevent distress on the charged items for rent, rates and taxes.[261]

However these charges, even if uncrystallised, prevented execution.[262] If a warrant of control has been issued and the enforcement agent has reason to believe that the debtor is a farmer, it is possible for either the court or the agent to ask that the creditor provide an official certificate, dated not more than three days beforehand, of the result of a search at the Land Registry as to the existence of any charge registered against the debtor under the Agricultural Credits Act 1928. If the creditor fails to provide the official certificate referred within seven days of receiving the request, the court may - of its own motion or on the application of the enforcement agent - order that the creditor provide the certificate.[263]

10.22 Recent problem areas

Driven, primarily, by the pressure of having to levy to be able to exact the higher fees allowed by the fee scales, private bailiffs have sometimes in recent years attempted a number of questionable procedures when seizing goods. These have included:

No goods levies
These were cases where no goods of significant value were seized. Proper practice should have dictated that in such cases, if there was genuinely nothing worth levying upon, the bailiff returned the warrant or liability order to the instructing creditor. In order, it seems, to be able to exact fees as well as to be able to convince creditors that they were effective, seizures have been made where goods were of no or negligible value.

All goods levies
For similar reasons, there have been frequent examples of bailiffs claiming to seize all goods on the premises. This practice was already of uncertain legality; it is hoped that the new Act will exclude the possibility of it continuing in future.

Exempt goods levies
Frequent examples have been encountered of cases where inventories included items which should plainly have been exempted - for example, levies upon all forms of seating in a household. It is probably that in poorer households the motivation for this practice was a desire to 'fill up' the inventory so that, again, the seizure looked more convincing than it was and thereby put more pressure upon the debtor to pay. Sometimes this practice was defended by bailiffs by making a wholly spurious distinction between seizure and removal. It was admitted that the goods had been levied upon, but it was argued that there had never been

any serious intention to remove. This was an indefensible position: the statutory exemptions of goods excluded them from being levied upon in the first place; the possibility of a later removal was immaterial.

Levies upon vehicles subject to HP
Particularly for fines and road traffic penalties, there was a persistent tendency for bailiffs to seize goods that were subject to hire purchase/ conditional sale or Motability agreements and which were not the property of the liable person. Part of the reason for this seems to be that, in cases where a motoring offence or parking violation has occurred, the bailiffs are aware that a motor vehicle is owned and will aim to seize that and nothing else. Issues of proportionality between the debt and the value of the vehicle, and issues of ownership, seem often to have been overridden by the attractions of the vehicle - its value, its accessibility outside the house and the inconvenience that its loss might cause to the debtor. The clear exemption of third party goods under the new Act should hopefully terminate such levies.

It has often been argued by enforcement agents that it is possible to take goods on hire purchase into control and then to agree their sale with the finance house. As already established, there seems to be not justification for this under the Act,[264] nor does thee seem to be any clear legal basis on the wider law. A taking of goods subject to hire purchase/ conditional sale is illegal, as they are not the debtor's property. The fact that lenders, faced with what appears to be a *fait accompli*, have assented to what is presented to them as a lawful act does not render the process legal. They have acted to protect their assets in the ignorance of the true situation. A taking under legal process may breach the credit agreement and have the effect of terminating it, incontestably ending any claim by the debtor (or bailiff). Secondly, by consenting to sale in these circumstances, the finance company may be breaching the provisions of the Consumer Credit Act, effectively appointing the bailiff company as their agents and repossessing the goods without following the correct procedures. The penalty for this is reimbursement to the debtor of all sums paid under the credit agreement.

The form of the new legislation ought to preclude the continuance of most of these practices: principles that formerly had solely been enunciated in case law are incorporated into statute.

Footnotes
1 Schedule 12 para.9 & 11(1)(a).
2 Sch.12 para.10.
3 Sch.12 paragraph 3(2).

4 *Cooper v Willomatt* [1845] 1 CB 72; *Manders v Williams* [1849] 4 Exch 339.

5 *Scott v Scholey* (1807) 8 East 467.

6 *Planet Earth Productions Inc. v. Rowlands* [1990] 69 DLR 715.

7 LGO complaint against Rossendale BC, 09 003 990.

8 Para.60.

9 Sch.12 para.11(1)(b).

10 Sch.12 paragraph 11(2).

11 Reg.10 TCG Regs.

12 Sch.12 paragraph 12.

13 Paragraph 50(3).

14 Paragraph 12(3).

15 Sch.12 paragraph 3(1).

16 Reg.4(1)(a) TCG Regs.

17 Re: Sherman (1915) 32 TLR 231.

18 Reg.4(2) TCG Regs.

19 [1971] 3 WWR 289; [1966] 1 OR 655.

20 See, respectively, *Buzard v Carter* (1993) *The Times*, December 15th, 15b; *The Times* February 2nd 1906 3f; *Thompson v Bertie* (2007) EWHC 2238 (QB).

21 (2007) EWHC 2238 (QB)- and see *Bailiff Studies Bulletin* issue 10.

22 *The Times* December 17th 1857, 8d; [1908] 2 KB 118.

23 *Lavell v Ritchings* [1906] 1 KB 480 and *The Times* Feb. 24th, 3c.

24 *Western Foundation Borings (Alta) Ltd v Walters Construction* (1966) 57 WWR 178; *Re: Belliard* (1994) 86 FTR 174.

25 See *Sources of bailiff law* c.4 p.116.

26 Regulation 10(2).

27 *The Times* November 16th 1844, 7d; *Yost Typewriter Co Ltd v Herinch* (1903) Estates Gazette Digest, p.55.

28 *Brookes v Harris* (1995) *The Times*, April 22nd; see too *Tyman v Eden* (1882) *The Times*, May 15th, 5d: plough horses are still essential to a farm's work even if they are unharnessed from the plough and in their stable to rest and eat.

29 *Read v Burley* (1597) Cro Eliz 550; *Simpson v Hartopp* (1744) Willes 512; *Benham v Weller* (1863) *The Times* April 21st, 11c; *Bray v Fitzwilliam* (1863) *The Times*, July 16th, 13c (Nisi Prius); *The Times* November 14th 1872 9e & July 30th 1873 11d.

30 *Longdon v Allen and Taylor* (1835) *The Times*, April 24th, 3c and April 30th 1836 6a; *Benham v Weller* (1863) *The Times* April 21st, 11c; in *Fenton v Logan* (1833) 2 LJ 102 a threshing machine was lawfully seizable on a Monday having last been used on a Saturday.

31 *Storey v Robinson* (1795) 6 TR 139.

32 *Bissett v Caldwell* (1791) 1 Esp 206.

33 (1989) 19 WL 649926 - see *Sources of bailiff law* c.7 p.211.

34 (1926) 1 DLR 216; see too *Impey v Porcupine Credit Union* (1993) 115 Sask 73.

35 *ITCO Properties (1982) Ltd v Melnyk* (1987) 50 Alta LR (2d) 35; *Kelemen v Continental Bank of Canada* (1985) 40 Alta LR (2d) 399.

36 *Amalgamated Credit Union Ltd v Letwin* (1982) 23 Alta LR (2d) 30.

37 *Burns v Christianson* [1921] 60 DLR 173.

38 *Boyd v. Bilham* [1909] 1 KB 14.

39 *W W Gleave Construction Ltd v Hampton* (1986) 31 DLR 478.

40 *Bank of Nova Scotia v Jordison* [1963] 40 DLR 790.

41 (1961) 30 DLR 742; [1959] 22 DLR 258.

42 *Hy's Steak Loft Ltd v Pitoulis* (1988) 76 CBR (NS) 51.

43 *Armstrong v Terry* (1967) 1 OR 588; *Bank of Nova Scotia v Jordison* [1963] 40 DLR 790; *Cook v Avco Financial Services Canada Ltd* (1976) 6 WWR 756.

44 *Canada v Smith* (1983) 48 CBR (NS) 272.

45 *ITCO Properties (1982) Ltd v Melnyk* (1987) 50 Alta LR (2d) 35.

46 [1928] 3 DLR 478.

47 (1992) 104 Sask 28; [1993] 2 WWR 605; (1982) 21 Alta LR 12 & (1981) 11 Sask. R 121; (1966) 1 OR 655- see also *Re: General Steel Wares Ltd v Clarke* [1956] 20 WWR 215; (1976) WWD 65.

48 *Pead's Ltd v Yeo* (1980) 31 NBR 581; *Mayner & Mayner v Cariboo Fir Co Ltd* [1956] 19 WWR 233.

49 *Delta Acceptance Corporation v Schauf* (1965) 51 WWR 505/ 50 DLR 570; *Metro-Cab v Munro* (1965) 1 OR 555.

50 Respectively *Bank of Montreal v Clarke* (1978) 7 Alta LR 353; *York v Flatekval* [1971] 3 WWR 289; *Haywards Builders Supplies Ltd v MacKenzie* [1956] 20 WWR 591; *Zelenisky v Isfield* [1935] 2 WWR 45; *Re: Bell* (1938) 2 DLR 754; *Gray Beverage (Alberta) Ltd v Wong* (1981) 29 AR 385; *Greenwood v Beneficial Finance Co* (1971) 4 WWR 764.

51 *Re: Belliard* [1994] 86 FTR 174.

52 *Mooney v Prince Albert Credit Union* (1994) 121 Sask LR 318; *Re: Lyons* (1934) 1 DLR 432.

53 *Burns v Christianson* [1921] 60 DLR 173.

54 [1959] 22 DLR 258.

55 *Capaniuk v. Sluchinski* (1963) 44 WWR 455.

56 *Re: Kreutzweiser* [1967] 2 OR 108.

57 *Gauntelett v King* (1857) 3 CBNS 59), though readers should note that *Halsbury's Laws* doubted this (vol 13 para 249 n4) and *Woodfall* was cautious on the point (para 9.059).

58 Co Litt 47.

59 *Iveson v Smithies* (1817) *The Times*, Sept 15th, 3c (Assizes); *Nyman v Ward* (1862) *The Times* August 18th, 11a (Assizes); *Benham v Weller* (1863) *The Times*, March 12th, 9d (Nisi Prius).

60 *Vosper v Curtice* (1888) *The Times*, Jan.28th, 5a (QBD).

61 *The Times*, June 23rd 1886, 15e; *Lavell v Ritchings* [1906] 1 KB 480 and *The Times* Feb. 24th, 3c.

62 *The Times* September 15th 1890 13c; *Estates Gazette* vol.38 p.60 (1891) & vol.49 p.955 (1897); *Law Journal* vol.34 p.504 (1899); *Law Times* vol.114 p.39 (1902); *Property Market Review* vol.13 p.927 (1905); *Singer Manufacturing Company v Fletcher* (1906) 40 ILT 88; *Law Times* vol.129 p.578 (1910).

63 *Gormally v Langmead, The Times* November 10th 1860 11a.

64 *Smith v Thomas & Wilberforce*, April 21st 1899, *Estates Gazette* vol.53 p.710; *Brown v Atkins*, July 14th 1894, *Property Market Review* vol.2 p.491; *The Times* August 8th 1892 14e; August 12th 6a and October 22nd 3e; *Bushbridge v Harvey*, January 13th 1897, Bow county court, *Estates Gazette* vol.49 p.254.

65 *Endrizzi v. Peto & Beckley* [1917] 1 WWR 1439.

66 *Addison v Shepherd* [1908] 2 KB 118.

67 *Rodi &. Weinberger AG v. Kay* [1959] 22 DLR 258.

68 *Re: Belliard* [1994] 86 FTR 174.

69 *Churchward v Johnson* [1889] 54 JP 326; *Master v Fraser* (1901) *The Times*, November 8th, 14e.

70 *Taylor v Ashworth* (1910) *Manchester Guardian* Oct.6th p.5; *Wertheim v Cheel* (1886) 12 VLR 46.

71 (1993), High Court, unreported - see my discussion in *Sources of bailiff law*.

72 *Rai & Rai v Birmingham City Council* (1993) unreported, see my *Sources of bailiffs' law* c.4 p.112.

73 *Taylor v Ashworth* (1910) 129 LT 578; (1905) 13 PMR 963; (1902) 114 LT 39.

74 Reg.4(1)(b) TCG Regs.

75 Reg.4(1)(c).

76 *The Times* April 22nd 1995; see too *Lavell v Ritchings* [1906] 1 KB 480.

77 Reg.5 TCG Regs.

78 reg.10(2).

79 Reg.10(3).

80 Coke 1 Inst 47; *Francis v Nash* (1734) 95 ER 32.

81 *Planet Earth Productions Inc. v. Rowlands* [1990] 69 DLR 715.

82 *Dennis v Whetham* [1874] 9 QB 345 @ 349.

83 *Pitcher v King* (1844) 5 QB 758.

84 *Scarlett v Hanson* [1883] 12 QBD 213; *Miller v Solomon* [1906] 2 KB 91 @ 96.

85 [1807] 8 East 467; *In Re: Duke of Newcastle* [1869] 8 Eq 700.

86 Mortgage - *Re: Lusty* (1889) 60 LT 160; bill of sale - *Holroyd v Marshall* (1862) 10 HL Cas 191. *Halsbury's Laws* vol.17, para.480, note 3 stated that ancient Chancery practice was to grant an order to the sheriff allowing seizure of an equitable interest or to validate a prior seizure, for example from a trustee. The note continues to the effect that the High Court may therefore still have the power to grant leave to seize such property - *Pit v Hunt* [1681] 2 Cas in Ch 73; see also *Horsley v Cox* [1869] 4 Ch App 92 @ 100.

87 Sch.12 para.6(2)(b), 37(2) or 38(b).

88 Magistrates' Courts Rules 1981 r.54(2) as amended by Tribunals, Courts & Enforcement Act 2007 (Consequential, Transitional & Saving Provision) Order 2014 Sch.para.1(d).

89 Sch.12 para.3.

90 Policy - *Re: Sargent's Trusts* [1879] 7 LR Ir 66; monies - *Re: New York Life Assurance Association Co. & Fullerton* [1919] 45 OLR 244.

91 *Dundas v Dutens* (1790) 1 Ves Jnr 196.

92 For example *Willows v Ball* (1806) 2 Bos & Pull 376.

93 *Walsh v. Walper* (1901) 3 OLR 158.

94 *Tener v. Booth* Ir Cir Rep 625.

95 *Dundas v Dutens* above; *Taylor v Jones* 2 Atk 600; *Nantes v Corrock* 9 Ves 177.

96 *Evans v Stephen* [1882] 3 NSWLR 154.

97 See *Brown v Cooper* [1870] 1 VR(L) 210; *British Mutoscope & Biograph Co Ltd v Homer* [1901] 1 Ch 671; *Wifley Ore Concentrator Syndicate Ltd v. N. Guthridge Ltd* (1905) 27 ALT 70.

98 *Ex. p. Foss* 2 De G &J 230; *Re: Baldwin* (1858) 2 De g & J 230 @ 237.

99 *Brown v Cooper* [1870] 1 VR(L) 210.

100 *Squire v Huetson* (1841) 1 QB 308; Re: Rollason [1887] 34 Ch D 495.

101 Schedule 12 para.3(1).

102 Para.36(1)(b).

103 Para.50(6).

104 Reg.13 Fees regulations 2014.

105 See *Farrar v Beswick* (1836) 1 M&W 682; *The James W. Elwell* [1921] P.351.

106 *Hulme v Brigham* [1943] 1 KB 152.

107 [1867] 5 Eq 72 citing *ex p Barclay* 5 DM & G 410.

108 *Boswell v Crucible Steel Co* [1925] 1 KB 119.

109 (1851) 6 Exch 295.

110 *Re: Richards ex p Astbury & Lloyds Banking Co* [1869] 4 Ch App 630; *Wood v Hewett* (1846) 8 QB 913.

111 *Provincial Bill Posting Co v Low Moor Iron Co* [1909] 2 KB 344.

112 *Snedeker v Waring* (1854) 12 NY 170 approved in *Elitestone v Morris* [1997] 1 WLR 687.

113 *Liford's Case* (1614) 11 Co Rep 46b; *Hellawell v Eastwood* (1851) 6 Exch 295.
114 Plugged in - *Vaudeville Electric Cinema Ltd v Muriset* [1923] 2 Ch 72; wired in - *Gray v Fuller* [1943] KB 694; *Young v Dalgety* (1987) 1 EGLR 117.
115 *Berkley v Poulett* (1976) 241 EG 911.
116 *Walmsley v Milne* (1859) 7 CBNS 115.
117 *Holland v Hodgson* [1872] 7 CP 328.
118 *Re: De Falbe* [1901] 1 Ch 523.
119 *Leigh v Taylor* [1902] AC 157.
120 [1996] EGCS 149.
121 [2013] EWHC 1658 (Ch).
122 *Billing v Pill* [1954] 1 QB 70.
123 Looms - *Boyd v Shorrock* [1867] 5 Eq 72; beer pump - *Dalton v Whittem* [1842] 3 QB 961; press - *Hulme v Brigham* [1943] KB 152.
124 *Melluish v BMI (No 3)* [1994] 2 WLR 795; screen - *Vaudeville Electric Cinema Ltd v Muriset* [1923] 2 Ch 72; millstones - *Wystow's Case* (1523) YB 14 Hen VIII fo 25 pl 6; rink - *Howell v Listowel Rink & Park Co* [1886] 13 OR 476; dairy - *Assiniboia Land Co v Acres* [1915] 25 DLR 439; sign - *Re: Thomas* (1881) 44 LT 781; letter boxes - *Bruce v Smith* [1923] 3 DLR 887; tracks - *Turner v Cameron* [1876] 5 QB 306.
125 Chairs - *Lyon & Co v London City & Midland Bank* [1903] 2 KB 135; machine - *Parsons v Hind* (1866) 13 WR 860; railway - *Chamberlayne v Collins* (1894) 70 LT 217; horses - *London & Eastern Counties Loan & Discount Co v Creasey* [1897] 1 QB 768.
126 *Lee v Gaskell* [1876] 1 QBD 700; *British Economical Lamp Co v Empire, Mile End* (1913) 29 TLR 386.
127 *Horwich v Symond* (1915) 84 LJKB 1083.
128 Appliances - *Allan v Lavine* [1942] 1 DLR 731; ovens - *Winn v Ingilby* (1822) 5 B & Ald 625; fitted units - *Gray v Fuller* [1943] 1 KB 694- see du Parcq LJ @ 712.
129 *Moore v Drinkwater* (1858) 1 F&F 134; *Beck v Denbigh* (1860) 29 LJCP 373.
130 *In Re: Sir Edward Hulse* [1905] 1 Ch 406.
131 See for example *Meux v Jacobs* [1875] 7 App Cas 481; *In Re: Yates* [1888] 38 Ch D 112; *Gough v Wood* [1894] 1 QB 713.
132 *Sanders v Davis* [1885] 15 QBD 218.
133 *Sheffield & South Yorkshire Permanent Benefit Building Society v Harrison* [1885] 15 QBD 338; *Hobson v Gorringe* [1897] 1 Ch 182.
134 *Holland v Hodgson* [1872] 7 CP 328; *In Re: Richards ex p Astbury & Lloyds Banking Co* [1869] 4 Ch App 630.
135 *Longbottom v Berry* (1869) 5 QB 123; *Climie v Wood* (1868) 3 Exch 257 - in this case an engine screwed to thick planks laid on the ground and set in brickwork.
136 *Re: Armytage* [1880] 14 Ch D 379; *In Re: Rogerstone Brick & Stone Co Ltd* [1919] 1 Ch 110.
137 *Small v National Provincial Bank of England* [1894] 1 Ch 686.
138 *Day v Bisbitch* (1595) 78 ER 622; *Pooles Case* (1703) 1 Salk 368.
139 *Webb v Frank Bevis* [1940] 1 All ER 247.
140 *Dumergue v Rumsey* (1863) 2 H&C 777.
141 *Duke of Beaufort v Bates* (1862) 6 LT 82.
142 *Never Stop (Railway) Ltd v British Empire Exhibition* (1924) Inc [1926] Ch 877.
143 Plant - *Whitehead v Bennett* (1858) 27 LJ Ch 474; collieries - *Lord Dudley v Lord Ward* (1751) Amb 113; pumps - *Smith v City Petroleum* [1940] 1 All ER 260; pub - *Elliott v Bishop* (1854) 10 Exch 496; brewery - *Lawton v Lawton* (1743) Atk 13.
144 Sheds - *Penton v Robert* (1801) 2 East 88; *Mears v Callender* [1901] 2 Ch 388.
145 *Young v Dalgety, Elliott v Bishop* earlier.
146 *Mears v Callender* [1901] 2 Ch 388.

147 *Buckland v Butterfield* (1820) 2 Brod & B 58.
148 Panelling etc - *Spyer v Phillipson* [1930] 2 Ch 183; bookcases etc - *Bishop v Elliot* [1885] 11 Exch 113; pictures - *Buckingham v Pembroke* (1672) 3 Keb 74; blinds - *Colegrave v Dias Santos* (1823) 2 B&C 76; cupboards - *R v St Dunstan (Inhabitants)* (1825) 4 B&C 686; *Re: Gawan ex p Barclay* (1855) 5 De G M & G 403; bookshelves - *Birch v Dawson* (1834) 2 A&E 37; cornices etc - *Grymes v Boweren* (1830) 6 Bing 437.
149 *Place v Flagg* (1821) 4 M&R 277; *Barnard v Leigh* (1815) 1 Stark 43.
150 *Farrant v Thompson* (1822) 5 B&Ald 826.
151 Termination - *Pugh v Arton* (1869) 8 Eq 626; disclaimer - *In Re: Lavies ex p Stephens* [1877] 7 ChD 127; *In Re: Roberts ex p Brook* [1878] 10 ChD 100.
152 *In Re: Moser* [1884] 13 QBD 738.
153 Vesting - *In Re: Maryport Haematite Iron & Steel Co Ltd* [1892] 1 Ch 415; holding over - *Weeton v Woodcock* (1840) 7 M&W 14.
154 Section 10(1).
155 Section 10(7), (2) & (8).
156 s.8(1).
157 Section 8(2), (5) & (7).
158 Dutch barns - *Dean v Allalley* (1799) 3 Esp 11; free standing barns - *Culling v Tufnal* (1694) Bull NP (5th Edn) 34; *Wansborough v Maton* (1836) 4 A&E 884; staddles - *Wiltshear v Cottrell* (1853) 1 E&B 674.
159 [1997]1 WLR 687.
160 *Wolfe v Summers* (1811) 2 Camp 631; *Sunbolf v Alford* (1838) 3 M & W 248.
161 *Bissett v Caldwell* 1 Esp 206; *Baynes v Smith* 1 Esp 206.
162 *Parke & Moss v. Howe*, Dalton, p.529.
163 [1875] 1 CP 554; *Colonial Bank of Australia v. Cooper* (1876) 2 VLR 41.
164 *Jennings v Mather* [1901] 1 QB 108.
165 *Re: Johnson* [1880] 15 Ch D 604.
166 *Farr v Newman* (1792) 4 TR 621; *In Re: Morgan* [1881] 18 ChD 93.
167 *Ray v Ray* (1813) Coop 264.
168 *Moseley v Rendell* [1871] 6 QB 338; *Abbott v Parfitt* [1871] 6 QB 346.
169 *Quick v Staines* (1798) 1 B&P 293.
170 *In Re: Evans* [1887] 34 ChD 597.
171 *Dowse v Gorton* [1891] AC 190; *In Re: Johnson* [1880] 15 Ch D 548.
172 *In Re: Oxley* [1914] 1 Ch 602.
173 *Sykes v Sykes* [1870] 5 CP 113.
174 *In Re: Brooke* [1894] 2 Ch 600.
175 E.g: *Grant v Grant* [1883] 10 PR 40; *Kingston City v Rogers* [1899] 31 OR 119.
176 *Haythorn v Bush* (1834) 2 Cr& M 689; *Belcher v Patten* (1848) 6 CB 608.
177 *Belcher v Patten* [1848] 6 CB 608.
178 *Edmunds v Ross* (1821) 9 Price 5; *Dicas v Warne* (1833) 10 Bing 341.
179 Abandoned - *Crowder v Long* [1828] 8 B&C 598; irregular - *Blades v Arundale* [1813] 1 M&S 711; satisfied - *Harwell v Burwell* Sir W Jones 456.
180 *Barrow v Bell* (1855) 5 E&B 540; *Re: Cuthbertson ex p Edey* [1875] LR 19 Eq 264.
181 See too *Reddell v Stowey* (1841) 2 Moo & R 358.
182 Reg.4(1)(d)-(f) TCG Regs.
183 Traffic Management Act 2004 s.92.
184 (1992) 100 Nfld & PEIR 12.
185 LGO complaint against Rossendale BC, 09 003 990.
186 *Rivers v Cutting* [1982] 3 All ER 69 CA.
187 CPR Part 70 Practice Direction 6A.1.
188 *Re: Frank Hill ex p Holt & Co* [1921] 2 KB 831; *Ellis v Wadeson* [1899] 1 QB 714.

189 *Clark v Cullen* [1882] 9 QBD 355; *Jackson v Litchfield* [1882] 8 QBD 474.

190 *Penoyer v Brace* (1697) 1 Ld Raym 244; *Clark v Clement* (1796) 6 TR 525.

191 *Herries v Jamieson* [1794] 5 TR 556.

192 CPR Part 70 Practice Direction 6A.3 & 6A.4.

193 *Wigram v Cox* [1894] 1 QB 792; *Davis v Hyman & Co* [1903] 1 KB 854.

194 *Peake v Carter* [1916] 1 KB 652; *Smith v. Ogg* (1864) 35 CR(NSW) 6.

195 [1916] 1 KB 662.

196 See my detailed discussion of these in 'Emblements & executions- the seizure of growing crops for debt', chapter 4 in *More popular than the hangman - the Victorian sheriff's officer*, KDP, 2012.

197 Mature crops - *Cameron v Gibson* [1889] 17 OR 233; potatoes - *Evans v Roberts* (1826) 5 B&C 829.

198 Trees - *Scorell v Boxall* (1827) 1 Y&J 396; grass - *Late v McLean* [1870] 8 NSR 69; seeds - *Bagshaw v Farnsworth* (1860) 2 LT 390; fruit - *Rodwell v Phillips* (1842) 9 M&W 501.

199 *Belair v Banque d'Hochelaga* [1923] 2 WWR 771; *Kidd & Clements v Docherty* [1914] 27 WLR 636.

200 *Pickard v Sears* (1837) 6 A&E 469.

201 *Freeman v Cooke* (1849) 4 Exch 654; *Dawson v Wood* (1810) 3 Taunt 256.

202 *Dunstan v Paterson* (1857) 2 CBNS 495.

203 S.89(2)(b).

204 EWHC 1270 (QB).

205 *Gas Light & Coke Co v Hardy* [1886] 17 QBD 619; and *Gas Light & Coke Co v Herbert Smith & Co* (1886) 3 TLR 15.

206 *Hayne's Case* (1614) 12 Co Rep 113.

207 *Hunter v Westbrook* (1827) 2 C&P 578.

208 *Garrett v Wilkinson* (1848) 2 De G & Sm 244 @ 246; *Beanland v Bradley* (1854) 2 Sm & G 339 @ 343; delivery - *May v May* (1863) 33 Beav 81 @ 87.

209 *Holmes v Brigg* [1818] 8 Taunt 508; *Manby v Scott* [1663] 1 Mod Rep 124.

210 CPR Part 21.

211 s.1(a) Law Reform (Married Women & Tortfeasors) Act 1935.

212 [1918] 1 KB 75; [1922] 1 KB 236.

213 [1894] 2 QB 18; [1966] 2 All ER 187; see also *Antoniadi v Smith* [1907] 2 KB 589 - a case of a man and his mother in law.

214 see s.1 Married Women's Property Act 1964.

215 [1951] Ch 572; [1965] Ch 450.

216 *Heseltine v Heseltine* [1971] 1 All ER 952 @ 956.

217 22 Ed IV 11; *Duncan v. Garrett* (1824) 1 C&P 169.

218 *The Ile de Ceylon* [1922] P 256; *Proctor v. Nicholson* (1835) 7 C&P 67; *AdanacTire & Retreaders Ltd v. Sheriff of Edmonton* [1979] 9 Alta LR 66.

219 [1907] 2 KB 522 ; *Legg v. Evans* (1840) 6 M&W 36.

220 *Massey Manufacturing v. Clement* (1893) 9 Man LR 359; *Dunn v. Bank of New South Wales* (1866).

221 *Rogers v. Kenmay* (1846) 9 QB 592; *Mather* para 9, p96.

222 *Squire v. Huetson* (1841) 1 QB 308; *In Re: Rollason, Rollason v. Rollason* [1887] 34 Ch D 495.

223 *Hopkins v Gudgeon* [1906] 1 KB 690

224 Section 7(2) as amended.

225 Form - *Roberts v Roberts* [1884] 13 QBD 794; shares - *Saunders v White* [1902] 1 KB 472; repayments - *Re: Cleaver ex p Rawlings* [1887] 18 QBD 489; interest - *Edwards v Marston* [1891] 1 QB 225; times - *Hetherington v Groome* [1884] 13 QBD 789; interest - *Blankenstein v Robertson* [1890] 24 QBD 543; void bills - s9 1882 Act and see *Davies v Rees* [1886] 17 QBD 408.

226 s.10 1882 Act.

227 *Matthews v Buchanan* [1889] 5 TLR 373

228 Description - *Thomas v Kelly* [1888] 13 App Cas 506; too vague - *Witt v Banner* [1887] 20 QBD 114; general words - *Davidson v Carlton Bank* [1893] 1 QB 82; inventories - *Svaigher v. Rotaru* [1906] 3 WLR 486; *Wilson v. Kerr* [1858] 17 UCQB 168/ 18 UCQB 470 (CA)).

229 Machinery - *Hawtry v Butlin* [1873] 8 QB 290; power plant - *Topham v Greenside Glazed Firebrick Co* [1887] 37 Ch D 281; fixtures - *Re: North Wales Produce & Supply Co Ltd* [1922] 2 Ch 340; exempt goods - *Re: Burdett* [1888] 20 QBD 310; real chattels - *Cochrane v Entwistle* [1890] 25 QBD 116

230 Instalments - *In Re: Young* [1880] 43 LT 576; void - *Heseltine v Simmons* [1892] 2 QB 547

231 s10 1878 Act and see *Pickard v Marriage* [1876] 1 Ex D 364; *Youngs v Youngs* [1940] 1 KB 760

232 s.8 1882 Act.

233 Void - *Fenton v Blythe* [1890] 25 QBD 417; execution - *Jenkinson v Brandley Mining Co* [1887] 19 QBD 568

234 *Heward v. Mitchell* [1853] 10 UCQB 535 (CA); *Ritchie Contracting v. Brown* [1915] 30 WLR 723; *Averill v. Caswell & Co Ltd* [1915] 31 WLR 953; *Official Assignee of Casey v. Bartosh* [1955] NZLR 287; *Althen Drilling Co v. Machinery Depot Ltd* (1960) 31 WWR 75; *Askin v. Robinson* (1960) 1 CBR 257; *Spruhs v. Gregoryk* [1930] 1 WWR 378.

235 Wife - 2 IR 71; stock - *Svaigher v. Rotaru* [1906] 3 WLR 486; key - *Taylor v. Commercial Bank* (1854) 3 UCCP 447; moving goods - *Dominion Lumber v. Alberta Fish Co* [1921] 62 DLR 93.

236 *Taylor v Eckersley* [1877] 5 Ch D 740; *Donaghue v Campbell* [1901] 2 OLR 124.

237 Post levy - *Gladstone v Padwick* [1871] LR 6 Exch 203; binding - *Thompson v. De Lissa* (1881) 2 LR(NSW) 165.

238 Mortgaged goods - *Holroyd v Marshall* [1862] 10 HL Cas 191; *In Re: Cuthbertson ex p Edey* [1875] 19 Eq 264; *Wimbledon Local Board v Underwood* (1892) 61 LJNS 484; assigned goods - *Condy v Blaiberg* [1891] 55 JP 580.

239 Account - *Evans v Wright* [1857] 2 H&N 527; pay off - *Edmunds v Wallingford* [1885] 14 QBD 811.

240 See rule 4, s.18 Sale of Goods Act 1979, but note that the mere fact of seizure of the goods in execution is not such retention to render the property passed - *Re: Ferrier* [1944] Ch 295.

241 See *Aluminium Industrie Vaassen v Romalpa Aluminium Ltd* [1976] 2 All ER 552.

242 *Borden (UK) v Scottish Timber Products Ltd* [1979] 3 All ER 961 CA; see also *Re: Bond Worth* [1979] 3 All ER 919 CA.

243 *Re: New City Constitutional Club Co ex p Russell* [1887] 34 ChD 646.

244 *Duck v Tower Galvanising Co Ltd* [1901] 2 KB 314.

245 *Simultaneous Colour Printing Syndicate v Foweraker* [1901] 1 KB 771.

246 *Re: Roundwood Colliery Co* [1897] 1 Ch 373.

247 *Davey & Co v Williamson & Sons* [1898] 2 QB 194.

248 *Wildy v Mid-Hampshire Railway Co* [1868] 16 WR 409; *In Re: London Pressed Hinge Co Ltd* [1905] 1 Ch 576.

249 *Evans v Rival Granite Quarries* [1910] 2 KB 979.

250 *Taunton v Sheriff of Warwickshire* [1895] 2 Ch 319 and see *8.2 above*.

251 *Re: Opera* [1891] 3 Ch 260.

252 *Heaton & Dugard Ltd v Cutting* [1925] 1 KB 655 or *Robinson v Burnell's Vienna Bakery Ltd* [1904] 2 KB 624.

253 *Heaton v Dugard Ltd & Cutting Bros Ltd* [1925] 1 KB 655.

254 Re: ELS [1995] Ch 11.

255 ([1994] BCC 974; *Pegge v. Neath District Tramways* [1895] 2 Ch 508.

256 *Edwards v Edwards* [1875] 1 ChD 454.

257 (1910) 74 JP 25.

258 *Richards v Overseers of Kidderminster* [1896] 2 Ch 212.

259 *Taggs Island Casino Hotel Ltd v Richmond upon Thames Borough Council* [1967] RA 70; (1901) 17 TLR 232.

260 [2001] EWCA Civ 1934.

261 1928 Act ss.5 & 8(7).

262 This is according to Keith, Podevin & Sandbrook @ p44 - but contrast Mather pp.100-102 which follows s.7(1) of the Act and treats agricultural charges like charges under debentures i.e. they are not effective against execution or distraint whilst they are still floating and have not crystallised - see the previous subsections above.

263 CPR 83.21.

264 Sch.12 para.10.

Chapter 11

Payment, removal and sale

11.1 Tender and payment

As suggested before, the purpose of taking control is to provoke payment through the threat of goods' sale and removal rather than those steps actually being taken. Consequently the bailiff aims either to either receive a lump sum or to agree instalment payment. The latter is the most common result of the bailiffs' call. On average over ninety five percent of levies lead to instalments being arranged.

11.1.1 Instalment arrangements

Difficulties may arise for both parties when an affordable payment cannot be agreed. This is often because of the timescales for recovery laid down by creditors. Local authorities have, in respect of local taxes, been happy to see instalments accepted, but will often wanted them only to run for two or three months. Magistrates' courts and local authorities collecting road traffic penalties did not tend to accept instalments at all. In either case if the debtor was on low income the options open to the bailiff could be limited. Attitudes may, perhaps be altered by the fact that warrants remain valid and enforceable for twelve months under the new regulations.[1] NSEA also provides some very clear guidance on the affordability of payments. It is stressed that debtors must not be pressed to make unrealistic offers and should be asked to consider carefully any offer they voluntarily make. Where a creditor has indicated they will accept a reasonable repayment offer, enforcement agents must always refer these onto them.

Bailiffs in the civil courts can be made to accept instalments and withdraw if the court consents to suspending the execution on terms (*see Chapter 6*). The terms of such suspensions can be quite low offers over extended periods. In other forms of seizure there is no option for the debtor to make application to the court and s/he will have to rely on negotiation with the bailiff or creditor. For all that, it is clearly the expectation of the new regulations that instalments will be possible at two points in the process- after issue of an enforcement notice and under controlled goods agreements (at least). The former situation is discussed at 7.5.1. In the latter situations the Taking Control of Goods Regulations 2013 require that the agreement should document "the terms of the arrangement entered into between the enforcement agent and the debtor for the repayment, by the debtor of the sum outstanding."[2] This could, of course, be an agreement to pay a lump sum to discharge the total debt after a certain period of days. Nevertheless, the form of this document should be contrasted to the notices required after entry, levying or after removal which simply make reference to 'making payment of the sum due to prevent sale.'[3] What is notable about payment arrangements made after goods have been taken into control is that the regulations fail to make any detailed provision as to the effect of instalments. It may be that they postpone the deadline for sale (see 11.3.3 below) but this is not explicitly stated.

11.1.2 The nature of tender

Over and above any contractual requirement imposed on the bailiff regarding payments, there are both common law and statutory restrictions as to how payment may be made by the debtor, when it must be accepted by the bailiff or creditor and the impact thereof. Reference is often made to 'tender' of payment of a debt and costs. Tender may be defined as an unconditional offer to pay, whether by means of cash or a banker's draft or building society cheque, and the money should be produced at the time of making such an offer.

A tender under protest, reserving the right to dispute the sum claimed later, is still a valid tender provided that no conditions are imposed on the creditor. The creditor should not refuse the offer, simply because the payer preserves the right to take legal action later. Where the sum due is disputed, a request for a receipt is not such a condition as will invalidate a tender, unless the receipt is requested to specify that it covers the sums due for a certain period and the periods for which the sum is due are disputed.[4] Tender by a third party who is neither co-debtor nor co-tenant is only acceptable if they act as agent for the debtor - whether their agency has prior authorisation or later ratification. In Smith v Cox [1940] an action for illegal distress for rent by the plaintiff failed when he admitted that payment of the rent had been made by a stranger without his knowledge or consent.[5]

Enforcement will therefore continue unless there is a specific agreement to suspend or postpone the seizure or sale.[6] Offering a current account cheque or other means of payment does not qualify as valid tender, though of course the bailiff or creditor may accept such a method of settling a debt and may suspend enforcement until the cheque is cleared, rather than withdrawing the levy altogether. Providing a promissory note in payment is not satisfaction of a debt until the monies are paid over. The ordinary rule is that acceptance of a cheque is not absolute satisfaction of a debt but conditional payment and operates to suspend a creditor's remedies until it is either met or dishonoured. Where a landlord did accept a bill of exchange from a tenant for rent due, it was held to be evidence of an agreement to suspend the remedy of distress during the currency of the bill. The tenant was therefore entitled to recover his goods.[7]

The creditor has the choice, if the cheque is dishonoured, of either suing on the cheque or pursuing the debt as normal. Thus in *Bolt & Nut Co (Tipton) Ltd v Rowlands, Nicholls & Co* [1964], a judgment entered after receipt of a cheque to settle the claim was set aside as irregular. The court however suggested that, if judgment had been entered before the cheque was taken, it could have been argued that a better course of action for the creditor might be to levy execution rather than sue on the cheque.[8] Note also that payment by tender of a cheque that later is dishonoured has been held not to be obtaining pecuniary advantage by deception under s.16 Theft Act 1968.[9] Payment by instalments is handled in the same way as payment by cheque. It is not valid tender, with the consequences that flow from that, but enforcement may be stayed whilst payments are maintained.

11.1.3 Tender or payment before seizure

If there is no actual tender, the debtor's mere presence on the premises will not prevent a levy taking place. Equally the readiness to pay must have continued until the moment of seizure.[10] Tender must be of the full sum of debt and costs, though less than the full sum due may be accepted without prejudice to the right to pursue the outstanding balance. Tender may be to the creditor or bailiff and either should accept. The bailiff can receive a payment and ought not to be told to refuse it by the creditor, but a bailiff's assistant cannot receive a tender. In execution it seems tender should be to the HCEO or the creditor. In *D'Jan v Bond St Estates* [1993] the Court of Appeal held that a landlord was not entitled to reject a tender by banker's draft either because it is less than the full amount claimed or because s/he feels that a large sum should be paid in cash.[11]

If tender of the full sum due is made before control of goods is taken, any subsequent levy would be illegal as there would no longer be any debt due. The seizure would be a trespass. Refusal of a valid tender gives the debtor the right to make a claim.[12]

11.1.4 Tender or payment after seizure

Where the debtor pays the amount outstanding in full after the enforcement agent has taken control of goods but before they are sold or abandoned.[13] No further enforcement action can be taken and if payment is made the enforcement agent has removed the goods, he must as soon as reasonably practicable make them available for collection by the debtor; no further step may be taken under the enforcement power concerned. Note that the new Act refers only to payment, not to tender of payment. It remains to be seen if the courts will assume tender is included in the meaning, as in the former cases.[14]

For the purposes of determining the total sum which the debtor should pay, the amount outstanding is reduced by the value of any controlled goods consisting of money required to be used to pay that amount, and the duty to return seized property does not apply to that money. The amount outstanding is defined as the sum of the amount of the debt which remains unpaid (or an amount that the creditor agrees to accept in full satisfaction of the debt) and any amounts recoverable out of proceeds in accordance with regulations under paragraph 62 (costs).[15]

If a further step is taken in the enforcement process despite the bar upon such action in paragraph 58(3), special rules apply. To continue recovery action after payment will be a breach of the Act for which the debtor could recover damages under para.66 of Sch.12.[16] However, the enforcement agent is not liable unless he had notice, when the step was taken, that the amount outstanding had been paid in full. This applies as much to a related party as to the enforcement agent. If a sale of any of the goods takes place the purchaser acquires good title unless, at the time of sale, he or the enforcement agent had notice that the amount outstanding had been paid in full. A person will be deemed to have notice that the amount outstanding has been paid in full if he would have found it out if he had made reasonable enquiries. The foregoing does not affect any right of the debtor or a co-owner to a remedy against any person other than the enforcement agent or a related party.[17]

As stated, the amount outstanding includes costs. The difficult issue has been to define what amount of costs should be paid or tendered in a situation where the recovery action is an ongoing process and costs are mounting. The Court of Appeal gave helpful guidance on the issue of costs and the calculation and acceptance of tenders to discharge the sums due in *Wilson v South Kesteven DC* [2000].[18] The case was a claim for damages for illegal distraint. During a levy for NNDR a sum in settlement of the amounts due was tendered by the debtor and refused by the bailiff, who was engaged in removing the goods from the premises. This refusal was held to be wrongful by a county court circuit judge. The Court of Appeal reversed this decision and held that, under the relevant local tax regulations, there were two distinct opportunities to make payment - either:

1. before any goods are seized; or,
2. after seizure and before sale.

The county court judge assumed there was a "continuum of opportunity" to pay, so that tender could be made lawfully during the process of seizure. Simon Brown LJ rejected this partly because of the form of the regulations and partly because of the practical difficulty of determining charges which could be accruing minute by minute. In terms of practice for bailiffs, he recommended that the required memorandum of charges is presented either:

1. upon, or shortly after, first entry to the premises, giving the debtor a chance to pay "before the process gets fully underway and charges begin to escalate"; or,
2. a further memo would be required after seizure has occurred, detailing charges so far and warning that further charges (such as removal) may be incurred.

The judgment is still of some relevance, despite the much revised fee structure. Under the new scale, there are clear points at which payment can be made to avoid further sums falling due and, additionally, stages at which certain disbursements have been incurred which may not be immediately quantifiable but for which the debtor will be liable once a particular process has been initiated: for example, locksmith's charges or perhaps removal or other expenses allowed in 'exceptional' cases (*see chapter 12*).

11.2 Re-entry and removal

Removal and sale is a last resort where acceptable payments cannot be agreed or maintained. In the past removals and sales only happened in a tiny percentage of cases. However, this may change because of changes to rights of re-entry (*see next section*). The former law on the right of forced re-entry was very simple; the new rules are considerably more complicated. It should be re-emphasised that removal for sale is an activity distinct from removal for the purposes of taking control of goods and that they are treated separately in the legislation. Re-entry and sale are intimately related to each other in the new legislation, as will emerge in the following paragraphs.

11.2.1 Re-entry - general issues

It may be necessary for the enforcement agent to force re-entry to premises in order to check on goods previously taken into control or (more commonly) to remove them for sale. The right of re-entry is governed generally by Sch.12 para.16 which applies where goods on any premises have been taken into control and have not been removed by the enforcement agent. The enforcement agent is granted the right to enter the premises to inspect the items or to remove them for storage or sale. This paragraph also authorises repeated re-entry to the same premises. 'Reasonable force' may be used to regain entry to premises. The meaning of this phrase is discussed *at 8.6 above*. NSEA cautions agents that the power of forced re-entry should only be used to the extent that it is reasonably required and only after the debtor has been given notice of the enforcement agent's intention to re-enter.

It should be re-emphasised that the general rules already described in chapter 8 relating to the day and time of initial entry also apply to re-entries. Re-entry to premises may accordingly take place:

- On any day of the week;[19] and,
- Between 6am and 9pm. However, where the goods to be taken into control are located on premises which are used (either wholly or partly) for the purposes of carrying on a business and those premises are open for business. Lastly, the court, on specific application for this purpose from an enforcement agent, may make an order permitting a bailiff to re-enter premises outside the permitted hours.[20]

Any re-entry should (like initial entry) only be made through a normal access route (a door or gate). An agent may not re-enter if only a child or a vulnerable person are present alone at the premises.[21]

In a complaint brought under the former law, it was found by the Local Government Ombudsman that bailiffs had abused their powers when, on returning to premises in order to remove goods, they first called at neighbours' homes to enquire where the debtors were - identifying themselves as bailiffs when doing this. The bailiffs then searched the debtor's house, located an address book and began to ring some of the telephone numbers contained in it in an effort to locate the debtors. These actions were condemned as a serious breach of confidentiality in excess of the bailiffs' lawful rights, for which £200 compensation was awarded.

11.2.2 Forced re-entry

Re-entry to premises may be forced by an enforcement agent without any other prior proceedings under Sch.12 para.18 or 19 if certain prescribed conditions are met. These are that the enforcement agent has power to re- enter the premises under paragraph 16 (i.e. there are controlled goods on the premises) and that either:

- *the bailiff is acting on a warrant issued to enforce a criminal penalty* under s.76(1) of the Magistrates' Courts Act 1980;[22] or,
- *the agent reasonably believes that the debtor carries on a trade or business* on the premises and that the agent is acting under an enforcement power in respect of certain specific debts. These are defined as being:[23]
- *executions* - a writ or warrant of control issued for the purpose of recovering a sum payable under a High Court or county court judgment for what is most likely to be a trade debt;
- *income taxes* - under section 61(1) of the Taxes Management Act 1970;
- *national insurance contributions* - under section 121A(1) of the Social Security Administration Act 1992;
- *indirect taxes* - under section 51(A1) of the Finance Act 1997; and,
- *stamp duty land tax* - under the Finance Act 2003.[24]

11.2.3 Re-entry after breached controlled goods agreement

Whilst for the former debts re-entry may be forced without the need for any prior proceedings, for all other debts notice of the intention to re-enter to inspect the goods or to remove them must have been given to the debtor following a failure to comply with the terms of payment laid down in a controlled goods agreement.[25] Provided that notice has been given, reasonable force may be used to enter.[26] The Taking Control of Goods Regulations 2013 specify the details of the notice.

Notice of an intention to re-enter should give not less than two clear days warning of the planned return visit (not counting Sundays, bank holidays, Good Friday or Christmas Day). However, a court may on application order that a lesser period of notice is given but only where it is satisfied that, if the order was not made, the debtor's goods would be likely to be moved from the premises where they were taken into control, or might be disposed of, in order to defeat the levy. The application will be made to the court on N244 without notice to the debtor. It must be accompanied by evidence demonstrating that, if the order requested is not made, it is likely that goods of the debtor will be moved or will be disposed of in order to avoid the enforcement agent inspecting or removing them.[27]

The notice must provide details of the debtor, the controlled goods agreement that has been breached and repayment terms that were made (and the debtor's default on these), the balance of the debt remaining due, the means by which payment may now be made and the deadline for doing this. The debtor will, naturally, be warned that if payment is not now made entry will be forced to the premises in order to remove the goods for storage and sale and that this will incur further costs (the sale stage fee and any associated disbursements - see chapter 12). The notice should be dated and bear any reference numbers.[28] Re-entry notices should be served by one of the following means - by:[29]

- · fax or other means of electronic communication;
- · delivery by hand through the letter box of the place, or one of the places, where the debtor usually lives or carries on a trade or business;
- · affixing the notice at or in the place that it is likely to come to the attention of the debtor in those cases where there is no letterbox at the premises;
- · to the debtor personally, where the debtor is an individual; or,
- · where the debtor is not an individual (but is, for example, a company, corporation or partnership), by delivering the notice to -
  - · the place, or one of the places, where the debtor carries on a trade or business; or,
  - · the registered office of the company or partnership.

The enforcement agent is responsible for ensuring that the notice is given and must keep a record of when it is served.

It will be seen that a key element of the notice of re-entry, like the controlled goods agreement that preceded it, is the repayment arrangement made with the debtor. If no payment terms were agreed, there will be no right to serve notice or to force re-entry. The bailiff still retains a right of re-entry, but this could only be exercised peaceably and with the debtor's consent. Forced re-entry could perhaps be made with a court warrant, but application for this will necessarily demand an explanation to the court of the bailiff's failure to agree the mandatory repayments terms required by the Regulations.[30]

11.2.4 Re-entry where goods secured on premises

If, rather than entering into a controlled goods agreement, the bailiff secured the goods on the premises by locking them in a room, clamping them, or similar, subsequent re-entry to remove those goods for sale at a later date is rather more difficult.

The notice of intention to re-enter is issued only where a controlled goods agreement has been breached. Issue of the notice justifies a subsequent forcible entry. In other cases, it will be necessary to make application to a court for a warrant permitting the use of reasonable force to re-enter.[31] Application will be on N244 but the Civil Procedure Rules do not make detailed provision for these cases.[32] A constable may be required by the court to assist in the re-entry.[33]

11.2.5 Re-entry to inspect goods

An enforcement agent may re-enter premises to inspect goods previously taken into control- whether by securing them there by some means or by a controlled goods agreement. If the return visit to inspect the assets follows the making of a controlled goods agreement, a notice of intended re-entry may be served as described *at 11.2.3*. Force may then be used to gain access if it is felt to be appropriate. Otherwise, force would only be permissible with a court warrant (*see 11.2.4*).

If the bailiff re-enters premises without any use of force merely to check upon goods taken into control on a previous occasion, no further notice of entry under reg.30 need be provided.[34] However, if the goods are to be removed for storage or sale, notice will be required under reg.32 (*see below*). Having re-entered, a bailiff may remain to inspect outside the hours permitted (see above) only so long as no more than a 'reasonable time' is occupied doing this.[35]

11.2.6 Removal

Following re-entry, it is emphasised that a bailiff may remain to remove goods outside the hours permitted (see above) only so long as no more than a 'reasonable time' is occupied doing this.[36] Finally recall that the enforcement agent is required to leave the premises as effectively secured as he finds them.[37]

Once removal is complete, controlled goods cannot be sold within a minimum period of seven clear days after the date of removal.[38] Exceptions are made if the assets are of declining value (*see 11.3.2*).

11.2.7 Notice after removal

The regulations stipulate that an enforcement agent must provide a written and signed notice to the debtor when goods are removed from a property for the purposes of sale.[39] In addition to the information required by reg.30 (*see chapter 9 above*) the notice will also have to inform the debtor of:[40]

 · The fact that the goods have been removed for storage or sale;
 · The list of items removed if this is different to those listed after

taking control (otherwise the inventory supplied previously will suffice - *see chapter 9 above*);[41]

· The date of the removal for sale;
· The procedure for making payment so as to prevent the sale of the goods.

If any of this information is not immediately available to the agent at the time of removal, it should be provided to the debtor as soon as is reasonably practicable.[42] The prescribed form of notice also warns of the storage costs which will accrue daily or weekly (these are recoverable as a disbursement from the debtor - *see chapter 12*). The NSEA supplements this statutory duty by requiring that a receipt for the goods removed should be given to the debtor or left at the premises.

The reference to the difference between the first inventory and the goods actually removed might appear to imply that additional valuables might be taken into control if they are found, in contradiction of the previous legal rules. The former rule was that, on return, only what was previously seized may be removed. If extra goods were discovered after the seizure and notice had been presented, they could not be included in the levy and to remove them would have been a trespass.[43] There seems no reason to suppose that this rule has been changed by the new Act. We are only concerned with goods already taken into control and, it will be remembered, bailiffs' rights to make repeat visits with a view to taking more goods into control are highly circumscribed.[44] Certainly, by the point of attendance to remove for sale, it will be too late for the agent to add to the inventory. A repeat visit under reg.24 may be made in exercise of the rights of entry included in Sch.12 paras.14 and 15 - but not the right of re-entry made under para.16.

The kinds of circumstance envisaged by the regulation in which a new inventory may be included in the removal notice appear to be those where less needs to be removed than was initially anticipated, perhaps because:

· The debt has been reduced in the interim by payments by the debtor;
· Certain items have been removed from the initial inventory because it has been accepted that they are third party property or should be regarded as exempt from taking;
· Items have since broken or depreciated;
· Items have been wrongfully removed by the debtor;
· The liability itself has been adjusted- for instance by an award of council tax benefit during the financial year or because the person has left a property in question and liability for council tax has ceased; or,
· Possibly, items on the initial inventory have been replaced or

substituted with replacement goods by the debtor. It might conceivably be possible to take these instead of those previously identified.

11.2.8 Care of controlled goods

Where an agent removes goods (other than securities) that had been taken into control from premises or from a highway, they should be kept in the same condition as that in which they were found.[45] If they are being removed for sale, the goods may be removed straight to an auction house provided that it is secure and is suitable for ensuring that there is no damage or deterioration to the goods. Goods should not be removed to any location where they might cause some contravention of law- this particularly must relate to motor vehicles and the right of an enforcement agent to move a vehicle found on the highway before clamping it.[46]

Agents must take care of assets while they remain controlled goods. If a bailiff acts negligently, the debtor will be able to claim damages under Sch.12 paragraph 66. The standard set for this care has been said to be the same as that exercised by a person of ordinary discretion and judgment over his/her own property.[47] If the goods are stored at an auction house, the auctioneer must exercise ordinary care and diligence in keeping them and is liable for any damage or loss arising from default or negligence. Equally the auctioneer's possession gives an interest in the goods which entitles him/her to sue for any trespass or conversion of the goods, so, if a debtor sought to rescue the goods, the auctioneer could take action. The NSEA adds that agents must ensure that goods are handled with reasonable care so that they do not suffer any damage whilst in their possession and should have insurance in place for goods in transit so that if damage occurs this is covered by the policy.

The principles applicable hitherto were that a bailiff should not use items taken into control for his own purposes but might use items if that was necessary for their preservation and for the benefit of the owner- for example, milking cows. Modern examples might include the fact that a bailiff may not drive a motor vehicle seized from a debtor but may be entitled to periodically operate certain equipment that would otherwise deteriorate if not regularly used. In *Bagshaw v Goward* (1607) a defendant seized a stray horse and rode it. The court held such use to be a misdemeanour as seizure gave only a custody and no property in the items. Consequently the seizure was wrong from the beginning and the plaintiff was entitled to damages for the value of the item. In *Chamberlayn's Case* (1590) the court held that livestock should be made available to the owner to feed during impounding.[48]

If impounded items were damaged or lost as a result of the neglect of the impounder, the owner may sue for their value.[49]

11.3 Sale

The Act provides a comprehensive set of rules upon the conduct of sales which apply to all cases except those where securities are involved (*for which see 11.3.5 below*) or where sale is by exchange of one currency for another.[50]

11.3.1 Best price & valuation of goods

The general duty on sale is for the enforcement agent to sell or dispose of controlled goods for the best price that can reasonably be obtained.[51] This does not apply to money that can be used for paying any of the outstanding amount, unless the best price is more than its value if used in that way.

To assist in achieving the optimum proceeds from the sale, a new duty is created for the enforcement agent. Immediately after removal of goods for the purposes of their sale, an agent must make or obtain a valuation of the controlled goods and for the agent to give the debtor, and separately any co-owner, an opportunity to obtain an independent valuation of the goods.[52] This must be done within seven clear days of either the date of the notice of disposal of securities or the date of removal of goods for sale.[53]

As will be seen, re-entry, removal and the conduct of a sale of goods are inextricably interlinked concepts. A removal for the purposes of sale is defined by the fact that a valuation of the goods follows from it. Two situations will be therefore encountered:

- *Goods secured on the premises are removed* - in these circumstances, for example after default upon the terms of a controlled goods agreement, it will generally be clear that sale is the next stage in the process and the seven day deadline for valuing the assets will run from the date of their removal from the debtor's home or business;
- *Goods already removed for storage* - where items have previously been taken into control by removing them from the debtor's premises to store them elsewhere, it is more difficult to define when 'removing for sale' takes place. Presumably, if goods are taken from the warehouse to the auction house, that action will trigger the seven day period for conducting the valuation. If no such move is necessary, it is not clear from the Regulations when the period starts.

No form of notice is prescribed for enforcement agents to use to inform debtors about valuation. It will be necessary for firms to devise their own letters, stating that a valuation will be carried out and that the debtor or co-owner is entitled to arrange their own. If either chooses to do so, liaison with the enforcement agent will be required to arrange access to the removed goods.

A valuation must be in writing and should be signed by the enforcement agent.[54] It should set out the agent's name and reference number and should be dated. Where appropriate, a separate value for each item taken into control should be stated. The debtor and any co-owner should both be provided with copies. If the agent does not conduct the valuation personally, only a qualified, independent valuer should be used.[55] The third party valuer must comply with the same conditions for the valuation as apply to the bailiff.

Under the now repealed Distress for Rent Act 1689, landlords used to have a duty to appraise (value) goods seized. Some of the principles developed in connection with this may be of guidance in interpreting the new regulations. If there was loss due to a failure to (properly) appraise, the debtor could sue for special damages based on the value of the goods less any sums due.[56] Even though there might have been an appraisement, the resulting valuation was not conclusive proof of the goods' value.[57] Enforcement agents should note particularly that the courts ruled that the exact procedure laid down for appraisal had to be strictly observed in order to entitle the creditor lawfully to sell.58 The former case of *Biggins v Goode* (1832) may provide authority for stating that, if a sale proceeds without a mandatory valuation taking place, the debtor will be entitled to compensation, the measure of the damages being the value of the goods less the debt due.[59]

The duty to conduct a valuation is closely linked to the duty to avoid excessive levies (see later) and emphasises the need for the bailiff to ensure that there is proportionality between the value of the goods taken into control and the debt and costs due. This principle operates both ways: it can apply just as much to levies where the goods are worth far less than the debt due as to those where the value of the chattels in far in excess of the liability. It may be that both may be the subject of a complaint of excessive seizure; certainly the Local Government Ombudsman has treated a levy upon goods of nil or negligible value as maladministration. This includes cases where multiple levies take place upon only the one chattel or set of chattels.[60]

The exact relationship between the price suggested by the mandatory valuation and the 'best possible price' to be achieved at auction is not explained. As described here, it is probably intended that the valuation provides a minimum or reserve price at auction, but this is not explicitly stated. Other purposes of the mandatory valuation may be as a guard against excessive takings in breach of Sch.12 para.12 and as a protection against agents proceeding with levies that cannot be justified by the value of the assets available. Although the debtor has the right to obtain his/her own valuation it must be stressed that no procedure is provided for resolving disagreements over conflicting or disputed valuations.

11.3.2   Timing of sale

A sale must not be held before the end of a minimum period of delay. The regulations specify that this minimum period before a sale may lawfully be held is seven clear days from the day of removal or, in the case of perishable goods, the day after removal.[61] Perishable items are defined as those which, were sale to take place after the elapse of the minimum seven day waiting period, would become unsaleable or would have their sale value extinguished or substantially reduced.62 This will include the contents of food shops, such as greengrocers and fruiterers, but also seasonal or time limited goods such as cards for festivals or other events.

11.3.3 Notice of sale

In another innovation, before the sale, the enforcement agent must give in every case notice of the date, time and place of the sale to the debtor and any co-owner.[63] The regulations specify the minimum period of notice, which is seven clear days before the date of sale. If the goods removed are perishable items the notice may be given the day before the sale.[64]

The notice of sale is a prescribed form. It must be in writing and must be signed and dated by the enforcement agent. It must state:[65]

- · The name and address of the debtor and of any co-owner of the goods;
- · The bailiff's name and reference numbers;
- · A list of the goods providing sufficient details to enable the debtor or co-owner to identify them, such as their model, make, serial or registration number, colour, usage or other identifying feature;
- · That sale is conditional upon a satisfactory purchaser being found. An offer must be received which at least covers the 'reserve price' (which is, it is assumed, the value set by the mandatory valuation- see earlier- as the term is not defined in the regulations). If these conditions are not met, another sale will be arranged;
- · The amount of the debt due including costs at the date of the notice;

- How and when payment may be made to prevent sale proceeding; and,
- Where payment is made and the goods are redeemed, how they may be collected by the debtor or co-owner.

The enforcement agent may replace a notice with a new notice, subject to any restriction in regulations. These are that:

- The date, time or location of the sale has had to be re-arranged;
- The notice given by the new notice should not be less than that given by the initial sale notice; and,
- The replacement notice makes it clear that it replaces any previous notice served.[66]

Any notice of sale must be given within the permitted period which, unless extended, is twelve months beginning with the day on which the enforcement agent takes control of the goods. Any extension to this deadline must be by agreement in writing between the creditor and debtor before the end of the period. They may extend the period more than once. It is to be presumed that these extensions are particularly likely to be agreed in the context of instalment arrangements made with the debtor and secured by a controlled goods agreement. Rather like the postponement of the date for taking control of goods, it will be a term of such an arrangement that every payment will have the effect of extending the one year deadline for arranging sale. This is not made explicit in the legislation (unlike for instalments agreed at the enforcement notice stage) but makes practical sense in that, otherwise, all instalments arrangements agreed after goods had been taken into control would have to run for no more than one year.

As it is possible for a bailiff to remove goods already taken into control on premises simply to store them at a more secure location, rather than for the purposes of an imminent sale, it appears that this second taking into control would replace the earlier. This would substitute a new, and later, 52 week deadline for arranging the sale.

The other situation in which the one year deadline for sale may be extended is where a claim is made to ownership of goods or for their exemption from taking. The deadline will run for twelve months from the conclusion of the claim.[67] The regulations add that any new sale notice that may be issued must comply with the time limits set out in 11.3.2, must provide all the information detailed above and must make it clear that it is a further sale notice.[68]

The notice of sale may be served by one of several methods:[69]

- by post addressed to the debtor at one of the addresses at which s/he usually resides or trades;
- by fax or other electronic means;
- by hand delivery through a letter box at one of the addresses at which s/he usually resides or trades;
- personally to the debtor if s/he is an individual rather than a company or partnership; or,
- where companies, corporations or firms are involved, by delivery to the registered office or one of the addresses at which the debtor usually carries on business.

11.3.4 Mode of sale

The sale must be by public auction unless the court orders otherwise.[70] The court may make an order permitting a different form of sale only on an application by the enforcement agent. Four alternative modes of sale may be permitted by a court, which are:[71]

- Private contract;
- Sealed bids;
- Advertisement; or,
- Such other method as the court considers appropriate.

An "alternative sale application" may be made by an enforcement agent on N244.[72] In the 'alternative sale application' the enforcement agent must state whether he has reason to believe that an enforcement power has become exercisable by another creditor against the debtor or a co-owner. If the enforcement agent states that he does believe that another bailiff is instructed, the court may not consider the application until notice of it has been given to the other creditor (or until the court is satisfied that an enforcement power is not exercisable by the other creditor against the debtor or a co-owner). If there are other enforceable instruments, the application must be accompanied by the following information:

- a list of the names and addresses of every other creditor that the agent has reason to believe has an exercisable enforcement power against the debtor or co-owner and a explanation of why the agent has such a belief; and,
- a copy of the notice of application and proof that the notice has been served on such other creditors not less than four days before the day fixed for the hearing of the application.[73]

The notice of the alternative sale application must be in writing, signed by the enforcement agent and must provide the name and address of the debtor and the details of the agent.[74] A copy of the court application must be included. The notice may be handed to the other creditor or may be served by one of several methods:[75]

- · by post addressed to the creditor at one of the addresses at which s/he usually resides or trades;
- · by fax or other electronic means;
- · by hand delivery through a letter box at one of the addresses at which s/he usually resides or trades;
- · personally to the creditor if s/he is an individual rather than a company or partnership; or,
- · where companies, corporations or firms are involved, by delivery to the registered office or one of the addresses at which the debtor usually carries on business.

Every person to whom notice of the application was given may attend and be heard on the hearing of the application.

This expansion by the new law of the modes of sale possible is a major improvement over the erstwhile obligation of bailiffs to use only public auction. All parties should benefit from this change, as it should hopefully enable better prices to be achieved (or enable a buyer to be found who otherwise might not have been).

11.3.5 Place of sale

It is stipulated that, generally, every sale should take place at a public auction house or through an online or internet site.[76] However a sale may be held on the premises where the goods were found if those premises are used solely for trade purposes and the debtor consents to this.[77]

If the sale is held on the debtor's premises, the enforcement agent and any person permitted by him may enter the premises to conduct or attend the sale and may bring equipment onto the premises for the purposes of the sale.[78] Repeated entries may be made to the premises by the enforcement agent for the purposes of organising and holding the sale there. If necessary the enforcement agent may use reasonable force to enable the sale to be conducted and any person to enter.[79] The enforcement agent must on request show the debtor and any person who appears to him to be in charge of the premises evidence of his identity and his authority to enter and hold the sale on the premises.[80] The request for the production of identification may be made before the enforcement agent enters the premises or while he is there. The final stipulation is that, on departure, the enforcement agent must leave the premises as effectively secured as he found them.[81]

11.3.6 Conduct of sales

The 2013 Regulations make further provision about the sale of controlled goods. A qualified auctioneer - or an independent and reputable provider in the case of online auction site - must be employed.[82] The new legislation does not go deeper into the conduct of the sale than this, trusting in the professionalism of auction providers. It may prove in future useful to make reference to the wealth of case authority on this subject under the old law.

The previous law was that a sale of some description had to take place; the goods could not be handed over to the creditor,[83] but both the creditor and the debtor could buy them at the sale.[84] Existing case authority has also established that, if the goods are of a specialist nature, it is the bailiff's duty to obtain advice on the mode of sale - for instance advertising in specialist press to encourage bids by creating "an excitement or an opposition".[85] Restrictive conditions should not be laid down that will effect the sum raised.[86] Any conditions preventing the best price being achieved would give rise to a claim for damages by the debtor. The best price is not necessarily that offered by the highest bidder if this is still greatly under the item's value and no reasonable price can be obtained.[87] If the goods have been appraised but do not reach the reserve price, the sale may proceed for the best price that can be obtained. It may be necessary for several attempts to be made to reach the appraised price at successive auctions before sale for a lesser sum is reasonable.

As stated, the purpose of the mandatory valuation must be assumed, in large measure, to provide guidance as to the best price to be achieved at sale. In the past it was accepted by the courts that a claim could be made for not selling at the best price, giving evidence of mismanagement in connection with the handling of the goods at the sale. From the old authorities it may be extrapolated that the sorts of mishandling for which a claim might be made will include:

· *Mishandling the goods* - for example, where goods were left in the rain and inadequately lotted;[88]
· *Mishandling the sale* - by improper lotting and hurrying the sale, thereby failing to achieve the best price possible;[89]
· *Failing properly to advertise the sale* - care must be taken to ensure adequate publicity which can attract the largest number of potential buyers;[90]
· *Delaying sale* - just as hurrying a sale might be wrongful, undue delay in conducting a sale was held to be an irregular distress for which damages could be recovered;[91]

· *Selling too much* - a bailiff acted wrongfully by seizing and selling more than was "reasonably sufficient" to cover the debt and costs, though obviously there must be a margin for error and a reasonable amount may be seized in the first place.[92] The bailiff's duty was to closely monitor a sale to make sure that too much was not sold.[93] If several items, each worth more than the debt due, were seized and all of them were subsequently sold, this would give grounds for a claim.[94] Thus in a case where the sale was extended over two days, but where enough was sold on the first day, it was trespass to continue with the sale on the second day, even if there was a fear that actual delivery of the goods might somehow be prevented by loss or accident.[95]

If, despite acting with due diligence, the bailiff is unable to find buyers for the goods seized he is not liable in negligence, though sufficient efforts should be made to sell before voluntarily abandoning goods of sufficient value. If a bailiff is to be sued for being negligent in the conduct of a sale only nominal damages will be recoverable unless actual loss and damage can be shown by the creditor.[96]

11.3.7 Remedies

If the rules on the conduct of sale are not observed, an aggrieved debtor may have a claim under Sch.12 para.66. Under the common law rules applicable formerly, if goods were sold for greatly under their value the debtor was assumed to have a substantial grievance upon which a claim for damages could be based.[97] However the onus was on the claimant to show that there was substantial difference between the price realised and the value at the date of sale. In the absence of such proof the bailiff was protected from proceedings. The auction price is not conclusive proof of the value of the goods, as was confirmed in *Khazanchi v Faircharm Investments* [1998]:

"The price realised at auction is not necessarily the best evidence of value at any particular date but if there is no evidence... to the effect that the auction had not been properly advertised or conducted it is evidence a judge is entitled to accept".

It was also confirmed that evidence as to prices fetched for goods on the second hand market may be acceptable, but in the absence of such indications of worth the value of goods if bought new at the time of seizure could not be relied upon as evidence as to the value of seized items sold some years earlier. The judgment also contained useful guidance on the matter of accounting for VAT in the course of assessing the price obtained.[98]

11.3.8 Disposal of securities

Special provisions apply to the sale or disposal of securities as controlled goods.[99] To repeat, securities include promissory notes, bills of exchange and bonds. They may be disposed of by sale, assignment or by court claim. An enforcement agent may hold such securities until they mature but, during this time, must ensure that they receive the same protection from damage, destruction, theft or unauthorised or fraudulent interference as they had before they were taken into control.[100]

The creditor has the right to issue a claim in the name of the debtor, or in the name of any person in whose name the debtor might have claimed, for the recovery of any sum secured or made payable by securities, when the time of payment arrives.[101] Before any proceedings are commenced or the securities are otherwise disposed of, the enforcement agent must give at least seven clear days' notice of the disposal to the debtor and any co-owner.[102]

The notice must be in writing and signed and dated by the enforcement agent and must set out:[103]

- The name and address of both the debtor and any co-owner of the securities;
- The name and reference numbers used by the enforcement agent;
- Sufficient details of each security to enable the debtor or co-owner to identify correctly;
- Notice that the securities may be disposed of by realising the sums secured or made payable by them and the date and time when this realisation may take place
- That the creditor may issue proceedings in the name of the debtor (or in the name of any person in whose name the debtor may have issued a claim) - or may assign the right to issue a claim - for recovery of the sums due when the time for payment arrives. In such cases the notice should also provide details of court proceedings - the name and address of the applicant and defendant(s) and the amount to be claimed (both on each security and in total);[104]
- The sums due to the creditor at the date of the notice; and,
- How and when payment may be made to prevent disposal of the securities and how those securities may then be released back to the debtor or co-owner.

The enforcement agent may replace a notice of sale with a new notice. A new notice may only be issued if the method of disposal of the securities has changed or the date and time of the disposal has had to be re-arranged.[105] Any notice must be given within the permitted period which, unless extended, is 12 months beginning with the time of payment. Any extension must be by agreement in writing between the creditor and debtor before the end of the period. They may extend the period more than once. The new disposal notice must give the same period of notice as the original, must contain the same information as is set out above and must make it clear that it is a new notice replacing a previous notice, the date of which must be stated.[106]

These notices may be served by one of several methods:[107]

- by post addressed to the debtor at one of the addresses at which s/he usually resides or trades;
- by fax or other electronic means;
- by hand delivery through a letter box at one of the addresses at which s/he usually resides or trades;
- personally to the debtor if s/he is an individual rather than a company or partnership; or,
- where companies, corporations or firms are involved, by delivery to the registered office or one of the addresses at which the debtor usually carries on business.

11.3.9 Proceeds of sale

The proceeds from the exercise of an enforcement power must be used to pay the amount outstanding. The proceeds are defined as the sums raised by a sale or disposal of controlled goods and any money taken in exercise of the power- this presumably means payments received from the debtor rather than cash taken from the person.[108] The 'amount outstanding' is defined as being the sum of the amount of the debt which remains unpaid (or an amount that the creditor agrees to accept in full satisfaction of the debt) and any amounts recoverable out of proceeds in accordance with regulations under paragraph 62 (costs).[109]

If the proceeds are less than the amount outstanding, their distribution is determined in accordance with regulation 13 of the 2104 Fees Regulations, which states that payment should be made in the following manner:

- co-owners receive payment for their share of the goods sold;
- the auctioneers receive settlement for their commission and expenses;
- the enforcement agent recovers the compliance fee (*see chapter 12*); and,
- the enforcement agent and creditor will then receive a pro-rata share of the remainder.

The most significant thing about this regulation is that it demotes the bailiff from the priority claim to recovery of fees which heretofore applied. It is to be noted that this order of distribution assumes a sale which fails to produce the total debt and costs outstanding. If part-payments are made by the debtor towards the sums due, this formula should also be applied. The co-owner's and auctioneer's shares will not be relevant, so that the first payment(s) received by the enforcement agent will go to paying the compliance fee, after which every instalment received will have to be distributed proportionately between the reducing balances of debt and costs.

If the proceeds are more than the amount outstanding, the surplus must be paid to the debtor. If there is a co-owner of any of the goods, the enforcement agent must first pay the co-owner a share of the proceeds of those goods proportionate to his interest and then deal with the rest of the proceeds as already described. If there is a dispute over the share to be paid to a co-owner, application may be made to the court to decide the matter. The application is made on general application form N244 and must be supported by the following:

· evidence of the enforcement power being exercised;
· a copy of the itemised list of goods sold or otherwise disposed of;[110]
· a copy of the statement of the sum received in relation to each item;[111]
· a copy of the statement of the proceeds required by regulation 14(1)(b)(ii) of the Fees Regulations - *see 11.4 below*;
· a copy of the statement of the application of the proceeds;[112] and,
· evidence that the share of proceeds paid to the co-owner was not proportionate to the co-owner's interest in the goods sold.

Notice of the application must be served on all the other parties - the creditor, debtor, enforcement agent and any other co-owners as applicable.[113]

The former case law found that the balance of the proceeds, after satisfying any debt and costs, constitutes a debt from the bailiff to the debtor. If the surplus money is paid direct to the debtor, his/her receipt of it is not necessarily acceptance in satisfaction and s/he may still question any fees charged etc.[114]

11.3.10 Passing of title

A purchaser of controlled goods acquires good title, with two exceptions - which only apply if the goods are not the debtor's at the time of sale.[115] The first exception is where the purchaser, the creditor, the enforcement agent or a related party has notice that the goods are not the debtor's. A related party is any person who acts in exercise of an enforcement power, other than the creditor or enforcement agent. The second exception is where a lawful claimant has already made an application to the court claiming an interest in the goods. A lawful claimant in relation to goods is a person who has an interest in them at the time of sale, other than an interest that was assigned or transferred to him while the property in the goods was bound for the purposes of the enforcement power.

Earlier authority suggests that, if the sale of the goods occurs before a person has had any chance to make a claim to them, the sale will not pass good title. Contrast this general rule with the result in *Goodlock v Cousins* [1897] where a sale of goods which took place in default of a claimant complying with the conditions laid down in interpleader procedure was held to pass good title.[116]

On the matter of notice by a claimant, a couple of older cases may be helpful. It was held that good title was not passed if it could be shown that notice of a third party claim was received or that on 'reasonable enquiry' an agent should have ascertained that the goods were not the property of the judgment debtor. In *Pilling v Teleconstruction Co Ltd* [1961] the defendants were held liable for damages in trespass and costs. They were judgment debtors at whose rented premises the plaintiffs left industrial machinery. The equipment was seized by a county court bailiff and sold. As bailees the defendants should have notified the bailiffs and the court of the situation, whilst the court did all it had to try to establish the facts. In contrast in *Observer Ltd v Gordon* [1983] a sheriff's officer was not found liable in conversion. The defendant had repaired pianos, which were seized and sold for a judgment creditor. The owners of the pianos then made claims but the sheriff was held not to have had notice of ownership nor would it have been reasonable for him to make enquiries in the circumstances of the case. There had been no indication that the pianos were not the judgment debtor's, despite repeated visits by the bailiff to the shop. It was reasonable that he did not make further enquiries as the removal and sale occurred after the judgment debtor's death, so that goods were removed from an unoccupied shop, and, the court felt that even if he had made enquiries, the true facts would not have been revealed to the sheriff's officer in a reasonable period of time.[117] A purchaser in good faith was entitled to protection against other executions which should have had priority, even if the writ itself was void through fraud unless s/he was aware of or party to this.[118]

Title in goods sold at auction passes at the instant the hammer falls. This will terminate any right to take control of those goods and it would be wrongful for an auctioneer then to satisfy a claim because of a threat to seize goods already sold.[119]

11.3.11 *Limitation of liability for sale or payment of proceeds*

Any liability of an enforcement agent or related party to a lawful claimant for the sale of controlled goods is excluded except in two cases.[120] The first exception is where at the time of the sale the enforcement agent had notice that the goods were not the debtor's, or not his alone. The second exception is where before sale the lawful claimant had made an application to the court claiming an interest in the goods. A lawful claimant in relation to goods is a person who has an interest in them at the time of sale, other than an interest that was assigned or transferred to him while the property in the goods was bound for the purposes of the enforcement power.

Similarly, any liability of an enforcement agent or related party to a lawful claimant for paying over proceeds is excluded except in two cases.[121] The first exception is where at the time of the payment he had notice that the goods were not the debtor's, or not his alone. The second exception is where, before that time, the lawful claimant had made an application to the court claiming an interest in the goods. A lawful claimant in relation to goods is a person who has an interest in them at the time of sale.

The above provisions do not affect the liability for wrongful sale of a person other than the enforcement agent or a related party and do not apply to a creditor who also acted as enforcement agent. The enforcement agent or a related party will be treated as having notice of something if it would have found it out by making reasonable enquiries. A 'related party' is defined as being any person who acts in exercise of an enforcement power, other than the creditor or enforcement agent. It is interesting to note that this definition is different to that used in the following paragraph of Schedule 12, which deals with debtors' remedies (*see 13.7*); it might include auctioneers, locksmiths and removals contractors employed by an enforcement agency.[122]

11.4 Accounts

There used to be very little regulation of the bailiff's duty to provide information on receipts and expenses to any of the parties at the conclusion of the enforcement process. This has been remedied by the new Fees Regulations. Directly upon sale or disposal of goods, the enforcement agent must provide the debtor and any co-owner of goods of whom s/he is aware with a statement detailing the following items:

- · the items sold or otherwise disposed of;
- · the sum received in relation to each item;
- · the proceeds of sale;
- · the application of the proceeds of sale; and,
- · the disbursements recoverable under these Regulations and incurred in relation to the goods (*see 12.2 below*).[123]

The enforcement agent must provide the debtor and any co-owner with a copy of all receipts for the expenses incurred in respect of sale by a qualified auctioneer- whether at an auction house or at the debtor's premises (*see 12.2.5 below*). This duty does not apply if the goods are sold by internet auction or by other means of disposal.

Where the debtor pays, or seeks to pay, the amount outstanding at any time after the enforcement agent has incurred disbursements- but before sale or disposal of the goods takes place - the enforcement agent must provide the debtor with the following information:

- · a statement of disbursements recoverable (*see 12.2 below*);
- · any receipts for disbursements unless they relate to sale by internet auction or any form of sale other than public auction ; and,
- · a statement of any fixed and percentage fees charged.

In the case of High Court writs and county court warrants of control, either the creditor or debtor may serve a notice on the enforcement agent or enforcement officer requiring reasonable information about the execution of a writ or warrant. The agent or officer must then send such information to the person requesting it within seven days of service of the notice. If the agent or officer fails to comply, the party who served the notice may apply to the court for an order directing the agent or officer to provide the information required.[124]

The NSEA also stipulates that, on returning any un-executed warrants, the enforcement agency should report the outcome to the creditor and provide further appropriate information, where this is requested and paid for by the creditor.

11.5 Repeat levies

The following issues are not dealt with in the Act, so it must be presumed that the common law principles on further levies will continue to apply should any such problems arise in future.

The frequently stated rule was that a second levy could not be conducted. In fact this principle dealt with two issues under the same heading. A bailiff could not distrain again for the same debt after a completed levy. This is because the second levy was rendered illegal by the fact that no debt was any longer due. Secondly, the bailiff could not split the demand and try more to levy than once under the same warrant because he realised he had not seized enough the first time around. There was an exception to the second instance for execution as repeat levies could be made in any circumstances where any portion of the debt remained outstanding.

11.5.1 Second levies

The following principles on second levies may be derived from the old case law. A bailiff could not levy more than once - even though the levies are only separated by a few hours[125] - if:

· it was for the same debt after a complete levy had satisfied it already;[126]
· the bailiff had levied for too little previously and simply failed to get enough through his "own folly";[127]
· the bailiff had 'abandoned' seized goods (see 9.10). In *Bagge v Mawby* [1853] a landlord withdrew after receiving a notice that another creditor intended to petition for the tenant's bankruptcy. After the order he distrained again. It was held that if there was no lawful cause for not following the levy through, he should have continued. The notice from the creditor was not a good cause or excuse- rather it was a mere idle threat from a stranger with no right to interfere in the distress. The landlord ought to have proceeded and couldn't levy again. The same rule would appear to have applied in execution. An allegation of abandonment which thereby bars further levies could also arise where the bailiff was withdrawn by the creditor on reaching an arrangement with the debtor. A new warrant would need to be issued;[128]
· if seizable goods were lost to the creditor either because the goods that were seized were of inadequate value when the bailiff had a fair opportunity to levy for more or because those goods that had been levied upon were lost through negligence on the part of the bailiff;

· the total debt due was split between separate warrants in order to give a series of small levies. Separate rents could be enforced separately as could separate instalments of rent. This could be in any order, and did not have to be in the sequence in which the sums fell due.[129]

A wrongful second levy could be resisted by the means described in chapter 6. However second levies of distress and execution were permissible and lawful where:

· *there were insufficient goods* on a first visit upon which to levy execution. Writs remained in force until the whole sum due has been collected- they were a continuing power to seize any goods that became available until such time as the debt was clear. Thus in one case it was held permissible to complete the levy some eleven years after the first seizure. Equally, a further levy might have been permitted where, on the first levy, it was found that all the goods then available had been seized by another bailiff or where more effects were discovered at a later date. Bailiffs were allowed to make a partial levy but were entitled to wait until the levy can be completed rather than make a return of no goods. Bailiffs were also allowed to distrain in 'instalments' where they were concerned to avoid an excessive levy.[130] This ability to make successive moderate levies is endorsed by both earlier writers as to the advantage of the debtor, as otherwise items of great value might have had to be seized on the first visit. Finally, a further levy was held to be legal if on the first occasion the bailiff acted out of 'moderation or tenderness' and did not levy for full value;[131]
· *the bailiff made a reasonable mistake* because of the uncertain or illusory value of the items;[132]
· *the levy was obstructed* - for instance, because the debtor obstructed or attacked the bailiff or refused entry. On such a second levy the bailiff did not need to confine himself to the goods seized on the previous occasion. Equally a second levy might have been justified if circumstances at the auction prevented the best price being obtained. See for example *Rawlence & Squarey v Spicer* [1935] where demonstrations and threats by the debtor prevented a sale or *R v Judge Clements ex p Ferridge* [1932] where a crowd prevented the sale by attending the auction, harassing bidders and making ridiculous offers;[133]
· *seized cattle died in the pound* by an act of God.[134]
· *the first attempted levy was trespass* and thus void *ab initio*. This could have been where a levy on goods was made, but it transpired that none of the goods were the debtor's;[135]
· *the first distress was withdrawn*, at the request of the debtor. This

might have been because the debtor simply asked the creditor to forbear and postpone the distress or because instalments were agreed. If the arranged payments were not made, the bailiff could then distrain again;[136] and,

· the debtor went bankrupt so that the first levy was withdrawn, but the bankruptcy was later annulled.[137]

11.5.2 *Second warrants*

The previous section dealt with repeat levies under the same warrant. Various regulations permit repeat warrants to be issued, as many times as are necessary, for the same debt.[138] A second warrant should not be issued whilst the first is still in the bailiff's hands even if the levy has been abandoned. If the bailiff is withdrawn on the instructions of the creditor, following an arrangement between debtor and creditor, a new warrant will have to be issued to permit the bailiff to return. A new warrant can be issued if the first was inoperative due to prior seizure and assignment of goods to a third party.[139]

11.6 Abandonment

The 2007 Act gives a new and simple meaning to the term 'abandonment.'[140] Controlled goods are abandoned if the enforcement agent does not give the debtor or any co-owner notice of sale within the permitted period of twelve months beginning on the date of taking control. The consequences of abandonment of controlled goods are that the enforcement power ceases to be exercisable and, as soon as reasonably practicable, the enforcement agent must make the goods available for collection by the debtor, if he removed them from the place where he found them.[141] Readers should note, however, that the Act stipulates that where the enforcement power was under a writ or warrant of control, an abandonment does not affect any power for the creditor to issue another writ or warrant. Under the Civil Procedure Rules if a creditor requests that a warrant of control is withdrawn by the court, the warrant will be marked as withdrawn by the court and it will be treated as abandonment of the goods.[142]

When an enforcement agent makes controlled goods available for collection by the debtor after they have come to be treated as abandoned, all immobilisation devices that have been applied must be removed by the agent on (but not before) the day of collection.[143] Where the agent removed the goods for storage from the place where they were found, the debtor must be given a written notice, as soon as reasonably practicable, signed the enforcement agent and setting out the following information:

- the name and address of the debtor;
- the agent's name, reference number(s) and the date of the notice;
- a confirmation of the fact that the controlled goods are abandoned and the reason why;
- a list of those goods which have been abandoned along with a sufficient description of them so as to enable the debtor to be able to identify them correctly, including, where applicable-
    - the manufacturer, model and serial number of the goods;
    - in the case of vehicles, the manufacturer, model, colour and registration mark of the vehicle; and,
    - the material, colour and usage of the goods or any other identifying characteristic;
- a statement that the goods are available for collection by the debtor;
- information on the procedure for collection of the goods by the debtor; and,
- a warning that, if the debtor fails to collect the goods within 28 days from the date on which the goods were made available for collection, the enforcement agent will make an application to the court for determination of how those goods are to be disposed of.

The method of giving the notice is the method required under regulation 8(1) to which reference has already been made.

Where the debtor fails to retrieve the abandoned goods within 28 days of the date upon which the goods were made available for collection, the enforcement agent must make an application to the court for determination of how the uncollected goods shall be disposed of. The application is made by means of general application form N244 in which the bailiff will have to explain why it is not appropriate to extend the time allowed to the debtor to collect his or her goods.[144]

On hearing the application, the court may make one of the following orders:

- that a further period of time, to be determined by the court, is to be allowed to the debtor for collection of the goods;
- that the goods are to be given to a charitable organisation nominated by the court or are to be destroyed; or,
- that the goods are to be made available for collection by the debtor during a further period of time to be determined by the court and, if not collected during that period, are either to be donated to a charity or destroyed.

Finally, separate provision is made concerning the abandonment of securities.[145] Securities are abandoned if the enforcement agent does not give the debtor or any co-owner notice of disposal under paragraph 49 within the permitted period. The Act states that regulations may prescribe other circumstances in which securities are abandoned, but this has not in fact been done.[146] If securities are abandoned then the enforcement power ceases to be exercisable and, as soon as reasonably practicable the enforcement agent must make the securities available for collection by the debtor, if he removed them from where he found them. Where the enforcement power was being exercised under a writ or warrant, the rules on abandonment do not affect any power to issue another writ or warrant.[147]

Footnotes

1 See reg.9(1) TCG Regs.
2 Reg.15(2)(f).
3 Regs.30(2)(f)(iii), 32(1)(e) & 39(1)(i).
4 Under protest - *Manning v Lunn* [1845] 2 C&K 13 and *Greenwood v Sutcliffe* [1892] 1 Ch 1; no refusal - *Scott v Uxbridge & Rickmansworth Railway Co* [1866] 1 CP 596; receipt - *Richardson v Jackson* [1849] 8 M&W 298; periods covered by receipt - *Finch v Miller* [1848] 5 CB 428.
5 3rd party - *Smith v Egginton* [1855] 10 Exch 845; co-tenant - *Smith v Cox* [1940] 2 KB 558.
6 *Simpson v. Howitt* (1876) 39 UCQB 610.
7 *Palmer v Bramley* [1895] 2 QB 405
8 *Re: Romer & Haslam* [1893] 2 QB 286; *Gunn v Bolckow, Vaughan & Co* [1875] 10 Ch App 491; [1964] 2 QB 10.
9 *R v Locker* [1971] 2 QB 321.
10 Presence - *Horne v Lewin* (1700) 1 Ld Raym 639; willingness to pay - *Cranley v Kingswell* (1617) Hob 207.
11 Full sum - *Finch v Miller* (1848) 5 CB 428; to whom - *Smith v Goodwin* (1833) 4 B & Ad 413; to bailiff - *Hatch v Hale* (1850) 15 QB 10; man in possession - *Boulton v Reynolds* (1859) 2 E&E 369; execution - *Taylor v Bekon* (1678) 2 Lev 203; [1993] NPC 36.
12 Illegal - *Branscomb v Bridges* (1823) 1 B&C 145; refusal - *Bennet v Bayes* (1860) 5 H&N 391 & Smith v Goodwin (1823) 4 B & Ad 413.
13 Sch.12 para.58.
14 Tender before removal - *Loring v Warburton* (1858) EB&E 507; before impounding - *Vertue v Beasley* (1831) 1 Mood & R 21 and *Evans v Elliot* (1836) 5 Ad & El 142.
15 Sch.12 para.50(3).
16 For example, failing to return goods after tender used to be treated as conversion - *West v Nibbs* (1847) 4 CB 172; it was also held that if the debtor tenders or pays the debt, an execution would be discharged and the officer could not then sell - *Taylor v Baker* (1677) 3 Keb 788/ 2 Lev 203, *R v Bird* (1679) 2 Show 87 and *Brun v Hutchinson* 2 D&L 43.
17 Paragraph 59(5).
18 [2001] 1 WLR 387; see *Sources of bailiff law* c.5 p.154.
19 Reg.21(2) TCG Regs.
20 Reg.22.
21 Regs.21 & 23 TCG Regs.
22 Sch.12 para.16.
23 Sch.12 para.19(2).

24 Schedule 12 paragraph 1A.
25 Para.19A.
26 Sch.12 para.17
27 Reg.25 TCG Regs; CPR 84.8.
28 Reg.26.
29 Reg.27.
30 Sch.12 para.16 & para.20.
31 Reg.20.
32 CPR 84.9 is not applicable as it refers to reg.28 TCG Regs.
33 Sch.12 para.22(2).
34 Reg.30(3) TCG Regs.
35 Reg.22(4).
36 Reg.22(4).
37 Sch.12 paragraph 30.
38 Sch.12 para.39 & reg.37(1) TCG Regs.
39 Taking Control of Goods Regulations 2013 regs 30 & 32.
40 Reg.32(1) TCG Regs.
41 Reg.32(3).
42 Reg.32(2).
43 *Smith v Torr* [1862] 3 F&F 505; *Bishop v Bryant* [1834] 6 C&P 484.
44 Reg.24 - *see 8.11 earlier.*
45 Sch.12 para.35; reg.34(1) Taking Control of Goods Regulations 2013.
46 Reg.34(2).
47 *Kennedy v. Grose* (1914) 7 WWR 74.
48 Yelv 96; 74 ER 202
49 *Perkins v Butterfield* [1627] Het 75 - though note that in this case in a dissenting judgment Hitcham J felt that trespass did lie for such mistreatment and that loss of goods seized could render the levy trespass *ab initio*).
50 Para.38.
51 Para.37.
52 Sch.12 paragraph 36.
53 Respectively, for securities Sch.12 para.36(2)(a) & para.49 or for goods Sch.12 para.36(2)(b) & para.39.
54 Regulation 35 Taking Control of Goods Regulations 2013.
55 Reg.35(3).
56 *Knotts v Curtis* (1832) 5 C&P 322; *Whitworth v Maden* (1847) 2 C&K 517.
57 *Cook v Corbett* (1875) 24 WR.
58 See for example *Lamb v Cloves* (1847) 10 LT 231. See too *Westwood v Cowne* (1816) 1 Stark 172 - the distrainor may not appraise and *Burroughs v Smith* (1869) 4 LJ 22 - damages for failing to leave surplus with sheriff- though not being able to find the tenant is a good excuse for failure! (*Stubbs v May* (1822) 1 LJCP 12)
59 (1832) 2 C&J 364.
60 LGO complaint against Slough BC, 10 007 469; complaint against Blaby DC 11 007 684.
61 Sch.12 para.39 & reg.37(1) TCG Regs.
62 Reg.37(2).
63 Para.40.
64 Reg.38(1) & (2).
65 Reg.39(1).
66 Reg.39(2) & (3).
67 CPR 83.4(7).
68 Reg.39(3).

69 Reg.40(2) applying reg.8(1).
70 para.41.
71 Reg.41(1).
72 Schedule 12 para.41(2).
73 CPR 84.11.
74 Reg.41(2).
75 Reg.41(3) applying reg.8(1).
76 Sch.12 para.43; reg.42(1) Taking Control of Goods Regulations 2013.
77 Reg.42(2).
78 Sch.12 paragraphs 44 to 46.
79 Para.44(3).
80 Para.45.
81 Para.46.
82 Sch.12 para.42 & reg.43 TCG Regs.
83 *Thomson v Clark* (1596) 78 ER 754; *Holm v Hunter* (1701) Holt 494.
84 *Re: Rogers ex p Villars* [1874] 9 Ch App 432 or *Stratford v Twynan* (1822) Jac 418.
85 *American Express v Hurley* [1985] 3 All ER 564.
86 *Ridgway v Lord Stafford* (1851) 6 Exch 404; *Hawkins v Walrond* [1876] 1 CPD 280.
87 *Keightley v Birch* (1814) 3 Camp 321.
88 *Poynter v Buckley* (1833) 5 C&P 512.
89 *Wright v Child* [1866] 1 Exch 358; *Cameron v. Eldorado Properties* [1981] 113 DLR(3d) 141.
90 *Edge v Kavanagh* [1884] 24 LR IR 1.
91 *Langtry v. Clark* (1896) 27 OR 280.
92 *Gawler v Chaplin* (1848) 2 Exch 503; *Cooke v Palmer* (1827) 6 B & C 739.
93 *Batchelor v Vyse* (1834) 4 Moo & S 552.
94 *Wooddye v Coles* (1595) Noy 59.
95 *Aldred v Constable* (1844) 6 QB 370.
96 *Guardians of Naas Union v. Cooper* 18 LR Ir 242; *Bales v Wingfield* (1843) 4 A&E 580.
97 *Sayer's Case* Cro Jac 526; *Sly v. Finch* Cro Jac 514.
98 *Neumann v Bakeaway* [1983] 1 WLR 1016; [1998] 2 All ER 901, Morritt LJ @ 920f; see also 919 & 921 b & c - see *Sources of bailiff law* c.5 p.131.
99 Sch.12 paragraphs 48-49; Part 4 Taking Control of Goods Regulations 2013.
100 Reg.45.
101 Paragraph 49.
102 Reg.46(1) TCG Regs.
103 Regulation 46(2).
104 Reg.46(3).
105 Reg.46(4).
106 Reg.46(5).
107 Reg.46(6) applying reg.8(1).
108 Para.50(2).
109 Paragraph 50(3).
110 Reg.14(1)(a) Fees Regulations 2014.
111 Reg.14(1)(b)(i) Fees Regulations.
112 Reg.14(1)(b)(iii) Fees Regulations.
113 CPR 84.15.
114 Liability to debtor - *Harrison v Paynter* (1840) 6 M&W 387; fees - *Lyon v Tomkies* (1836) 1 M&W 603.
115 Sch.12 para.51.

116 *Crane & Sons v Ormerod* [1903] 2 KB 37; [1897] 1 QB 348.

117 [1961] 111 L J 424; [1983] 1 WLR 1008.

118 Priority - *Imray v Magnay* (1843) 11 M&W 267; writ void - *Bessey v Windham* (1844) 6 QB 166 and *Shattock v Craden* (1851) 6 Exch 725.

119 *Sweeting v Turner* (1872) 36 JP 597.

120 Para.63.

121 Sch.12 para.64.

122 Sch.12 para.65.

123 Reg.14 Fees Regulations.

124 CPR 83.8.

125 *Wallis v Savill* [1701] 2 Lut 493.

126 *Wotton v Shirt* [1600] Cro Eliz 742; *Owens v Wynne* [1855] 4 E&B 579.

127 *Dawson v Cropp* [1845] 1 CB 961; *Wallis v Savill* [1701] 2 Lut 493; *Anon* Moore 7.

128 [1853] 8 Exch 641; execution - *Castle v Ruttan* [1854] 4 CP 252; withdrawn - *Shaw v Kirby* [1888] 52 JP 182.

129 Split debt - *Forster v Baker* [1910] 2 KB 636; *Rothschild v Fisher* [1920] 2 KB 243; separate rents - *Sheppard's Touchstone of Common Assurances* 81; separate instalments - *Anon* Moore 7; *Gambrell v Earl of Falmouth* [1835] 4 A&E 73; order - *Palmer v Stanage* [1661] 1 Lev 43.

130 *Anon* Cro Eliz 13; *Jordan v Binckes* [1849] 13 QB 757; *R v Sheriff of Essex* [1839] 8 Dowl PC 5.

131 Prior levy - *Edmunds v Ross* [1821] 9 Price 5 and *Drear v Warren* [1833] 10 Bing 341; more goods found - *Hopkins v Adcock* [1772] 2 Dick 443; 'instalments' - *Hudd v Ravenor* [1821] 2 Brod & Bing 662; 'moderation' - *Hutchins v Chambers* [1758] 1 Burr 580.

132 *Hutchins v Chambers* [1758] 1 Burr 579.

133 Obstruction - *Lee v Cooke* [1858] 3 H & N 203; no restriction - *Gislason v Rural Municipality of Foam Lake* [1929] 2 DLR 386; [1935] 1 KB 412; [1932] 2 KB 535.

134 *Anon* [1568] 3 Dyer 280 pl 14; *Anon* [1700] 12 MR 397; *Vaspor v Edwards* [1796] 12 Mod Rep 658.

135 *Grunnell v Welch* [1906] 2 KB 555; *Re: A Debtor ex p Smith* [1902] 2 KB 260.

136 *Bagge v Mawby* (1853) 8 Exch 64; *Thwaites v Wilding* [1883] 12 QBD 4.

137 *Crew v Terry* [1877] 2 CPD 403.

138 For example, reg 52(3) CT(A&E) Regs.

139 Execution - *Lee v Dangar, Grant & Co* [1892] 2 QB 337; unreturned warrant - *Chapman v Bowlby* [1841] 8 M&W 249; abandoned - *Miller v Parnell* [1815] 5 Taunt 370; after withdrawal - *Shaw v Kirby* [1888] 52 JP 182; prior seizure - *Dicas v Warne* [1833] 10 Bing 341.

140 Sch.12 para.52.

141 Sch.12 para 54.

142 CPR 83.22(2).

143 Reg.47 Taking Control of Goods Regulations 2013.

144 CPR 84.12.

145 Para 55.

146 Para 56.

147 Para 57.

Chapter 12

Charges

12.1 Introduction

The Tribunals, Courts and Enforcement Act 2007 itself has little to say in detail about the fundamental issue of charges, relegating all the vital details to regulations. However, some broad statements of principle are laid down. Schedule 12 para.62 reads:

> "62(1) Regulations may make provision for the recovery by any person from the debtor of amounts in respect of costs of enforcement-related services.
>
> (2) The regulations may provide for recovery to be out of proceeds or otherwise.
>
> (3) The amount recoverable under the regulations in any case is to be determined by or under the regulations.
>
> (4) The regulations may in particular provide for the amount, if disputed, to be assessed in accordance with rules of court.
>
> (5) 'Enforcement-related services' means anything done under or in connection with an enforcement power, or in connection with obtaining an enforcement power, or any services used for the purposes of a provision of this Schedule or regulations under it."

This brief paragraph confirms that the two established approaches to the control of bailiffs' fees continue. Charges for all aspects of taking control of goods will continue to be regulated by government laying down a framework, the only fees recoverable will be those specified in the scale whilst the scale's application in individual cases will be supervised by the courts.

It seems reasonable to assume from the legislation that the case law relating to certain existing principles as to bailiffs' fees will continue to apply. These principles are that:

- Only the fees allowed by law may be charged - only those sums permitted by the fee scale may be charged lawfully to debtors. Any higher or additional fees would be unlawful (*see 12.5*);[1]
- Bailiffs may only charge for work actually and necessarily done (*see 12.6*); and,
- Any fees received should not breach the bailiffs' duties to the creditor under agency law (*see chapter 13*).

At this point certain general principles of practice on fees contained in guidelines may also be noted. The NSEA states that:

- Agents should provide clear and prompt information to debtors and should in particular explain the fees charged so far and those possible in the future;
- Whenever a fee is incurred, notice of this and all fees previously charged to the account should be given; and,
- On written request, a full and detailed breakdown of the fees charged on the account should be provided.

The second point may be of particular relevance. The new regulations contain no prescribed notice of a visit - only a notice after entry. At the same time, visits either to attempt to take control or to remove goods for sale mark the transition to a new stage of the enforcement process and the addition of a further fee. In light of this, most agencies will prefer to produce their own visit notices to record the work done and to justify the charge made.

12.2 Charge scales

It has been the practice for many centuries for Parliament to regulate bailiffs' fees by means of fee scales. The purpose of a scale is to regulate what is charged to individuals and to prevent the 'extortion' of 'helpless debtors' by the levying of any 'unfairly large sum'.[2] The new fee scale continues to try to attain this goal, balanced against a wish to provide a fair remuneration to enforcement agents.

Paragraph 62 of Schedule 12 sets out the broad principles on fees; the Taking Control of Goods (Fees) Regulations 2014 provide the detail.[3] In this chapter these will be referred to simply as the Regulations; any reference to other regulations will specify which are meant.

12.2.1 Introduction to new charge scales

The new Fees Regulations take a radical and simple approach to the calculation of bailiffs' fees. Regulation 4 sets out the structure for the main fees to be recovered. These are either fixed fees or fees calculated as a percentage of the sum to be recovered, which is defined as the debt which remains unpaid- or the amount that the creditor agrees to accept in full satisfaction of the debt.[4]

The fixed fees are applied to three stages of the enforcement process.

Compliance stage
This covers the following activities: receiving instructions from creditors and setting up accounts, confirming the personal details of the debtor, initial contacts and negotiations with the debtor, processing payments received, general office administration, handling complaints and managing instalment plans.

Enforcement stage
This comprehends the 'levy' process, from the first attendance at premises, through the taking into control of goods until a debtor's default in payments and the decision to remove. It also will also include supervising controlled goods agreements, dealing with insolvencies, undertaking HPI and DVLA checks and managing claims that goods either belong to third parties or should be given exempted status. This stage is split into two for High Court (*see 12.2.3*). The stage runs from the initial visits to 'premises.' These are defined in the Fees Regulations by reference to Sch.12 para.3(1) of the Act; this gives a very broad meaning to the term, as may be recalled, covering "any place" and including vehicles, vessels and moveable structures. On this basis it would appear that the enforcement fee may be applied after either a visit to the debtor's home or business or after discovery of a car on the highway. It is worth observing that the enforcement stage begins with the first visit to premises, yet no mandatory notice is prescribed for use between the enforcement notice and entry notice. Regardless, if an attendance is made but there is no contact with a debtor, but it is recommended that a notice should be left at the premises for reasons of clarity and good practice.

Sale or disposal stage
The last stage extends through all aspects of the concluding parts of the process, from attending to remove goods for disposal- or starting to prepare for sale if it is held on the premises, through the conduct of the sale to dealing with proceeds, the return of goods unsold and final reports to creditors. Where the goods which have been taken into control are securities, this stage commences with the provision of a notice of disposal in accordance with paragraph 49(2) of Schedule 12 of the Act.

As soon as one of these stages has been commenced, the fixed fee is chargeable, even though all the activities covered by the stage may not have been carried out or completed.[5]

It is stipulated that these sums are to be recovered out of the 'proceeds' of the enforcement process. The proceeds are defined as monies received from sale or disposal of goods and any money received in payment from the debtor.[6] The Act suggests that fees may be recovered by other means, but the Regulations make no provision for any such alternatives.[7]

In addition to the fixed fees, enforcement agents will be able to recover a percentage fee based upon higher value debts. These fees are calculated on the amount by which the debt being collected exceeds a specified figure. This amount is "the sum to be recovered", which is defined as "the amount of the debt which remains unpaid."[8] These phrases seem to imply that the fee is worked out on the basis of the current balance outstanding at the time of the calculation rather than on the sum for which the warrant was issued. Accordingly, if the debt is reduced by payments under a controlled goods agreement (for example) the percentage allowable will be calculated on a lower balance at sale stage than at enforcement stage.

Lastly, certain prescribed disbursements and expenses (see 12.2.4-12.2.6). It is notable that most of these latter charges which may be passed on to debtors arise towards the end of the recovery process and particularly only at the final, 'sale', stage, meaning that only a minority of debtors are likely to become liable for them.

Debtors should be able to keep track of the fees and expenses charged to them through the succession of notices which must now be served at key stages of the process. Moreover, at the end of the whole procedure, there is an obligation for a final account of sums received and paid to be provided.[9]

12.2.2 'Standard' fee scale

For all debts except High Court a single fee scale applies. This will be referred to as the 'standard' scale and is as follows:

- Compliance - £75;
- Enforcement - £235; and,
- Sale or disposal - £110.

In cases where the debt exceeds £1500, the enforcement and sale fees may be increased by an additional 7.5% of the amount over the £1500 base.[10]

The only distinction made in the fees regulations is between High Court and all other work. However, it is understood that county court bailiffs will not make the charges set out above and will instead simply rely upon the fees charged to judgment creditors for issue of warrants. This option is available as reg.4(1) states that agents "may recover from the debtor the fees indicated...;" a discretion remains not to pass on the charges.

12.2.3 High Court fee scale

For High Court enforcement, some significantly higher fees and a slightly different fee structure apply as follows:

- Compliance - £75;
- First enforcement - £190;
- Second enforcement - £495; and,
- Sale - £525.

As will have been observed, the enforcement stage is split into two stages for HCEOs. The boundaries between the stages are as set out below:

- *Compliance* covers all actions to the beginning of the first or second enforcement stage (as appropriate - see below);
- *First stage* - applies where the HCEO and the debtor enter into a controlled goods agreement and covers all activities relating to enforcement from the first attendance at the premises until the agreement is completed or breached. The difference between this first stage enforcement fee and that allowed to all other agents must be noted: in the High Court the fee is technically conditional upon contact with the debtor and agreement with that person, whilst in other cases the fee may be applied as soon as a visit is made. In fact, as the first stage fee will always be added on regardless of outcome (see next paragraph), this provisional aspect is not a problem;
- *Second stage* - the second enforcement stage applies as follows:
  - where the HCEO and the debtor do not enter into a controlled goods agreement, the second enforcement stage covers all activities relating to enforcement from the first attendance at the premises in relation to the instructions until the commencement of the sale or disposal stage; or,
  - where the enforcement agent and the debtor enter into a controlled goods agreement but the debtor breaches that agreement, the second enforcement stage covers all subsequent activities relating to enforcement of the writ from the time at which the debtor breaches the agreement until the commencement of the sale or disposal stage.[11]

Where the HCEO and the debtor enter into a controlled goods agreement which the debtor does not breach, only the first enforcement stage fee may be recovered from the debtor. Where, either, the HCEO and the debtor enter into a controlled goods agreement which the debtor later breaches, or no controlled goods agreement is made at all, both the first and second enforcement stage fees may be recovered from the debtor by the HCEO.[12] There may be cause for concern here, as economically there is no reason for an HCEO ever to seek to make a payment arrangement with a judgment debtor. Additionally, for debts in excess of £1000 a 'mark-up' of 7.5% on sums exceeding the £1000 base is permitted on the first enforcement stage and sale fees.[13]

Readers should note that the former fee scale for HCEOs levying execution on writs has largely been repealed in respect of writs of control.[14] However, the controversial para.12 of the former fee scale, which allowed 'miscellaneous' extra fees to be recovered where a court made an order to this effect has been left in place.[15] This is unlikely to have any impact upon the charges made for taking control of goods under the 2007 Act because the fees regulations make specific provision for 'exceptional expenses' (see 12.2.6) whilst at the same time making it very clear that no charges other than those permitted under the new regime will be permissible (see in particular 12.4 and 12.5 below).

12.2.4 Disbursements

Strictly limited out of pocket expenses may also be recouped from debtors by enforcement agents. Regulation 8 states that the following expenses are recoverable provided that they are "reasonably and actually" incurred:

- · the cost of storing goods which have been taken into control and removed from the premises or highway;
- · the cost of hiring a locksmith to use of reasonable force to enter premises and to secure premises following the forcible entry in line with Schedule 12; and,
- · court fees payable for any applications made by the enforcement agent in relation to the enforcement power in respect of which the application is granted. The costs of N244 applications to court may be passed onto debtors- but only if that request is successful.

The specification in reg.8(2) that agents may pass on to debtors only such disbursements as have been reasonably and actually incurred builds upon former case authority.[16] These principles are examined in further detail in section 12.6. The restriction upon expenses in this regulation is reinforced by the obligation on bailiffs that, when rendering a final account to debtors, they are mandated to provide copies of receipts for all expenses claimed - except those for sales other than by auction at a public auction house - see 11.4 for further discussion.[17]

Two further restrictions are explicitly imposed. These out of pocket expenses may only be recovered from the proceeds of the enforcement process. Secondly, no other disbursements may legitimately be recovered.[18]

12.2.5 Sale costs

Disbursements for the expenses of conducting a sale or other disposal of assets seized are recoverable in addition to the prescribed scale fees. These are calculated under reg.9 of the Fees Regulations. It would seem proper that these sums cannot be charged until at least after the notice of sale has been served upon the debtor, before which no expenses connected with a sale can possibly be incurred.

Where the sale is held on premises provided by the auctioneer conducting the sale, the enforcement agent may recover from the debtor -

· a sum in respect of the auctioneer's commission not exceeding 15 percent of the sum realised by the sale of the goods;
· the auctioneer's out of pocket expenses. These amounts are clearly disbursements such as travel and other identifiable costs incurred by the auctioneer, which may be passed on to the enforcement agency and, in turn, to the debtor. They are obviously not fees of any description and receipts must exist to substantiate any claim; and,
· reasonable expenses incurred in respect of advertising the sale.

Where the sale is held on other premises in accordance with paragraph 43 of Schedule 12, the enforcement agent may recover from the debtor the same sums and expenses set out in the previous paragraph, except that the auctioneer's commission is limited to 7.5 percent of the sum realised by the sale. Where the goods are sold through an internet auction site or are sold other than by auction, the enforcement agent may recover from the debtor 7.5 percent of the sum realised by the sale of the goods. These sale costs may only be recovered from the proceeds of the enforcement process. No other expenses relating to sale may legitimately be recovered.[19]

12.2.6 Exceptional costs

In very limited circumstances, it will be possible for enforcement agents to seek to recover fees outside the statutory structure described so far. Under regulation 10, provided that the consent of the creditor has been obtained, the enforcement agent is entitled then to apply to court for an order that s/he may recover from the debtor exceptional expenses not otherwise recoverable under the Fees Regulations.

The court may not make such an order unless it has been satisfied that the expenses to which it relates are necessary to effective enforcement of the sum to be recovered, with regard to all the circumstances including -

· the value of that sum; and,
· the nature and value of the goods which it is sought to take into control.

An application under this regulation is made on application form N244. It must be accompanied by the following evidence:

· of the creditor's consent to the application; and,
· that the disbursements to which the application relate are necessary for effective enforcement of the sum recoverable, having regard to all the circumstances of the case, including -
    · the amount of the debt to be recovered; and
    · the nature and value of the goods which have been taken into control, or which the bailiff seeks to take into control.

Where such an application is made before the goods are taken into control, it may be made without notice.[20] The costs allowed by the court's order may only be recovered from the proceeds of the enforcement process. No other such costs may legitimately be recovered.[21]

12.2.7 Multiple warrants

An effort has been made in the regulations to cap the sums that may be charged to debtors where they face the enforcement of multiple instructions simultaneously. This builds upon previous case law that, where there is essentially only one levy for two or more debts, only one set of fees should be recoverable.[22]

Regulation 11 applies to all the fees and expenses that might be charged by the enforcement agent in cases where the right to take control of goods could "reasonably be exercised at the same time." Although the enforcement agent is entitled to recover the compliance stage fee in respect of each instruction received, s/he must - except where it is impracticable to do so - take control of goods in relation to all such instructions on the same occasion and sell or dispose of all goods taken into control on the same occasion. In such cases, the enforcement and sale fees must be calculated as follows:

· the fixed fee for each stage may be recovered only once, regardless of the number of instructions being enforced; and,

- the percentage fee due for each stage, if any, is calculated on the basis of the total amount of the sums to be recovered under all warrants or writs held by the agent.[23]

The regulation concludes with a general rule: the enforcement agent must, as far as practicable, minimise the expenses recoverable from the debtor by dealing with the goods to which the instructions relate together and on as few occasions as possible.[24] The structure of the new fee scale is likely to reinforce this exhortation. For smaller debts in particular, the fact that the percentage fees are only available to bailiff for sums over £1500 will probably serve to encourage agencies to consolidate instructions wherever possible so as to maximise income.

12.2.8 Vulnerable debtors

Under regulation 12 where the debtor is a vulnerable person, the fee or fees due for the enforcement stage(s) - and any related expenses- are not recoverable from the debtor unless the enforcement agent has given the person an adequate opportunity to get assistance and advice on the enforcement process before proceeding to remove goods which have been taken into control.

As described previously in the context of entry and taking control, vulnerability is not defined in the regulations. Resort will have to be made to guidance and codes of practice. Equally, this regulation is also flawed by the subjective nature of its requirement that the bailiff give the debtor reasonable time to get advice. The questions of whether the debtor is vulnerable and whether s/he has had time to seek assistance will be entirely at the discretion of the bailiff and will doubtless be a source of dispute between parties.

12.2.9 VAT on enforcement fees

In March 2014 HMRC issued guidance on the charging of VAT on the fees allowed by the Regulations for enforcement activities. That guidance is reproduced here without extensive commentary.

- *High Court judgments* - the services of HCEOs are taxable and liable to VAT. Other people who may be involved in High Court debt recovery work, for example locksmiths, auctioneers or storage firms, are also regarded as making taxable supplies in the course of their businesses. The value of these supplies for VAT purposes is the amount each enforcement agent gets as their share of the statutory fee and any expenses charged. The full amount charged, including any irrecoverable VAT if applicable, is recoverable from the debtor.[25]

The services of HCEOs and their agents are regarded as supplies to the judgment creditors. Services of other people in connection with the enforcement of the judgment debts are supplies to the High Court Enforcement Officers and their enforcement agents where appropriate. Therefore, where the judgment creditors are registered for VAT and the debt relates to their taxable business activities the VAT on the HCEOs' services may be recovered by the judgment creditors. VAT invoices for the services must be addressed and sent to the creditors. Any documents issued to debtors should make it clear that they are not VAT invoices.

· *County court judgments* - when a warrant is issued by a County Court the recovery action is carried out by a civil servant. VAT is not chargeable on the cost of their services because these enforcement agents are employees. Where necessary the Court will appoint independent businesses such as storage, locksmiths or auctioneers to carry out specific duties. These businesses provide standard-rated services to the Court. The costs of enforcement, including irrecoverable VAT, are recoverable from the debtor.

· *Magistrates' court fines* - HM Courts and Tribunals Service contract out their recovery work to enforcement agents who are not employees and who are separate persons for VAT purposes. Therefore services provided by these enforcement agents to enforce court fines are liable to VAT. These services are supplied to HM Courts and Tribunals Service and the tax on them is recoverable under section 41(3) of the VAT Act 1994 by the Ministry of Justice, under whose control the courts fall.

· *Local authority debts* - recovery action in respect of road traffic penalties, council tax and business rates can be carried out by employees of local authorities or may be contracted out to separate enforcement agencies. Where the recovery action is carried out by local authority employees VAT is not chargeable on the cost of their services. Where recovery is carried out by independent enforcement agencies, their services are taxable and liable to VAT. The services of enforcement agents in these circumstances are supplied to the creditor, the local authority that instructs them. Guidance on recovery of VAT by local authorities is contained in the HMRC manual on VAT for Government and Public Bodies and VAT Notice 749. The services of auctioneers, storage and locksmiths engaged by the enforcement agent are supplied to the enforcement agent. However, if a local authority employs its own bailiffs the services of auctioneers and tradesmen are supplied to the local authority.

· *Child support maintenance* - CSA contract out the recovery of arrears to enforcement agents who are not employees. They are separate persons for VAT purposes and their services provided are taxable and liable to VAT. These services are supplied to Child Support and the tax on them is recoverable under section 41(3) VAT Act 1994 by the Department for Work and Pensions, under whose control Child Support fall.

· *Tax debts* - when enforcement action is taken by HMRC for the recovery of a debt the recovery action is carried out by an enforcement agent who is a civil servant. VAT is not chargeable on the cost of their services because these enforcement agents are employees. Where necessary, HMRC will appoint independent businesses such as storage, locksmiths or auctioneers to carry out specific duties. These businesses provide standard-rated services to HMRC. The costs of enforcement including irrecoverable VAT are recoverable from the debtor.

· *Value of supply* - the value of the enforcement agents' services is the total amount of fees and expenses recovered under Taking Control of Goods (Fees) Regulations 2014. The full amount charged, including any irrecoverable VAT (if applicable), is recoverable from the debtor.

· *Invoicing, accounting and input tax* - to support their entitlement to input tax deduction an enforcement agent has to have tax invoices from the auctioneer, storage firm or other tradesmen. The MoJ, HMRC and DWP need a tax invoice from the enforcement agent to support their claim under section 41(3) VAT Act 1994. A local authority and Transport for London need tax invoices from the enforcement agent to support its claim under section 33(1) of the VAT Act 1994. An enforcement agent can issue an invoice for the statutory fees and expenses. An enforcement agent may submit periodic invoices to a local authority or Transport for London for the total services supplied within the period. Where they do so, these invoices can show the individual charges as a single comprehensive total. However, the invoice must be cross-referenced to the documents relating to the individual fees included on the invoice. Copies of these subsidiary documents must be available for inspection at both the agents and the local authority's premises. Documents supplied to debtors by enforcement agents must be endorsed "this is not a tax invoice" so that they cannot be taken for tax invoices. VAT incurred by enforcement agents and other registered persons on their own overhead expenses may be treated as input tax and deducted in accordance with the normal rules.

The position of HMRC is very clear: the bailiff is supplying taxable services to a client (the creditor) and will be required to charge VAT on those. Both creditor and enforcement agent will then account for the tax in their quarterly returns. 'Irrecoverable VAT' refers to situations where the person paying the VAT is unable to charge it to a customer. This most typically applies to those unregistered for VAT - perhaps a small partnership or sole trader - and would relate to the tax charged to them by suppliers such as locksmiths and storage companies. This should generally not be of concern to a debtor.

In conclusion, debtors should not be asked to pay VAT. They are liable to pay the fees due under the 2014 Fees Regulations, but no more. The tax is recovered from the creditor by submitting a 'VAT only' invoice.

12.2.10 County court fees

Ministry of Justice issued a table of revised fees for use in county courts some time after the new scales were issued for taking control of goods. These fees do not acknowledge the change in the law, even in their terminology. Courts will charge:

· For issuing a warrant of control, £100. The bulk centre will charge £70 and a reissued warrant will cost £30;
· Removals attract "reasonable expenses;"
· Appraisement [sic] will be charged at 5p in the pound; and,
· Sales will be charged for at 15p in the pound or, if the sale is withdrawn, 10p in the pound.

12.2.11 Conclusions

As will be apparent to many readers, the new scale is considerably less complicated than any of its predecessors; the fees are (for most forms of seizure) significantly higher than those charged under the old law. It is hoped that the consequence of these changes will be two-fold.

Firstly, by drastically simplifying the wording of the scales, it is hoped to remove ambiguity about the meaning of fees and disputes as whether the charge for a certain stage has (or should have) arisen. This should remove a great deal of the contention from the process. Secondly, by increasing the fees, it is hoped that there will be no need for strategies on the part of enforcement agencies to generate extra revenue which are of less certain legality and which again produce complaints and litigation. Additionally, higher fees will enable the industry to pay for better trained and qualified staff and thereby raise standards in enforcement generally. All in all, the aspiration is that any grievances over the higher fees will be more than offset by greater clarity in the process, a reduction in real or perceived fee abuse and a general improvement in the profession.

12.3 Checking fees

To challenge fees, it is necessary for debtors to have the evidence upon which to base a claim. The statutory fee scale is of course one element; the other is a breakdown of what is being charged on the account. Obtaining this information could prove a challenge to individuals under the old law. Under the new regulations, there will be a constant flow of notices providing information on the sums due and accruing fees. Additionally, under reg.14 of the Fees Regulations there is a duty on the bailiff to provide a final account to the debtor after sale or disposal of the goods, giving a breakdown of the distribution of proceeds (*see 11.4*).

Debtors were assisted by the introduction of the NSEA and the valuable right to insist upon receiving a detailed breakdown of fees on making a written request. If disputes arise before a final account has been rendered, it may well still prove necessary to rely upon the revised National Standard.

If disparities are detected, these matters can be taken up with the bailiff company and, it is recommended, with the creditor. If it is not possible to resolve the questions raised at this level, a number of further options arise. Complaint may be made to the relevant trade body (see later); complaint may be made also to the appropriate ombudsman if the creditor's own complaints procedure is not helpful. A significant number of the local authority bailiff complaints considered by the Ombudsman concern disputes about fees. Overcharging and making charges not found in the statutory scale have been condemned by the ombudsman, with local authorities' bailiffs being required to refund these amounts and pay compensation. See for example *Fry v. Tameside Borough Council* where an unjustifiable charge for a removal vehicle was refunded or the case of Mr A. where incorrectly calculated charges were waived.[26] Finally there are legal remedies, which are discussed later in *section 12.7*.

12.4 Liability

The new Regulations set out very clearly the rights of enforcement agents to recover the permissible fees. As mentioned already, the fixed and percentage fees and expenses are recoverable solely from the proceeds of the enforcement procedure - that is, from sums raised by sale or disposal or from money paid by the debtor to prevent loss of goods.[27] NSEA underlines this fact by reminding agencies that they must not seek to enforce the recovery of fees where an enforcement power has ceased to be exercisable.

Secondly, the order in which these sums are to be recouped when the amount recovered by the bailiff is less than the total debt outstanding is laid down in regulation 13. This sets out a precise sequence for dealing with monies:

- Firstly, the claims of co-owners to a share of the proceeds are settled. If any dispute arises regarding co-owner's share of proceeds, application may be made to court to resolve the matter by the enforcement agent, the creditor, the debtor, or a co-owner of goods. The court will then determine the amount of the proceeds payable to that co-owner;[28]
- Where the goods are sold or disposed of at public auction (other than by internet auction), the proceeds must then be applied to payment of the auctioneer's fees calculated in accordance with regulation 9(2) or (3) as described earlier;
- the enforcement agent may then recover the compliance fee(s) due;
- the proceeds must then be applied pro rata in payment of the sum to be recovered and any remaining amounts recoverable in respect of fees and expenses payable to the enforcement agent in accordance with the Regulations. Where the creditor and the enforcement agent are the same legal person (for example, HMRC tax collectors), the proceeds must be applied in payment of the enforcement fees prior to payment of the remaining debt.

These rules only apply to cases where less than the full amount outstanding is produced. It appears that, if the full debt is recovered, the enforcement agent has a freer hand in dealing with the proceeds, although co-owner's rights will always be given preferential treatment.

The Regulations state categorically that fees and expenses are not recoverable where the enforcement process ceases. Under reg.17, enforcement agents are prohibited from recovering fees or expenses in relation to any stage of enforcement where the relevant enforcement power has ceased to be exercisable. This is likely to apply where an instruction has been withdrawn or a warrant or writ has been set aside. However, this bar does not apply where the enforcement power ceases to be exercisable because the debtor has paid the amount outstanding. In cases of rent arrears, where a court makes an order under section 78(1)(a) of the Act setting aside an enforcement notice, the enforcement agent may not recover any fees or disbursements from the tenant. Where the order is made under section 78(1)(b) postponing the effect of the enforcement notice, the enforcement agent may recover fees and disbursements from the tenant in accordance with these Regulations only if the court has made an order permitting further steps to be taken under CRAR.

The pre-reform case law may provide clarification on a few additional points. If the debt was paid to the creditor and the bailiff was instructed to withdraw, the bailiff would not be able to proceed to recover any costs by sale as it would be conversion and would not pass good title.[29] If the creditor instructed the bailiff to withdraw any authority to sell was lost, as the bailiff was acting as the creditor's agent. If the creditor lost the right to enforce, the bailiff could not sell goods for fees.[30] The costs of previous unsuccessful levies could not be included in later levies as these were only payable out of proceeds of the first and could not be carried over to another: the debtor was under no personal liability for them.[31] Lastly, whenever a levy was withdrawn, satisfied, stopped or failed, the principle in execution law was that the bailiff is entitled to the same fees from the creditor as if the execution had been completed.[32] This is preserved in the new regulations. The High Court Enforcement Officers Regulations 2004 are amended to make it clear that where an HCEO takes control of goods and the proceeds (if any) are insufficient to cover the compliance fee, the fee or its balance must be paid by the judgment creditor.[33]

12.5 Non-statutory charges

It is anticipated that the new, enhanced scale of charges will obviate any perceived necessity for enforcement agencies to seek to recover sums for additional activities not covered by the scale. The fees are higher and the wording of the scale so broad as to enable all legitimate charges to be covered. However, it may be worth briefly restating the former position on the recovery of charges not explicitly allowed by the scale. It may be worth noting in this connection that the new legislation stresses that the regulations establish the parameters for what may or may not be charged. For example, in respect of disbursements, sale costs and exceptional expenses, it is specifically stated that no other sums may legitimately be recovered by enforcement agents.[34] These rules give statutory form to the longstanding principle found in the case authority.[35]

Under the former law, the courts' position on attempts to charge fees extra to those allowed by Parliament was very clear - they were unlawful - and there is no reason to suppose that judges' interpretation of the new statute would be any different. In *A.W. Ltd v Cooper & Hall Ltd* [1925] during the course of his judgment Salter J observed:

> "In the absence of any special bargain [between bailiff and creditor], the rights of the bailiff to his fees are purely statutory. He may in some cases have contractual rights to fees arising by bargain..."[36]

As there was no bargain in this case, the bailiff could only claim the sums set in the relevant statutory scale. There is nothing in the legislation specifically precluding special agreements for extra remuneration, even though these may be contrary to the provisions of the law.[37] However it is clear that, whilst special arrangements with creditors may be conscienced by the court, there will be great reluctance to endorse similar arrangements with debtors due to their weak bargaining position. The purpose of fee scales has always been, primarily, to protect debtors from oppression and abuse.

There are numerous cases illustrating the court's attitude to bailiffs charging debtors fees extra to the scale figures allowable.[38] For example, in *Day v Davies* [1938] the Court of Appeal reviewed the permissible charges a bailiff could make under the Distress for Rent Rules 1920.[39] The bailiff was not permitted to charge fees "for doing any act in relation [to a levy], other than those specified and authorised" by the Rules. On this basis the court held that any charge for actions related to distress not covered by the rules was directly prohibited, and as the charge being made by the plaintiff was not in the rules, it could not be recovered. In particular the Court observed:

> "As for special agreements, where a prohibition under statute is absolute, it cannot be waived by the party for whose benefit it is made. If an act is prohibited, it cannot be the subject of a valid contract. No special agreement as to charges for an act of distress, other than those permitted by the rules, can be made and the agreement relied upon to justify a [non-statutory charge] cannot be enforced."

It is clear that in most cases the courts have felt that the statutory bar on extra fees should have been final and that there was exasperation that the rule was regularly flouted and that illegal charges were still made despite clear judicial and statutory prohibitions.[40]

12.6 Charges actually due

The established principle of bailiffs' fees (and, for that matter, detailed assessments - *for which see 12.7*) was that charges should only be made for steps actually and necessarily taken by the bailiff. This was a rule of general application.[41] The onus lay on the bailiff to show that the charges were properly and reasonably incurred.[42] Only actual expenses might be recovered, and the bailiff could not aim to make a profit in addition to recovering the actual and necessary expense.[43] This principle has been restated in the new Regulations (*see 12.2.4*).

The previous legal position on the recoverability of charges was very clear. In *Cohen v Das Rivas* the court declared that "the bailiff cannot charge for what he does not do."[44] It does not seem to be any violation of the language to paraphrase this as 'the bailiff cannot charge for what he has not done.' This simple position is underlined by two other judgments. In *Re: H.K. Stinton* (1900) it was ruled that the full fees could not be charged if the actions allowed for are not fully performed. In this case, the sheriff charged for lotting and cataloguing seized goods, neither of which action was actually carried out. On appeal against a detailed assessment, the court revised its order and reduced the fees allowed.[45] Clearly such a challenge would still be open to a debtor, but avoiding the cause for litigation must surely be preferable. Thirdly, in *Hippisley v Knee* the court stressed that only what had actually been paid out as disbursements could be passed on to the paying party.[46] This case, incidentally, has some very telling and interesting things to say about honest and honourable conduct by agents.

Bills should not therefore be issued including sums which might arise, dependent upon a range of unpredictable factors. For the sake merely of clarity and certainty, this should be the case. The inclusion of speculative or potential fees only serves to create an impression of underhand or extortionate practices, however valid the reasons for their inclusion on bills.

12.7 Remedies for disputed charges

Generally specific remedies will have to be employed for challenging disputed charges. It will probably not be possible to sue for trespass, as an overcharge alone was not treated as being so wrongful as to render a seizure unlawful.[47] It is conceivable that remaining in possession solely to receive unlawful charges might cause a court to view the bailiff's presence as no longer legitimate or reasonable, and hence wrongful.

The regulation 16 of the Regulations states that "In the event of a dispute regarding the amount recoverable under these regulations, the amount recoverable may be assessed in accordance with rules of court." This refers to the process of detailed assessment (*see next paragraph*). It is to be noted that this remedy will only apply where the subject matter of the contention is fees and expenses set out in the new Regulations. Detailed assessment will be concerned with such issues as the calculation of percentage fees and the permissibility of expenses. If the complainant's case is that the sums charged were illegal, being wholly outside the Regulations, it appears that other remedies would apply, such as a claim for recovery of any sums paid.

12.7.1 Detailed assessment

An aggrieved individual can apply for a court to assess an enforcement agent's bill.[48] This can be done where -

· there is a dispute about the amount of fees or disbursements, other than exceptional disbursements (which , of course, are only allowable under court order anyway), recoverable under the Fees Regulations; and,
· a party wishes the court to determine the amounts lawfully recoverable.

The application is made on form N244 and must be accompanied by:

· evidence of the amount of fees or disbursements in dispute;
· evidence that the fees or disbursements in dispute were not applicable, because the debt had been settled before the stage where it would have been necessary to incur those charges;
· evidence that the enforcement agent was instructed to take control of the goods of a single debtor in respect of more than one enforcement power when those powers could reasonably be exercised at the same time (so that regulation 11 of the Fees Regulations should have been applied);
· evidence that the fee due and any disbursements for the enforcement stage, first enforcement stage, or first and second enforcement stage, as appropriate, are not recoverable because a vulnerable person had not been given adequate opportunity to get advice or help; or,
· where the dispute concerns the amount of the percentage fee calculated in accordance with regulation 7 of the Fees Regulations, evidence of the amount of the sum to be recovered.

The form of the Civil Procedure Rules appears severely to delimit the grounds for dispute open to individuals (although the much simpler fee scales will also have this effect in any case). If a complaint does not fall within the criteria listed above, it seems that no application for assessment may be made. If the debtor's objection is that the fees charged were wholly outside those permitted by the 2014 Regulations, it appears that s/he is not inhibited by the form of the Rules and may take other legal action - whether issuing a claim or perhaps initiating a prosecution.

Experience of assessment of solicitors' bills under Part 44-48 of the Civil Procedure Rules may be some guide to the conduct of hearings under the new rules. The focus of the assessment will be the bailiff company's files containing its record of an individual levy. A key principle of assessment is that the 'receiving party' (the enforcement agency) has the burden of proof in convincing the court that a fee is allowable and reasonable. Should the enforcement agency fail to do this, the fee may be disallowed. As a general rule in assessments, unreasonable amounts unreasonably incurred are likely to be disallowed. In reaching a decision on propriety and amount, judges are expected to consider a variety of factors:

· The conduct of the parties;
· The level of the debt;
· The complexity of the case and the specialist, skilled knowledge required; and,
· The time involved.

The court also has a general duty to take account of 'proportionality', which will be discussed first. Proportionality is a concept with a pervasive influence. We have discussed in an earlier chapter the role of proportionality under the ECHR: any enforcement agency acting for a public body will be under a duty to comply with human rights principles. The courts are also required to apply proportionality to all aspects of their procedure and the concept has been of considerable significance in detailed assessments: all charges are subject to the tests of reasonability and proportionality. The idea may prove to be of some application in determining cases where enforcement on multiple instructions ought to have been consolidated.

As stated, certain specific criteria are also considered by judges in assessments:

· *The parties' conduct* - if a debtor has been uncooperative, for example, this may have made expenses necessary which otherwise would not have been incurred. That said, only conduct relevant to the fees should be considered. A debtor's conduct in incurring a liability is irrelevant to assessing fees; the person's behaviour during the recovery process is highly pertinent.[49]
· *Lower value claims* - there is clearly a risk that fees can rapidly outstrip a small debt. This will always be the case where small sums of money as being claimed and it is accepted that the relationship between the total charges and the amount due may not be a reliable guide to whether costs are disproportionate. The court can certainly not apply any fixed percentage measure and say - for example - that any charges exceeding 100% of the debt will be unreasonable. Recompense for proper and necessary work must be allowed, so that some balance between remuneration and the fair

treatment of debtors must be sought. That said, the guidance is that costs should be controlled in smaller cases. Expenses should not be allowed to escalate disproportionately.[50] This will clearly be a significant principle in dealing with 'multiple warrant' cases.

Lastly, costs are usually assessed on the so-called 'standard' basis. In such cases the court will only allow costs which are proportionate to the matter and any doubts about the proportionality or reasonability of any charge will be determined in favour of the 'paying party' (the debtor). The other type of assessment is the 'indemnity basis.' The principle of this approach is to place a cap upon the sums that may be recovered by the 'receiving party' (the bailiff company). The indemnity basis is only applied in exceptional cases, for example, where there has been unreasonable or misleading conduct. Although rare, indemnity costs were quite recently awarded against a bailiff's company which presented an exaggerated bill containing many elements it was unable to justify, leading to a 90% reduction by the judge.

The court can allow the bailiff the costs of the assessment or allow costs to a debtor who is successful in opposing the fees. A person cannot appeal sums decided by assessment, but the principles of the process can be appealed.[51]

12.7.2 Pay and issue a claim

An alternative civil remedy for debtor who is aggrieved by an impermissible charge would be to make a county court claim for money 'had and received'. A number of cases illustrate the application of this remedy in the case of charges and confirm that there would be grounds for an action against a bailiff.

The debtor's course of action is to pay the disputed debt under protest and then issue a Part 7 claim to recover any sums wrongfully paid, on the grounds that they were paid under coercion. This is technically known as claim for money 'had and received' by the bailiff and is found as such in the older case reports. The debtor claims to recover money paid to the bailiff but which rightfully belongs to him/ her. This procedure is not a claim for damages: the defendant's liability to the claimant is that s/he has unjustly benefited from the latter's money. The debtor may issue a claim not only against the bailiff but the principal who instructed the bailiff.[52]

Payment under duress in the context of taking goods means compulsion under which a person pays money to a bailiff through fear for their property (or the property of a close family or household member) being wrongfully seized or detained. The taking in question may be threatened or actual.[53] The payment must not be voluntary (defining which can be difficult) but the debtor should be expected to have made it clear that they were paying the sum claimed under protest.[54] Ideally the fact that payment was being made under protest should have been conveyed by unambiguous words or in writing, but the court may find that the circumstances of payment or the claimant's conduct were sufficient indication of their intention. Establishing that payment was made under protest is important to the claimant because the general rule is that seizure under a lawful warrant is not illegal pressure and any payment made by the debtor to release goods is simply submission to that form of legal process. Money paid to release goods in the custody of the law is thus not paid under duress and can't be recovered.[55] Consequently there must be some wrongful element in the levy and the debtor, in paying, would have to make clear that this was not seen as an end to the matter but simply a way of retaining use of the goods rather than being deprived of them during lengthy litigation over the alleged illegality.[56]

This remedy is available to dispute both excessive fees[57] and illegal fees.[58] A clear element in all cases seems to be that there has been extortion of the debtor by a public officer.[59] There can be no action where the defendant has received goods instead of money unless the goods in question can easily be converted to money (e.g. securities).[60] Electing to issue a claim in this form extinguishes any right to damages on the part of the debtor, although it is possible for a person to separately make a claim for trespass or money had and received on the same claim form.

12.7.3 Criminal remedies

There are several remedies for overcharging available in principle through the criminal courts, although there is very little evidence of them ever having being successfully used.

A complainant might contemplate prosecution of the bailiff under the Theft Act 1968 for either:

- *deception* - under s15 a person who by any deception dishonestly obtains property (including money) belonging to another with the intention of permanently depriving the other of it, shall on conviction on indictment be liable to imprisonment for a term not exceeding 10 years; or,
- *blackmail* - a person is guilty of blackmail under s21 if, with a view to gain for himself or another or with an intent to cause loss (monetary or property) to another, s/he makes (either verbal or written) any

unwarranted demand with menaces. Menaces include any threats of action detrimental to or unpleasant to the person addressed. Words or conduct are menaces if they are likely to operate on the mind of a person of ordinary courage or firmness so as to make him/her accede unwillingly to the demand. A defence could be that the bailiff acted in the belief that there were reasonable grounds for the demand or the use of menaces is the proper means of re-enforcing the demand. On conviction the person is liable to up to fourteen years imprisonment.

Readers may also encounter the Fraud Act 2006 being cited as the basis for a challenge against disputed fees. How valid is this suggestion? The first point to note is that the Act is quite new and there is little case law yet developed. As a result, we must largely rely on the wording of the Act alone. The potential penalties for conviction for fraud are severe: on summary conviction by a magistrates' court there may be a sentence of up to 12 months in prison or a fine up to the maximum figure of £5000; after conviction on indictment in a crown court gaol of up to 10 years or a fine, or both, are possible.

The Act identifies various forms of fraud. Enforcement agents will be concerned with "fraud by false representation" which is defined in section 2 of the Act as 'dishonestly making a false representation, intending by that to make gain for himself or others.' A representation is false if it is known to be untrue or misleading and 'representations' include oral or written statements as to facts or as to the law. Section 12 of the Act makes it clear that a company can be found liable if the offence is committed with the consent or connivance of its directors or other officers. Readers will readily see that the users of consumer advice forums have easily applied the Act to contentious fees charged for enforcement. A bailiff company's breakdown of fees on a notice of seizure, and any subsequent letter justifying those fees, could be seen as intentionally false statements about the legality of those fees under the applicable fees scale. It is worth noting here that fraud is a 'conduct offence'- there doesn't have to be actual gain (in the sense of the fees being paid) for the offence to be committed.

How real is the threat of prosecution under the Act? The key question for the courts to determine will be whether there was deliberate dishonesty on the part of the accused. By the standards of reasonable, honest people, did the accused person knowingly act in a dishonest way? Did the defendant know that his/her statements would (or might) mislead the other person and did s/he intend to gain by that?[61]

The police and Crown Prosecution Service would have to determine whether a particular interpretation of a fee scale was applied without any genuine belief that it was correct - and this, of course, in a situation where many fee scales are notoriously ambiguous. If case law exists to support a reading, it would be even harder to argue that a person was consciously and purposely setting out to mislead and defraud. It seems that the cases will be very rare where such a threat of prosecution under the Fraud Act would succeed.

There is lastly a specific remedy in s.78 of the Magistrates Court Act for overcharges made on debts still enforceable under the old procedure of distraint. This is described in c.1.[62]

12.8 Recent problem areas

Fees have been one of the most difficult areas of bailiffs' law for many years. Poor regulation, lack of payment to enforcement agents by creditors and miserly fee scales all conspired to make abuse of fee scales possible and prevalent. Amongst the practices encountered in recent years are the following:

· *unlawful charges* - charges for such items as damage to clamps, for clamping and unspecified general charges for 'enforcement' or 'administration' have all been seen, when none of these were allowed by the relevant fee scales;
· *ghost visits or levies* - charges for actions for which there was no proof or record have been very common;
· *'warning charges'* - a more recently seen practice was the addition of charges which might have become due if further visits and chargeable actions had taken place;
· *Charges made earlier than permitted* - the addition of fees for attendances with vehicles or for the costs of abortive sales have been added to accounts as a matter of course by some firms, frequently well before the work involved had been done - or had even been contemplated;
· *Charges exceeding the sum due* - especially in the collection of fines and road traffic penalties, there have been problems with firms adding on large fees, especially for multiple attendances at properties, which quickly escalate total due and which are grossly disproportionate to the original penalty due. Often these sums are added on before any entry or seizure is made- that is, before there is any satisfactory evidence that goods exist to satisfy the debt and costs.

All of these practices have of course compounded the existing debt problems of those being visited by the bailiffs. It is to be hoped that the new fee scale, combined with more vigorous regulation and enforcement through the courts, will end many of these practices, by removing both the motivation and the opportunity. If the new fee scale fails, it risks the whole Act.

Footnotes

1 See for example *Salter & Arnold Ltd v Neepawa (Town)* [1933] 4 DLR 371 - the town was liable for the bailiff's actions; he tried to make a profit by charging extra sums for storage; he also miscalculated the auctioneer's fees; Re: Duckworth (1930) 11 CBR 445- an "incompetent and careless" miscalculation led to an "excessive and unwarranted" fee being charged.

2 See Lord Coleridge CJ in *Roe v Hammond* [1877] 2 CPD 300; *Phillips & Another v Rees* [1889] 24 QBD 17.

3 SI 1/2014.

4 Reg.4(1) & 2(1).

5 Reg.4(3).

6 Reg.4(2) & 2(1) and 2007 Act Sch.12 para.50(2).

7 Sch.12 para.62(2).

8 Regs 7 & 2.

9 Reg.14.

10 Reg.7(a).

11 Reg.6(1)(b) & (c).

12 Reg.4(5).

13 Reg.7(b).

14 Tribunals, Courts & Enforcement Act 2007 (Consequential, Transitional & Saving Provision) Order 2014 Sch.para.8.

15 High Court Enforcement Officers Regulations 2004 Sch.3 Part C.

16 See also the cases of ex p Arnison (1868) & Lumsden v Burnett [1898] discussed in *Sources of bailiff law* pp.170-171.

17 Reg.16(2).

18 Reg.8(3) & (1).

19 Reg.8(3) & (1).

20 CPR 84.14.

21 Reg.8(3) & (1).

22 See for example *Glasbrook v David & Vaux* [1905] and *Throssell v Leeds City Council* (1993) in *Sources of bailiff law* pp.176 & 186.

23 Reg.11(1)-(4).

24 Reg.11(5).

25 Irrecoverable VAT is the tax charged to a trader that cannot be set off against VAT charged to customers because the trader is not VAT registered.

26 98/C/4810; 96/A/3626.

27 Reg.4(2) & 8(3).

28 Reg.15 & paragraph 50(6)(a) of Schedule 12.

29 *Harding v Hall* (1866) 14 LT 410.

30 *Sneary v Abdy* [1876] 1 Ex D 299.

31 *Re: W M Long & Co ex p Cuddeford* [1888] 20 QBD 316.

32 *Mortimer v Cragg* (1879) 3 CPD 216.

33 Tribunals, Courts & Enforcement Act 2007 (Consequential, Transitional & Saving Provision) Order 2014 Sch.para.8, inserting new para.3A into 2004 Regs.

34 Reg.8(3) & (1); equally fixed and percentage fees are restricted to what the Regulations permit by reg.4(1).

35 See for example *Day v Davies* [1938] in *Sources of bailiff law* p.178.

36 2 KB 816.

37 *Robson v Biggar* [1907] 1 KB 690.

38 *Usher v Walters* [1843] 4 QB 553, *Jenkins v Biddulph* [1827] 4 Bing 160; *Phillips v Viscount Canterbury* [1843] 11 M&W 619; *Braithwaite v Marriott* [1862] 1 H&C 591; *Megson v Mapleton* [1884] 49 LT 744; *R v Smith & Others ex p Porter* [1927] 1 KB 478; *Headland v Coster* [1905] 1 KB 219 (confirmed on appeal [1906] AC 286 HL).

39 1 All ER 686.

40 *Woodgate v Knatchbull* [1787] 2 Term Rep 148; *Philips v Rees* [1889] 29 QBD 17.

41 See *Day v Davies* (1938) 2 KB 74; *Holmes v Sparks & Nicholas* (1852) 12 CB 242; *Cohen v Das Rivas* (1891) 64 LT 661; *R. v. Barton* [1921] 27 BCR 485; *Noble Investments Ltd v. General Collections Ltd* (1965) 48 DLR (2d) 638.

42 *McGregor v. Klotz* [1929] 4 DLR 792.

43 *Toth v. Hilkevics* (1918) 11 Sask LR 95.

44 (1891) 64 LT 661/ 39 WR 539.

45 Reported in *Law Times* vol.109 no.2997 (Sept.8th 1900), 'Bankruptcy law & practice' p.427. Reference is also made in this report to an earlier decision by Cave J to the effect that, unless each item on the fee scale is fully performed, the full fee will not be allowable. I have been unable to trace a report of this judgment.

46 [1905] 1 KB 1.

47 *Shorland v Govett* [1826] 5 B&C 485, though it should be noted that the court in *Hickman v Maisey* [1900] 1 QB 752 observed that the decision in Shorland might have been otherwise had the facts been slightly different.

48 Schedule 12 para.62(4), reg.16 and CPR 84.16.

49 *Hall v Rover Financial* [2002] EWCA Civ 1514.

50 *Jefferson v National Freight* [20010 EWCA 2082.

51 *Butler v Smith* (1895) 39 SJ 406; *Townsend v Sheriff of Yorkshire* [1890] 24 QBD 612; *Re: Beeston* [1889] 1 QB 626.

52 *Dawe v Cloud & Dunning* (1849) 14 LTOS 155.

53 *Maskell v Horner* [1915] 3 KB 106.

54 *Atlee v Backhouse* (1838) 3 M&W 633.

55 *Liverpool Marine Credit v Hunter* [1868] LR 3 Ch App 479.

56 *Green v Duckett* [1883] 11 QBD 275.

57 *Blake v Newburn* (1848) 17 LJQB 216; *R v Judge Philbrick & Morey ex parte Edwards* [1905] 2 KT 108; *Loring v Warburton* (1858) EB & E 507.

58 *Dew v Parsons* (1819) 2 B& A 562; *Nott v Bound* (1866) 1 QB 405; *Hills v Street* (1828) 5 Bing 37.

59 *Dew v Parsons* (1819) 2 B&A 562; *Clarke v Dickenson* (1858) EB&E 148.

60 *Leery v Goodson* (1792) 4 TR 687.

61 *R v Ghosh* [1982] 2 All ER 689 CA.

62 But note the potential problem that, as already stated, s.54(4) of the new Act renames all warrants of distress as warrants of control. That being so, it would appear to mean that s.78 of the 1980 Act should now be read with the necessary modifications to make it applicable to the new procedure of taking control, so that it will apply to all fines enforcement.

Chapter 13

Remedies for wrongful taking

Section One - Determining liability

13.1 Liability

As will be described in the next section of this chapter, the new Act creates a new structure for dealing with the wrongful acts of enforcement agents. However there are other parties involved in the process who may have liability for wrongful acts arising in the course of a levy; it appears that their liability is still governed by the former rules and principles.

13.1.1 *Justices' liability*

In the case of magistrates' court warrants the scope for action against justices is limited because of the effect of ss.44 and 45 Justice of the Peace Act 1979. Under s.44 justices may not be sued for any act or omission in the execution of their duty in respect of any matter within their jurisdiction. This is despite any negligence on their part, informality or irregularity.[1] Even when the justices act beyond their jurisdiction, s.45 provides that any act or omission in purported execution of their duty may only be the subject of an action if done in bad faith. Acting in excess of jurisdiction thus may not be actionable if it is the result of an error or misdirection - for instance, for lack of sufficient evidence.[2] Under s.50 of the Act the High Court or county court may set aside with costs any action wrongly brought against a justice of the peace.

13.1.2 *Constables' and other officers' liability*

Constables or other officers enforcing a warrant issued by justices have a duty to act strictly according to the terms of the warrant. If they do not they can be sued. However if the officer acts in obedience to the warrant, s/he has a good defence to any action in tort as s/he is protected by s.6 Constables Protection Act 1750. Provided that s/he complies within six days with any written demand for sight of, or an opportunity to copy the warrant, the officer will not face judgment as a result of any defect in the justices' jurisdiction. If the officer complies with the demand for the warrant the justices must be sued as co-defendants and judgment cannot be given against the officer for any defect in the justice's jurisdiction. The officer merely needs to produce the warrant at the trial to be entitled to judgment in his/ her favour. As already described, it may be very difficult to enter any judgment for trespass or conversion against justices nowadays, though if a judgment is entered against them, even though the case is dismissed against the constable or officer, costs can be awarded against the justices. If no demand for a copy of the warrant is made, the constable may be protected from damages for seizing goods under an illegal warrant.[3] A constable is under a duty to enforce a justices' warrant, even though it is known to be defective, so resisting the execution can be an offence and the proper procedure will be to challenge the magistrates jurisdiction following the procedure under the 1750 Act.[4]

Section 6 has been held to apply to any person acting by order of a constable[5] and to any 'officer', not just a constable, enforcing a magistrates' warrant. Thus "all inferior officers" enforcing a warrant issued for rates were entitled to protection in any action, for instance for conversion, where the validity of the warrant is disputed.[6] Today it will probably not be possible to count warrants of control issued under liability orders for local taxes and child support maintenance as equivalent to distress warrants issued for rates by justices under previous legislation. As a result the 1750 Act will no longer be relevant to such bailiffs and will only apply to those bailiffs and CEOs enforcing magistrates' orders for fines, maintenance and civil debts by taking control of goods.

Case law has considered the details of the nature of the demand for sight of the warrant.[7] A demand is not invalid because it requires compliance in less than six days. The person charged with execution of the warrant must receive the demand, not a subordinate.[8] If the officer refuses or neglects to comply with the demand, action may be begun immediately, but if it is delayed, the constable may still comply before the writ or summons is issued. A substantial rather than literal compliance with the section may be sufficient to protect the officer.[9]

A distinction needs to be made between cases where an action may lie against the justices for exceeding their jurisdiction and actions against the officer for exceeding the authority of the warrant.[10] Thus in an action against the bailiffs for a wrongful and malicious excessive taking, there was no need to demand the warrant under s.6 prior to commencing action as the bailiffs had clearly not been acting in obedience to their authority.[11] Thus an action for an unauthorised taking control of goods will not require prior compliance with s.6, nor will a claim for an excessive seizure.[12] If it is doubtful whether the officer was acting in obedience to the warrant, it should be demanded.[13] A constable is protected if s/he obeys an unlawful warrant, but not if s/he executes a lawful warrant in an unlawful way, in which case the officer may be sued, but not the justices. A constable may be sued even though s/he believes that s/he is acting under the warrant- for example, by taking the wrong person's goods, by levying excessively or by levying without having the warrant available (see 7.1.2).[14]

The Act protects against defects in jurisdiction, not against defects in the form of the warrant. If there are faults with the form, the bailiff's protection may be derived from the Magistrates Court Act 1980 (*see 13.9 below*).

13.1.3 Auctioneers' liability

Auctioneers will probably not be liable in trespass for receiving illegally seized goods, as they are receiving goods in the custody of the law and are not concerned with the circumstances of their seizure (this is argued by analogy with the position of pound keepers, who were held not to ratify a seizure merely by receiving the distrained goods). An auctioneer is not liable in conversion if no sale actually takes place.[15] Equally auction rooms will not be liable for sale of goods wrongfully levied provided that the sale itself is conducted in a proper manner. Sale at a gross undervalue may be the basis for a claim for damages, but given the low prices to be seen at most public auctions this could be very difficult to prove.[16] Auctioneers will be liable - both to creditors and, presumably debtors - if goods stored by them are not treated with reasonable care so that they deteriorate or are lost through negligence whilst on their premises (*see 11.2*).[17] Auctioneers may also be liable for a wrongful sale under Sch.12 paragraphs 63-65 of the new Act (*see 13.3.12*).

13.2 Agency & liability

> "[The] person appointing an agent must have a better idea of his character than the third parties with whom he deals and the principal, having delegated acts to the agent, it is not unjust if he, having the benefit of success, bears the risk of the agent's exceeding his authority in matters incidental to the doing of the delegated acts"[18]

Local authorities in particular have long been encouraged to contract out their functions to private sector agencies. This is seen explicitly in the Local Authorities (Contracting out of tax billing, collection and enforcement functions) Order 1996, which deals specifically with the collection of council tax and business rates, but it was also implicit in such regulations as the Enforcement of Road Traffic (Certificated Bailiff) Regulations 1993.

Regardless of the detailed terms of any such contract, the effect of it is generally understood to be that it makes the bailiff the agent of the creditor so that, besides all the explicit terms of any agreement, there will be certain terms implied by common law as a result of the relationship of principal and agent.

13.2.1 Agents' duties

The status of agent brings with it additional duties which supplement the obligations already imposed by the courts and legislation. An agent should:

- *Protect the principal from liability for wrongful acts* - the creditor is responsible for the actions of the agent when undertaking the role for which they are contracted. Plainly, any potentially unlawful acts should be avoided if for no other reason than to protect the principal from claims for damages. A creditor can sue enforcement agents for losses arising from imperfect performance of their duties - for example, to recover the damages that had to be paid out following an excessive levy of distress, as compensation for the failure to recover a debt because the bailiffs' negligence allowed a rescue to take place,[19] or for failing to act sufficiently promptly, or at all, so that a chance to levy was lost;[20]
- *Refrain from making un-permitted charges* - the agency agreement will generally stipulate the remuneration of the agent. Charges in excess of this can be treated as fraud of the principal; and,
- *Exercise ordinary care in performing their functions* - it is this issue that will be examined in detail in this section.

Over the centuries, the courts have delineated a number of standards which agents should meet when performing functions for their principals; failure to fulfil these could provide the grounds for a claim for damages for negligence.[21] The most significant for our purposes are as follows:

- *Agents should act with diligence and within a reasonable time* - or otherwise inform the principal promptly if this is not possible. In enforcement terms, a levy should not be delayed without good justification so as to reduce the risk of fraudulent removal or rescue of goods;[22]
- *Agents should exercise such care and skill as is considered usual or necessary for the proper conduct of the profession or business in which they are engaged* - or which is reasonably necessary for the proper performance of the duties they have undertaken.[23]

This latter duty of care can be further analysed to give specific examples of the standards which bailiffs should seek to attain:

- *Goods should not be sold for less than the best price possible.* The fair value should be carefully estimated (and, ideally, notified to the principal) and if the goods are sold for less than this, even at public auction, there may be an indication of negligence on the part of the agent;[24]
- *In exercising any discretion on the part of the principal, agents should use proper care and skill.* This could include such issues as assessing whether or not to refrain from action because of a debtor's vulnerability or determining whether or not to treat certain goods as exempted from seizure;
- *They should ensure the lawful conduct of the work undertaken* and that all statutory and common law rules are observed, otherwise work undertaken for a creditor may not be valid or effective.[25]
- Professional agents should be properly qualified and have the proper knowledge to perform their business. In addition, agents should keep themselves up to date with current developments in the field.[26] As professionals, a higher level of skill may be expected to be exercised.[27] Of course, a successful outcome cannot be guaranteed for a client, but an agent must be competent. A genuine mistake, or a misinterpretation of an aspect of bailiffs' law which is obscure or wholly new and unexplored, is not something for which a professional agent should be held liable.[28] However, if an agent is ignorant of or fails to follow basic principles or rules of procedure, s/he will be liable for any losses that arise from their mismanagement.[29]

As will be seen, the duties to act lawfully, diligently and with the highest levels of professional care and attention are applicable to enforcement agents from two different sources. In respect of the debtor and the courts, these duties are imposed as part of the certification process. In respect of creditors, the duties arise as an aspect of the agency relationship between the two parties. The rules on agency thus reinforce the broader enforcement duties.

13.2.2 Lawful actions

One implied term of an agency agreement is that the agent has the powers of the principal, but cannot exceed those powers. Thus, where statute gives a creditor the power to levy in a certain way, the bailiff may exercise those same powers, but may not go beyond them. There is an implied authority to do all subordinate acts necessary or incidental to the exercise of that authority - though these may be restricted by codes of practice and the like (*see chapter 4*). Where an agreement is vague, an agent acts in good faith if s/he uses discretion, places a reasonable construction on the principal's authority and seeks to act in the best possible manner for the principal. If the agreement is clear, there is no right to exercise discretion. Authority cannot be given to act illegally and the agent cannot seek reimbursement from the principal for performing any illegal act.

13.2.3 Lawful charges

As the agency relationship is a fiduciary one, there is an implicit term that the agent must not acquire any profit or benefit from the agency which was not contemplated by the principal at the time of making the contract. To receive such sums is a breach of duty.[30] This duty is combined with the requirement that the agent should not put their agency in conflict with their own interests and therefore must not enter into any transaction likely to produce that result, unless it has been fully disclosed to the principal and consented to by him/ her. Any profit must be accounted for to the principal and the whole benefit paid over less any commission and expenses - it cannot be pocketed by the agent.[31] This appears to have implications for separate agreements with debtors over the payment of 'non-statutory' fees as discussed in chapter 12. Note the case of *Erskine, Oxenford & Co v Sachs* [1901] in which it was held that such a 'secret' profit made out of a share deal should be accounted for to the creditor - and also that failing to separate private and agency elements in the deal and treating it all as one transaction to the benefit of the agent made the agents liable to make payment to the principal. The agent cannot defend such a claim on the basis that in acting for the principal, the agent incurred a possibility of loss.[32] See too *Salter & Arnold Ltd v. Town of Neepawa* [1933] in which the court held that a bailiff acting as agent in a levy cannot make for himself any sums other than those allowed by statute.[33] This is a very clear authority on this important issue.

13.2.4 Creditors' liability

Generally the principal will be responsible for those acts of the agent that are expressly authorised or procured or are within the scope of the agent's apparent or implied authority. There is therefore a general duty imposed on the principal to supervise the agent's actions to ensure that they are performed lawfully.[34] Thus if the agent exceeds that authority, the principal may become responsible for wrongful acts and may be pursued along with or instead of the bailiff.[35] The principal will be liable whether the bailiff's wrongful act is deliberate or arises from carelessness, provided that it was in execution of the warrant and for the benefit of the principal.36 A principal will be responsible for the actions of his agent if an unsuitable person is chosen to act and s/he is then guilty of gross misconduct. In *Craig v. Sauve* [1940], the court found a landlord liable for wrongful distress as an unlicenced person was appointed to act as bailiff. An enforcement agency will normally be responsible for the actions of its staff. Thus it will be liable for any error made by the individual bailiff to whom execution of a warrant was entrusted.37

If the act in question is wilful and completely outside the agent's authority, there can be no joint and several liability. See for example *Richards v West Middlesex Waterworks Co* [1885] in which the company was held not to be liable for an assault committed by a bailiff executing a warrant in their name as such an excessive action was not within the fair scope of the bailiff's duty; see also *Ferrier v. Cole* (1858) in which the landlord was found not to be liable for a seizure of property off the demised premises, as he had not caused or procured this action to be done, nor had he subsequently ratified it.38

13.2.5 Ratification

The principal is liable for any acts of the agent that are ratified. S/he then becomes liable for any wrongful act as well.39 Ratification must be a clear adoption of the acts in full knowledge of the facts. Thus receipt of proceeds of sale of wrongfully seized fixtures without knowing the source of the money is not ratification, nor is offering to compromise an action.40 However, keeping goods illegally seized with knowledge of the illegality is evidence of ratification, as is receiving the proceeds of their sale, and it has been said in one case that ratification also arose where the landlord was aware of a dispute but left it up to the bailiff to resolve.41 Ratification relates back so an action done without authority becomes legal if it is later authorised by the principal- for example, if a bailiff distrained without authority but later received it he will thus ceased to be liable.42 The principal will also be liable for acts that are a breach of his/ her personal duty as principal and, of course, for acts jointly undertaken with the agent. The position of a collector of taxes who employs a bailiff to assist with a levy which he undertakes himself is uncertain. It was held in *Fraser v. Page & Robins* (1859) that a tax collector was not liable for a disputed seizure of third party goods in use. The court speculated that if the collector had interfered with or ratified the seizure, he would have clearly been liable but it did not give a final ruling on this point.43

13.2.6 Agents' liability

The agent is personally liable for any wrongful act or omission done on behalf of the principal as if it was done on his/ her own behalf and will have a duty to indemnify the principal. Examples of such liability include refusal of a tender of payment, illegal seizure of exempt goods and an agent's conversion of third party goods to the principal's use, which rendered him liable to the true owner for the full value.[44]

13.2.7 Authority

The issue of the bailiff's authority as agent is linked to the earlier discussion on codes of practice (see chapter 4). Where an agent purports to do anything as agent of the principal s/he is deemed to warrant that s/he has, in fact, received authority from the principal to act in that way. If there is no such authority the agent may be sued by the third party for "breach of warranty of authority". Thus if a bailiff acts outside a code of practice, even though those actions may not amount to wrongful taking, those actions may still form the basis for a complaint by the debtor or other aggrieved individual.

The damages that may be obtained in an action for breach of warranty of authority are the losses engendered by the absence of authority. The measure is based on what normally applies in cases of breach of contract, that is any fair and reasonable loss actually sustained as the natural or probable consequence of the breach. These damages reflect the position that the plaintiff would have been in had the representation been true and the position the person is in because it is untrue. Finally if the agent makes wilfully false statements about his/ her authority an alternative course of action is for the debtor to sue for deceit or to consider prosecution for obtaining pecuniary advantage by deception.

13.2.8 Public bodies and maladministration

The position of the Local Government Ombudsman has been that a public authority is liable for the actions of its bailiffs. From this it has followed that, if a wrongful action is drawn to the authority's attention, which it fails to investigate or to rectify, maladministration will have occurred.[45]

13.2.9 National Standard

The NSEA sets out a number of key principles for creditors to observe in their relations with their enforcement agents. Generally it is stated that, for the enforcement process to work effectively, creditors must be fully aware of their own responsibilities. These should be observed and set out in terms of agreement with their enforcement agent/ or agency. Creditors should consider carefully any specific requirements for financial guarantees or the like so that these are adequate, fair and appropriate for the work involved. In particular creditors:

· must not seek payment from an enforcement agent or enforcement agency in order to secure a contract;
· must notify the enforcement agency of all payments received and other contacts with the debtor;
· have a responsibility to tell the debtor that if payment is not made within a specified period of time, action may be taken to enforce payment;
· on agreeing the suspension of a warrant or making direct payment arrangements with debtors, must give appropriate notification to and should pay appropriate fees due to the enforcement agent;
· must not issue a warrant knowing that the debtor is not at the address, as a means of tracing the debtor at no cost;
· must provide a contact point at appropriate times to enable the enforcement agent or agency to make essential queries particularly where they have cause for concern; and,
· should inform the enforcement agency if they have any cause to believe that the debtor may present a risk to the safety of the enforcement agent.

13.3 Service concessions and liability

As described in the preceding sections, the long established view of the relationship between creditor and bailiff has been that of agency. However, in recent years a different interpretation has emerged, which radically changes the position of the two parties. Much will depend upon the nature and wording of the specific agreements and contracts and these will need to be examined carefully.

13.3.1 Court of Appeal judgment

The change in analysis of the relationship stems from a court judgment. In *JBW Group Ltd v Ministry of Justice* [2012] the Court of Appeal held that the procurement of bailiff services by the Ministry of Justice was a 'service concession' and therefore fell outside the scope of the Public Contracts Regulations 2006 (the Regulations).[46]

Those tendering for contracts to collect fines with Ministry of Justice were required to specify on a schedule in the invitation to tender documents the fees which they proposed to charge to debtors. Tenders were given marks according to whether the fee structure proposed was felt to be efficient, effective, economic and fair to debtors. Contractors were not guaranteed any particular level of work and the numbers of warrants issued would depend upon the numbers of fine defaulters, a figure which varies over time. The Ministry stipulated the levels of service that had to be achieved and laid down financial sanctions for non-performance. There was an 'operational protocol' detailing how warrants would be enforced, plus specification of the detail that would have to be supplied if a warrant was to be returned un-enforced (such as the minimum number of visits that should be made to the premises). Certain data had to be provided periodically to enable Ministry of Justice to monitor performance. Finally, work could be allocated to a reserve contractor in the event that the performance targets were not met by the main contractor.

JBW Group was unsuccessful in its tender. The company alleged that Ministry of Justice officials had acted improperly, leaking information and providing assistance to a rival bidder in a manner which breached EU regulations on the making of public service contracts. When the disagreement could not be resolved amicably with the Ministry, JBW issued court proceedings complaining of a breach of the Regulations and, alternatively, breach of an implied contract created by the invitation to tender read in conjunction with JBW's tender in response to it and which imposed obligations of transparency and equality of treatment as under the Regulations. JBW did not allege breach of EU Treaty rules as there was no cross-border interest in the contracts.

The Ministry applied for summary judgment on the claim (or alternatively its striking out) on the basis that the contracts were 'service concessions' which were excluded from the scope of the Regulations and that no contract could be implied as alleged by JBW. The Ministry was successful on both points before a High Court Master. Because of the importance of the case the appeal from the Master went directly to the Court of Appeal, which gave a definitive judgment.

A services concession contract is a public services contract under which the consideration given by the contracting authority consists of, or includes, the right to exploit the service or services to be provided under the contract.[47] The Ministry relied on several recent decisions in the European Court of Justice to argue that it was sufficient to satisfy the definition of services concession that payment to the contractor came from third parties- rather than the contracting authority - and that some risk was transferred from the contracting authority to the contractor, even if that risk was small having regard to the nature of the services to be provided.[48]

Although the Court of Appeal considered that the arrangement at issue was not "a paradigm case of a concession" - one in which the contractor is put in charge of a business opportunity which he could exploit by providing services to third parties and charging for them - the Court nonetheless held that the enforcement contract was a service concession. Its reasoning was as follows:

- there was some transfer of risk from the Ministry to the bailiffs in the running of the bailiff service;
- there was no direct payment by the Ministry to the bailiffs for the performance of the service;
- a 'service' was provided to third parties in that they were subjected to a regulated and lawful system of debt enforcement; and,
- lastly, it did not matter that those third parties were unwilling recipients of these services.

The Court also rejected the argument of JBW that there could be an implied contract incorporating the terms akin to the duties found in the Regulations (that is, the duty to conduct negotiations in a fair, transparent and non-discriminatory manner). Such terms were not necessary to give efficacy to the agreement; there could have been no common intention to imply these obligations as the Ministry had always proceeded on the basis that the Regulations did not apply; and lastly the Ministry had an express power to depart from the terms of the tendering document, a fact which was inconsistent with implying the EU principle of transparency. The Court held that the only 'contract' that could be implied was one limited to a duty to consider tenders submitted as required by the invitation to tender, and also to consider them in good faith.[49]

There are several importance aspects to this decision:

1. It is the first time that the Court of Appeal has ruled on service concessions in England and Wales and it clarifies the nature and scope of such agreements in English law;
2. It redefines the nature of the bailiff and creditor relationship and seems to displace the principal-agent relationship which has been accepted as governing the contract previously; and,
3. It makes clear that a disappointed tenderer cannot rely on an implied contract to bring EU procurement obligations to bear on the tendering process even when the tender falls outside the scope of the EU rules.

13.3.2 Public service concessions

As article 1(4) of the EU Directive 2004/18/EC baldly states, a public service concession is "a contract [in which] consideration consists solely in the right to exploit the service or in this right together with payment." If this right of 'exploitation' is passed to a contractor (often termed a 'concessionaire' or concessionary), along with the risk of supplying the service involved (however great or small that risk may be) and provided that the contracting authority (that is, the local or central government department or agency) makes no direct payment for the service provided, a 'concession' is created. In the narrow terms of the JBW judgment, this therefore exempted the Ministry of Justice from the 2006 Regulations and from the 2004 Directive governing the process of tendering and contracting.

A concession (rather than a contract) will be created even though:

- the 'market' is limited - there will be a limited number of fine defaulters each year and there will be no scope to increase the market or to attract extra 'customers;'
- the 'market' is entirely composed of unwilling service users and no 'contract' is made between them and the bailiffs;
- the fees paid by the recipients of the service may be fixed by statute or, as in the Ministry of Justice case, by the terms of the agreement, (or indeed by both) so that the degree of 'exploitation' of the reluctant debtors that may take place is limited;
- the Ministry of Justice retained an interest in the service in the sense that it benefited from the successful enforcement of debts just as much as the bailiffs did; and,
- other controls may be imposed on the contractor's conduct.

The advantages to public authorities of entering into concessions rather than traditional public service contracts are:

- all the risks and costs of the service are transferred to an outside agency. The divesting of all these responsibilities onto a third party is the major attraction to concession agreements and give rise to savings which far offset any loss of control or even income. The creditor may not recover the debt being enforced, of course, but the expenses of pursuing the defaulter lie with the bailiff - as does the risk that nothing at all may be recovered, or that only enough may be raised to cover the debt but not the fees;
- a high and detailed degree of control may still be retained; and,
- the Regulations and Directive do not apply to the tendering process, nor do the general principles of EU law.

Both the High Court and the Court of Appeal appreciated that the bailiff services tender was not a 'classic' concession agreement, and that to speak of debtors facing seizure of their goods as the "beneficiaries" of the bailiff's service was, according to the High Court master, "an ugly use of language." Nonetheless, the weight of the factors was in favour of treating the arrangement as a concessionary one.

13.3.3 Implications

The judgment in *JBW Group Ltd v Ministry of Justice* has a number of potentially far-reaching implications for the relationship between public sector creditors and the enforcement service providers whom they use - as well as for the detailed process of tendering for and entering into agreements. The natural tendency is to fear that there will be less formality in tendering, that creditors will exercise less day to day control over the bailiff companies acting on their behalf and that there will be less stipulation made about levels and incidence of fees. As will be explained, this is a genuine risk, but it need not be so. There are cogent reasons why public bodies should wish to retain control and oversight of their enforcement procedures, but it will be readily evident that there are equally strong reasons why many officers will find the concession approach attractive - the primary one being, of course, the fact that for the creditor the cost implications are lower overall.

- *How are creditors affected?* Creditors' control over- and remedies against- enforcement agencies may be reduced by the judgment. The essence of a concession is that responsibility and risk are transferred to the concessionaire. This is clearly advantageous to the creditor entering into the arrangement but as this relationship no longer appears to be one which may be classified as being that of principal and agent, all the rights of and sanctions against the principal will be lost. Amongst these (for example) is the loss of redress against the agent for abuse of the agency role: for example, by taking profits not contemplated in the agency agreement. It may be necessary for each creditor authority to protect its position by enhancing the terms of the agreement made with the concessionaire to ensure that issues of quality control and fiduciary safeguards are covered.
- *How are debtors affected?* Just as creditors lose the remedies against their agent, debtors lose the remedies against the principal described in 13.2.
- *What about existing arrangements?* The majority of public sector creditors will have entered into agreements with bailiff companies on the assumptions that the Public Contracts Regulations 2006 applied and that the longstanding relationship of principal and agent continued to operate. The Court of Appeal judgment indicates that these assumptions need not have been made, but this does not of course detract from the contractual arrangements that have been entered into and which continue to apply at present.

Creditors may wish to reappraise their position in future in light of the judgment, but their present arrangements are no less lawful and valid for that.

· *No contradiction between control and concession* The Court of Appeal remarked upon the high degree of control retained by Ministry of Justice over the performance of the contract. Creditors may therefore impose controls, specify detailed criteria for the conduct of bailiffs and insist on feedback on a regular basis without making a concession into a contract.

· *A contract document can exist without there being a contract* The tender documents and specifications supplied during the tender process were extensive and detailed. Even so, such a written agreement would not make the relationship contractual provided that the key elements of a concession applied- the right to 'exploit' (i.e. to receive fees) plus the acceptance of risk.

· *How does the Act effect service concessions?* It is arguable that the Act may reinforce the status of bailiffs as concessionaries rather than as agents. This is because it provides regulation of enforcement powers independently of the debts being collected. Rather than granting powers to creditors, who may in turn choose to devolve those to their contracted bailiffs, the 2007 Act is largely concerned with the rights and duties of the bailiff alone (even though reference is made throughout to 'enforcement agent'.) This change of emphasis is particularly to be noticed in respect of fees- no longer is the fee the creditor's, which the bailiff is allowed to collect; the Act is concerned with the remuneration of enforcement agents as such.

Section Two - Informal remedies

13.4 Statutory declarations

If there is a dispute about the ownership of goods, or about whether an item should have been treated as exempt by the bailiff, the obvious first step for the claimant is to take the matter up as a written complaint with the bailiffs, copying in the creditor at the same time. Supporting evidence to back up a claim clearly needs to be provided a promptly as possible. This might be a hire or hire purchase agreement or some other document relating to ownership or status. A useful tool can be the statutory declaration. This is a sworn statement of facts made in prescribed form under the Statutory Declarations Act 1835. The declaration may be used by the debtor to set out the facts of ownership they wish to confirm to the bailiffs, or may be used by a third party in order to assert their claim to goods. The format of the declaration is as follows.

"I [name] of [address] solemnly and sincerely declare that:

[the facts to be affirmed are set out in numbered paragraphs, the last paragraph to read as follows]:
1) ...
2) ...
3) ...
4) AND I make this solemn declaration conscientiously believing the same to be true and by virtue of the provisions of the Statutory Declarations Act 1835.

SIGNED AND DECLARED AT ___

In the County of ___

This __day, the ___ of ___ 2014

Before me ____.
Solicitor/ Commissioners for Oaths"

The completed declaration can be sworn by a commissioner for oaths. The fee for this should be modest (around £5) and the document may then be served upon the bailiffs and creditors. Should they fail to heed it and a county court claim has then to be issued, the declaration will provide absolute proof for the court of the ownership claim that has been made (*see 13.6 below*).

13.5 Complaints

Whenever an individual is aggrieved over the conduct of a levy for a debt, or over the behaviour of an enforcement agent, the matter should always initially be dealt with by complaint to the agency and to the creditor. If the outcome of the complaint is unsatisfactory, there is still the option of proceeding to a more formal complaint to the appropriate ombudsman or trade body rather than taking the risk of litigation (*see below*). In almost every case, an informal resolution is probably to be preferred but in cases of gross misconduct or substantial loss, court action may seem more appropriate.

13.5.1 Internal complaints

All creditors and most bailiffs' firms will operate some sort of internal complaints procedure which should in most cases be the first stage in any effort to resolve a dispute. Any internal complaints procedure which a public body operates must be used before complaint is made to either the Local Government or Parliamentary Ombudsman. Creditors are reminded by the NSEA that they should have clear complaints procedures in place to address complaints regarding their own enforcement agents or external enforcement agents acting on their behalf.

The NSEA expects enforcement agencies to operate complaints and disciplinary procedures, with which their agents must be fully conversant. The complaints procedures should be set out in plain English, have a main point of contact, set time limits for dealing with complaints and an independent appeal process where appropriate. A register should be maintained to record all complaints. Agencies are encouraged to make use of the complaints and disciplinary procedures of the professional associations (see 13.5.2). The enforcement agent must make available details of the comments and complaints procedure on request or when circumstances indicate it would be appropriate to do so. Agencies are further cautioned by the NSEA that the method for making a complaint should be easily ascertainable by a debtor and that obstacles should not be placed in the way of complainants.

13.5.2 Trade bodies

There are two key trade bodies for the enforcement sector, both of whom offer complaints resolution to aggrieved individuals:

High Court Enforcement Officers Association
The Association exists to regulate its members, maintain professional standards and lobby government. The Association's website states that, as a responsible professional association, it takes complaints about its members seriously. A robust complaints procedure is operated. Details of this and of the Association's code of practice and membership will be found on the website. Those aggrieved by the actions of an officer should consult the website and may complain by e-mail or in writing to the Association's secretary. In cases of very serious misconduct, it may be possible for the Association to refer members to the High Court for revocation of their authorisation to be considered. This is, of course, at the discretion of the complaints panel of the Association and is not a remedy available to all members of the public, unlike certification of other bailiffs in the county court (see 13.11). The professional body mediates access to the judicial sanctions.[50]

CIVEA

The Civil Enforcement Agents Association represents the bulk of bailiffs who do not operate as HCEOs; it has 41 corporate members and a number of personal members. The Association represents its members to government, sets standards backed by training, operates a mandatory code of practice and also has a good practice guide. Individuals unhappy with the conduct of a member can seek redress under the Association's complaints procedure.[51]

Section Three - Judicial remedies

As described in the previous section, court action is available as a last resort for intractable cases where a negotiated settlement cannot be achieved or where there is evidence of serious abuse or illegal activity.

All of the existing common law rules on wrongful acts by bailiffs such as irregular and excessive seizure, and the associated remedies, such as replevin, are intended to be replaced by the Act.[52] Instead the new act provides a set of new remedies for dealing with disputed cases where enforcement agents have taken control of goods. We are however left with a conundrum as a result of these changes. Whilst the common law rules on excessive seizure and replevin are abolished, for some reason the statutory procedures linked to these remain in place, primarily we must assume, for the purposes of those forms of seizure of goods which remain unreformed. How this is to be interpreted will be down to the courts, but I have retained in the present text an outline of the surviving statutory provisions and any judicial interpretation of them, as they may still be available for use.

13.6 Third party claims to goods

Instead of interpleader and other such remedies, a third party may now make an application to the court claiming that goods taken control of are his and not the debtor's.[53] The court in these provisions means the High Court, in relation to an enforcement power under a writ of the High Court, a county court, in relation to an enforcement power under a warrant issued by a county court and, in any other case, the High Court or a county court. As mentioned previously, the various notices given to debtors at the time of taking control of goods do not alert them to the existence of this remedy.

13.6.1 Initial claim

Any person making a claim to be owner of goods which have been taken into control as goods of the debtor must as soon as practicable after the taking, but in any event within 7 days of the goods being removed by the enforcement agent, give notice in writing of their claim to the enforcement agent who has taken control of the goods.[54] This notice must include certain information:

- the claimant's full name and address, and confirmation that the address given may be used for service of documents;
- a list of all those goods in respect of which the claim is being made; and,
- the grounds of the claim in respect of each item on the list. It will obviously be important in many cases for the claimant to provide evidence to substantiate the claim to ownership, whether this is a receipt, bill of sale or statutory declaration (*see 13.4*).

On receiving a valid notice of claim to controlled goods, the enforcement agent must within three days give notice of the claim to the creditor and to any other person who might also be making a claim to the same controlled goods.

13.6.2 Creditor's response

The creditor, and any other claimant to the goods, must respond within seven days after receiving from the bailiff the notice of claim to the controlled goods. This is done by giving written notice to the enforcement agent stating whether the claim to the controlled goods is admitted or disputed in whole or in part. The enforcement agent must in turn notify the claimant to the goods in writing, and within three days of receiving the response to the claim, whether that claim is admitted or disputed.

A creditor who gives notice admitting the third party's claim to controlled goods will not be liable to the enforcement agent for any fees and expenses incurred after receipt of that notice by the agent. If the claim is admitted, the enforcement power ceases to be exercisable in respect of the goods and, as soon as is reasonably practicable thereafter, the enforcement agent must make the goods available for collection by the claimant if they have been removed from where they were found.

It is clearly essential for creditors to give very careful consideration to claims if they are received. Whilst they may initially rely upon the professional skill and judgment of their agents, at this stage the principal needs to impartially and thoroughly examine the evidence supplied. This is especially important given that, at any future trial, costs are likely to be awarded against the unsuccessful party and also because a claim might also be made against the creditor under Sch.12 para.65(1).

Where the creditor, or any other claimant to the controlled goods to whom notice was given, fails to respond within the seven day period allowed, the enforcement agent may make an application seeking the directions of the court and an order preventing the bringing of any claim against them for, or in respect of, their having taken control of any of the goods or having failed so to do.

13.6.3 Court application

Where either the creditor, or any other claimant to those goods, disputes all or part of a claim to controlled goods, and wishes to maintain their claim to those goods, the onus falls upon the claimant to initiate further proceedings if s/he wishes to do so.[55]

A person who wishes to maintain the claim to particular controlled goods must make an application to court which must be supported by the following evidence:

- a witness statement specifying any money, describing any goods claimed and setting out the grounds upon which their claim to the controlled goods is based; and,
- copies of any supporting documents that will assist the court in determining the claim.

In the High Court, the claimant to controlled goods must serve the notice of the application and supporting witness statements and exhibits on the creditor, on any other claimant to controlled goods of whom the first claimant is aware and on the enforcement agent. In the county court when the application is made the claimant to controlled goods must provide to the court the addresses for service of the creditor, of any other claimant to controlled goods of whom the claimant making the application is aware and of the enforcement agent; the court will then serve the application notice and any supporting witness statement and exhibits on these 'respondents.' The application must be made by the claimant to either the court which issued the writ or warrant conferring power to take control of the controlled goods, or, if the power was conferred under an enactment, to the debtor's home court.

After receiving notice of the application the enforcement agent must not sell the goods, or dispose of them (in the case of securities), unless directed by the court. The court may direct the enforcement agent to sell or dispose of the goods if the applicant fails to make, or to continue to make, certain required payments into court. These required payments are as follows:

· firstly an amount equal to the value of the goods, or such proportion of it as is directed by the court. It will be appreciated that, in the case of expensive assets such as motor vehicles, a person may be required to pay several thousand pounds into court as security for the item claimed- and this in addition to a court fee. At the same time, though, the court retains discretion to set the amount of the deposit and may choose to order lesser amounts for those facing genuine financial hardship (for example, a self employed person losing custom because a van used in the business has been taken into control).[56] A claimant must seek such a direction immediately after issue of the application, on notice to the creditor and to the enforcement agent.   Nonetheless, even though an applicant may make the payment as directed by the court, the enforcement agent may dispute the value of the items in question. Any underpayment will be determined by reference to an independent valuation carried out by a qualified valuer. Any sum which may be determined to have been underpaid should then be paid within 14 days of provision of the copy of the valuation to the claimant.[57]; and,
· secondly payment, at certain times (on making the application or later), of any amounts prescribed in respect of the enforcement agent's costs of retaining the goods. The court will determine what amount of a bailiff's costs are to be payable and when this sum is to be paid.

The exact purpose of the deposit paid into court is not made entirely clear in either the Act or the Civil Procedure Rules. The sums are not mentioned thereafter and presumably their ultimate disposal is left to the discretion of the judge. It is very likely that the former practice in civil court interpleader proceedings will act as a guide. The deposit accepted by High Court or county court could be a solicitor's undertaking, a bond from a bank or insurance company or a guarantee from a person with two other sureties. The purpose of the deposit was to provide the court and judgment creditor with security which became the subject matter of the dispute. The goods themselves were released to the claimant and could not then be seized again by that creditor.[58] If less than the value was deposited the court could order the bailiff to retake possession if necessary.[59] If a second execution was made against goods already the subject of interpleader proceedings, the existing deposit could not be relied on in further proceedings and the claimant had to provide a further sum of security.[60]

Even though a third party claimant may make the payment(s) required, the court may still direct the enforcement agent to sell or dispose of the goods before the court determines the applicant's claim, if it considers it appropriate. Any sale will be carried out in line with the rules contained in the Act, and the regulations made under them (*see chapter 11*), subject to any modification directed by the court.[61] The enforcement agent must pay the proceeds of sale or disposal into court.

The application notice will be referred to a Master or District Judge who then may do one or more of the following:

· give directions for further evidence from any party;
· list a hearing to give directions;
· list a hearing of the application;
· determine the amount of the required payments, make directions or list a hearing to determine any issue relating to the amount of the required payments or the value of the controlled goods;
· stay, or dismiss, the application if the required payments have not been made;
· make directions for the retention, sale or disposal of the controlled goods; and,
· give directions for determination of any issue raised by a claim to controlled goods.

13.6.4 Determination of claims

At any hearing of any application claiming ownership of goods the court may make one or more of the following orders:

· determine an application summarily;
· give directions for the determination of any issue raised by such application;
· order that any issue between any parties to a claim to goods subject to enforcement be stated and tried, and give all necessary directions for trial;
· give directions for the purpose of determining the amount of the required payments or any underpayment thereof;[62]
· summarily determine the amount of those required payments or any underpayment;
· make directions for the retention, sale or disposal of goods subject to enforcement and for the payment of any proceeds of sale; or,
· make orders on any other issues that the court considers appropriate.

Where a claimant to goods subject to enforcement does not appear at any hearing listed on the application or, having appeared, subsequently fails or refuses to comply with an order made in the proceedings, the court may make an order barring that claimant from ever prosecuting their claim against the creditor or any other claimant to the goods. Such an order will not affect the rights of any other claimants to the goods subject to enforcement as between themselves.

Where a claimant to goods subject to enforcement alleges that they are entitled to the goods under a bill of sale or by way of security for debt, the court may order those goods or any part thereof to be sold. The court then may direct that the proceeds of sale be applied in such manner and on such terms as may be just and as may be specified in the order.[63]

If the claim ultimately goes to trial, the court may give such judgment or make such order as finally to dispose of all questions arising in the application.[64] In particular, the court may make such order as to costs as it thinks just. Where a claimant to goods subject to enforcement fails to appear at a hearing, the court may direct that the enforcement agent's or officer's costs and creditor's costs will be assessed by a Master, District Judge, Costs judge or Costs officer.[65]

Lastly, note that the one year deadline for sale of goods taken into control will be extended is where a claim is made to ownership of goods. The deadline will run for twelve months from the conclusion of the claim.[66]

13.7 Statutory remedies for debtors

Instead of the previous remedies of replevin and claims for illegal distress, and the like, Sch.12 para.66 of the new Act aims to supply a complete remedy for debtors for all disputed cases of taking control. It applies where an enforcement agent breaches a provision of Sch.12, or acts under an enforcement power under a writ, warrant, liability order or other instrument that is defective. It should be noted that this remedy specifically applies to the debtor alone. Aggrieved spouses, partners, children, lodgers, other family or household members and third parties presumably still have remedies in tort - for wrongful interference with goods, for trespass or for other wrongs (see *13.11*) - and by way of replevin (*see 13.10*).

Paragraph 66(2) specifically states that any breach or defect does not make the enforcement agent, or the person for whom he is acting, a trespasser. The abolition of the principle of an illegal seizure- one that renders an entire levy void *ab initio* - is a significant loss of protection for the debtor. How well the protection provided by para.66 substitutes for this will remain to be seen. Claims for trespass to land and for wrongful interference will no longer be possible (*but see 8.15 on entries*). Certain other claims for trespass to the person may however remain possible (*see 13.11 below*).

An aggrieved debtor is entitled to bring proceedings under para.66 to seek redress for any wrongful or irregular act by an enforcement agent. These proceedings may be brought in the High Court, in relation to an enforcement power under a writ of control issued by the High Court, in a county court, in relation to an enforcement power under a warrant issued by a county court or, in any other case, in the High Court or a county court.[67] Application is made to the relevant court under Part 23 CPR (that is, on form N244). The notice of application is accompanied by evidence, either showing how Sch.12 of the 2007 Act has been breached or how the instrument under which the bailiff acted was defective.[68]

In the proceedings the court may order goods to be returned to the debtor and may order the enforcement agent or a related party to pay damages in respect of any loss suffered by the debtor as a direct result of the breach or anything done under the defective instrument. A 'related party' is either of the following (if different from the enforcement agent) - the person on whom the enforcement power is conferred or the creditor.[69] It is however stated that the powers of the court to grant relief are without prejudice to any other powers of the court.[70] In addition the power of the court to award damages does not apply where the enforcement agent acted in the reasonable belief that he was not breaching a provision of this Schedule or, as the case may be, that the instrument was not defective. Although claims for general damages in trespass will no longer generally be possible, special damages might be claimed for a number of consequential losses which are the natural and direct result of a seizure, such as:

· the loss of use of a vehicle and the hire charges of a replacement;
· the cost of repairs to goods or to property. The damages can top up the resale value of items if they are permanently impaired;
· The costs of alternative accommodation;
· The loss of profits due to the disruption of a business, such as the fall in value of stock that couldn't be sold or the loss of hire income from a chattel;
· Other expenses incurred as a result the wrongful taking of control; and,
· The excess value of goods seized disproportionately (*see 13.9 later*).

In cases where the enforcement agent continues to enforce despite settlement by the debtor, the agent is protected from any proceedings if he acted without notice of payment but still the debtor or co-owner have a remedy against the creditor or any other liable person.[71]

13.8 'Pay and claim'

It would be open to a third party owner of goods to simply pay the debt due in order to safeguard the items and then to make a claim against the debtor, as it is a principle of law that where one person's goods are taken to satisfy another's debts, the owner shall have a remedy against the debtor for an indemnity.[72] The action would be either for the sum paid out to the bailiff or the value of the goods if they have been sold.[73] An exception may be made by the courts where the third party claimant is personally liable to the debtor or where s/he has left goods at the debtor's property for his/ her own convenience and could have removed them to avoid seizure.[74]

If the debtor denies the validity of the seizure or feels exempt goods have been seized, it is also open to him/ her to pay off the debt and costs to the bailiff and then sue to recover those sums from the creditor. Although payment under protest in such circumstances is not the only option open to the debtor to alleviate an alleged unlawful interference with his/ her property, any such payment is involuntary, being made under the duress of a threatened seizure of goods, and a claim may be commenced to recover it.[75] For the use of this remedy to recover disputed fees, *see 12.7.*

13.9 Excessive seizure

Section 65 of the new Act states that it replaces the common law rules which differentiate between excessive levies and other irregularities. However, the common law position was confirmed and codified by two medieval statutes which both still remain in force, despite the coming into force of the new Act. As only 'common law rules' are abolished it appears that these two statutory provisions remain available for use against enforcement agents acting wrongfully under the new procedures for taking control of goods.[76] It is to be noted that unlike, for example, the County Courts Act 1984, which has been amended to make it clear that the sections dealing with interpleader and rescue no longer apply to TCEA powers, no such amendment has been made to the two medieval statutes. Although the older statutes refer to distress, s.64(4) of the new Act renames all warrants of distress as warrants of control. That being so, it would appear to mean that the older statutes should now be read with the necessary modifications to make them applicable to the new procedure of taking control, in which case it may still be possible for a taking control of goods under a warrant of control to be excessive. In this regard, it is notable that the Insolvency Act 1986 has not been amended to remove all references to distress and execution - this is presumably taken to be done automatically by TCEA s.64(4) (*see chapter 5*).

Even if the preceding arguments are mistaken, it will still be possible under Sch.12 para.66 TCEA to raise complaints about excessive levies which may arise in the manner described earlier.

13.9.1 Statutory remedy

Given therefore that these ancient statutes are both un-repealed and un-amended, it is worthwhile quoting the relevant provisions in full. The first to mention is the Statute of Marlborough of 1267. Chapter 4 remains in force and reads:

> "Moreover, distresses shall be reasonable, and not too great; and he that takes great (or undue) and unreasonable distresses, shall be grievously amerced for the excess of such distresses."[77]

The second ancient statute remaining in force is the Statute of Exchequer.[78] The statute makes various provisions concerning seizures "for the King's debt, or the debt of any other man, or for any other cause" and repeats the previous statute's stipulation that "such distresses be reasonable, after the value of the demand [and by the estimation of neighbours and not by strangers] and not outrageous."

An excessive seizure can arise in two ways - either the sum levied for is an overestimate, and an overlarge quantity of goods are taken into control,[79] or (more usually) the enforcement agent takes more than is reasonably required for the debt. These will be examined in more detail later. I have retained in the text cases which cited the statutes rather than purely common law principles.

13.9.2 Amercements

An amercement, in medieval and early modern legal procedure, was a punishment in the nature of a fine. A person found guilty of a violation was "in the mercy" of the lord of the court (the monarch or the manorial lord) and had to make a settlement in satisfaction (a 'fine' to finalise and resolve matters). This would suggest therefore that the remedy for an excessive distress would be a private prosecution. However it has been held that it is not a criminal offence to levy in an excessive manner and no information or indictment can be laid.[80] Viner's Abridgment terms an excessive seizure in breach of statute a 'private offence' and rather than prosecution the remedy for excessive distress is an action in case founded on the statute. In modern parlance, a Part 7 claim would be issued under the Civil Procedure Rules, the measure of damages generally being the value of the excess chattels taken. It has been generally accepted that the above mentioned statutes apply to all forms of seizure of goods.[81]

13.9.3 Damages

It has been argued that as an excessive levy of distress is a breach of statutory duty under the Statute of Marlborough, some damage will always be presumed in the debtor's favour, though only nominal or nearly nominal damages will be allowed if no substantial damage is actually proved - despite the statute's reference to grievous amercements.[82] The measure of damages will include losses of use of the excess goods taken, loss of the ability to sell them and any costs incurred in legal proceedings. It may be arguable that a modern understanding of 'grievous amercement' could be that punitive damages will be awarded. Exemplary damages are a punitive award made where, in certain specific cases, it is necessary to teach the wrongdoer that tort does not pay.[83] The specific circumstances in which they may arise are:

- if they are expressly permitted by statute;
- if a public officer can be shown to have acted in an oppressive, improper or arbitrary way. A public officer is anyone who, under common law or statute, exercises functions of a governmental character. This definition has, of course, been expanded by the Human Rights Act (see 4.3);[84] and,
- if a desire for personal profit could be shown on the part of the creditor or of the bailiff, where the defendant sought to gain, at the expense of the plaintiff, that which s/he could not otherwise get, or could only get at great expense.[85]

It is likely that cases where exemplary damages are considered appropriate will be rare and that the courts will always consider first whether an award of aggravated damages is not on its own sufficient compensation. It will only be considered inadequate where the defendant's behaviour has been truly 'outrageous' or where the bailiff has acted both maliciously as well as wrongfully - thus a mistakenly excessive levy is wrong but does not justify exemplary damages.[86] Punitive damages were recently refused in a Canadian case in which a landlord distrained on the busiest shopping day of the year for arrears of service charge unpaid by the tenant after the landlord had refused to provide a breakdown of the sums due. The court felt neither party was blameless and awarded only general damages. Another example of the potential level of an award for exemplary damages is *Bhatnagar & Elanrent v Whitehall Investments* (1996). A landlord levied distress on the entire contents of business premises after both re-entry and a judgment for the arrears in the High Court. It was held that the landlords' actions (an excessive as well as illegal levy) indicated that they were motivated by a desire to make a profit and, in addition to an award of general damages of £54,500 for conversion based on the value of the goods seized, the court awarded exemplary damages to the plaintiffs of £12,500- plus interest.[87]

13.9.4 Claims

There is no need to prove malice in the claim but the excess will have to be disproportionate rather than trifling.[88] A modern example of an excessive levy is *Rawlins v. Monsour* (1978) in which it was held grossly excessive to seize goods with a wholesale value ten times the rent due and a retail value twenty times the size of the debt. If the proceeds of an auction turn out to be slightly more than the debt due, there is unlikely to have been an excessive levy. There is certainly little basis for a claim if the value of the goods taken is less than the sum actually due. No special damage need be shown for the plaintiff to succeed, but if the plaintiff only establishes an entitlement to nominal damages s/he may be deprived of the costs of the action.[89] The price realised at sale by auction, rather than in the normal course of the plaintiff's business, is *prima facie* evidence of the item's value and will generally be the measure of damages. This standard of valuation may be confirmed by the Taking Control of Goods Regulations. In assessing the quantity of business assets exempted from seizure, a ceiling set at the "aggregate value" of £1350 is specified. It is very likely that this figure will be determined by reference to the resale value of goods. Normally, the debt and costs due will be deducted from the amount of damages awarded to cover the excess.

A claim can be begun even when the goods are not yet sold, the measure of damages then being the loss and inconvenience to the debtor occasioned by the goods' removal, though this may be nominal.[90] A claim may even be made where the goods have remained on the premises if excessive sums were paid to prevent removal. Damages for consequential losses are also recoverable: these could cover such claims as a loss of use and enjoyment. If there is no inconvenience, for example where a controlled goods agreement was made, no damages may be awarded. For instance, in one case sheriff's officers attended at the plaintiff's shop and said they must take charge of everything there. The plaintiff signed a walking possession agreement under protest and then sued. The court held the seizure to have been valid, if excessive. The excessive seizure caused no damage as the trader was able to carry on dealing with the stock in the course of business. In a claim for an excessive levy any bailiff should not appear as a witness for the creditor unless released from their agency.[91]

In addition to reliance on medieval statute, it is worth noting that the NSEA requires enforcement agents to seize in a proportionate manner, so any excessive seizure could always be a matter of a complaint to the firm and them on to the trade body or to the creditor/ ombudsman. Equally, a disproportionate act on the part of an enforcement agent might be a breach of the ECHR and could be pursued by this route.

13.9.5 When does the statute apply?
Excessive levies may come about in two separate ways.

Excessive demands
This is a situation where the sum demanded, and upon which the levy is founded, is too high. The matter at issue is therefore not the conduct of the levy but the creditor's mistaken or fraudulent calculation of the arrears.[92] Excessive demands can arise for a number of reasons. For example, seizure may take place after tender has been made or the seizure may be for sums not yet due.

Taking too much into control
This is the classic or conventional understanding of 'excessive.' In order to argue that more has been taken into control than was required, it is of course necessary to determine what those goods were worth and the scale of the disparity between their value and the debt. By and large, cases up until the mid-nineteenth century relied on the debtor's valuation of his/her own goods and seemed to accept that anything over double the sum due was 'obviously excessive'.[93] Judicial opinion shifted significantly in the second quarter of the nineteenth century and it is this more recent attitude which now seems to be the orthodox approach. The reliance on the auction price as the test of value was well summarised in the recent judgment in *Steel Linings Ltd v Bibby* [1993]. The case concerned seizure of business goods valued at £46,340 for a business rate debt of £7385. Simon Brown LJ stated that:

> "It should be noted… that to be proved excessive the value of the goods seized must be clearly disproportionate to the arrears and

charges, taking into consideration the conditions under which a forced sale of the effects must take place; to avoid an excessive distress all that is required is that the distrainor should exercise a reasonable and honest discretion in estimating what the goods will realise at auction; he need not consider what value the ratepayer himself could have obtained for them or what they would be worth to a business successor."

Simon Brown concluded with a significant warning: "Where, as here, the allegation advanced is one of excessive distraint, debtors should expect a generally sceptical reaction to their own estimation of their goods' worth."

In *Bhatnagar & Elanrent v Whitehall Investments* (1995) electrical goods worth £54,500 were seized from a shop for rent arrears of £8906. The court felt that the landlord had acted with a view to personal gain, which explained his excessive levy on items worth six times the debt due, and, in consequence, exemplary damages were awarded in addition to damages based upon the value of the goods.[94] Both of these more recent cases suggest that now the Statute of Marlborough will be of most likely to be applicable in cases where trade goods worth several hundred per cent or more of the debt due have been levied. That said, the substantial disparity between the debt due and the value of many motor vehicles which are seized may also give rise to successful claims. There has been a tendency to levy upon a vehicles irrespective of their value in proportion to the debt due for reasons convenience and effectiveness. Irrespective of such considerations, the bailiff's duty is to seek goods of a value near to that of the debt due and only if there is nothing else to seize should an expensive item be taken. Constant care should be exercised to ensure that levies are proportionate.[95] Repeated attempts to again access to premises, or a search of premises without finding anything suitable, should have to be proved to defend a claim for excessive seizure.

Taking too little into control
Lastly, it must be observed that the wording of the 1267 Statute does not use the term 'excessive.' Instead, it discusses instances where the levy has been undue or unreasonable. This implies that there may be two interpretations to 'excessive': the bailiff may take too much into control or s/he may proceed with a levy when there is simply too little to justify the action, given the costs being incurred and the likely proportion of the debt which could be recovered on sale. Certainly, this was the interpretation given to the Statue by the Local Government Ombudsman in a recent decision.[96] If this is correct, and if the interpretation of the new Act is more narrow, it may be that it is in

this respect that the ancient remedy continues to perform a function for debtors.

13.10 Replevin

The county court remedy of replevin has not been abolished by the 2007 Act, although the common law rules relating to the process have been. This appears to indicate that the remedy remains available for use in cases of goods taken into control, although without the assistance of much of the case authority developed over previous centuries. For the purposes of completeness, the following paragraphs outline the remedy as it survives. However, such are its practical drawbacks that it is neither anticipated nor recommended that an aggrieved individual resort to replevin in preference to the statutory remedies discussed in *section 13.7 earlier*. This is so even though replevin offers a person a means of immediate recovery of goods which have been illegally taken (subject to proving the illegality of that seizure at a subsequent trial).

Section 144 of the 1984 Act simply gives effect to the procedure outlined in Schedule 1 to the Act. This reads as follows (the replevisor is the person applying for replevin):

"Para.1(1) The sheriff shall have no power or responsibility with respect to replevin bonds or replevins.[97]

(2)The district judge for the district in which any goods subject to replevin are taken shall have power, subject to the provisions of this Schedule, to approve of replevin bonds and to grant replevins and to issue all necessary process in relation to them, and any such process shall be executed by a bailiff of the court.

(3)The district judge shall, at the instance of the party whose goods have been seized, cause the goods to be replevied to that party on his giving such security as is provided in this Schedule.

Para.2(1) It shall be a condition of any security given under paragraph 1 that the replevisor will -

(a) commence an action of replevin against the seizor in the High Court within one week from the date when the security is given; or

(b) commence such an action in a county court within one month from that date.

(2) In either case -

(a) the replevisor shall give security, to be approved by the registrar having power in the matter, for such an amount as the registrar thinks sufficient to cover both the probable costs of the action and either -
    (i) the alleged rent or damage in respect of which the distress has been made; or,
    (ii) in a case where the goods replevied have been seized otherwise than under colour of distress, the value of the goods; and,
(b) it shall be a further condition of the security that the replevisor will -
    (i) prosecute the action with effect and without delay; and
    (ii) make a return of the goods, if a return of them is ordered in the action."

A right of possession was not considered enough to found a replevin claim: the claimant should have property in the goods, though a person with use or enjoyment of goods by the consent of the owner has enough special property to justify a replevy. It used to be said that seizures under the order of an inferior court - i.e. either a county court or magistrates court - could not normally be replevied unless the warrant in question was issued in excess of or completely outside the court's jurisdiction. Replevin was not available where a levy is lawful but could be used in any case of illegal seizure, for instance, where there is no debt due, an illegal entry occurred or exempt goods were seized.

The term 'with effect' in paragraph 2(2)(b)(i) means that the action must be pursued to a successful conclusion - if not, the security is forfeit.[98] Delay should be avoided as otherwise the action may be regarded as having been abandoned, in which case again the security may be forfeit for breach of the conditions.[99] The district judge is empowered under CPR Part 25.12 to determine the terms and manner of the security, which must be accepted provided that it is adequate.[100] All forms will need to be drafted from precedents by the claimant as standard court forms do not presently exist. The district judge then instructs the court bailiff by warrant to deliver the goods to the replevisor. The replevisor must then begin the action without delay and undertake to return the goods if ordered. If the bailiff does dispose of the goods, despite notice of the replevy, he may be sued.

The replevin action must then be commenced by claim filed in line with CPR Part 8. A hearing follows with the bailiff (the seizor) as defendant. If successful, the replevisor could expect to recover the expenses of the replevy plus damages to be assessed as in an action for trespass. As the goods will usually have been returned, the measure of the damages will normally be the value of the replevin bond itself, though if the goods are not recovered the full value of the goods plus damages for detention may be awarded. No further action could then be taken in respect of damages. If the seizor is unsuccessful, it is not usually possible to appeal the decision, even on payment of the costs. This is because it is generally seen as unfair to the sureties to renew their liability and to expose the claimant once more to the risk of paying full costs, whilst there is normally some other remedy available for the debt due. If the seizor (the bailiff) is successful, s/he is entitled to an order for the return of the goods and to recover costs.

If the conditions of the replevin bond are not satisfied distrainors have two remedies. They may either:

· claim the sum secured by the bond; or,
· make a court claim for whatever damages are caused by the breach.

Breach of the bond may occur, for instance, the claimant does not prosecute the case within a reasonable time, but the court will protect the claimant if there are good reasons for the delay, such as delay by the seizor or the death of the replevisor.

13.11 Certification complaints

As described much earlier in *section 3.1* it is possible to complain against an individual bailiff's certificate issued by a county court. It is a judicial remedy like much that has already been described, except that it will generally be handled much more quickly and cheaply than other court processes.

13.11.1 *Making a complaint*

Any person who considers that a certificated person is not a fit person to hold a certificate whether by reason his/her conduct in acting as an enforcement agent - or for any other reason - may submit a complaint in writing to the court.[101] No fee is payable to the court for submitting such a complaint.

A complaint must provide details of the matters complained of and explain the reason or reasons why the certificated person is not a fit person to hold a certificate. Practice Direction 84 of the Civil Procedure Rules specifies the form to be used, EAC2, which will elicit all the required information. It is simple to complete being only one side of A4. The complaint must be sent to the county court hearing centre that issued the certificate.[102]

13.11.2 Bailiff's response

No complaint may be considered by the judge until the certificated person has been provided with a copy and given an opportunity to respond to it in writing. The certificate holder will receive the copy form at least 14 days before the hearing date set by the court. S/he may file a written response or may simply await the appearance before the judge, but the clear risk of the latter course of action is that it guarantees a hearing, aside from any appearance of ignoring the matter.[103]

If, on considering the complaint and the certificated person's response to it, the judge is satisfied that the bailiff remains a fit and proper person to hold a certificate, the complaint must be dismissed. If, however, the certificated person fails to respond to the complaint or, on considering the grievance and the bailiff's explanation or justification of his/her conduct, the judge is not satisfied that the individual remains a fit and proper person to act under the legislation, the complaint must be considered at a hearing.[104]

13.11.3 Hearing and consequences

If it is decided by the judge that a complaint is to be considered at a hearing the certificated person must attend for examination and may make representations. Similarly, the complainant may attend and make representations, or may simply make further representations in writing.[105]

If, after hearing the parties' evidence, the judge is satisfied that the certificated bailiff remains a fit and proper person to hold a certificate, the complaint must be dismissed. There is no scope for appeal by a complainant against the dismissal of a complaint by the judge, either before a hearing or at its conclusion.[106] In contrast, a bailiff against whom an adverse decision is made may appeal, either from the district judge to a circuit judge or from the county court to the Court of Appeal.

If, following consideration of a complaint at a hearing, the judge is satisfied that the bailiff is no longer a fit and proper person to hold a certificate, s/he may either cancel the certificate or suspend it. If the certificate is cancelled, the judge may order that the certificated person must, before making any further application to be issued with a certificate, have fulfilled such requirements as to training or any other conditions that are considered necessary for him/her to have become a fit and proper person. The bailiff will be required to surrender the cancelled certificate to the court that issued it, unless the judge orders otherwise. The security must also be cancelled and the balance of any deposit returned to the certificated person following surrender (see 13.11.4). If the certificate is suspended, rather than cancelled outright, the judge may order that the suspension is not to be lifted until the certificated person has fulfilled such stipulations as to training or any other conditions the judge considers necessary.[107]

Whether the certificate is suspended or cancelled the court must consider if it is appropriate to make an order as to the continuing validity of the certificate. If, before the cancellation or suspension of a certificate, the certificated person took control of goods, the goods continue to be controlled goods and the certificate normally continues to have effect as if it had not been cancelled or suspended. The court nonetheless may make an order invalidating any levy if it chooses.[108]

Under the former Distress for Rent Rules 1988 there was only one reported complaint in recent decades which can provide any guidance on contemporary judicial attitudes (but see 3.1.6). This was the case of *Manchester City Council v Robinson* [1991]. The council's housing advice team applied for revocation of the defendant's certificate on the grounds that he had distrained after a suspended possession order had been made in the county court, that he had used invalid forms, that he had entered illegally by using his own pass key to gain access to the premises and that he was director of the landlord company, despite undertaking in his certificate application not to distrain where he was regularly employed in rent collection. The county court held that, whilst the landlord may have acted illegally in some respects, his misconduct was not serious enough to warrant cancellation of his certificate. This was justified particularly by the fact that the defendant gave the court an assurance that he would not use the out-dated forms again. Whilst it was suggested that the use of the key was illegal entry, only £100 costs were awarded against the defendant.[109]

This case indicates that the attitude of courts is likely to be that the wrong complained of will have to be very serious, and certainly more than a 'technicality', to warrant revocation or a heavy financial penalty. As a guide, it is probably only appropriate to use the certification complaints procedure, with its sanction of potential loss of livelihood, where very serious abuses of position or gross violations of the law have taken place. In the recent past, use of the complaints procedure for less substantial complaints has led to costs awards against complainants, a risk which will be lessened in future but not entirely eradicated (see *next section).* It should be stressed that this is a complaint against an individual. Where s/he has merely been following the policy and procedures of an employer, courts may be reluctant to impose severe sanctions. In such cases, a claim against the employer under Sch.12 para.66 may be more appropriate, reserving certification complaints for cases of clear personal unfitness.

13.11.4 Compensation and costs

If, at a hearing, a judge is satisfied that a complaint is well founded, s/he may also order that the bailiff's security be forfeited either wholly or in part. The forfeited amount may be paid to the complainant, in such proportions as the judge considers to be appropriate, by way of compensation for failure in due performance of the certificated person's duties as an enforcement agent or for the complainant's costs or expenses in attending and making representations. Additionally, where costs or expenses have been incurred by the court in considering the complaint at a hearing, the judge may order payment to Her Majesty's Paymaster General by way of reimbursement of those costs or expenses.[110]

Compensation may be awarded by the court whether or not the certificate is cancelled or suspended. If a payment of compensation or costs is ordered from the security, but the certificate is not cancelled at the same time, the bailiff will be required to provide a fresh bond.[111] If the certificate is cancelled, the security must, be cancelled and the balance of any deposit, following payment of any amounts ordered to be forfeited, returned to the certificated person *(see 3.1.4).*

Whilst the bailiff may incur expense and loss as a result of a successful complaint, the new legislation deliberately protects most complainants. It is clearly stated that a complainant will not be not liable for any costs incurred by the certificated person, in responding to the complaint, except in limited circumstances. The court may order the complainant to pay such costs as it considers reasonable if it is satisfied that the complaint both disclosed no reasonable grounds for considering that the bailiff was not a fit person to hold a certificate and that it amounted to an abuse of the court's process.[112] 'Abuse of process' is unfair or wrong conduct on the part of the complainant that 'offends justice and propriety' and means either that the person complained against is unlikely to get a fair trial or, even, that it is not fair to try them at all. It can include litigation, possibly malicious, for an ulterior motive, as well as misuse or manipulation of court procedures, such as by delay, by issuing a complaint without any intention of pursuing it or by complaining after agreeing not to pursue the matter.

The new rule as to costs awards is a significant alteration of the previous situation, though it must be noted that a costs order could conceivably be made against a complainant not only at the hearing but following consideration by the judge of the initial complaint form and the bailiff's written submissions. Part of the motivation for this change was to encourage advice agencies to bring complaints on behalf of their clients as a whole. Nonetheless, the much reduced risk of being liable for legal costs may make certification a more attractive form of redress than any of the other statutory remedies provided by the new Act.

13.12 Claims to exempt goods

The procedure for dealing with claims by third parties to the ownership of goods (see 13.6) is also adapted to allegations by debtors that their property should be treated as falling within one of the statutory exemptions. As noted before, though, it is unfortunate that the mandatory notices issued upon taking control of goods do not alert debtors to the availability of this procedure.

Although this remedy is an adaptation of the process for third parties claiming goods, its statutory basis is another part of the Act. It is a specific form of relief under Sch.12 para.66, although it borrows most of its rules from third party claims under CPR Part 85. This has major consequences. As exempt goods claims do not, like third party claims, derive from Sch.12 para.60 they do not share some of the features of latter. On the positive side, in exempt goods claims no payment into court is required from the debtor to cover the value of the goods or the bailiff's costs.[113] On the downside, the statutory stay on sale triggered by an application under Sch.12 para.60(2) does not apply, which may mean that aggrieved debtors may need to proceed to court very promptly if suspension of continuing enforcement cannot be agreed with the agent.

13.12.1 Initial claim

If a debtor wishes to making a claim that certain goods that have been taken into control should be treated as exempted, s/he must, as soon as is practicable after the taking and - in any event - within 7 days of the removal of the goods, give written notice in of the claim to the enforcement agent who took the items into control. This notice must contain certain specified information:

- the debtor's full name and address and confirmation that the address may be used as their address for service;
- a list of all the goods in respect of which exemption is being

claimed; and,
· details of the grounds of the claim in respect of each item.

On receipt of a notice of claim to exempt goods, the enforcement agent or relevant enforcement officer must within three days give notice of it to the creditor; and to any other person making a claim under CPR Part 85.4 or 85.6 to the goods subject to enforcement (*see earlier 13.6*).[114]

13.12.2 *Creditor's response*

The creditor, and any other claimant to the goods subject to enforcement, must respond within seven days of receiving the notice of the claim that the goods should be treated as exempted, to the enforcement agent or enforcement officer. They must inform in writing them whether the claim to exempt goods is admitted or disputed in whole or in part. On receipt of this response, the enforcement agent or officer must then within three days notify the debtor in writing whether the claim is admitted or disputed.

A creditor who gives notice admitting a claim to the exempt status of controlled goods is not liable to the enforcement agent or officer for any fees and expenses incurred after receipt of that notice. If an enforcement agent or officer receives a notice admitting the claim from a creditor and from any other claimant the enforcement power ceases to be exercisable in respect of those particular goods. As soon as is reasonably practicable the enforcement agent or relevant enforcement officer must then make the goods available for collection by the debtor if they have been removed from where they were found.

Where the creditor, or any other claimant to the goods, fails, within seven days of service of the claim to give the required notice, the enforcement agent or relevant enforcement officer may apply to the court for the directions and for an order preventing the bringing of any claim against them for, or in respect of, their having taken into control any of the goods (or for their having failed to do so). Such an application must be made to the court which issued the writ or warrant conferring power to take control of controlled goods or, if the power to take control of controlled goods was conferred under an enactment, to the county court hearing centre which is nearest to the debtor's home.[115]

If the creditor or the third party claimant chooses to dispute the claim to exemption, a hearing may follow (*see next section*).

13.12.3 Court application

If a creditor, or any other claimant to goods, gives notice that the claim to exemption is disputed, and that they wish to maintain their claim on the goods subject to enforcement, court proceedings must be commenced by the debtor ifs/he wants to pursue the matter.

The debtor must make an application within seven days of receiving a copy of the notice sent to the bailiff by the creditor. The application must be made to the court which issued the writ or warrant or, if the power to take control of controlled goods was conferred under an enactment, to the debtor's home court. This application will be on form N244 and must be supported by the following evidence:

- a witness statement which describes any goods to which a claim to exemption is made and which sets out the grounds upon which such claim is based; and,
- copies of any supporting documents that will assist the court to determine such claim.

In the High Court the debtor will have to serve the application notice and supporting witness statements and exhibits on the creditor, any other claimant to the goods of whom they are aware and on the enforcement agent or officer. In the county court the debtor must, a the time of making the application, provide the addresses for service of the creditor, any other claimant and the enforcement agent, and the court will then serve the application and supporting documents on them.

The application notice will be referred to a Master or District Judge, who may give directions for further evidence, list a hearing to give directions, list a hearing of the application, make directions for the retention, sale or disposal of the goods subject to the claim to exempt goods or give directions for determination of any issue raised by the exempt goods claim.[116]

13.12.4 Determination of claims

At any hearing of any application that goods are exempt from seizure, the court may:

- determine an application summarily;
- give directions for the determination of any issue raised by the application;
- order that any issue between any parties to a claim to goods subject to enforcement be stated and tried, and give all necessary directions for trial;

- make directions for the retention, sale or disposal of goods subject to enforcement and for the payment of any proceeds of sale (perhaps because items are perishable or of declining value); or
- make any other order that the court considers appropriate.

Where the debtor making the claim does not appear at any hearing listed on the application or, having attended, fails or refuses to comply with an order made in the proceedings, the court may bar that person, and all persons claiming under him/her, from prosecuting their claim against the creditor or any other claimant to the goods. Such an order will not affect the rights of any other claimants to the goods subject to enforcement as between themselves. The court may make such order as to costs as it thinks just.

Where the debtor in a claim to exempt goods fails to appear at a hearing, the court may direct that the enforcement agent's or officer's costs and creditor's costs will be assessed by a Master, District Judge, costs judge or costs officer. In a claim to controlled goods a debtor may request the court to assess the costs incurred by an enforcement agent, in which case the court will apply the Taking Control of Goods (Fees) Regulations 2014 to such assessment.[117]

The former case law may provide some guidance to judges on these issues. If an item is obviously exempt then it seems that its seizure is simply prohibited.[118] The High Court has held that the burden of proof of exemption is on the debtor and that this proof should be more than a bald assertion on oath, especially where a large number of goods are concerned.119 Canadian authorities suggest that the onus would then shift to the creditor to disprove it.[120] It would seem reasonable to insist that any claim to exemption should be made within a reasonable time of seizure (within a few months for example), and certainly before sale takes place. Otherwise the exemption will be presumed to have been waived.[121] It is probable that only the debtor can make such a claim for exemption and that a bailee or mortgagee may not.[122] If, after seizure, a successful claim for exemption is made by the debtor, the debtor may still be held liable for the bailiffs' costs.[123] The High Court has also noted that whilst there is no duty upon a bailiff to advise a debtor of the right to claim exemption, but it would undoubtedly be good practice for a bailiff to give such a warning.[124]

Lastly, readers should note that the one year deadline for sale of goods taken into control may be extended is where a claim is made for their exemption. The deadline will run for twelve months from the conclusion of the claim.[125]

13.13 Other claims for damages

The scope for claims for damages for unlawful seizures may have been deliberately restricted by the TCEA, but the opportunity for certain other claims in tort still exists.

13.13.1 Misfeasance in public office

An aggrieved person may sue to recover damages for any loss, injury or damage resulting from an administrative action known by the relevant authority or officer to be unlawful or done maliciously.[126]

The key elements of the tort of misfeasance are an abuse of power leading to damage, whether financial or loss of reputation and the like. There are two ways in which the tort may arise. Those actions motivated by malice are clearly misfeasance. Malice renders an action both ultra vires and tortious. Alternatively, if it can be shown that the defendant knew his/ her actions to be illegal and likely to cause loss to the claimant there may also be the basis for a claim in misfeasance.[127] In these cases instance it must be shown that the officer knew their actions were unlawful, or was reckless about whether they were acting within their powers or whether damage would be caused. Recklessness may be proved by showing that the officer suspected that they were behaving in an ultra vires fashion, but failed to take reasonable steps to check the true position. The quantum of damages will include compensation for the plaintiff's losses, but may also include an exemplary element.

Any public authority may be sued, as may any individual officer. The action lies for both abuse of the individual's and the authority's power. The authority is not liable for the officer's action if the person behaved in a way that s/he knew to be deliberately unlawful and beyond his/ her powers.

The application of misfeasance to the area of seizing goods has only been examined in one case, that of *R v Hampstead Magistrates Court & another ex p St Marylebone Property Company* (1995).[128] In his judgment Carnwath J acknowledged that, despite the lack of proper pleadings or evidence on the matter, there were reasons for imputing to the local authority, Camden Borough Council, knowledge that their acts were unlawful: "one would have thought it possible to infer, in the absence of evidence to the contrary, that those responsible for rates were aware of something as basic as the ordinary requirements for service" of demand notices for NNDR. However, the problem was that the levy of distress in question naturally rested upon a liability order from the magistrates' court. The validity of the order had not been challenged, therefore the council was entitled to rely upon it and regard the distraint as lawful. As knowledge of the illegality of one's acts is an important element in proving misfeasance, the judge did not find the claim proved in this case. From this it may be suggested that levies based on some form of court order or judgment are unlikely to be susceptible to challenge by this route. Those warrants issued by public officers without prior recourse to court (for instance, income tax and VAT) may still be. It may however be useful to note a related Canadian case on this point. In *McGowan v. Betts* [1871] a fisheries officer was held liable in trespass for failing to deal with seized goods as the relevant statute required. The court observed that an officer exceeding his authority may be sued for malfeasance- by abusing or not following his legal authority he will have acted illegally.[129]

13.13.2 Negligence

An alternative means of bringing a matter to court may be by means of an action for damages for negligence on the part of the Crown department or local authority, as they will be vicariously liable for the torts of their servants. Taking action for negligence may be preferable simply because there is no need to prove malice or deliberate illegality. It would also be possible to sue a bailiff's employer for a person's negligent conduct of their job or to sue the principal instructing an enforcement agent. In such cases there would be joint liability on the part of bailiff and employer.

Where an operational task is carried out negligently or in excess of statutory power, there may be liability for negligence. Negligence can arise where a public body uses its powers in such a way that care is not taken to avoid foreseeable and proximate damage or where it fails to act fairly, reasonably or with justice. The duty of care must be established, but a person is entitled to assume that a public body will comply with statutory regulations and seek to avoid any probable harm that could arise from their activities. As negligence is concerned with the defendant's conduct, it may be possible to claim for damages for both negligence and for another tort committed at the same time, for instance, trespass. There is no duty of care if a body is acting within a statutory discretion. Any matter of policy concerned with the exercise of discretion is not actionable - so an authority cannot be sued for choosing to issue a warrant as against another remedy, but it may be sued for the manner in which warrant was levied.

The claimant can sue only for such actual damage as can be proved. There is no right to receive nominal damages. The court may of course feel that no duty of care is owed in the exercise of certain statutory powers and duties, in the context of the statutory framework or if alternative remedies exist. An authority's defence may be that they were acting in good faith in a reasonable manner within their statutory powers or that the action complained of was outside the authority given to an employee and outside the scope of their employment.

13.13.3 *Trespass to person*

A bailiff might also be sued for damages for trespass to person. This covers three separate wrongs - assault, battery and unlawful imprisonment.

Assault
Assault is any intentional or reckless act that causes a person to fear the use of immediate unlawful force or personal violence. It is an overt act indicating an immediate intent to commit battery, combined with an ability to carry that through. A person cannot sue for shock and fear alone: there must be a physical consequence of the emotion, such as illness arising from shock. Threats, gestures and abuse on their own are not assault, without capacity to carry them out. As there does not need to be any physical contact or injury in assault, the emphasis being the reaction of the victim, it will be possible for claimants to sue in any situations where there has been a clear physical menace of violence (with the ability to commit it) against them or, it appears, where there has been a simply a verbal intimation of violence. Assault must be shown by the claimant to be intentional or negligent on the part of the defendant.

Battery
Battery is the infliction of any unwanted physical contact, force or violence in excess of everyday contact and without the person's consent. It may be a blow, spitting or pushing. There is no need to show that any harm was inflicted or intended.

False imprisonment
False imprisonment is an enforcement example is the case of *Cave v. Capel* [1954].[130] This was an interpleader case concerned with the seizure of a caravan owned by a third party. The aggravating factor in the seizure was that the van was removed from the debtor's premises with his mother inside. The van was secured in a barn for four days, the main door of the barn being locked. The mother eventually escaped through a side door, having been kept in "a state of some humiliation." The sheriff was refused protection through interpleader against her claims of false imprisonment, trespass to person and wrongful execution.

As a form of trespass assault is actionable in all cases without proof of injury. The compensation recoverable may be as follows:

· Nominal damages should be recoverable, whilst substantial damages may be possible where there has been discomfort, inconvenience or injury to dignity, even though there has been no physical injury. If there is physical injury, damages are calculated as in personal injury cases.
· Consequential damages for specific pecuniary and non-pecuniary losses are recoverable In addition to general damages for physical or mental injury - for example medical expenses, loss of earnings and compensation for pain and suffering and loss of amenities of life.
· Aggravated and exemplary damages may be possible (see earlier), though any award of aggravated damages may be reduced or eliminated if there was any provocation from the claimant. Aggravated damages will be appropriate where there has been injury and discomfort, embarrassment and injury to dignity and also shock, particularly where there has been physical injury but possibly in other cases too where the distress caused to the person is substantial and directly linked to the assault. The trespass ab initio principle should also apply.[131]

Any wilful act or statement by the defendant, intended to cause physical harm to the claimant, which in fact causes such harm, infringes the person's legal right to personal safety and is tortious and actionable.[132] If proved, damages may therefore be recovered for any false statement giving rise to nervous shock or physical illness. If the acts were unjustifiable there is a good basis for a claim, and it is no defence to say that more harm was done than was intended. To prove such a wrong the claimant must show an intention to produce the effect produced, having regard to the action's impact on a person of ordinary mental and physical health, and must show that the grave effects produced were not too remote. Finally, assault is also an offence under ss.42-45 Offences against the Person Act 1861. Criminal proceedings can bar a civil action.

Footnotes

1 Negligence - *Everett v Griffiths* [1921] AC 631; informality - *Ratt v Parkinson* (1851) 15 JP 356; irregularity - *Bott v Ackroyd* (1859) 23 JP 661.
2 *Palmer v Crone* [1927] 1 KB 804; *R v Cardiff Justices ex p Salter* [1985] 149 JP 721.
3 *Palmer v Crone* [1927] 1 KB 804.
4 *R v Royds ex p Sidney* (1860) 1 QSCR 8; R v Rapay (1902) 7 CCC 170.
5 *Jones v Chapman* (1845) 14 M&W 124.
6 Conversion - *Lyons v Golding* (1829) 3 C&P 586; validity - *Harper v Carr* (1797) 7 TR 270; see also *Nutting v Jackson* (1773) Bull NP 24.
7 See *Clark v Woods* (1848) 2 Ex 395; *Jory v Orchard* (1799) 2 B&P 39.
8 Period - *Collins v Rose* (1839) 5 M&W 194; service - *Clarke v Davey* (1820) 4 Moo 465.

9 *Jones v Vaughan* (1804) 5 East 445; *Atkins v Kilby* (1840) 11 Ad & El 777.

10 *Milton v Green* 2 B&P 158.

11 *Hoye v Buck* (1840) 1 Man & G 775.

12 Unauthorised - *Kay v Grover* (1831) 7 Bing 312 and *Cotton v Kaldwell* (1833) 2 Nev & M KB 399; excessive - *Stirch v Clarke* (1832) 4 B&A 113.

13 *Price v Messenger* (1800) 2 Bos & P 158.

14 Unlawful act - *Horsfield v Brown* [1932] 1 KB 355; justices' liability - *Money v Leach* (1765) 3 Burr 1742; belief - *Price v Messenger* as above.

15 *Badkin v. Powell* (1776) 2 Cowp 476; *Whitworth v Smith* (1832) 5 C&P 250.

16 *Von Knoop v. Moss & Jamieson* (1891) 7 TLR 500.

17 *Rook v Turner* (1870) 14 Sol Jo 941.

18 Middleton JA in *Craig v. Sauve* [1940] 1 DLR 72.

19 *Megson v Mapleton* (1883) *The Times*, December 11th, 3c; *Chard v Beale* (1861) June 5th, 11a (CP); *May v Hadley & East* (1878) Aug.3rd, 4c (CP); *Barton v Hankey* (1880) May 4th, 4e (CP); *Trent Bros v Hodgson* (1885) Fe.17th, 3c, (QBD); *Stocks v Combe* (1887) Feb.19th, 5c (QBD).

20 *Coton v Hunter* (1886) *The Times* June 20th, 8c (Exch).

21 *Fletcher v Whittaker* (1900) *Manchester Guardian* Feb.10th p.6.

22 *Varden v Parker* (1798) 2 Esp 710; *Barber v Taylor* (1839) 5 M&W 527; *Smith v Lascelles* (1788) 2 TR 187; *Prince v Clark* (1823) 1 B&C 186.

23 *Beal v South Devon Railway* (1864) 3 H&C 337.

24 *Solomon v Barker* (1862) 2 F&F 726.

25 *Grant v Fletcher* (1826) 5 B&C 436; *Neilson v James* [1882] 9 QBD 546.

26 *Park v Hammond* (1816) 6 Taunt 495.

27 *Lanphier v Phipos* (1838) 8 C&P 475; *Lee v Walker* [1872] 7 CP 121.

28 *Simmons v Pennington* [1955] 1 WLR 183; *Pitt v Yalden* (1767) 4 Burr 2060; *Laidler v Elliott* (1825) 3 B&C 738; *Kemp v Burt* (1833) 4 B&A 424.

29 *Russell v Palmer* (1767) 2 Wils 325; *Godefroy v Dalton* (1830) 6 Bing 460.

30 <u>*Rogier v Campbell*</u> [1939] Ch 766

31 Respectively *Phipps v Boardman* [1965] Ch 992; *De Busscher v Alt* [1878] 8 Ch D 286.

32 2 KB 504; *Williams v Stevens* [1866] 1 PC 352.

33 4 DLR 371

34 *Brown v Thompson & Ratcliffe* (1904) *Manchester Guardian* March 25th p.3; also see March 20th 1908 p.10.

35 *Megson v Mapleton* (1884) 49 LT 744; *Re: Caidan* [1942] Ch 90.

36 *Dawe v Cloud & Dunning* (1849) 14 LTOS 155.

37 [1940] 1 DLR 72; *Bowden v Waithman* (1821) 5 Moore CP 183.

38 Respectively 15 QBD 660; 15 UCQB 561; see too *Kinsella v. Hamilton* 26 LR Ir 671 - the landlord was not liable for an illegal distress which culminated in the death of a man resisting the levy as none of this was within his express instructions.

39 For examples of acceptance of illegal distraint see *Carter v St Mary Abbot's Vestry* (1900) 64 JP 548 or *Whitehead v Taylor* (1837) 10 A&E 210.

40 Ratification - *Green v Wroe* (1877) WN 130; mere receipt - *Freeman v Rosher* (1849) 13 QB 780, *Lewis v Read* (1845) 13 M&W 834 and *Haselar v Lemoyne* (1858) 5 CBNS 530; offer to settle - *Roe v Birkenhead Railway* [1851] 7 Exch 36.

41 Keeping goods - *Becker v Riebold* (1913) 30 TLR 142; receiving proceeds - *Dick v. Winkler* (1899) 12 Man LR 624; dispute - *Montgomery v. Hellyar* (1894) 9 Man LR 551.

42 *Potter v North* (1669) 1 Wms Saund 347(c); *Hull v Pickersgill* (1819) 1 Brod & Bing 282.

43 18 UCQB 327

44 Tender refused - *Bennett v Bayes* (1860) 5 H&N 391; exempt goods - *Lowe v Dorling* [1906] 2 KB 772; conversion - *Stephens v Elwall* (1815) 4 M&S 259.

45 LGO complaint against Blaby DC 11 007 684.

46 EWCA Civ 8.

47 Reg. 2(1) of the 2006 Regulations.

48 The relevant cases include *Parking Brixen GmbH v Gemeinde Brixen und Stadtwerke Brixen AG* [2005] ECR 1-08585, *Wasser v Eurowasser Aufbereitungs* [2009] ECR 1-08377 and *Stadler v Zweckverband fur Rettungsdienst und Feuerwehralarmierung Passau*, Case C-274/09.

49 *Blackpool Aero Club v Fylde BC* [1990] 1 WLR 1195.

50 High Court Enforcement Officers Association Limited, PO Box 180, Winsford, CW7 2WP; www.hceoa.org.uk.

51 For more information see www.civea.co.uk or contact CIVEA, 513, Bradford Road, Batley, WF17 8LL.

52 s.65(2)(a)-(c). However see excessive seizures later and see also the potential problem that s.62(4) of the new Act renames all warrants of distress as warrants of control. That being so, it would appear to mean that the unrepealed or amended s.78 of the Magistrates Court Act 1980 should now be read with the necessary modifications to make it applicable to the new procedure of taking control, so that the former offence of irregular distraint will still apply to all fines enforcement.

53 Sch.12 para.60.

54 Sch.12 para.60(1); CPR 85.4.

55 CPR 85.5.

56 Under Sch.12 paragraph 60(4)(a).

57 Reg.49 TCG Regs.

58 *Haddow v Morton* [1894] 1 QB 565.

59 *Miller v Solomon* [1906] 2 KB 91.

60 *Kotchie v The Golden Sovereigns Ltd* [1898] 2 QB 164.

61 Sch.12 paragraphs 38 to 49. Sale will of course pass good title - *Goodlock v Cousins* [1897] 1 QB 558.

62 Under Sch.12 paragraph 60(5) & reg. 49 of the TCG Regulations.

63 CPR 85.10

64 CPR 85.11.

65 CPR 85.12.

66 CPR 83.4(7).

67 Para.66(4).

68 CPR 84.13.

69 Para.66(5) & (6).

70 Para.66(7).

71 Sch.12 para.59 applies in cases of a breach of paragraph 58(3) - see chapter 11.

72 *In Re: Button ex p Haviside* [1907] 2 KB 180; *Edmunds v Wallingford* [1885] 14 QBD 811.

73 *Groom v Bluck* [1841] 2 Man & G 567; *Lampleigh v Brathwaite* 1 Sm LC 151; *Dering v Winchelsea* 1 W&T 106.

74 *England v Marsden* 1 CP 529.

75 *Kanhaya Lal v National Bank of India* [1913] 29 TLR 314.

76 By the same token, it is to be observed that para.57 refers to the common law rule on irregularities. No such common law rule ever existed. Irregular distress was a creation of statute introduced initially by the Distress for Rent Act 1737 to overcome the problem of the common law rule that all errors, no matter how trivial, rendered a distress trespass and illegal. Nonetheless, the repeal of most of the relevant statutes and statutory instruments will mean that there will no longer be any basis upon which to claim an irregular seizure - for instance for

local taxes, child support maintenance, county court judgments or road traffic penalties. A statutory form of irregularity still survives in magistrates' court - see 13.1.3 earlier and chapter 1.

77 See too *Sources of bailiff law* c.1 p.16.
78 Date uncertain - often allocated to the reign of Henry III but dated at 1322 on the government's statute law database.
79 *Sells v Hoare* (1824) 1 Bing 401.
80 *R v Ledgingham* 1 Vent 604.
81 *Bradby* at p.275 cites Coke 2 Inst 107.
82 See *Hessey v. Quinn* [1910] 21 OLR 519 citing *Rodgers v Palmer* (1856) 18 CB 112, *Lucas v Tarleton* (1858) 3H&N 116, *Piggott v Birtles* (1836) 1 M&W 441, *Chandeler v Doulton* 3 H&C 553.
83 *Rookes v Barnard* [1964] AC 1129.
84 *Broome v. Cassell & Co* [1972] AC 1027.
85 *Tufuya v. Haddon* [1984] NZ Recent Law 285.
86 Outrageous - *Bradford MBC v. Arora* [1991] 2 WLR 1377 CA; mistake - *Moore v. Lambeth County Court Registrar* [1970] 1 All ER 980.
87 *Dalfen's Ltd v. Bay Roberts Shopping Centre Ltd* (1990) 81 Nfld & PEIR 127; (1996) 5 CL 166.
88 *Roden v Eyton* (1848) 6 CB 427.*Fitzgerald v Longfield* (1855) 7 Ir Jur 21.
89 Gross excess - (1978) 88 DLR (3d) 601; slight excess - *Fitzgerald v. Longfield* Ir Jur OS 21; no special damages - *Chandler v Doulton* (1865) 3 H&C 553.
90 *Chandler v Doulton* (1865) 3 H&C 553; *Thompson v Wood* (1842) 4 QB 493.
91 *Piggott v Birtles* (1836) 1 M&W 441; no inconvenience - *Watson v Murray & Co* [1955] 1 All ER 350.
92 *M'Guckin v Dobbin* (1863) 15 Ir Jur 311.
93 *Chandler v Doulton* (1865) 3 H&C 553.
94 [1993] RA 27 - see *Sources of bailiff law* c.7 p.221; (1995) Current Law Digest, May, p.61.
95 *Sullivan v Bishop* (1826) 2 C&P 359.
96 LGO 10 007 469.
97 This was the High Sheriff of the county.
98 *Jackson v Hanson* (1841) 8 M&W 477.
99 *Axford v Perret* (1828) 4 Bing 586 - a delay of two years; *Morris v Matthews* (1841) 2 QB 293; *Evans v Bowen* (1850) 19 LJQB 8.
100 *Young v Broughton Waterworks Co* (1861) 31 LJQB 14.
101 Certification Regulations reg.9.
102 CPR 84.20.
103 Certification Regs reg.9(4) & CPR 84.20(3).
104 Certification Regs reg.9(5) & (6).
105 Certification Regs reg.9(7).
106 Certification Regs reg.9(8) & (9).
107 Certification Regs reg.10 & 12; CPR 84.19(2).
108 Certification Regs reg.10(4) & 13.
109 10 *Legal Action* 1991.
110 Certification Regs reg.11.
111 Certification Regs reg.11(2) & 3) and reg.6(4).
112 CPR 84.20(4) & (5).
113 Sch.12 para.60(4).
114 CPR 85.8(1) & (2).
115 CPR 85.8(3)-(8).
116 CPR 85.9.

117 CPR 85.10-12.

118 *Rodi &. Weinberger AG v. Kay* [1959] 22 DLR 258; *Canadian National Railways v Norwegian* [1971] 1 WWR 766.

119 *Moffat v Lemkin* (1993) unreported, following *Sheriff of Bedford & Toseland Building Supplies Ltd v Bishop* [1993] CA unreported; see too *Hotchkiss v. Hurst Construction* (1994) 18 Alta LR 206.

120 *ITCO Properties (1982) Ltd v Melnyk* (1987) 50 Alta LR (2d) 35; *ET Marshall & Co v. Fleming* (1965) 55 WWR 11.

121 *Pilling v Stewart* [1895] 4 BCR 94; *In Re: Trenwith* [1922] 3 WWR 1205; *Roy v Fortin* [1915] 26 DLR 18 - in which a delay of several months before making a claim was held too long.

122 *Young v Short* [1886] 3 Man LR 302.

123 *Selil v. Humphreys* (1886) 1 BCR 257.

124 *Sheriff of Bedford & Toseland Building Supplies Ltd v Bishop* [1993] CA unreported.

125 CPR 83.4(7).

126 See *Bourgoin SA v Ministry of Agriculture* [1986] 1 QB 716; also *Jones v Swansea City Council* [1989] 3 All ER 162.

127 *Three Rivers DC v Governor & Company of the Bank of England* [1996] 3 All ER 558.

128 *Legal Action* Sept.1996 p.21.

129 13 NBR 296

130 1 QB 367

131 Though see *Smith v. Egginton* [1837] 7 A&E 167 and *Wiltshire v. Barrett* [1966] 1 QB 312.

132 *Wilkinson v. Downton* [1897] 2 QB 57.

Chapter 14

Conclusions

The new code of powers contained in the Tribunals, Courts & Enforcement Act 2007 promises many enforcement agencies higher fees for their work. However, this gain is balanced by higher risk and increased responsibilities.

There is now a clear duty of openness and clarity as demonstrated by the succession of notices that must be served. There is a duty to make enquiries as to co-owners, third party claimants, exempt status of goods and vulnerable status of individuals. All of this will increase the time that must be spent on levies- in particular at the point of entering premises for the first time and taking control of goods. Overall, then, there are increased duties and far more deadlines for bailiffs to observe. This increases the risk of facing court claims for breach of the new code under Sch.12 para.66 of the 2007 Act.

The new code has simplified recovery for many debts- indeed, for most and definitely for all the most significant ones. Nonetheless, in a sense the law is now more complex and potentially confusing than it was previously. The old laws of distress and execution persist for just a few debts, with their case law, their special rules and their unique remedies, whilst in parallel the new statutory remedy governs the majority of enforcement work. In addition to this, there are still a variety of remedies which resemble seizures of goods, without formally being recognised as such. I have described many of these in my book *Powers of distress*.[1] Here, to conclude, I describe one that is very close to the power of taking control by immobilising vehicles on a highway: magistrates' court clamping orders.

14.1 Clamping for fines enforcement

As described in earlier chapters, the Courts Act 2003 created a new regime for the collection of fines. Amongst the 'further steps' permitted for the recovery of an unpaid penalty is an order allowing the fitting of an immobilisation device to, and eventual sale of, a motor vehicle.[2] The detail of these clamping orders is contained in the Fines Collection Regulations 2006 Part 4 - all subsequent references are to these regulations unless otherwise stated.[3] It seems that this process has been little used since its introduction and, with the clear legalisation of clamping as a form of taking control of goods, whether clamping orders will have any function in future remains to be seen.

This form of clamping was wholly new and is distinct from similar powers already described. Before a clamping order can be made the court's fines officer must be satisfied that the defendant has the means to pay and that the value of the car exceeds the fine outstanding plus the likely costs of clamping and sale.[4] The form of the clamping order is specified by regulation 17, although regulation 21 provides no defect in the order invalidates it or renders the clamper a trespasser. The order is sent to a clamping contractor along with details of the defaulter's address and vehicle.[5]

Vehicles may be clamped in any public places as well as on any private land to which access may be gained without opening or removing any gate, door or other barrier. A right to enter such land is granted by the regulation 19. Vehicles not registered in the defaulter's name, those which display a disabled badge or which appear to be for a disabled person's use and those which are used by a doctor or the emergency services cannot be clamped.[6] If the vehicle to be clamped would contravene any traffic or parking regulations if it were left clamped, the contractor can move it to the nearest suitable place and, if that is out of sight of its original position, should leave a prominent notice indicating that the vehicle has been moved and clamped. Regulation 22 requires that a notice should also be put on the clamped vehicle specifying certain prescribed information, such as the details of the order how to arrange release and contact details for the court and contractor. It is an offence to remove, or to attempt to remove, a vehicle clamp or a clamping notice. The penalty is a fine up to level 3.[7]

If the sums due are paid either to the contractor or to the court office, the vehicle should be released - within a maximum of 4 hours if payment is made to the court or contractor's office and within 2 hours if the clamper himself is paid. Part payments go first to the costs of the process. A receipt in prescribed form is issued.[8]

A clamped vehicle must remain in place at least 24 hours. After that if the fine is unpaid and if no challenge has been made to the clamping, the clamper must remove the vehicle to secure and suitable premises. Notice of this must be posted to the defaulter in prescribed form.[9] The vehicle must remain in storage for up to one month from the date of the clamping before it can be sold and if the fine and costs have not been paid. Ten days after the clamping the fines officer must apply to the court for a sale order. The defaulter will receive notice of this and a hearing will take place no earlier than 21 days after the clamping. At the hearing the court may order sale of the vehicle or may order its release to the defendant (with or without payment of the charges due). If sale is ordered the contractor will be instructed to make the necessary arrangements. On sale the ownership will vest in the purchaser and the contractor will arrange registration of the transfer with DVLA. The contractor receives the proceeds of sale, deducts the costs due and passes the balance to the fines officer. After paying the outstanding penalty, an remaining balance should be remitted to the defendant within ten working days with a written statement of account. If all or part of the fine then remains unpaid, other enforcement action will be taken.[10]

If a vehicle is wrongfully clamped, removed or stored in breach of the regulations a person can seek its release of return. Initially the request should be made to the fines officer (if the breach was in the content or making of the order) or to the contractor (if the manner of execution of the order is challenged). If a request is made to the wrong person, s/he should refer it to their counterpart. A written decision should be supplied within seven working days. If the request is accepted, the vehicle shall be released without charge. If the request is refused- or if no decision is made within the time scale - a person can apply to the court for a release order. Application should be made within ten working days of the refusal though the court can allow more time. The court may order release without charge or may refuse the application.[11] In addition, under regulation 21(3), a person is entitled to make a claim for special damages arising from any defect in the order or irregularity in its execution.

Footnotes

1 Wildy, Simmonds & Hill, 2009.
2 Courts Act 2003 Sch.5 Pt 9 para 38 & 41
3 SI 501, made under Courts Act 2003 Sch.5 Pt 10.
4 Reg.16.
5 Reg.18.
6 Reg.20.
7 Courts Act 2003 Sch.5 para.49
8 Reg.23; note that in the analogous clamping regime for road traffic penalties, DfT guidance is that clamps should be removed within one hour and at most within two' the parking adjudicator has found that immobilised vehicles should be released as quickly as is reasonably possible (*Watts v Westminster CC* (2002)).
9 Reg.24
10 Reg.26.
11 Regs.27 & 28.

Appendix 1

Glossary of Abbreviations

Repeated reference will be made to a number of statutes and statutory instruments plus other subjects generally known by acronym. To save space the commonest will be referred to by abbreviations:

CCA 84	County Courts Act 1984
CCR 81	County Court Rules 1981
CPR	Civil Procedure Rules
Crim PR	Criminal Procedure Rules
CSA (the)	Child Support Agency
CSA (with section number)	Child Support Act 1992
ERTDO	Enforcement of Road Traffic Debts Order 1993
LGFA 1988/ 1992	Local Government Finance Acts 1988/ 1992
MCA	Magistrates Court Act 1981
NNDR	National non-domestic rates (business rates)
NSEA	National Standard for Enforcement Agents
RSC	Rules of the Supreme Court 1965
RTA	Road Traffic Act 1991
TCEA	Tribunals, Courts and Enforcement Act 2007
TCG Regs	(the) Taking Control of Goods Regulations 2013.
VATA	Value Added Tax Act 1994

Index

Lightning Source UK Ltd.
Milton Keynes UK
UKHW022139271220
375841UK00008B/769